ISBN 978-1-331-83411-3
PIBN 10239837

THE SHORES AND CITIES OF THE
BODEN SEE.

CONSTANCE.

THE

SHORES AND CITIES

OF

THE BODEN SEE

RAMBLES IN 1879 AND 1880

With Maps of the District ;

and

Numerous Original Etchings on Stone by H. Schmidt-Pecht.

BY

SAMUEL JAMES CAPPER

AUTHOR OF "WANDERINGS IN WAR TIME," AND "SKETCHES OF AND FROM
JEAN PAUL RICHTER."

LONDON:

THOS. DE LA RUE & CO.

1881

PRINTED BY

THOMAS DE LA RUE AND CO., BUNHILL ROW, LONDON.

CONTENTS.

―・◇・―

CHAPTER I.

GENERAL DESCRIPTION OF THE LAKE OF CONSTANCE.

CHAPTER II.

LAKE OF CONSTANCE—*continued*.

CHAPTER III.

APPENZELL.

CONTENTS.

CHAPTER XIV.

THE COUNCIL OF CONSTANCE.

CHAPTER XV.

JOHN HUSS AND JEROME OF PRAGUE.

CHAPTER XVI.

THE FLIGHT OF POPE JOHN XXIII.—ELECTION OF A NEW POPE AND CLOSE OF THE COUNCIL.

CHAPTER XVII.

THE HISTORY OF THE CITY OF CONSTANCE SUBSEQUENT TO THE PERIOD OF THE GREAT COUNCIL.

CHAPTER XXI.

THE FROZEN BODEN SEE.

CHAPTER XXII.

CONSTANCE IN THE SPRING.

CHAPTER XXIII.

THE THIRTY YEARS' WAR ON THE BODEN SEE.

CHAPTER XXIV.

THE INHABITANTS OF THE WATERS OF THE BODEN SEE.

CHAPTER XXX.

DAVOS AM PLATZ.

LIST OF ILLUSTRATIONS.

PREFACE.

I FEAR that this book is a bold experiment. I have invited the reader to accompany me on a journey around the Lake of Constance, and up the Rheinthal into the sunny Prättigau, and to sojourn with me for nearly two years. Whatever has interested me, I have asked him to share—excursions, personal adventure, books, and even sermons.

In the summer of 1879 I addressed a letter to the *Times*, under the title "Can cheapness be combined with enjoyment in foreign·travel?" which was followed, in the course of the autumn, by a series of letters with the title of the present work. It appeared to me that the Boden See was little known and less appreciated in England, and that much of its history and legend was a sealed book to the merely English reader. If, in this work, I have not succeeded in showing, that the Lake of Constance and the cities on its shores, are full of interest to the historical student, as well as to the traveller, I am profoundly conscious that I alone am to blame.

The reader will be greatly assisted in following my narrative by the map of the Boden See, as well

b

as by the sketch-map of the Prättigau, to be found in this volume. To the artist, Herr Heinrich Schmidt-Pecht, of Constance, I feel myself under a great obligation, for the pains-taking care and fidelity which he has exercised in the preparation of the original etchings, with which my narrative is illustrated. Of the manner in which he has executed the task assigned to him, it is un-necessary for me to speak, but I will venture to express my thanks to him for the feeling and enthusiasm which he has thrown into his work, thus converting a matter of business into a labour of love. The Introductory Chapter is intended for the class for whose benefit my first letter to the *Times* was pub-lished, for those namely, who, however great may be their culture, possess but little cash, and desire to employ it to the best advantage in foreign travel.

One word as to the spelling of German words. As my book is intended for English readers, many of whom may not be German scholars, I have thought it best to adopt the plan likely to be most convenient to them, which is not in all cases that used by Germans. The system of word-building is very simple when you once understand it, but an English reader might well be appalled by such a word as Rheinundmainschleppdampfshifffahrtgesellschaft, the title of a tug company on the Rhine.

Without having quite such long words to deal with, I have written Bodensee —- Boden See, Friedrichshafen—Friedrichs-hafen, &c., and I have often, instead of using the *umlaut* as in Thür, a door, written Thuer ; and Vögel, birds, Voegel. Thanks to the efforts of radical spelling-reformers, German spelling is now in a state of absolute chaos. This seems the greater pity, as the system, adopted until within the last few years, was singularly simple and intelligible. The new reformers have made war, and successful war, upon all unnecessary, or what they regard as unnecessary, consonants and vowels : thus " Muth," courage, has become " Mut," " Rath," counsel, has become " Rat," " That," a deed, has become " Tat." The German Minister of Education has ordered that the new spelling shall be used in the schools, though it is said Prince Bismarck will have none of it ; and some of the leading newspapers have adopted it, so that those of us who had the misfortune to learn our German twenty-five years ago, feel, on looking through a broad sheet, as if we were trying to make out an unknown tongue. An incident which recently occurred in Berlin, aptly illustrates the inconvenience, at any rate, of the transition-state between the new spelling and the old. A gentleman of high rank advertised for a governess of specially good education. A lady applied who had just completed an elaborate course of study in a government college where the new system of spelling was used. Her testimonials were unexceptionable, her qualifications everything that could be desired, but her letter of application was written in the new style, and the gentleman replied that he regretted exceedingly his inability to avail himself of her services, but that it was impossible for him to engage, as teacher for his daughters, a lady who did not know how to write her own language!

The names of places and of men seem to be spelt in the most varied fashion : thus old Reichenthal is often called " Richental," or even " Rikental." I have endeavoured, as far as possible, to adopt a uniform and consistent plan, but if I have not always been successful, I may, I think, under the circumstances, justly crave the indulgence of my readers.

I cannot close this preface without acknowledging the very great kindness I have received from many gentlemen in lending me books, and securing them for me from libraries, books which I 'have found invaluable, and which, without this kind courtesy, would have been quite inaccessible to me, where I write, in this Alpine retreat. Among those to whom I am thus indebted, I desire especially to mention Herr Dr. Stizenberger, Herr Ludwig Leiner, and Herr Hermann Müller, of Constance, and Herr Franz Xaver Ullersberger of Ueberlingen.

S. J. CAPPER.

Seewis, Prättigau,
Switzerland, *December 6th, 1880.*

PRINCIPAL AUTHORITIES CONSULTED IN THE PREPARATION OF THIS WORK.

———•◦•———

" Der Boden See nebst dem Rheinthale."—GUSTAV SCHWAB. Cotta, Stuttgart und Tübingen, 1840.

" Rund um den Boden See."—DR. K. TH. ZINGELER. Würzburg.

" Reisen in einige Klöster Schwabens, durch den Schwarzwald, und in die Schweiz."—ZAPF, 1781.

" Schwäbisches Stadtewesen des Mittelalters."—JÄGER, 1831.

" Beschreibung des Boden Sees."—Ulm, 1783.

ULRICH VON REICHENTHAL'S " Chronik des Konzils in Konstanz. Manuskript mit illuminirten Handzeichnungen."

" Das Conzil zu Kontanz in den Jahren, 1414-1418."—Bearbeitet von J. MARMOR. Fritz, Kontanz, 1874.

" Réformateurs avant la Réforme ; XVᵉ Siècle."—EMILE DE BONNECHOSE, 1860.

" Hus und Hieronymus."—J. A. HELFERT, Studie. Tempsky, Prag, 1853.

" Das Leben J. H. Von Wessenberg's."—WAGNER, Freiburg, 1860.

" Schriften des Vereins für Geschichte des Boden Sees und seiner Umgebung." —STETTNER, Lindau.

" Das Thierleben im Boden See."—DR. AUGUST WEISMANN, Professor in Freiburg i. Br.

" Ueber das Tiefseeleben der Meere und Seen mit besonderer Berücksichtigung des Boden Sees."—A. STEUDEL, Professor in Ravensburg.

J. HEIDER'S " Tagebuch über den Verlauf der Belagerung Lindau's durch die Schweden 29 Dec. (8 Januar) 1646—28 Februar (10 Marz)."

" Die Genfer-Kolonie in Konstanz."—DR. MARMOR.

" Der Boden See ist zugefroren im Winter, 1880."—ANTON METZ. Feyel, Ueberlingen.

" Sebastian Bürster's Beschreibung des Schwedischen Krieges, 1630-1647, nach der Original-Handschrift im General-Landes-archiv zu Karlsruhe."—Herausgegeben von DR. FRIEDRICH VON WEECH, Gr : Bad. Archivrath. Hirzel, Leipzig.

" Die Reformation in den Bisthümern Chur und Como."—C. J. KIND. Grubenmann, Chur, 1858.

" Die Schweizer Daheim und in der Fremde."—EDWARD OSENBRÜGGEN. Hofmann, Berlin.

" Gedichte von Johann Gaudenz von Salis-Seewis."—ORELL FÜSSLI. Zürich, 1869.

" Das Buch vom General Dufour."—SENN-BARBIEUX. Altwegg-Weber, St. Gallen, 1878.

" Germany: Present and Past."—By S. BARING-GOULD, M.A. Kegan Paul & Co., London, 1879.

INTRODUCTION.

THE whole art of travel has undergone many revolutions since the blind bard of Chios spoke of the advantage of becoming acquainted with many men and many manners. The wise Ulysses combined much adventure and piracy with the extension of his general culture, brought to him by his travels. Speaking generally, however, the idea of travelling for pleasure was quite foreign to the ancients. Travel meant toil and hardship, and was only engaged in by the young and the adventurous as a means of conquering fortune, or by insatiable lovers of knowledge, like the father of history, to whom everything that related to his fellow men was full of interest. The Romans were universal conquerors, and therefore great travellers; but it is doubtful whether travel, as such, had any great charms for them. The early Christian missionaries, with St. Paul as their great prototype, were too conscious of the tremendous issues offered to mankind by the faith which they proclaimed, to have an eye for the beauties of nature or the triumphs of art, which their long and toilsome journeys opened up to them. A narrow and fierce piety, combined with the " *auri sacra fames,*" was the origin of the adventurous journeys alike of the Crusaders, and of Cortez, Pizarro, and their compeers. Then came the time when the cadets of almost all noble Scotch houses, and of many English, sought fortune and knowledge of the world in military service abroad ; and wherever in the world quarrels were to be fought out, there the hardy Swiss mercenary was to be found in hundreds or in thousands.

This custom produced not merely professional "soldados," of whom Sir Dugald Dalgetty is the inimitable type—not mere soldiers of fortune, like the Butlers and Gordons of the Thirty Years' War, but generals of European reputation like Leslie, and David Barclay, of Ury. Probably this habit of taking foreign service was the immediate forerunner of the custom of every English nobleman, or man of family, making the grand tour before settling down to the serious business of life. But the future of the world belongs to democracy, and in nothing is this more strikingly true than in the matter of travelling. Where fifty years back one English "milor" drove along in his gorgeous travelling coach with mountains of luggage and many servants, thousands of his humbler fellow-countrymen, with or without the kindly offices of Mr. Cook or Mr. Gaze, now fill the second and third-class carriages ot railways which everywhere open out what in a former generation was a "*terra incognita*" to their class. The phrase that the future of the world belongs to democracy surely means that, in the time to come, the world, with its possibilities of enjoyment and culture, will be for the many, and not alone for the favoured few. The cheapening of the necessaries of life and of the cost of conveyance, and the shortening of the hours of labour, all point in this direction, and the general extension of education at once awakens the taste for intelligent enjoyment, and helps to make its accomplishment possible.

There are those who regret this change, who think it the natural and proper order of the world that the many shall toil, and the few—of course *they* are among the number—shall enjoy. This sentiment has never been so well or so tersely expressed as by James Russell Lowell in the " Biglow Papers " :—

" The mass ough' to labor, an' we lay on soffies."

These would-be aristocrats are always ready with the observation that there always have been Helots, and that there always will be ; if you give culture and education and enjoyment to the hewers of wood and the drawers of water, who will draw water or hew wood for us ? The answer to this question is not easy, but we must remember that the constitution of Sparta was upon no Christian model, and that science is every day teaching us how to make Nature do the rough work of life—the hewing of wood and the drawing of water—for us. The hard exhausting work of agriculture—the ploughing, the reaping, the threshing, the grinding, once all done directly by men and women—are more and more done, and done well, by machinery ; and this applies with even more force to almost every laborious craft and manufacture. The powers of Nature—wind, water, or steam—supply the brute force ; man gives the directing intelligence. Is it too much to hope that with the advance of science, humanity may be relieved from all degrading and brutalizing drudgery, and thus the hindrances to the enjoyment and culture of the masses be removed ?

Those who hold that education, art, science, and indeed every higher enjoyment should be reserved for the select few, including, of course, themselves, are especially strong upon the subject of travel. What do vulgar shop-keepers, much less greasy mechanics, want

with travel? It is absurd to suppose that they can
enjoy, much less appreciate, the beauties of Nature.
"Let them not come between the wind and our
nobility!" These, not too generous, critics forget
that one hundred and fifty years since, 'Squire Western
and his hunting compeers were not one whit more
capable of appreciating the beauties of Nature than
the most self-indulgent Sheffield artizans are now.

No doubt the eccentricities of the "personally conducted" tourists of Mr. Cook or Mr. Gaze form an easy
butt for the more or less good-humoured satire of
those who have had greater advantages, and who,
accustomed from their youth to travel, do not require
to be "personally conducted;" but who can measure
the amount of rational pleasure and broadening culture
which these agencies have rendered possible to a class,
to whom, without them, it would have been impossible?
I know that it is possible for a man to travel far and
wide, and to only grow narrower in the experience,
but in such a case the fault is all his own.

The vulgar rich man, who travels to make a display
of his wealth, who abuses every place at which he
stays as a "beastly hole," and demoralises every one
with whom he comes in contact by prodigality and
lavish expenditure, will not gain more from his travels
than the vulgar poor man,—who glories in screwing
hotel-keepers, guides, and the like, down to the
lowest possible price, and whose mind is so completely absorbed in this ignoble task as to have little
energy left for other enjoyment. Both these classes
have, I believe, always been exceptional, and we
will hope are becoming more so.

On the other hand, there is every year an increasing
number of assistant schoolmasters and schoolmistresses,
commercial clerks and students, and others whose

purses are but slenderly endowed, who desire to derive the utmost benefit, physical and intellectual, from an inexpensive continental tour. In speaking thus of *foreign* travel, I would not for a moment seem to disparage our own beautiful country; but, unfortunately the science of keeping moderately good hotels at anything like reasonable prices is in its infancy in Great Britain. Scotland, with its magnificent scenery, and glorious historical memories, is too costly for the class of tourists of whom I am speaking. Even the district of the English lakes, a sort of miniature Switzerland, with an unsurpassable loveliness all its own, presents none of the advantages of excellent but cheap *pensions* and hotels, such as are to be found in Switzerland. Then, too, nothing is so useful to, or so much desired by, the jaded professional man, or man of business, the wearied clergyman or clerk, as a complete change of air and scene, of language, and even of diet. There is a pleasure, not altogether unmixed with surprise, to the untravelled Briton, in hearing even little boys and girls discoursing fluently in French or German, as the case may be. It is a great thing also to have put a strip of salt water between you and your cares, whatever they may be, and a pleasant thing to see and feel the bright hot sun, so often veiled to us by our insular fogs and clouds. An interesting shilling volume, entitled "A Continental Tour of Eight Days for Forty-Four Shillings, by a Journeyman," shows how much may be done with very small expenditure. I have never travelled quite so cheaply as this, but considerable experience in Normandy and Brittany has shewn me that a pedestrian, if he avoid the large and expensive hotels, may live very comfortably for eight francs a day, or say five pounds for a fortnight. Add to this the lowest fare to and from St. Malo, and the cost of the holiday will not be more than, with a little saving and self-sacrifice during the year, very many young men and young women engaged in arduous occupations might reasonably indulge in. Brittany and Normandy are exceeding rich in historic and archæological interest, and contain gems of architectural beauty, such as the Abbey-Fortress on the Mont St. Michel and the Church of St. Ouen at Rouen. The rocky shore and great Atlantic billows rolling in are a constant charm, and much of the land is so rich and fertile as to be at once corn-land and orchard. This region has also the great advantage of being easily and cheaply accessible from England.

But if the tourist be able and willing to come further afield, there is no country that presents such abundant attractions as Switzerland. The most glorious scenes in Nature,—mountain, lake, and glacier,—await him there. The keeping of hotels, too, has there been made one of the fine arts, and you obtain the maximum of comfort at the minimum of cost. The visitor to Switzerland has, it is true, to add the cost of the long journey there and back to that of his holiday sojourn there, and this probably cannot be estimated, at the very lowest, at less than £6. My experience is that, if the smaller and more modest hotels are chosen, about eight francs a day will cover hotel expenses, so that, if the traveller have a month's holiday, and be contented to thoroughly visit some particular district of limited area, he need not spend more upon it than £16 to £20. If he wish to compass the whole of Switzerland and Savoy he will, of course, find his expenditure very much greater. My first visit to Switzerland was in 1860. We had twenty-four days' leave of absence from Liverpool to Liverpool. We entered Switzerland at Schaffhausen, and, after walking all through the Bernese Oberland, climbing the St. Gotthardt as far as the summit of the pass, crossing the Gemmi, and visiting the monks on the Great St. Bernard, we spent three days at Chamouny, and returned by Geneva and Paris. Our expenses were £24 each; all the passes we did on foot, and there was no extravagance. The tour was an admirable one, but it covered far too much ground; and having been planned by a man of great physical power, it involved far greater exertion than was consistent either with enjoyment or health. This was a mistake which many young people still make, and the result is that you constantly see young men come home from their annual holiday looking jaded and worn out, instead of bringing back a store of health and strength for their work. Far better is it to choose some small district, study well its physical characteristics, history, &c., before you start, and determine to see it well, leaving other districts for other years. This plan is in every way more satisfactory, and it is far cheaper. But it is not only young people who travel, and a time of life comes when we are quite satisfied not to have walked twenty-five or thirty miles every day, and when to sleep in a fresh bed every night does not increase our happiness, or enhance the enjoyment of our holiday. For those who, when they have found a beautiful place, wish to stay there, and quietly drink in the scenery around, while they rest from the labours of the work-a-day year, Switzerland presents peculiar advantages in what is well known to all sojourners there as the *pension* system.

The principle upon which the hotel proprietor can

receive guests for a week and longer at something like two-thirds, or even one-half, the charge he would make to occasional visitors, is that the prolonged stay saves him an infinitude of trouble, and the *personnel* and material of the hotel an immense amount of wear and tear. In the matter of bed-linen alone this is considerable.

In Geneva you may live at *pensions* kept in palatial buildings, supplied with a good table, and provided with elegant drawing-room and other requisites of a first-class hotel, at a cost of six francs to eight francs *per diem*, everything except wine and candles included. At Lausanne, the beau tiful capital of the Pays de Vaud, prices range about the same, and both in Geneva and Lausanne there are simpler establishments where visitors remaining for months, may be comfortably entertained at from 100 to 150 francs per month. The whole of the winter of 1878-9 my wife and I passed in the residence of a retired pastor, a lovely villa just above the Château de Chillon. I doubt if there is a more beautiful situation for a house in the whole world; with Lac Leman stretched in front and the Savoy Alps beyond, while the precipitous Rochers de Naye rise behind. The garden was full of fine trees and lovely flowers, and the estate, which included many acres of vineyard, extended right up into the mountains, on the gentler slopes of which grew a magnificent wood of ancient Spanish chestnuts. Our host, a man of more than fourscore, had resided for many years in Florence as Protestant pastor connected with the Prussian embassy in that city. Italian was, therefore, a second native tongue to him. It was said of him, that if the whole of the *Iliad* were lost he could have restored it, as he knew every line of it

by heart. He used often to tell me that, when sleep-
less at night, he found nothing so soothing as to recite
the *Iliad* in the original. His recollections of life
during the great Napoleonic wars, in whose armies
his brother was an officer, and of Parisian society
immediately after the restoration in 1815, were intensely interesting. The *mènage* here was very
simple, and we paid 125 francs a month each,
or a little more than four francs a day. Four-and-
a-half francs a day was not an uncommon price at
Montreux during the same winter.

On the lakes of Brienz and Thun *pension* may be
found at about six francs, or perhaps a little less; if
early in the season, say in May or early June,
probably four-and-a-half francs would be accepted.

Even at the. fashionable Mürren, where everything
has to be carried on horse or man's back to 5,600 feet
above sea level—the only road being a mountain track
from the valley of Lauterbrunnen—*early in June*, the
proprietors of the two hotels—Hotel de Mürren and
Hotel des Alpes—will probably be glad to receive
guests at about eight francs, though a few weeks later
twelve-and-a-half to fifteen francs is the lowest price.
There are hotels at lovely points on the Italian lakes
—Maggiore, Como, and Lugano—where visitors are
very well treated for about eight lire, which, in consequence of the depreciation of Italian paper money,
amounts to considerably less than as many francs.

To return to the classic shores of Lac Leman.
About 3000 feet above sea-level, and consequently
about 2000 feet above Montreux, on the ancient roadway which in the Middle Ages served as the sole
means of communication between the eastern shores
of Lac Leman and the cantons of Freiburg and
Berne, on the bridle path which leads over the Col de

Jaman, stands the little hamlet of Les Avants. Here, twenty to thirty years ago, a worthy couple who had been in domestic service established a little mountain hostelry, where they received guests at a charge of three francs per diem, everything included, and, as I am informed by visitors of those early days, treated them so liberally, that they rapidly established an attached *clientèle*, The old-fashioned châlet-inn has long since passed away,—so also have the old people. Their children have built a spacious (not to say magnificent) hotel, with I know not how many bed-rooms, and a *salle-à-manger* where 150 guests can sit down to dinner at one time. The plenteous but homely table of former days has given place to an exquisite and—in fairness I must add—most abundant Parisian *cuisine*, and of course the prices have of necessity gone up. Still, when my wife and I were there in 1878, the prices ranged from six to nine francs, and the only fault we could find with the fare was that, if anything, it was too good. The two capital *tables d'hôte* every day were almost of the nature of a temptation to live not wisely but *too well.* I am only afraid lest the obliging proprietors should avail themselves of their well-won reputation to put up their prices. They will do well, however, to remember that in the long run their most valuable *clientèle* consists of those who would prefer a decrease in luxury to an increase in cost. Not but that many innkeepers make the mistake of imagining that fine scenery will take the place of good cooking, and that the stomachs of their guests may be trampled upon—figuratively, of course, I mean—with impunity, Within a bowshot of Mürren, with the Black Monk rising sheer opposite, and the everlasting snows of the Jungfrau above, there stands or stood a picturesque hostelry. Those who formed part of the happy company who sojourned there in July of 1878, will not soon forget the time. We were mostly disciples of the " Porch " rather than of the " Garden," and the greater number of us had been beguiled by the demon of economy, in the shape of a tariff of five francs per diem, from the excellent and luxurious hotels at Mürren. We were in the very *sanctum sanctorum* of the Alps, the air was magnificent, the scenery was superb; we thoroughly enjoyed one another's society. The host was also a local judge, and did not condescend to have much to do with attending to the comfort of his guests. His activity was principally confined to scolding his little wife if they were not satisfied. She, poor little woman, was very obliging, but cumbered with much serving and many small children, and we all felt great sympathy for her. At first we persuaded ourselves that the style of living was really a pleasant change from the great luxury we had been enjoying; but soon that important and long-suffering organ to which I have already referred, revolted, and cried out at the food put before us, and we began ruefully to confess to one another, that never before in our lives had we lived so badly. I believe that there is no member of that pleasant company who would not rejoice to see it again assembled; but we should unanimously vote that the meeting should not be under that too-Spartan roof. While upon the subject of hotels where moderate people may live at a moderate cost, I must not forget to mention those at Chateau d'Oex and in the Sarine valley. They stand as high as Les Avants, have glorious mountain air, with fine scenery and walks in the neighbourhood, and I believe are as cheap as any in Switzerland.

Simplicity does not always or generally mean bad

cooking, or insufficiency of appetizing food ; nevertheless the change is great from the sumptuous
establishments around the Lake of Geneva to some
of the hostelries around the Boden See. The
lofty *salle-à-manger*, where upwards of a hundred
guests discuss every delicacy that sea, lake, farm-
yard, and forest can provide, and the skill of a
French *chef* can prepare, gives place to the old-
fashioned Speise-saal where a homely German cookery
reigns. The Speise-saal often also serves for drawing-
room and reading-room as well, and many of the
guests are homely country bumpkins, whose knives
habitually do dreadful duty. As to cost, at
hotels of the second class, fairly comfortable but
simple establishments, my wife and I paid at Rorschach
four francs each *per diem;* at Lindau, four marks
or five francs ; at Ueberlingen, a little more ; and at
Kreuzlingen five francs. This was in the summer.
In the winter we had our two little children with us.
We spent five months at Kreuzlingen, and were able
to make an arrangement by which we were taken in
en pension for little over 300 francs *per mensem* for the
whole party. At Heiden, above Rorschach, it is difficult to obtain *pension* at less than seven or eight francs,
while at Seewis in the Prättigau, a description of which
will be found in the body of the work, there is one
pension which advertises that it receives guests at four
francs, while at the Kurhaus, where comfort and plenty
reign, the prices are five to seven francs. In the
Engadine it is almost impossible to get in under eight
to ten francs *per diem.*

I have gone into these particulars, because I am
anxious to show those of limited means just what a
short holiday or a prolonged residence in Switzerland
will cost them. I prefer as little as possible to recom-

mend particular hotels. Baedeker and Tschudi are
to be trusted, and if the visitor will go to those
recommended as good *second class* houses, he will
find the charges to be about what I have named.
Those contemplating a lengthened stay in Switzerland
would do well to advertise in the local papers of the
district they affect, stating their requirements, and
inviting offers. In this way they will often hear of
private *pensions* which may suit them better than
more public establishments, and perhaps also be
cheaper.

Though anxious that the enjoyment of travel should
be thrown open to a wider class than that which now
has the advantage of it; which is only possible by an
economical and wise expenditure, I am no friend to
bargaining with and beating-down innkeepers. There
is, however, no objection to the traveller's asking if
an inferior room, or one upon a top story, will not be
cheaper than that which has been shown to him ; and
the price of *pension* is sometimes regulated by the
number of dishes served at dinner or supper,

A very good rule in travelling, as in life, is to stint
yourself but not others. Take a small top room,
forego your glass of wine, or beer, or your cup of
coffée of an afternoon, or walk where you would have
preferred to drive, but do not try to beat down your
landlord to a starvation price, or refrain from giving
the hardworking servants little *douceurs*, which an
unwritten law has rendered not an act of generosity
but of justice. If ever there was an age when "high
thinking and plain living" was imperative it is the
present. The universal spread of education is extending to the million a capacity and taste for enjoyment
which a century ago belonged to very few. It were,
however, absurd to expect that affluence should spread

pari passu with culture.   On the contrary, we have no reason to expect that the extraordinary increase of wealth and the general diffusion of material prosperity brought about in the last generation by the multiform application of steam-power, and especially by its application to locomotion, will have any counterpart in the age upon which we are entering.   It will only be in very exceptional cases that education will bring wealth.   It will probably be unfavourable neither to public nor private virtue, if education and real culture become general among those whose means are narrow and must always remain so.   Perhaps our great English vice of extravagance and apeing the display of our social superiors—a vice directly traceable to our aristocratic system, and which I verily believe pervades all classes—will some day be seen by us in its naked vulgarity, and when thus seen will assuredly be abhorred.   In the prospect of the spread of culture among poor people, and of the taste for travel which culture brings, I have given all these details of cost; for the day will assuredly come when there will be thousands of young men and young women with a fair knowledge of French and German, and a great desire to enjoy foreign travel, but who will not, possibly, be able to spare more than £5, £10, or £15, as the case may be, for their annual holiday.

If the hints I have given in this introduction should be of service to that class, my object will be gained; for richer men and women, as I have warned them in the preface, this chapter is not intended, and if they find it base, prosaic, and uninteresting, they have only themselves to blame for reading it.

THE

SHORES AND CITIES OF THE BODEN SEE.

CHAPTER I.

GENERAL DESCRIPTION OF THE LAKE OF CONSTANCE.

First visit — Donaueschingen — Hollenthal — View from Friedrichs-hafen — Dimensions of Boden See—Ingenious calculation—Like the sea—Name of lake—Glacier period—First mentioned in history—Tiberius builds a fleet on the lake—Rhaetians—Vindelicians—Alemanni—Irish missionaries and the holy Gallus—Foundation of St. Gall—Death of Gallus.

IT was early in February, 1878, that I first saw the Boden See. Up to that time I had followed the advice of the guide books, and had always left the great lake upon one side, regarding its scenery as tame compared with that of the interior of Switzerland. Even then it was only the desire of visiting the scene of the martyrdom of Huss, which induced me, accompanied by my wife, to drive in a sledge through the Höllenthal, stop at Donaueschingen long enough to watch the infant Danube bubbling up in the fountain in Prince Fürstenberger's park, and so reach the old imperial town of Constance. A cold fog lay heavy upon the lake, and under such circumstances it was difficult to form much idea of its beauty and charm. After eighteen months' sojourn on the shores of Lac Leman, the lakes of Brienz, Thun, Maggiore, Luzern, and Zürich, we found ourselves in the summer of 1879 near the great sheet of water which separates Southern Germany from Switzerland. Much of that summer we spent upon its shores or upon its waters, and after

B

passing the five months from December, 1879, to May, 1880, again beside it, we feel an affection for it far transcending that which we have for any other Swiss lake.

It is true that coming fresh from the glories of Lake Leman or from the unsurpassable loveliness of the Vierwaldstädter See and approaching the lake of Constance from the south, whence the mountains are not visible, a feeling does come over one that Switzerland and Swiss scenery are quite left behind. The blue water, sometimes like a mirror, and at others stormy as the ocean, with the vine, pasture, and forest-clad undulations of Southern Germany as a back-ground, gives more the impression of "green fields beyond the swelling flood" than of Alpine grandeur. When, however, the lake is approached from the northern side all this is changed. Take, for instance, the view from the southern residence of the King of Würtemberg, at Friedrichs-hafen. To the east rise the mountains of the Vorarlberg and Graubünden, with Scesa Plana and Zimp raising their snow-clad crests high above all compeers. To the south-west Glärnisch stands out bold and sharp. Golden in the sunlight rises, round like a great white throne, the lofty Tödi, while still further to the west is the sharp point of Uri Rothstock, and the mountains around the Lake of Luzern, while above and beyond are the peaks of the Jungfrau, the Wetterhörner, and the Finsteraarhorn. Sea-mews sweep over and swallows lightly skim the blue waters, the waves of which are snow-crested with white foam. Seven to eight miles away across the lake is Switzerland, and from out of the green and breezy uplands of Appenzell rises the huge mass of the Hohe Sentis, his mighty front black and scarred save where great banks of snow rest upon him.

With the long serrated ridge of fantastic rocks, such as Doré delights to paint, which connect the " Sentis" with the "Alter Mann" and the Kurfürsten, the great mountain range presents a very similar appearance to that of Mont Blanc as seen from the Jura, above Lake Leman.

The reader will find the map of the Boden See given in this work of great service in assisting him to understand the particulars of its length, breadth, and geographical position, which follow :—

The extreme length from Bregenz to the farthest point on the Ueberlingen See is 63 kilometres, or rather under 40 miles, and the extreme breadth from Friedrichs-hafen to Arbon is 12 kilometres, or 7½ miles. Its circumference measures 193 kilometres, or a little over 120 miles. Its average water level is 394·21 metres, or say 1,293 feet above that of the German Ocean.

If we include the Unter See, the area of the whole of the Boden See is 9½ German square miles, or 201 English square miles ; excluding the Unter See, its area is 8½ German square miles, or about 180 English square miles. Between Langenargen and Rorschach a depth of 693 feet has been measured, and between Friedrichs-hafen and Rorschach of 849 feet. The result of careful soundings is to prove that the maximum depth is nowhere more than 900 feet.

A pains-taking German has made the following ingenious calculation, which shows at once the extent of what the Germans sometimes fondly call " Das Deutsche Meer," and the insignificance, so far as bulk is concerned, of the whole human race at present alive upon our planet.

A German mile contains 25,856 feet (Würtemberg), consequently a square German mile 668½ million square feet. The superficial area of the Lake of Constance, being 8½ German square miles, contains therefore 5,682 million square feet. There are living upon the surface of our globe, in round numbers, about 1,430 million human beings. Let every man, woman, and child have four square feet of standing room allotted to him, and if the lake were frozen over the whole human family might be assembled on its surface. Should the weight prove too great, and collective humanity be submerged, it would only raise the level of the lake six inches.

I have tested this calculation by working it out in English measurement, and find it correct, but that I make the standing room only 3½ English square feet for each individual. This discrepancy I attribute to the comparative shortness of the Würtemberg foot.

The waters of the lake wash the shores of no less than five different states—the Empire of Austria, the Kingdoms of Bavaria and Würtemberg, the Grand Duchy of Baden, and the Republic of Switzerland.

About thirty steamers—some very fine ones—constantly ply from port to port, and ingenious camel barges are so constructed as to carry whole trains of railway wagons laden with merchandise—of course minus the locomotives—from shore to shore, thus avoiding the trouble and cost of unpacking and re-loading.

It has been well remarked by Dr. K. Th. Zingeler, to whose little book, "Rund um den Boden See," I am largely indebted, that in one respect the Lake of Constance has a great advantage over other Swiss lakes, even over Lake Leman itself, and that is in its being like the sea. If you take your stand upon the ancient ramparts of the island city of Lindau when a strong west wind is blowing, huge breakers will come rolling in and will cover you with spray, while, however keen your vision, you will see only water and sky towards the setting sun.

For a short sojourn nothing can be more grand or delightful than the Vierwaldstädter See or the head of Lake Leman, with the glorious mountains rising almost sheer from the water ; but there are many who soon begin to feel themselves oppressed, shut in, and almost crushed by the mighty mountains towering around and above them : to such the wider horizons of the Lake of Constance are an unspeakable relief. Though you have still an astonishing panorama of mountains, they no longer seem to threaten you, but loom vast and shadowy in the distance.

Following the example of our French neighbours, we always speak of this great inland sea as the *Lake of Constance*, It has never, however, been known by this name by the inhabitants of its shores, who always speak of it as the " Boden See."

Strabo, in his description of the earth, 20 B.C., does not mention it by name, but speaks of a great lake formed by the inflowing of the Rhine. Pomponius Mela, about the commencement of our era, says,— The Rhine rushing down from the Alps here forms two lakes, " Venetus " and " Acronius," by which he means the Unter See and the Ober See, or proper Boden See.

Pliny first gives it the name of Raetiae Brigantinus. Subsequently, about the year A.D. 359, Ammianus Marcellinus, of Antioch, a learned Roman soldier, who was quartered on its shores, gives it the name by which it was known by its Rhaetian inhabitants, Brigantia. By the name of the Lake of Brigantia (Bregenz) it was known until the tenth century, while the name " Lacus Bodamicus " first appears in A.D. 890, from

which the name Bodam-see and Boden See. Some
centuries later the name *Suabian Sea*, "Schwäbisches
Meer," or in Mettel-hoch-deutsch, "Schwebische Mer"
appears in an old chronicle.

The popular notion that it was called " Boden See"
because it was so deep as to have no bottom or
" boden" will, manifestly, not hold water. It took its
name from the imperial castle of Bodmann or Bodam,
at the western extremity of the Ueberlinger See.

Written history tells us little of our lake, of its
shores, or their inhabitants much before the commencement of our era, but the science of geology carries us
back with authentic records, so far as the department is
concerned with which it has to deal, hundreds of
thousands, if not millions, of years. Without going
back so far as the Tertiary Period, when, as is proved
by the fossil remains, a tropical climate reigned, and
when the lake, there is every reason to believe, filled
up the whole of the Rhine valley as far as Chur, and
washed the bases of the Hohentwiel and of the other
heights of the Hegau, we may with safety refer to the
glacial period which followed, when the whole basin of
the lake must have been filled with ice, and at the
mouth of the Rhine valley, where Bregenz now stands,
there probably stood a mountain of ice 6,000 feet high.
Of what took place at that period we have unerring
witnesses—witnesses that cannot lie.

Scattered over the whole of the shores of the lake,
on mountain sides of an entirely different formation to
their own, are to be found great boulder stones, or
erratic blocks, that cannot have reached their present
site by accident, and can only have been borne there
by huge glaciers. Soon after this period the Boden
See probably assumed its present form, though its
level was much higher than it is now. There is

good reason to believe that a long time elapsed before the Rhine succeeded in forcing a passage through the wall of rock which hemmed its course at Schaffhausen. When at last the river succeeded in thus making its escape the level of the lake sank below what it is at present, as is proved by the discoveries that have been made of the remains of the villages of the lake-dwellers, " Die Pfahlbauten-reste."

From the level at which these dwellings have been found, it is evident that had the lake stood as high at that time as it now does, they would have been uninhabitable. The platform on which the huts stood must have been at least two feet above the nominal level of the lake, to allow for the wash of the waves.

Professor A. Steudel, of Ravensburg, who has most diligently studied the subject, is of opinion that the level of the lake was ten feet lower at the time of the lake-dwellers than at present. The configuration of the valley of the Rhine, between Chur and Rheineck, and the depression along which the railway now runs from Sargans to Zürich, past the Wallen See, would seem to show that at one period the whole or a great portion of the waters of the Rhine instead of flowing into the Boden See found their way into the Wallen See, the Lake of Zürich, and so seawards. If this were the case it would account for the present higher level of the Boden See.

Every year, at the time of low water in the winter, fresh discoveries are made of the remains of the lake-dwellers.

In the little Unter See, with an area of only twenty-one English square miles, the remains of no fewer than twenty-two settlements of these interesting people have been discovered, and one of these settlements at Wangen, on the Baden side, rested upon no less than forty thousand piles, and covered twenty-five acres. These piles are of oak, birch, beech, and pine, and are from four to six inches thick.   Probably, in proportion to its size, the Boden See was not so thickly studded by lake dwellings as its smaller neighbour, as the shallowness of the Unter See rendered it peculiarly suited for the operations of the pile-driving architects.

It is certain, however, that there was a large settlement at the lower end of the lake, where Constance now stands ; also at Rorschach, and at many other places.

We know so much about the lake-dwellers that we would fain know more.   We know that in pre-historic times the shallow waters of these and other lakes were all dotted over with their picturesque habitations.   Here in his wattled hut rising from a platform erected upon piles, primeval man led a toilsome life.   He grew wheat upon the shore, which he crushed between stones, and from the fibre of hemp he skilfully wove nets with which to obtain an ample supply of fish from the water below and around him.

He had flint hatchets and arrow-heads with which to fight his enemies and to pursue the wild beasts in the forests that encompassed his home.   Among these were the bear, the wolf, the aurochs, and the stag. The faithful dog was with him as friend and helper, but of his joys and his sorrows, his loves and his hates, we know little or nothing.

> " Rugged type of primal man,
>   Grim utilitarian,
>   Loving woods for hunt and prowl,
>   Lake and hill for fish and fowl,
>   As the brown bear blind and dull
>   To the grand and beautiful ;

Lake Dwellers on the Boden See.

" Not for him the lesson drawn
   From the mountain smit with dawn.
   Star-rise, moon-rise, flowers of May,
   Sunset's purple bloom of day,—
   Took his life, no hue from thence,
   Poor amid such affluence?

" Haply unto hill and tree,
   All too near akin was he :
   Unto him who stands afar
   Nature's marvels greatest are.
   Who the mountain purple seeks
   Must not climb the higher peaks.

" Yet who knows in winter tramp,
   Or the midnight of the camp,
   What revealings, faint and far,
   Stealing down from moon and star,
   Kindled in that human clod
   Thought of destiny and God?"*

As stone implements gave place to bronze, so
we know that the use of these latter had to yield
to the short two-edged iron sword of the Roman
legionary.

When, fifteen years after Christ, the Rhaetians and
Vindelicians fell with desperate fury upon the out-
skirts of the Roman empire, the Emperor Augustus
sent his adopted step-son, Claudius Drusus Nero,
against them into Upper Italy. The Roman legions
met the wild northern hordes at the foot of the
Tridentine Alps, and routed them with great slaughter,
driving them back into their mountain fastnesses.
But defeated here, the Rhaetians and Vindelicians
(supposed to be Wends settled upon the Lech)
burst with renewed fury upon transalpine Gaul, carrying fire and sword far and wide. Hereupon Augustus

* " The Grave by the Lake."—WHITTIER.

despatched Claudius Tiberius Nero—the subsequent
emperor Tiberius—to the assistance of his brother.
The young Cæsars advanced upon the foe in detached
armies. Drusus crossed the Alps (probably by the
Wormser Joch) into the Engadine, while Tiberius
appears to have approached the scene of conflict from
Gaul. This brought the Roman, probably for the first
time, to the shores of the Boden See. Tiberius found
it covered by the canoes of the Vindelicians, to con-
quer whom he caused a fleet of war galleys to be built,
and seized and fortified an island, probably Reichenau.
It is related that in the final struggle the barbarian
women took an active part, and, when all other missiles
were exhausted, dashed out the brains of their children
and hurled them at the Roman invaders, determined
thus, if in no other way, to save them from slavery.
But undisciplined valour was of little avail against
the skill of a Tiberius at the head of Roman legions,
and the Rhaetians and Vindelicians were brought
under the yoke of the world-conquerors. To hold
the inhabitants of the shores of the lake in subjection
strong places were built, and thus arose Brigantia
(Bregenz), Arbor Felix (Arbon), and Constantia
(Constance).

Towards the end of the third century A.D., we cease
to hear of the various distinctive names of Germanic
tribes, previously familiar to us in the pages of the
Roman historians, and in their place we read of the
Alemanni—origin of the modern French *les Allemands*.
The name Alemanni appears not to have been the
designation of a particular people but of a great confederation — " Allerlei Mannen " — " Alle Mannen."
These Alemanni gave infinite trouble to the Roman
government, and although Constantine the Great drove
them out of Gaul in A.D. 313, and fortified the Rhine

against them, they were a constant thorn in the side
of the Roman empire, until at last, when, in 455, that
colossus, with head of gold and feet of clay, began to
totter to its fall, Attila, the scourge of God, combined
in one great army all the warlike peoples from the
Caspian to the Rhine, and swept them in a destroying
flood towards Rome.   Constantia, Arbor, and Brigantia
were all given to the flames, and the devastating horde
probably passed up the Rhine valley and over into
Italy by Chur and the Splügen.

In A.D. 359 Ammianus Marcellinus thus describes
the Rhine and the lake :—

"In the inmost recesses of the highest mountains rises the Rhine
with a mighty gush.

"It carves for itself a way through opposing rocks, and without an
increase from other waters it flows on with a roar and crash like the
Nile through its cataracts.

"From its very source it would be navigable, for it has ample
waters, were it not that it is more a torrent than a stream.

"When it leaves the rocks, and deep clefts of its origin, and enters
a more open country, it flows into a round and immense lake, called
by the Rhaetians who dwell there Brigantia, 460 stadia long and as
many wide.

"It is unapproachable by reason of the horror of gloomy forests,
save where the ancient invincible Roman valour has made a broad
road : for the nature of the country and the unfriendliness of the sky
fight against the barbarians.   Through this swamp rushes the stream
with foaming waves, passes quickly through the lazy calm of its
waters, and cuts through them with a sharply-defined edge ; and, as if
a separate element divided from it by eternal discord, it leaves the
lake, with neither increased nor diminished volume, with its old
name and its old force, and suffering no pollution whatever, it
hastens on towards the remotest depths of the ocean.   And what,
indeed, is very wonderful, the placid waters of the lake are not
disturbed by the rapid passage of the stream, and the hurrying river
is not hindered by the floating mud beneath it.   The two bodies of
water neither unite nor mix.   If indeed actual observation did not
teach us that this really was so, we should believe that no power
in nature could possibly keep the two from combining."

There is, of course, much that is fanciful in this description by the old Roman. It will be seen that he makes the lake about fifty miles long by as many wide, or to cover an area of 2,500 miles. As to the non-mixing of the waters of the lake with those of the Rhine, it has been suggested that at that time the lake may have been largely overgrown with water plants. It is easy to imagine the effect produced upon the mind of one accustomed to the bright sun and unclouded sky of Syria, by the great lake surrounded by dense and impenetrable forest, and over which hung an almost perpetual fog, the exhalations of the rank vegetation, not yet brought within bounds by the civilising hand of man. The Roman historians have much to say of the robbery and murder practised by the Vindelicians, Rhaetians, Alemanni, and other barbarian peoples; but, as an anonymous describer of the Boden See of the last century quaintly says, if these latter had left us a history, they might have had a good deal to say about the robbery and murder practised by the Romans. Probably if Red Indians, Zulus, and Basutos, were literary people they would have a like story to tell about their civilised invaders.

In 496 the Alemanni were beaten by the Franks under the great king Clovis, and in 536 those dwelling on the Boden See were brought under subjection to the Frank power.

Although Clovis and his successors were Christians, the new religion was not forced upon the conquered people, so that up to the middle of the sixth century the people around the Boden See were almost all heathens. In 609, however, when in Arabia Mohammed was beginning to proclaim his counter-evangel, a band of fourteen cowled strangers reached the shores of the Boden See. They came from the monastery of Bangor, in Ireland, and Columban and Gallus were their leaders. From Arbon, where was already a Christian bishopric, the Irish apostles crossed the lake to Bregenz, where the reign of heathenism remained undisturbed. Here, in the later days of the Roman domination, a Christian church had been founded, and a chapel ·dedicated to St. Aurelia. The wild Alemanni had turned this chapel into a heathen temple, and ·in it had erected idols, supreme among which·ruled the mighty Woden and Thor. "These," said they, "are our primeval gods, the ancient guardians of this place, whose help and power have sustained us until this day."

Undismayed the Irish missionaries entered the temple, and Gallus addressed the heathen with fiery eloquence. The words in which he proclaimed the true God as revealed by Jesus Christ, had a great effect upon his audience, and waxing bolder he smote the idols and broke them to pieces, and the huge beer vessel shivered at his touch, and the sacred beer was all spilled.*

Three years the missionaries remained at Bregenz ; they built a cell, made clearings in ·the primeval forest, cultivated gardens, and planted fruit trees. It is related of the holy Gallus that he wove nets, by means of which he caught so many fish that he was not only able to meet his own wants and those of the brotherhood, but also to give away a great many to the surrounding people. The old monkish chronicles, as epitomised by Schwab, relate that once in the stillness of the night as Gallus stood by

---

* A huge vessel contained the sacred beer, probably the representative among our Germanic forefathers of the "Soma" which their and our ancestors worshipped and sang in the Vedic hymns in their far away primeval home at the base of the Himalayas.

the lake shore, and proceeded to cast his nets into the water, he heard a demon or wood spirit cry aloud from the height of the Bregenzer Wald, and address by name the water-spirit in the depth of the lake, who answered " Here am I." Then spoke the Wood Spirit, "Come thou to my help, that we may drive away these strangers who have come to us from the far distance. They have broken down my images in the temple, and have seduced the people that served me to themselves. Up! let us chase away our common enemies!" "Woe is me," replied the Water Spirit, "it is the truth that thou speakest. This I know, for one of them attacks me in the water and wastes my kingdom there, and I can neither break his nets nor otherwise withstand him, for on his lips is continually the name of the true God." The holy man protected himself with the sign of the cross, rebuked the devils in Christ's name, and hurried to his master Columbanus in his cell, who without a moment's delay summoned all the other brothers to a solemn conclave. Hardly had they begun to pray and sing praises to God, when the air was filled with the dreadful cries of the demons, who with wild and bitter lamentations departed away over the summits of the surrounding mountains. But, in truth, the brotherhood was not simply troubled by superstitious fears of the supernatural. Those of the heathen who were irreconcilable complained to Duke Gunzo, who ruled in Iburningen, (Ueberlingen), as a result of which he commanded them to leave Bregenz, and refused them any longer his protection. The heathen stole a cow from the monks, and two brothers who endeavoured to track it were found murdered in the woods.

Sadly the brotherhood decided that they must leave their fields and orchards, their huts and cell, and little church, and return to Arbon. Here Gallus lay almost sick unto death of a fever.

Now the deacon of Willimar, the bishop of Arbon, named Hiltibold, was like Nimrod, a mighty hunter before the Lord; he knew every recess of the woods, and every mountain fastness in the neighbourhood. To him Gallus, as he became convalescent, turned and asked him if he knew "of a place rich in springs of water, where also there was some good level land, where he might end his days in solitude." "I do, indeed, know of such a place," replied Hiltibold, "a solitude rich in springs of water, but desert and rude, full of steep hills and narrow valleys : beasts of prey, bears, boars, and ravening wolves, make their home there. I fear, brother, if I take thee thither, that thou wilt be swallowed up of such enemies." Gallus was not to be frightened, so they wandered through the woods behind Arbon, and over the hills until they reached a narrow high-lying valley, overshadowed by a spur of the great stony Alpine range, whose summits pierced the clouds. Here they came to a beautiful waterfall of the little river Steinach, caught some fish, broiled and ate them. On the way Gallus stumbled and fell into a thorny hollow. " Let me lie, it is God's will," said he ; " here will I stay." On this spot later arose the Abbey of St. Gall. The chronicle avers that even here the good man was not free from supernatural foes. When the deacon began to fish in the stream, two demons in the shape of naked water-nymphs appeared, abused him for having brought a stranger into their midst, and threw stones at him. Gallus exorcised them in the name of the triune Gód, when they disappeared over the mountains, amid the sad wailing of women's voices. He then consecrated the· place where he fell with prayer and fasting, marked the spot with a cross made of hazel sticks, shared his bread with a wonderfully tame bear, and returned to Arbon. Then he took leave of Bishop Willimar, and with his two comrades, Magnoald and Theodore, returned into the wilderness and built a hut, and began to make a clearing in the woods.

Shortly after this, Frideburg, the beautiful and only daughter of Duke Gunzo, at Iburningen (Ueberlingen), on the opposite shore of the lake, fell very sick, so that her father and all who saw her believed her to be possessed by an evil spirit. She was betrothed to the Frank king Sigebert, and he sent priests to her to help her recovery. These she laughed to scorn, but after a frightful paroxysm of her disorder, she asked that the holy Gallus might be sent for into the wilderness and brought to her.

The Duke's messengers at once sailed across the lake to Arbon, where they found Gallus on a visit to his friend Willimar. The humility of Gallus was such that he could not believe it his duty to obey the call to the ducal court, but hurried back with his two disciples to his cell, and thence into the Rheinthal to Quaradaves (Grabs), where he found a Christian deacon of the name of John, and hid himself with him in a cave. There Willimar sought and found him, and convinced him that it must be God's voice that called him to a work of love, and persuaded him to return with him, and to cross the lake to the Duke at Iburningen. His prayers prevailed to cure the maiden, and the old historian (Walafrid Strabo) adds that the evil spirit that tormented her flew out of her mouth in the shape of a raven.

The Duke, in the fulness of his gratitude, wished Gallus to become Bishop of Constance, which important see had just become vacant. The unfeigned humility of the man would not allow him to accept this honour, but he named for it John, the deacon of Quaradaves, who had studied the Holy Scriptures under his guidance. Gallus was present at the consecration of John, and availed himself of the opportunity to unfold to the new Christians around him the love of God as displayed in the creation and redemption of man.

He and John entered the pulpit together, and the latter translated into German what he spoke in Latin. The sermon, which is still extant, attests the genuineness of his Christian piety. When he returned to Arbon laden with the gifts of the grateful prince, he assembled the poor of the place around him and gave away all to them.

The representative of Duke Gunzo at Arbon was ordered to repair with ample assistance to the cell of Gallus, and there to prepare him a dwelling, and put everything into proper order.

By degrees, twelve brothers assembled around Gallus, and a church was built. They endured hardness in every sense, for in addition to the work of subduing and cultivating the wilderness, they travelled all around, teaching, preaching, healing, overthrowing the idols, and persuading the people to renounce their service. At length, in extreme old age, Gallus received an invitation from Willimar, the friend of so many years, to come again to Arbon. There he preached with great emotion on St. Michael's day. He was 95 years old, and the exertion brought on a violent fever, of which he lay ill for a fortnight. When his friend and former scholar, John, Bishop of Constance, heard of the sickness of his master, he quickly loaded a boat with food and drink suitable for him, and was rowed to Arbon.

As the boat approached the harbour of the *Camp*

(this was the name Arbon had retained since the time
of the Romans) the death-wail from the house of
the Presbyter told that he who was so well called
the "Apostle to the Germans" had passed away. Grief
did not permit the bishop to await the arrival of the
boat at the shore: he and his companion flung themselves into the water, hurried to the house of mourning,
and threw himself weeping upon the corpse of his
teacher.

It is related that when Gallus was distributing the
presents he had received from Gunzo to the poor at
Arbon, his disciple Magnoald said to him, " Father,
I have here a silver vessel, beautifully adorned with
carving; if thou art willing I will put it upon one side,
so that we may use it in the celebration of the· holy
mass." " My son," replied Gallus, "think of the
words of Peter to the man at the Beautiful Gate of
the Temple, ' Silver and gold have I none ;' that thou
may'st not be found unmindful of this wholesome
example, see to it that this vessel is given to the poor.
In brazen vessels my teacher Columbanus was wont
to celebrate the mass, and of brass were the nails
with which the Redeemer was fastened to the cross."

The interest of the subject has caused me to linger
too long on the introduction of Christianity into the
region of the Boden See ; what further of history we
have to tell will find its proper place as we visit the
separate cities on its shores.

CHAPTER II.

Romanshorn—Rorschach—Celebration of Frohnleichnamstag—Protestant service at Rorschach—Catholic Worship—Visitors at our inn—Class-distinctions in Germany—Sunset near Rorschach—Arbon—Conradin—Heiden—An Appenzell house—The Steinli—View from the Kayen—Rustic bath—Sermon at Heiden — Thunderstorm — Visitor from St. Sepulchre—Die Ahnen — St. Nicholas and Wolfshalden.

On the 11th of June, 1879, my wife and I left the pleasant and flourishing town of Zürich, where we had been spending some months, for the shores of the Boden See, determined in the first instance to make Rorschach our head quarters. A thunderstorm on the preceding day had cleared the air; there was no dust, and the various shades of green of meadow, orchard, and forest, were all in their pristine brightness.

Through Winterthur and Frauenfeld, with their cotton factories, we speed, and at Romanshorn we reach the shores of that huge reservoir of the Rhine, the Boden See.

Romanshorn is a flourishing town with 3,300 inhabitants, and is now one of the most important harbours on the lake ; for not only do many passenger steamers call daily, but, by an ingenious arrangement, at any water level, a whole train of goods wagons can be run on and off powerful steamers specially constructed for the service, which ply between Romanshorn and the opposite Würtemberg shore at Friedrichs-hafen. It is

also a junction for the railway from Zürich to Romanshorn, and from Constance to Rorschach.

The line now runs through vineyards and orchards,
close by the side of the lake, until we reach Rorschach.

Leaving our luggage at the station, we proceeded to
make a tour of inspection of the hotels, walking slowly,
and keeping to the shady side of the street, on account
of the hot sun.   The principal hotel of the place is the
Seehof, well situated close to the lake, with cool
verandahs and corridors and a shady garden in front,
reaching down to the water.   We were, however, in
search of something simpler, and ultimately found the
accommodation we needed in the hotel, " Zum Grünen
Baum," which I find Schwab mentions fifty-four years
ago.   A " Green Tree " is a shelter by no means to be
despised in this piping hot weather, and, on the whole,
we were well satisfied with our choice.

Across the road is a " Garten Wirthschaft," or open
space full of benches and tables, shaded by plane
trees, and within a stone's throw are capital bathing
places—large wooden structures built on piles on the
lake, not unlike the residences of the lake dwellers of
four thousand years ago—where for 2½d. you have a
comfortable box with steps descending into deep water,
whence you may swim out into the lake and over into
Germany, if so disposed, and if you happen to be gifted
with the powers of a Captain Boyton or a Captain
Webb.   Oh! how refreshing are those swims—moderate ones I mean—when the sun blazes down as it did
the first day we were at Rorschach.   We have a
pleasant little room, the windows of which look right
across the lake to the coast of Würtemberg.   Our bed
furniture is most dainty.   The pillows, so far as visible,
are of amber silk, which peeps through open-work
insertion, four inches wide, in the pillow cases.   The

linen sheets are also handsomely embroidered in satin-stitch.

Rorschach is the most important Swiss town on the Boden See, and has nearly 4,000 inhabitants—mostly Catholics.

Rorschach from very early times was a place of importance, as the most convenient halting-place for northern wanderers and traders desirous of crossing into Italy by the Splügen Pass. The readers of "Ekkehard"* will remember that it was at Rorschach that Dame Hadwig landed from her barge on the occasion of her visit to the Abbey of St. Gall—that visit fraught with such momentous consequences to poor Ekkehard.

In 1486, the then Abbot of St. Gall, being in constant feud with the inhabitants of the city which had grown up under the shadow of the cloister, determined to transplant the Abbey to Rorschach, and, choosing a magnificent site upon a slope above the town, he erected some very fine buildings. But the citizens of St. Gall, however much they might quarrel with the Abbot, did not relish the idea of the loss that would accrue to the town if the Abbey were removed, and they made all possible remonstrances with Abbot Roesch to dissuade him from his purpose. He was, however, supported by both Pope and Emperor, and absolutely refused to yield. Thereupon, on the night

---

* "Ekkehard," by Scheffel, is a romance of the tenth century, the scene of which is laid entirely on the shores of the Boden See. Scheffel takes considerable liberties with history, and there is an unpleasant flavour about the love story in the book, but the descriptions of scenery are very fine, and it has been given to few modern writers so completely to transplant their readers into the life of the middle ages.

The work has gained an extraordinary popularity in Germany, having run through I know not how many editions. The Rev. S. Baring-Gould, in his admirable work upon Germany, subjects it to unsparing and somewhat savage criticism.

of the 28th July, 1489, 2,000 men marched down from
St. Gall through the woods to Rorschach with the cry,
" Wohl uf, thut dem heiligen Gallus ein Ehrentag an,"
—" Up, we will do honour to St. Gall."

Then they destroyed the new buildings, and committed everything to the flames, which threw their
lurid glare far over the lake.   For this outrage the
citizens of St. Gall had to pay dearly, both in money
and in the surrender of valuable privileges, but the
transference of the Abbey was abandoned, and the
monastery which arose on the ruins at Rorschach was
simply a daughter house to the mother institution at
St. Gall.   The building is now most usefully employed
as a seminary for teachers, and later on we will pay it
a visit.   It is called " Marienberg." After the Reformation, when Constance cruelly suffered through the
bigotry of Charles V., Rorschach rose in importance
at the expense of her sister city, and not only became
the entrepôt of an important trade in corn, but also
developed a large manufacture of linen, which brought
great wealth to the citizens.   The corn trade remains,
and one of the most conspicuous buildings in the town
is a palatial corn warehouse, built 140 years ago ; but
the linen manufacture has gone.   During the time of
its prosperity the burghers of Rorschach spent a part
of their wealth in building, in the broad street that runs
by the lake, fine mansions adorned with the quaintest
bay windows imaginable, supported by grim-looking
lions, griffins, and men-at-arms carved in wood.

The day after our arrival was the feast of " Corpus
Christi," or, as they call it here, " Frohnleichnamstag."
A great hammering at 3 a.m. told us that the preparations for the festival were beginning.   The whole town
was decorated, and the decorations were a decided
success.   The · stone-paved streets were so thickly

strewn as to be literally carpeted with fresh cut grass, and the walls of the houses were tapestried with tall branches of beech, chestnut, and other trees.

Each house vied with its neighbour. From the windows hung gaily-coloured carpets, paintings, and engravings, among the latter of which we noticed one of Michael Angelo's prophets. Vases of gorgeous peonies and other flowers stood on the window-sills, and were relieved by festoons of greenery which passed from window to window, and from floor to floor. The bright flowers and leaves set off wonderfully the lions and griffins and other quaint wood-carving of the projecting upper-floor windows. All business was suspended. Exactly in front of our window stood a species of triumphal arch, some forty feet high, surmounted by a lofty green cross. The woodwork was entirely covered with moss and leaves, and festooned and garlanded with flowers. Immediately below the cross was the inscription "Der Herr segne und beschütze diesen Ort und seine Bewohner."—"The Lord bless and protect this place and its inhabitants." The archway led up to a temporary altar, also profusely adorned with flowers, of which there were at least five in different parts of the little town. Shortly after 9 a.m. the head of the procession, which had formed at the church, appeared underneath our windows, from which we could see and hear everything. The procession appeared far more numerous than we should have thought possible, though every man, woman and child in Rorschach had taken part in it. First came two banner-bearers in long crimson cloaks; then the school-boys and school-girls in a double line; then about twenty little girls dressed in white, with wreaths of flowers on their heads; then maidens also dressed in white from head to foot, carrying on their shoulders an image of the Virgin and Child; then followed half-a-dozen gorgeously-attired priests, bearing the Host under a baldachin. Arrived at the altar under our windows, one of the priests intoned the discourse on the bread of life, from the sixth chapter of John, so clearly that we did not lose a syllable. The elevation of the Host followed, when all present reverently knelt. Taking part in the procession, and kept well in regular order and line by beadles or marshals dressed in black, with long staves of office, were old and young, rich and poor, but all were well dressed, and all seemed thoroughly and devoutly to enjoy themselves. When the procession had dispersed we walked through the town to the church, which was overflowing with worshippers at all its doors, and which it was useless to attempt to enter.

Near the church was a Bambino, or representation of the Saviour as an infant in a cradle, round which were gathered delighted groups of children. Everywhere we met whole families pacing the streets to examine the decorations. While the procession was mustering there were evident signs of an approaching storm, and later in the day the rain came down very heavily. During the last two days passing thunder-showers have swept over the lake, with occasional vivid flashes of lightning. The lake is constantly changing—now perfectly smooth, and in a few hours, or even less, lashed into fury by the wind, and covered with great waves all capped with white. In the evening we walked to a little hill above the town whence we could see the whole lake of Constance stretched at our feet. Towards Constance itself, lies what was once also lake, but is now a flat and very fertile plain, so studded with fruit trees that it looks

like an immense orchard, and reminds us of the
landscape in Normandy and Brittany. The heat is
seldom so great as at Zürich, for, unlike that charming
old city, it is not shut in by hills, and the broad expanse
of the lake serves as a constant refrigerator. Upon
inquiring of our landlord, a Catholic, the hours of
the Protestant and Roman Catholic services, we
were informed, *inter alia*, that if the parish priest
preached we should have a good sermon, but that
his vicar was not worth hearing. The Protestant
pastor, on the contrary, was "ein wahrer Kanzel-
redner," a true pulpit orator ; so, at 9 a.m. on Sunday
morning, June 15th, we sallied out to worship with
the Protestants, and to listen to this evangelical
Boanerges. The beautiful little church stands on rising
ground above the town, and is embowered in trees and
exquisite flowering shrubs, among which the tamarisk,
with its feathery branches now covered with delicate
bloom, is conspicuous. The church was well filled with
well-dressed men and women, and clean, tidy, and
happy-looking boys and girls,—for at any rate in this
part of Switzerland there are no slovenly, ragged, unkempt, neglected poor, such as we have in England.
A short hymn, a prayer in which the Almighty was
briefly thanked for the Reformation, and then the
preacher mounted the pulpit and gave a really fine
address. A week ago, he said, he had given notice
that he would that day preach upon the Reformation.
Many had urged that it was unwise. Why, said they,
re-awaken strife, and kindle anew the fires of religious
hatred of long ago? One reason that weighed strongly
with him in disregarding this advice was, that after
witnessing the affecting solemnities of Frohnleichnamstag, it was well for them in Rorschach anew to
consider what Roman Catholicism was, and what it

meant.   There were two points of view from which
we could regard it—in its social bearings and in its
essential principles.   If wandering into the Swiss Uplands, in some remote valley, or amid the sublimities of
lofty Alpine peaks, where the orchard and the cornfield
smile upon the very edge of the glacier, we came
upon a little village the whitewashed church of which
with its tall spire was the centre of its life, we felt
how beautiful was the religion which hallowed and
controlled the life of these simple peasants and shepherds, and brought to them comfort and hope in death.
But when we descended into the plain and entered
any of our cities, and especially when we took in hand
our daily paper and read how steadily and determinedly
the papacy opposed itself, as ever, to all progress, how
it put the human intellect under its ban, and strove to
clip the wings of man's thought, we felt that we must
never falter in our opposition to it.   "It is too much the
fashion now-a-days," he added, "to speak of Luther and
Zwingli as of over-rated men—men full of prejudices
and extremely *borné*.   But let us consider a moment
what they accomplished!   Think how strong is the
Church of Rome now!   How little has the Old
Catholic movement been able to accomplish with all its
efforts, and with all the assistance it has received from
the civil power!   The most powerful States strike blows
at the papacy, expecting that they will prove highly
damaging to it, and the blows recoil upon the heads of the
strikers, who are obliged to retract their hostile measures.
Consider for a moment how much greater was the
power of the Church at the beginning of the sixteenth
century!   The *Servus Servorum* was really the master
of kings, and the arbiter of the destinies of the civilised
world.   Against him, arrayed in all the glory of
authority and backed by the prestige of the fifteen

Christian centuries, stood two men, one a simple monk of Wittenberg, the other 'ein Leut-Prediger,' a people's preacher in the Cathedral of Zürich. Yet these two simple men won the battle for humanity, and in securing spiritual freedom for the world, as greatly affected even its material destinies as did Columbus in discovering a new world." The sermon was followed by another short prayer, almost entirely confined to the subject of the Reformation, another verse of a hymn was sung, and the service was over, all within an hour, and we were surprised to learn that there was no other service, either on Sunday or during the week. The Roman Catholic church is much larger than the Protestant, and is handsomely painted inside and adorned with stained glass windows. It has recently been newly seated with handsome benches of polished walnut. It is of course open every day and all day, and on Sundays one service follows another from early morning till towards sundown. Servants and others who are busily at work all Sunday, will make a great effort to attend early morning mass. Thus, upon my remarking to a waitress at a refreshment and beer and cider (*Most*) room, that she must be terribly busy on Sundays, she replied, that it was true,—that every Sunday they were thronged with guests. "I am afraid you never have a chance of attending a place of worship," I continued. "Oh, yes," she replied, "I always go to the service at five. I should feel quite unhappy all day if I did not." Who knows how much of strength and support for her exposed and toilsome life she may draw from that service!

Hearing that there was to be a Catholic service at 1.30, we went to the church. There was no service until later; but the spacious and airy church was in many

parts crowded with reverent and silent worshippers,
mostly on their knees, and diligently studying their
prayer-books. As far as neatness and cleanliness were
concerned, there was nothing to choose between them
and the Protestants—greater could not be desired in
either; but the Catholics seemed to realise the idea of
worship more than the others. But for the gorgeous
altar, the really fine paintings, the stained windows,
and, I must add, the reverent attitude of the congregation, I could have fancied myself again in a Quakers'
meeting. Thus often in religion, as in life, do extremes seem to touch. At the end of half-an-hour the
tapers before the high altar were lighted, the organ
pealed, a sort of low mass was performed, and the
congregation joined in what is called a " Rosenkranz "
—the chanting of a number of prayers in German,
in which the Lord's Prayer is followed by the " Hail,
Mary." We shortly left. But I must not omit to
mention the reverent behaviour of the children, and
how the little "trots" entered and walked to their
seats with folded hands, and how thoroughly they all
seemed to enjoy the service. On another occasion
we attended Matins, when we heard a sermon upon
the virtues and miracles of St. Anthony of Padua.
The large church was quite full, the men on one side
and the women on the other, while there was a special
service for the children in the chapel of the former
monastery—the Marienberg. As each bench held
ten (and there are seventy-two benches), and as there
were in addition two large galleries quite full, and
many worshippers remained standing inside and even
outside the open doors, the congregation must have
numbered one thousand—this at eight in the morning, and out of a total population of less than four
thousand, of whom five hundred are Protestants.

Probably, however, some came from the surrounding country.

Our little inn pleases us better the longer we remain. Everything is very clean, and the quaint and familiar courtesy that is shown to us by every one in the house, from "mine host" downwards, is quite charming. Never do we sit down to a meal but he comes and "makes a leg" in capital style, and wishes us "besten Appetit." His pretty little wife is equally solicitous for our comfort, and some of the visitors are very amusing. One of these I must describe. He is a traveller in the wine trade who hails from the Vorarlberg, and looks much like one of the Goths Kingsley delighted to pourtray in "Hypatia." Gigantic in stature, with bright red hair and sanguine temperament, he is on the best of terms with everybody, from the guests and hotel proprietors down to the waiters, boots, and chambermaids. Above all, he is evidently on the best of terms with himself. We had first met with him at the Züricher Hof, Zürich, where the hearty, stentorian tones of his voice used to ring through the house, which re-echoed with his mighty laughter. He speaks some half-dozen Slavonic languages, besides German, French, Italian, English, and Dutch. He is an officer in the German Landwehr, who has served all through the campaign in France without ever being wounded, though you would suppose his enormous bulk would have presented a target that could not be missed. One would think a pessimist could not exist anywhere within half-a-mile of this exuberant being. The German adjective "lebensfroh" best describes him. We had not been long at Rorschach before he turned up at our hotel. Probably for the sake of coolness, he had had the red hair of his great leonine head polled down to about a sixteenth of an inch, and looked as if prepared to enter upon any project with the spirit and thoroughness which our trans-Atlantic cousins express by the phrase "going into it bald-headed." For some days there was with us a trader from the Toggenburg who had read Scott, Dickens, Thackeray, and George Eliot, and could criticise them intelligently. One morning when we came down to breakfast we found a stolid-looking man, not so much stout as large in every sense, with a tiny little wife. He proved to be a German from Silesia, probably a very well-to-do farmer. Hearing my wife read something aloud from the *Times*, he asked, in evident astonishment, "Is that German?" Upon being told it was English, he said, "I suppose everybody speaks English *here?*" The poor man's geography and ethnology were evidently at fault. When we explained that we were English visitors, it solved the mystery to him. He was furious at the extortions to which he had been subjected in Switzerland. At the Rigi Kulm he and his wife had been charged 12 francs for their beds, 2 for gas, 2 for bougies, and 2 for "service"—pretty well for one night; but his bitterness culminated as he spoke of the innkeeper at B——. Had the traveller been a Yankee, he would have expressed his opinion of this particular host by saying that he was the "meanest cuss" that he had ever met with; as it was, he exhausted the resources of the Teutonic tongue, aided by much pantomimic gesture, in expressing the same idea. He did not enter into particulars as to the enormities this vile extortioner had committed, so we could only presume that they were something beyond description. Upon our remarking that we had never met with anything of the kind, he asked us how long we had been in Switzerland,

and upon our replying, "A year and a-half," he fairly set his cup down, stared at us open-mouthed, and expressed his utter unbelief in an emphatic "Das glaube ich nicht," thinking that we were jesting. He was a very decent sort of man, but without the least pretence to breeding. This is, however, usual in his class in Germany, where the line of demarcation between the different ranks of society is drawn with a sharpness of which we have no idea in England. With us, a gentleman is a gentleman whether he be scholar, clergyman, lawyer, merchant, or trader; but in Germany you have the noble class, always military, the savants and professors, the clergy comparatively low down in the scale, and the merchants, manufacturers, and traders; and the ideas, habits, and reading of each class are so entirely distinct that they intermix but little. There are, of course, exceptions to this rule as to all rules; but the culture and refinement which so generally prevail among the English middle class are not to be met with in the corresponding class in Germany.

Rorschach makes a capital centre for excursions by steamboat. In about an hour you are conveyed to Friedrichs-hafen or to Lindau, and in half-an-hour longer to Bregenz. From Rorschach itself, or its immediate neighbourhood, the Sentis and its congeners are not visible, being hidden by the green heights of Appenzell; but before you reach the middle of the lake the whole panorama of the Alps comes into view.

The walks around Rorschach are numerous and delightful. Let us take that along the shore in the direction of Arbon. It is the evening of a stormy day in June, when, tempted by the temporary cessation of the down-pour, we stroll along the shore. About a mile from Rorschach a former queen of Würtemberg built herself a spacious and elegant wooden villa, now shaded by magnificent walnut and other trees, and surrounded by well-kept gardens, full of brilliant flowers. Just beyond the royal residence a spit of land runs out into the lake, from which we get a good view of our present home, the little town of Rorschach. The massive and palatial granary built for the accommodation of the corn trade in 1748, stands close to the harbour, and the town climbs up the hill-side behind it. Beyond are the green uplands which, from this point of view, shut out the high Alps from the prospect. They are deep in meadow grass, and are studded with innumerable fruit trees, against the green of which stands out an occasional patch of dark pine forest. Golden clouds, companions of the setting sun, are resting upon the low hills of southern Germany, while at another point a thunder-shower is darkly descending upon them. At the head of the lake our eyes rest upon the deep black purple of the mountains of the Bregenzer Wald, and the nearer peaks of the Vorarlberg just streaked with snow. The sound of church bells floats to us over the water. A solitary fisherman, with boat and tackle but little altered from those used by his predecessors of the period of the lake-dwellers, is drawing in his net in the gloaming. A hare starts from his form at our feet to seek shelter in one of the numerous clumps of trees which stud the lake-side as if it were a park, and we regret the thunder-shower which compels us to turn our faces homeward. Arbon, with its very ancient church, lies a little further to the west of Rorschach, bowered in and almost hidden by fruit trees, the great wealth of the Canton of Thurgau. In a good year not less than ten million pounds weight are exported hence to Germany, and the

dowry of a Thurgau maiden often consists, or did
consist until recently, of four or five great apple or
pear trees, which here attain the size of oaks or elms
in a less favoured clime.

The name " Arbor Felix," which the Romans gave
when they settled at Arbon—probably when they first
cleared the forest and planted the beneficent apple
tree—is at least as appropriate now as it was 1800
years ago. In the massive masonry of the walls
of the old castle is to be seen the handiwork of the
Merovingian period, and it is thought that the lower
part of the tower, fifty to sixty feet in diameter, is of
Roman origin. Here, about A.D. 1259, the last of the
great house of the Hohenstaufen, the unfortunate
Conradin, spent six months, and granted special
privileges to the citizens, on account " of the long
presence here of our servants and our Highness." At
present it is a flourishing little town of about 2000
inhabitants, who are mostly occupied either in the silk
manufacture or in agriculture.

Another very interesting walk from Rorschach is to
Rheineck, where from the ruins of the old castle,
a magnificent view is gained of the whole length of
the lake. It stands a little above the spot where the
young Rhine—already a broad and strong stream—
plunges into the lake. The frontier between Switzerland and Austria is in mid-stream, and the far shore
belongs to the Vorarlberg. It is well worth while to
visit the seminary for teachers on the Marienberg,
formerly a monastery. There are eighty-five youths
in the establishment, but upon the occasion of our
visit they were all away on their annual holiday
trip in Glarus. The great dormitory where they all
sleep reminded me much of a similar dormitory in
the settlement of the Moravian brethren at Ebersdorf.

D

What was once the refectorium of the monks, and is now the dining and music-hall, is of fine proportions, and the cloisters, which are in perfect preservation, present in their cool shade a most inviting appearance on a hot day. One side of them has been set apart as a workshop, wherein to teach the pupils carpenter's and other mechanical work. They also labour to some extent in the gardens and fields, so that they may have some practical knowledge of agriculture.

The old castles of St. Anne and Moettelli, dating from the fourteenth or fifteenth century, are both within an hour's walk of the town. They are now used as farm-houses or country inns. They are approached through greenest meadows, shaded by umbrageous apple and pear trees, while almost at every turn views of the blue lake of surpassing loveliness present themselves.

About three miles distant, and 1200 feet above Rorschach, surrounded by the green hills characteristic of Canton Appenzell, stands the charming village of Heiden. In the month of September, 1838, almost every house in Heiden was destroyed by one of those dreadful conflagrations which work such havoc among the wooden houses of Swiss villages. The fire threw a lurid glare over the whole of the Boden See, and ashes and other *débris* were carried by the wind, and fell in a thick shower at Lindau on the opposite side of the lake. Like the Phœnix, Heiden rose from its ashes, and is now a most prosperous hamlet of about 3000 inhabitants, much visited by invalids from all parts of the world. In addition to lovely views and pure mountain air, it affords abundant facilities to those invalids who wish to try the milk and whey cures. To induce an influx of visitors, a mountain railway has been constructed on the principle of that from the

Lake of Lucerne to the summit of the Rigi, and of that from the Lake of Zürich to Einsiedeln.

There is a fine church situated in a large square planted with trees, and the houses are large and roomy —mostly of wood. I do not know how to give an idea of the absolute neatness and cleanliness of the little town. Although but little after nine a.m. when we arrived, the sun was shining hotly down, and we were glad to find rest and shade in the comfortable hostelry of the " Krone." About five in the afternoon we thought we might venture upon a little walk to one of the picturesque hills clothed with pine, with which the village is, as it were, guarded. The air was as pure as air could be, but the heat was very great, and would have been intolerable but for the shade of the trees.

Though a very favourite summer resort, especially of the southern Germans, at this time (1879) it was but little visited by the English, and we were surprised to hear a lady and gentleman whom we met conversing in our language. They proved to be the Rev. D. H. and his sister-in-law. Mr. H. was for twenty-eight years a missionary on the West Coast of Africa, and is the author of "Seventeen Years in the Yoruba Country," a record of missionary zeal and suffering which ran through several editions some years back. Returning to Europe with his constitution shattered by so prolonged a residence in that exhausting climate, he was recommended to try Heiden, and, finding great benefit from the air, he and his sister had taken a charming little Appenzell house, commanding a noble view of the lake. What, then, is there especial or individual in an Appenzell house ? That it is almost entirely of wood will hardly distinguish it from other Swiss houses ; but what *is* remarkable is that the rooms seem entirely surrounded by windows. Sliding shutters can be run up, so that on the sunniest day you can have abundance of shade, but if the day be dark or cloudy you find yourself literally in a glass house.   As what is not window is covered with shingles, the exquisite cleanliness of an Appenzell house is a sight to see.   The blue smoke of the wood fire does not blacken and begrime like coal smoke.

Warned by the intense heat of the sun on the day of our arrival, we determined, if possible, to escape his more ardent rays by breakfasting at six ; after which, armed with our white umbrellas, we sallied out, turning westward down one of the main streets, the wooden Appenzell houses of which look as if they had just stepped out of a picture, so quaint and clean are they. Leaving the main road and threading our way through meadows and past farmsteads, we mount toward the " Steinli."   Though so early the heat is intense, and it is a great relief when our path takes us through a wooded dell where the interlacing leaves shield us from the sun's fiery rays.   The " Steinli" is a little hill-top, about a mile distant from Heiden, whence, towering above the green hills of Appenzell, a part of the huge mass of the Sentis is to be seen.   The immortal tinker of Bedford tells how, about half-way up the hill Difficulty, an arbour was placed for the rest and solace of pilgrims.   On the " Steinli" there is also an arbour open on all sides to the winds of heaven. On the stony hill-top around blooms in profusion the true Alpine thornless rose—not the Alpine rhododendron, commonly called Alpine rose, but a true wild rose with deep crimson petals.   The wind blew vigorously through the summer-house, and though it was the hot south wind, the Föhn, it refreshed us. Here then we sat and read, and were more fortunate than poor Christian in his arbour, for we left without any such sad loss as his.

The " Steinli " is at the lower extremity of a hog-backed hill, and as we followed a footpath along the ridge the refreshing breezes continued until we reached the shade of a pine wood, which extends to the higher summit of the hill called the Kayen.

Here we enjoyed the shade of the trees together with the coolness of the breeze which swept the meadows of still standing grass, causing that wavy, tremulous motion which was the original meaning of the Latin word *horror*. At our feet lay the Boden See in its whole extent, and around us was the green and fertile Canton of Appenzell, on whose hill-sides the rich pastures are dotted all over with smiling villages and farmsteads, while beyond, to the west, lies the low-level plain of Thurgau, which may be described as one great orchard. To the south is the whole range of the Sentis—a similar but nearer view to that from the lake at Friedrichs-hafen. More to the south-east rises the Scesa Plana and his snowy compeers of Graubünden, and just beyond Chur, white and shadowy, looms a peak that must overhang the Splügen Pass and be almost in Italy, while above the Vorarlberg mountains are some dazzling peaks, which we take to be the far distant Tyrolese mountains, the Orteler Spitze and the Stilfser Joch, or their congeners.

Long before the sun had reached the meridian we had gained the shelter of our hotel, and that afternoon the thermometer rose to 24° Réaumur, or 86° Fahrenheit.

A pretty little stream flows through Heiden, and thence finds its way to the lake through a deep ravine, both sides of which are densely wooded with beech and silver birch, and alder and willow, so

that there is always shade from the sun; just such a
spot, in fact, as that in which poor Ophelia met her
death.   Here the public-spirited inhabitants of Heiden
have thrown a dam of Portland cement across the
stream with a water door in it, and have thus converted
the bosky dell into a swimming bath 150 feet long.
En passant, be it remarked that it is not selfishly
monopolised by the coarser sex, but that for certain
hours during the day it is reserved for ladies.   Here
the sunlight glints through the overhanging roof of
verdure, while the air is perfumed with the blossom
of the meadow-sweet, with which one bank is white.

The handsome temple-like church of Heiden is in
the possession of a very "advanced" pastor, so by the
advice of Mr. H—— we attended the meeting-house of
a body who have broken away from the church.   The
service was held in a large upper room, constructed
and fitted up much like an old-fashioned Methodist
chapel.   The women occupied the body of the hall,
while the men were in two side galleries.   The sermon,
which was delivered in the harsh and guttural Schaffhausen dialect, was perfectly suited to the place and
people.   The rustic preacher, with his barbarous German, was, nevertheless, a true orator.   Not a word
was unnecessary, not a word was lost.   The text was,
"Godliness with contentment is great gain."   With
dramatic power he told the story of Diogenes and
Alexander, and contrasted with it an episode in the
life of the Emperor Otto.   The Emperor, hearing that
his conduct had been greatly censured by a celebrated
Christian saint, went to him and told him that, far from
blaming his freedom, he greatly admired it, and
desired that the saint should ask from him some
favour.   The saint replied that he had need of
nothing; the only favour he would ask of him was

that he should think of his own immortal soul. The preacher skilfully contrasted the haughty independence and egotistical self-satisfaction of the Greek philosopher, through every hole of whose rags pride peeped out, with the godly content of the Christian saint, indissolubly linked as it was with a yearning for the good of others. The whole sermon was fervent and practical, and calculated to raise the hearers to a higher spiritual level.

Though not so hot as the previous day, the afternoon was very sultry, and we rejoiced in the prospect of a thunderstorm. Towards evening it came. First the distant lightning flashed over the Boden See, lighting up Lindau and the Bregenzer Wald with a preternatural roseate light. Then the rain fell with tropical violence—indeed, literally in sheets—and the air seemed all aglow with lightning. For some time we estimated that there were twenty to thirty flashes each minute. From rose-colour the lightning changed to green, and finally to the usual brilliant yellow. The thunder was not so deafening as it is sometimes, and probably we were at some distance from the centre of the storm. Few spectacles are so grand as a thunderstorm in the Alps. The immediate effect of this storm was that the thermometer fell from about 85° to 53° Fahrenheit. Much damage was done by the rain. The charming bathing place was left a wreck. No one took thought to open the water door, and though the cement stood bravely against the pressure of the raging stream, a strong embankment in solid masonry, with a railing, steps, &c., was swept entirely away. Where the day before had been a deep reach of crystal-clear water, was now a turbid torrent, which, when it subsided, left the bath full of stones, soil, and mud. The stone buttresses of I know not how many small bridges, which spanned the stream at different points, were also carried away. On the roadside and on the hillsides, wherever the slope is steep, small landslips took place, the soil and turf slipping away into the road or stream, as the case might be, leaving only the bare rock. Land-drains burst and covered the meadows with stones, mud, and gravel. The people, however, did not lose heart, but were all busy on the morning after the storm trying to put to rights, where possible, the mischief it had occasioned. Whenever there is any sunshine, men, women, and children are also busy getting in the hay.

While at Heiden we were joined by a lady friend, who for some years had been an active member of one of the metropolitan boards of guardians. One would have thought that here, in Appenzell, she would be beyond the range of the influence of the august Board of (let us say) St. Sepulchre, and very unlikely to meet with one of her former clients. She had, however, hardly been with us a week when, one evening, coming down to dinner, I found a drunken, suspicious-looking fellow waiting in the hall, and, in the *salle-à-manger*, Miss D——, considerably puzzled by the following extraordinary epistle :—

"Miss D—— (her name was given correctly),

"Ci telle yuo ev bin here and dont have Monnay for schip. Do noi it if yuo plis for me. Plis uns ist moi.

"C. Stähli."

She could make neither head nor tail of this strange document, and it was only after consultation that we decided that it must be one of her poor people from St. Sepulchre, who had found her out in this remote place. I went out to see the man in the hall, who explained to me in German that his colleague, who

was just round the corner, had known Miss D—— in
St. Sepulchre. No doubt he had been in the workhouse there. He would call his friend if I liked. In
any case, any money with which I might entrust him
would be honestly divided between them. This I had
no reason to doubt ; but, before doing anything else,
I thought it well to return to the *salle-à-manger* to
learn what Miss D—— thought of her strange followers. Upon going back to the hall I found that,
during my few minutes' absence, the police had carried
off my friend, and that his "colleague," the author of
the strange *billet-doux*, had taken to his heels. I
make no doubt the poor fellow had, while in London
acquired a slight knowledge of English, but only pho-
netically, and that his letter might be translated :—

"MISS D——,

"This tells you I am here, and have no money for the ship
[probably to take him across the lake.] Do pay it, if you please, for
me. Please assist me.

"C. STÄHLI."

Our landlord, who is also a local judge, assured
me that they were a couple of tramps, and that the
ambassador—one would have thought that his mission
should have secured the inviolability of his person—
had been arrested for begging in the town. He would
receive a meal, be locked up for the night, and then,
if his papers were in order, he would be taken to the
frontier of the canton and there set at liberty. If his
papers were not in order, he would be detained to see
whether he were "wanted" by any other police authorities. This seems hard measure for wanderers without
papers and without money. The landlord said that
unless the cantonal authorities were very strict in
dealing with tramps they would be quite overrun with

them, from Germany and elsewhere. For their own poor they have an excellent system of relief, as we were able to assure ourselves when we visited the asylum for poor children and the almshouse for aged poor, both located on a height above the town.

Our company at the Krone was very pleasant: among others a judge from Nuremberg of the name of Danmer, with his wife, and the postmaster from Stuttgart, all of whom were religiously following the whey cure. The virtue of the whey is supposed greatly to depend upon the altitude at which it is prepared. That drunk at Heiden is prepared on the higher slopes of the Sentis, and, while still hot, is carried on men's backs for five hours so as to be ready for the patients before eight in the morning. It is not an exhilarating drink.

Mr. Danmer was kind enough to lend us "Ingro and Ingraban," the first in order of time of the series of historical romances by Freitag, called "Die Ahnen," "The Ancestors." In this series Freitag has endeavoured to portray the life of Germany from the earliest times downwards, and has adopted the curious and interesting plan of giving the fortunes of one family through different generations. Ingro lived in the fourth century after Christ, and his life is a grand old heathen idyll or war-song—a picture of the life of our ancestors, when Thor and Woden ruled supreme, and Hengist and Horsa had not yet swung their battle-axes upon British soil—there founding, amid blood and fire, the English nation. With Ingraban in the eighth century, we find ourselves in other times and among other manners. The cowled soldiers of the cross are carrying the glad tidings to the savage Germans. We breathe another atmosphere. Revenge ceases to be at once absolute duty and high virtue.

The idea of self-sacrifice dawns upon the rude warriors of the north. Thor and Woden bow their heads before the mild Christ. The book, too, shows admirably how in those far away centuries, when but a twilight civilisation obtained, the institution of the papacy was invaluable as giving unity to Christendom, and supplying an absolute and final high court of appeal in all civil as well as ecclesiastical disputes.

Another very beautiful walk from Heiden is to the Chapel of St. Nicholas, a little forest sanctuary on the crest of a hill some 700 or 800 feet above Heiden. From it you look right down into the Rhine valley, which is so immediately beneath, that it is difficult to believe that you could not drop a stone into the old town of Altstetten, 2000 feet below. The mountain view from here is very similar to that from the Kayen.

A mile from Heiden, on the road to Rheineck, is the beautifully-situated village of Wolfs-halden, or the Wolf Height. Here was fought a decisive engagement between the shepherds of Appenzell and their feudal lord the Abbot of St. Gall, aided by the powerful Frederick of Austria, in the year 1405.

As, however, we here touch upon a very interesting chapter in the history of the Cities and Shores of the Boden See, we will commence anew.

CHAPTER III.

APPENDZELL.

The Republic of Appenzell — Quarrels between the Abbeys of Reichenau and St. Gall—The shepherds of Appenzell rise against the Abbot of St. Gall— Appenzellers find a general in Rudolf of Werdenberg — Success of the Appenzellers — Siege of Bregenz — Family of Reding — Appenzell divided into Inner-Rhoden and Ausser-Rhoden.

FROM the time of its foundation, the Abbey of St. Gall shed a beneficent light of civilisation among the rude and savage people that dwelt in the fertile valleys, the green uplands, the dense woods, and the rocky fastnesses, comprised in the mountain regions where the Hohe Sentis and his congeners raise their snowy summits.

But although the benefits conferred on the neighbourhood by the monks were undoubted, and are not likely to be over-estimated, their rule was by no means an unmixed blessing. For, be it remembered, throughout the middle ages the Abbot of St. Gall possessed and exercised lordship over the whole of what now constitutes the Cantons of St. Gall and Appenzell, including almost the whole of the Rheinthal—and with the Abbots of Fulda, Kempten, and Reichenau, was reckoned among the richest and most powerful prelates in Christendom. Monks after all are but men, and the unnatural state in which they live is not conducive to the growth of the distinctively human virtues. Abbots were generally imperious, often proud, and sometimes cruel.

In 1084, sad to say, there was open war between the Abbeys of St. Gall and Reichenau, and later there were constant wars between the Abbey of St. Gall and the Bishopric of Constance. At the end of the twelfth century, when a certain Ulrich was abbot, there was a quarrel between the Abbey of St. Gall and the City of Arbon about a wood in Appenzell to which both parties laid claim. The men of Arbon caught one of the Abbot's men taking wood from this particular forest, and barbarously punished him by cutting off one of his feet. Shortly afterwards six men of Arbon fell into the hands of the Abbot, when he in revenge cut off both the feet of all of them. Yet this was an abbot who was specially honoured both by the Emperor and by Pope Innocent IV.

The Abbot of Reichenau, in 1366, caught five fishermen of Constance fishing in his waters, whereupon he with his own hand put out their eyes, and then sent them back blind into Constance. These instances show the savage side of the character of the times, and how constantly local feuds were likely to arise. By this time a considerable town had grown up under the walls of the Abbey of St. Gall, and the citizens began to feel the yoke of their priestly lord intolerable. The forest cantons had already bound themselves together by oath to support one another's independence, had overthrown the dominion of their feudal lords and had burned their castles. In the Suabian lowlands the free cities had united themselves under a solemn compact to defend their liberties against the nobility.

The cities were, however, by no means disposed to receive the discontented subjects of other lords into their confederacy; but the men of the four cantons were quite ready to join in fighting against tyranny, possibly against authority anywhere, especially if gold was to be earned in exchange for hard knocks.

In 1386, Leopold of Austria, with his lords and knights, gave battle to the men of Uri, Schwyz, and Unterwalden, at Sempach, and he and all his chivalry fell before the battle-axes and " morgensterns " of the redoubtable mountaineers.

The shepherds of Appenzell and the citizens of St. Gall felt that the oppression of the Abbot of St. Gall was intolerable—and they turned for assistance to the victors of Sempach, the men of the four cantons. Abbot Kuno, on his part, secured the assistance of the cities of Constance, Ueberlingen, Ravensburg, Lindau, Wangen, and Buchhorn (now Friedrichs-hafen). At the head of an army of 5000 men, composed of the contingents from the cities and great numbers of the nobility, the abbot now marched into Appenzell to coerce his refractory subjects. The shepherds waited for them in a favourable position at Speicher, com-pletely defeated them, killed 300 of the allied citizens, and captured the banners of Constance, Ueberlingen, Lindau, and Buchhorn, which are still hung up as trophies in the town of Appenzell. This was in 1404. The victorious shepherds carried fire and sword into their enemies' territory, and burned no less than fifty castles in Thurgau. The nobles, exasperated to fury, succeeded in obtaining the powerful assistance of Duke Frederick of Austria.

Things looked very black indeed for the handful of shepherds who lived on the slopes of the Hohe Sentis. Their courage was as high as the mountain that overshadowed their homes, and at the critical moment, when their fate was trembling in the balance, they gained that—for want of which undisciplined valour is so often displayed in vain—a skilful general.

Count Rudolf of Werdenberg had been driven by his cousin, Count William of Montfort-Bregenz, from his ancestral castle of Werdenberg, in the Rheinthal. Without land and without followers, he presented himself to the assembled men of Appenzell, and offered them his counsel and his sword. This they joyfully accepted, and he, to show how completely he made their cause his own, stripped off his knightly garments, and clothed himself in the simple shepherd's shirt or tunic of his allies. Duke Frederick of Austria advanced from the Tyrol, and established his headquarters at Arbon. Count William of Montfort-Bregenz was one of his principal generals. Constance and the other lake cities under Austrian dominion contributed their contingent of men. The plan of the campaign was that the ducal army should be divided into two corps, the one to march through St. Gall and on to the Häuptlisberg, the other to ascend the Rheinthal to Altstädten, there to climb through the mountain forest of the Stoss. Thus the men of Appenzell were to be taken in front and rear, and their destruction seemed inevitable. Any one, however, who stands at the chapel of St. Nicholas, and looks right down into the Rheinthal and on to the houses of Altstädten, will see how admirably suited the position is for defence. Count Rudolf of Werdenberg skilfully placed his men at a point of the mountain which commanded the road his enemies had to take. No sooner did they appear than huge rocks and trunks of trees came crashing down upon them. The horses took fright. A heavy rain had made the ground so slippery that the foot soldiers could hardly stand, much less advance. Rudolf of Werdenberg, like Lochiel on the field of Killiecrankie, took off his shoes, and, advising his soldiers to do the like, so as not to slip on the wet grass, rushed barefooted on the foe. The invaders, slipping about in the mud and staggering under the weight of their armour, were already perplexed and discouraged, when, to their horror, on another hill appeared another host clothed in the hated shepherd's shirt. It was the women of Appenzell who had thus come to the aid of their husbands. Wild panic seized the invaders, the battle was over, and the flight and butchery began, which lasted six hours.

One thousand enemies lay dead around the barricades of tree stems through which a portion of the invading army had been purposely allowed to enter. The attack on the Häuptlisberg and upon Wolfhalden, which Duke Frederick conducted in person, also signally failed, and he was glad to make good his retreat to Arbon and thence to Innsbrück. In the flight many of his knightly supporters were slain by the victorious shepherds.

In revenge for the attack upon their homes, the shepherds traversed a great part of what is now the Swiss shore of the lake, destroying all the castles whose owners refused to admit them and to renounce allegiance to Austria. They then went up the Rheinthal, doing the like there, until they came to Werdenberg, when they showed their gratitude to their leader by driving the Austrians out, and establishing him in full possession of his inheritance. For two years the men of Appenzell carried all before them. They conquered sixty-four places of some importance, and burned thirty castles. The peasants of Thurgau, of the Bregenzer Wald, of much of the Tyrol, and of southern Germany, all wished to become members of the Republic of Appenzell.

In 1407 the nobility and the cities banded themselves

resolutely together against the dreaded foe. The victors had become fairly intoxicated by success; they razed
every castle, and murdered every priest—as a practical
reply to the sentence of excommunication passed upon
them. The winter of 1408 was intensely cold: all the
streams were frozen, so also was the lake, except in
a very few places. The men of Appenzell had long
greatly coveted the possession of the town of Bregenz,
the headquarters of their great enemy, Count William
of Montfort. The town, from its position at the head
of the lake, would have been invaluable to them as a
place of arms. During nine long weeks, in the bitter
frost, and the still more trying thaw that followed,
the men of Appenzell besieged Bregenz. Among
their artillery was a favourite piece which threw
10 cwt., and was called " Die Appenzellerin." It was
during this siege that the town was saved by the
devotion of the maid or matron variously called
Hergothe or Gutha (that is Judith), which has been
made the subject of a charming poem by the gifted
Adelaide Anne Proctor. At length, on the 15th
January, 1408, in a dense fog which wrapped in its
thick veil the lake and its shore, a band of 8000
Knights of the Shield of St. George, came to the
rescue of the town, under the leadership of the Count
of Montfort-Scheer. A desperate battle ensued under
the walls of the town. The Appenzellers were defeated and their banners taken. In vain, however,
did one of the nobles, Beringer von Hohenlandenberg,
cry, " Up and let us follow them quickly to their
homes, and there let us spare neither woman nor child,
so that no seed of this accursed race may remain to
work the ruin of the nobility."

The Appenzellers were defeated but not demoralised,
and those that were left marched away in so iron a

E

phalanx, that the victors had no disposition to follow them. After this the conquests of the Appenzellers fell away, but they retained the independence they had so hardly won, and in 1410 the Republic of Appenzell was received into confederacy with the seven other little States which had already bound themselves by oath to one another, and laid the foundation of what is now Switzerland.

Throughout the fifteenth century there was almost constant warfare between the confederates and Austria, and the men of Appenzell bore themselves right· valiantly by the side of their brothers in arms—and again at Wolfhalden—the scene of their victory in 1405—defeated an Austrian army forty years later, in 1445. In this war a remarkable family came to the front. The confederates were commanded by Itel Reding, who distinguished himself by consummate generalship and by dauntless courage. During nearly 400 years members of the family distinguished themselves in almost every European war, and on the 18th July, 1808, a Spanish army, under the command of General Theodore Reding, inflicted upon a French army in the south of Spain the disastrous defeat of Baylen, which had much to do with the general rising of the peninsula against the yoke of Napoleon I. It was upon receipt of this news that the great world-conqueror is reported to have said: " Reding ! Reding ! I am always coming across these Redings !"

There is a great monotony about the fighting and butchery which continued to the end of the fifteenth century, with which I will not weary my readers. As a net result, the whole Rhine valley remained in the hands of the Swiss confederacy, to which the City and Canton of St. Gall were added, without, however, entirely depriving the Abbot of his time-honoured rights.

Thurgau, right up to the walls of Constance, became a member of the confederacy, as a result of the bloody Suabian war, in which the Swiss were everywhere successful, and the haughty Emperor Maximilian suffered the greatest humiliation at the hands of the invincible mountaineers.

Although this war hardly lasted a year, the misery and want caused by it were so great, that in some places the children, it is reported, were driven out to graze with the cattle.

Peace was for the time secured by the peace of Basle, 22nd September, 1499.

Of the Peasant War (1525), I shall have to speak when we reach Ueberlingen; but for our present purpose it is sufficient to say that the doctrines of the Reformation were joyfully accepted by that portion of the Canton of Appenzell beyond certain military limits called "Rhoden," and as steadily resisted by those within the "Rhoden." The two parties very nearly came to blows, but wisely determined to separate rather than tear their little republic to pieces by an intestine struggle, and thus the two half cantons were formed, and continue to this day, of Appenzell-Ausser-rhoden and Appenzell-Inner-rhoden. Both may be regarded as surviving specimens of pure democracies, as nothing of any importance can be decided upon by the government of either half canton until it has been ratified by the Lands-gemeinde, or general assembly of every male inhabitant. As I shall ask my readers to accompany me to the Lands-gemeinde of Appenzell-Ausser-rhoden, held at Trogen on the 2nd April, 1880, it will here be proper to insert a chapter upon the subject of the Swiss Lands-gemeinden.

CHAPTER IV.

THE LANDS-GEMEINDEN OF SWITZERLAND.

The Lands-gemeinden of Switzerland—Cantons that still hold them—Business: how conducted—Small pay of Swiss officials—Salary of President of Swiss Confederation — Napoleon's opinion of the Lands-gemeinden — Times of meeting.

IN England, Representative Government has been so long established, and has reached such a high state of development, that to most of us it seems little less than a law of nature. We esteem it a great privilege to be selected as the representative and mouthpiece of the feelings, views, and wishes of so many thousands or hundreds of thousands of our countrymen, as the case may be, in the great council of the nation. It is difficult for us to imagine a state of society where every adult male has a direct voice in public affairs, and we naturally suppose such a state of things could only exist in early and primitive times.

Yet at this moment there exist in Switzerland communities—little republics having the status of sovereign states—where every male citizen is a member of the local parliament, and as such is in duty bound to attend the Lands-gemeinde of his canton. Tacitus describes how the early Germans assembled, armed, to discuss all matters affecting the public well-being, and to this day there are Swiss mountaineers who gather throughout the length and breadth of their respective cantons, and come to the appointed place of conference precisely as their forefathers did two thousand years ago.

The cantons that maintain the practice of exercising immediately their sovereign rights are Uri, Glarus, the two half cantons of Appenzell-Inner-rhoden and Ausser-rhoden, and the two half cantons into which Unterwalden is divided—Nidwalden and Obwalden. Formerly the cantons of Schwyz and Zug used also to govern themselves by general assemblies of all their male inhabitants; but they have now so far yielded to the spirit of modern innovation as to be content that the members of their representative chambers shall vote for them in place of their exercising immediate self-government.

The general assemblies for the cantons of Uri and Glarus are held on the first Sunday in May; those for each of the two half cantons into which Appenzell and Unterwalden are respectively divided, upon the last Sunday in April. In addition to these meetings, whose time is fixed, and which, from the season of the year in which they are held, are called "Maien-landesgemeinden," the sovereign people is specially called together whenever any matter of importance has to be decided. It is only in the two half cantons of Appenzell that the legislators, according to im-memorial custom, arrive at the trysting-place, each armed with sword or spear.

The population of Uri, of Appenzell-Inner-rhoden, and of the two half cantons of Unterwalden is almost exclusively Catholic, and principally composed of herds-men, shepherds, and small farmers. Ausser-rhoden, on the contrary, is largely engaged in manufactures, principally that of embroidery, which has its centre in

the little city of St. Gall, while nearly 95 per cent. of
its inhabitants are Protestants ; and Canton Glarus has
also considerable industries, and not more than 20 per
cent. of its inhabitants are Catholics.   Whether, however, the canton is Protestant or Catholic, the annual
general assembly is regarded as a solemn religious
festival, as well as the most important political event of
the year.   A stranger naturally asks, How is it possible
that any political business, much less the whole, or
nearly the whole, of the political business of any com-
munity can be transacted in a few hours by the assembled manhood of the whole canton ?   It is not easy to
give an answer, but the difficulty is lessened by the fact
that weeks before the day of meeting, the Great Council
of the respective cantons sends out to every citizen
a statement of all the questions upon which the vote
will be taken at the Lands-gemeinde.   These questions
are then vigorously discussed in every house, in every
tavern, and upon every hill-side, so that when the great
day arrives most of the voters have made up their
minds as to how they will vote.   In the great Lands-
gemeinde of Appenzell-Ausser-rhoden, where 8,000
to 10,000 legislators usually assemble, discussion is
obviously impossible, and, after the opening speech of
the Landammann, which is very like a speech from
the throne, the business principally resolves itself into
taking the votes ; in the smaller Landtags, on the
contrary, interesting discussions often arise.   In the
Landtag at Glarus, held in 1872 or 1873 to consider
the revision of the Constitution of the whole of Switzerland, then under discussion, a venerable citizen of
Glarus, aged 98, who for some years had failed to put
in an appearance at the Landtag, was present, and
recorded his vote in favour of what he regarded as
the cause of progress and the true welfare of his Canton

and Fatherland.   In the Catholic cantons the priests are accommodated with seats of honour at the Landtag.

The men of Uri, after a solemn service in the church of Altdorf, march in procession to the place of meeting—a meadow bottom through which flows the River Reuss.   Above them tower the giant forms of the Uri-Rothstock and other peaks.   The Landammann, after his throne-speech, implores the divine blessing upon the proceedings, and the whole company uncover, and recite five Pater Nosters and five Ave Marias.   Similar are the proceedings in Obwalden, Nidwalden, and Appenzell-Inner-rhoden, in all of which the people are entirely Catholic, and the greatest deference is paid to the priests.   Throughout these Catholic cantons the inhabitants, like Jean Paul's grandfather, are exceedingly poor and pious ; and to judge from the remuneration given to their officials, they think it desirable that their poverty at any rate should remain beyond question.   In Appenzell no member of the government receives a higher salary than 200 francs, or £8 per annum, though he often has to devote his whole time to the service of the State.   So far as I know, there is no country in the world where so much hard public work is done for so little pay as in Switzerland, as what follows will illustrate.   I recently attended an examination held in the college for the education of teachers for the Canton of Thurgau, now housed in what was Kreuzlingen Abbey.   At the conclusion of the proceedings the minister of education for the Canton of Thurgau, who had presided throughout the examinations, made a speech congratulating masters and pupils upon the progress that had been made.   This speech was that of a practised orator, and was admirable both as to matter and manner.   His salary is 4,000 francs per annum, or £160 !

The President of the Swiss Confederation receives
12,000 francs, or £480 per annum; and it may be
safely said that no one in the associated republics
works so hard as he is obliged to do during his year of
office.   Yet I am informed that anything like corruption is unheard of, if it is not absolutely impossible, in
the Confederation.   To return, however, to the Lands-
gemeinden :—At the beginning of the century, when
all political institutions were in a state of flux and
change, an effort was made to abolish the Lands-
gemeinden as antiquated and unsuited to modern
needs and ideas.   They found, however, a potent
protector and advocate in a most unlikely quarter. .
The foremost man and greatest despot in all the
world, Napoleon Bonaparte, First Consul of France,
thus addressed the Swiss Embassy to the Consulate
on the 29th January, 1803 :—

"Without these democracies Switzerland would only present what
is to be seen everywhere else.   It would have no distinctive characteristic of its own.   Be careful, gentlemen, to áttach proper weight
to these unique institutions.   It is these that draw the attention of
the world to you, and prevent any other state from attempting to
unite you to itself.

"I am well aware that these popular governments have many
disadvantages.   They have, however, existed for centuries, and owe
their origin to the climate, the nature, the needs, and the earliest
customs of the inhabitants.

"They are in accord with the *genius loci ;* and, with questions of
sentiment and national feeling, logical reasoning is out of place.
The constitutions of the little cantons are anything but perfect, but
custom has given them solidity.

"When national habitudes come into conflict with abstract reason,
the latter always has to yield.

"You want altogether to do away with the Lands-gemeinden, or,
at any rate, greatly to limit their powers.   Be it so ; but if you do,
let no one henceforth speak either of democracies or republics.
Free peoples have never permitted the immediate exercise of
supreme power to be taken from them.   The new discovery of the

representative system, which destroys the real bases of republican forms of government, is unsuited for them."

The soundness of the above utterance may well be questioned. It smacks too much of the despotism, tempered by *plébiscites*, so dear to the Napoleons; but it is very remarkable, nevertheless, as coming from such a man; and probably it is partly owing to the support thus given to them by Napoleon that six Lands-gemeinden continue to exercise sovereign rights to this day.

For the benefit of any of my readers who may have opportunity and inclination to attend one of these interesting gatherings, I append a list of the places and times at which they are held. If in the neighbourhood about the time, a visitor may easily find out if any change has been made.

With this introduction I will now invite my readers to accompany me to the Lands-gemeinde for the half canton of Appenzell-Ausser-rhoden, which was held at Trogen on the 25th April, 1880.

Places and Times of holding the Annual Lands-gemeinden.

CANTONS.	PLACE OF MEETING.	TIME.
Obwalden	Landenberg, near Sarnen ...	Last Sunday in April
Nidwalden	Wyl, near Stans	,,
Appenzell-Inner-rhoden ...	Appenzell	,,
Appenzell-Ausser-rhoden ...	Alternately in Trogen and in Hundwyl	,,
Uri	Altdorf	First Sunday in May
Glarus	Glarus	,,

CHAPTER V.

THE LANDS-GEMEINDE AT TROGEN.

AT four on the afternoon of Saturday, the 24th
April, 1880, I took the steamer at Constance for
Rorschach *via* Friedrichs-hafen. The peculiar watery
sunlight, which permeates the air after and before
rain, gave extraordinary brightness and beauty to the
scenery. The great sheet of water gleamed like a
mirror, without a ripple upon its surface save those
made by our paddle-wheels. To our right lay outstretched the fertile Thurgau, its green fields and
vineyards dotted all over with innumerable fruit-trees,
some of which, even from the deck of the steamer,
showed white with blossom. Here and there a dark
patch of pine forest seemed actually black by contrast.
Tall church spires, usually painted a bright green, rise
from happy-looking villages, while grand old monastic
piles, like the abbeys of Kreuzlingen and Münster-
lingen, tell what were the civilising agencies on the
shores of the lake in the times of old. As we cross
the lake we gain a fine view of the Ueberlingen-see
and the island of Mainau, and the ancient towers of
Ueberlingen rise in beauty from the lake in the tender

sunlight. Meersburg, too, with its castles hoary with time, looks very grand. The fruit-trees on the German shore are even further advanced than those in Switzerland, and each pear-tree is a glorious mass of white. Great fleecy clouds hang upon the snow-streaked sides of the Vorarlberg Alps, while the whole of the Sentis is hidden by them. Between us and the higher peaks, the long, hilly tongue of land of Appenzell looks in the peculiar light a pale sea-green with dark belts of forest.

At five we are at Friedrichs-hafen, and at six we have again crossed the lake, and steam into the harbour of Rorschach. Here there is half-an-hour's delay, and then I get into the little mountain railway train for Heiden. The distance is only three miles, but we have to ascend 1,200 ft. There is just one carriage attached to the little locomotive. In the large compartment into which I enter there are so many enthusiastic votaries of tobacco, that I fear I shall soon be like a Yarmouth bloater. Before, however, the train starts a door is opened, which reveals a compartment for non-smokers, where I was rejoiced to make a retreat, and which was soon filled. After a few general remarks the gentleman in the seat opposite to me said, "You were, I think, at the ' Krone' at Heiden last summer?" and, upon my assenting, "and at the Zürcher Hof, Zürich, in the spring of 1878?" I replied that he seemed so well informed as to my movements, that I supposed he was right and I wrong; but that I certainly thought it was in 1879 that I was at the Zürcher Hof. We then spoke of the approaching Lands-gemeinde, and I found to my chagrin, that it was extremely doubtful whether a vehicle of any kind could be obtained to take me to Trogen on the morrow. My interlocutor further

asked me whether I was not going to stay at the
house of Mr. H—— (the African missionary), of
whom I have already spoken ; and, upon my replying
in the affirmative, said Mr. H—— was a friend of
his, and, if a vehicle had not been already engaged for
us, he believed he could himself offer me a seat in
his carriage. A member of the Regierungsrath of
Appenzell-Ausser-rhoden was with us in the carriage.
The position is about equivalent to that of a Cabinet
minister in England, only, as I think I have already
explained, no Cabinet minister in Appenzell receives
more than £8 (200 francs) per annum for his services.
The conversation turned upon the history of the
Canton, and upon the way the business of the morrow
was likely to go. When the disruption took place in
the republic of Appenzell at the time of the Reformation, that portion which clung to the old faith, Appenzell-Inner-rhoden, comprised sixty-three square miles,
and has now a population of 12,000, of whom only
124 are Protestants, while Appenzell-Ausser-rhoden
had a territory of ninety square miles, and now has a
population of 50,000, of whom 2000 are Catholics.
The Austrian and other banners, which were won by
the young and undivided republic upon many a hard-
fought field, remained with the small Catholic state,
and are hung up at Appenzell. The past may be said
to belong to it ; but the present and the future
belong to its flourishing Zwinglian neighbour. The
first business of the morrow's Lands-gemeinde, consisted of the passing of the accounts for the year
just expired, which takes precedence of all other
business.

Every male Appenzeller unconvicted of crime
receives a detailed programme of all the business
six weeks before the Lands-gemeinde. It consists of

more than 150 octavo pages. This includes the accounts, which are all given in detail. The total expenditure for the past year was about 400,000 francs or £16,000, of which £4,500, or more than one quarter, was spent upon the maintenance of the roads. The item for salaries, which includes the pay of all the members of the Cabinet, of the Rathschreiber (a sort of Clerk of the Council and Lord Privy Seal combined), of the Director of the Police, of the Commandant of the Military district, of all the necessary accountants, and descends to the beadles and foresters, amounts in all to 40,000 francs, or £1,600. The cantonal schools are a charge upon the budget of a little over £600.

An examination and analysis of the whole budget fills one with astonishment that it should be possible to do so much with what appear to be such ridiculously inadequate means. The only cantonal tax is one of 2½ per mille upon all property.

Against one mistake the untravelled Briton (if any such there be) must be guarded. Englishmen are apt to think of the Swiss cantons much as they think of their own counties. This is an error; each Swiss canton is a sovereign state. They were originally banded together only for purposes of defence.

The Sonderbund War of 1847 did much to increase the central authority, and to form the members of the Confederacy, till then but loosely held together, into one Swiss nation. The expenses of the central government are borne by taxation levied upon the whole of the Confederacy. When, therefore, I speak of a taxation of 2½ per mille, I refer only to the cantonal taxation.

After the passing of the accounts, came *second* upon the programme, the choice of Landammann and

members of the government, equivalent to our Prime
Minister and Cabinet, the people being the Sovereign.

Third. The choice of Judges.

Fourth. The acceptance or rejection of a revision
of the laws with regard to civil and criminal procedure
in the courts.

Fifth. The acceptance or rejection of an amend-
ment of the law by which dancing is to be absolutely
forbidden on Sundays and church festivals, and
subjected to a fine of ten francs for any one dancing,
and thirty to sixty francs for any one upon whose
premises the dancing should take place.

Sixth. The acceptance or rejection of a proposal of
the Government to establish a cantonal workhouse or
Zwangsarbeitsanstalt, a matter often proposed, but
long delayed on account of the cost, but which the
Government now consider imperative, as the relief of
vagabonds by sending them to the alms-houses intended
for deserving poor has been found to exercise a de-
moralising influence upon all concerned.

Finally. The oath of fealty to the fatherland of
Appenzell-Ausser-rhoden, first to be taken by the
Landammann, and then by him to be administered
to the whole assembly.

But to return to the miniature railway train, which,
while we have been digressing, has been slowly
ascending towards Heiden. It is between seven and
eight, and the gloaming is deepening. Cockchafers
are droning through the air, which is laden with the
odour of the blossoms of myriads of fruit-trees. Suddenly, at one of the most picturesque points of this
eminently picturesque " Berg-bahn," the full moon
rises in all her splendour upon us, and throws her sheen
upon mountain, lake, and hill-side. Yonder village
just across the gorge up which the line now takes us,

upon whose houses the moonlight is resting, is the Wolfshalden (the Wolf's Height), of which we have already spoken in a previous chapter.

Finding that my host, Mr. H——— had decided not to attend the Lands-gemeinde, I gladly closed with the offer of Mr. J. Züst-Brunnschweiler, my interlocutor in the railway carriage, who knew so much about me.

About 3 a.m. on the 25th of April, the discharge of guns began to murder sleep, though upon looking out of window no one appeared to be astir, and nothing seemed to break the calm of a lovely sabbath morning.

Precisely at five the sun leaped up above the horizon from behind the German hills on the other side of the lake. At eight, according to arrangement, I presented myself at M. Züst-Brunnschweiler's, where a roomy open carriage with a pair of dashing horses is waiting for us. M. Züst soon appears, with a handsome rapier at his side. It is a family-party who are going to Trogen, as M. Züst is taking his wife, his sister, and his wife's brother, who is also his sister's betrothed. I might well have reason to fear that I should be de trop, but the simple kindliness and hearty welcome of my new friends soon show that this fear is un-founded. To my surprise I found that M. Züst spoke English at least as well as I speak German, he having spent three years in London learning the English branch of his business—the business of this district,— the embroidery trade. While in England he acted as treasurer to the German branch of the Young Men's Christian Association. His sister, a charming girl, had also passed a few months in England. The driver on the box also addresses me in English, so I might well fancy that I had dropped into the midst of compatriots. His face seemed familiar to me, and I think I remember seeing him at the St. Pancras Hotel where he was for

some time.   Our road winds along the pleasant
Appenzell hills whose heights are clothed with pine.

The meadows are a deep green, and are dotted all
over with white cuckoo flowers and yellow cowslips,
while every little purling brook is fringed with the
bright golden yellow of the marsh marigold.   As we
drive through the woods we notice that the ground
is carpeted with wood anemones, and the delicately-
veined wood sorrel.   Ever and anon the song of the
cuckoo breaks upon our ear.   The road is thronged
with the law-makers all in their best " go-to-meeting "
clothes, almost all in cylinder hats ("toppers"), brought
out once a-year for this great occasion, and all, without
exception, with side-arms—mostly old sabres or cut-
lasses.   The sun being hot, many are to be seen
carrying their coats slung over their shoulders on the
handle of their sabres, which they hold by the point
of the sheath.   Until three years since, a fine of ten
francs was imposed upon any citizen of Appenzell-
Ausser-rhoden, under sixty years of age, who absented
himself from the Lands-gemeinde, half the fine to go
to the informer.   This was felt to be somewhat
unworthy, and so the fine was done away with, but
the people were charged to attend the Lands-
gemeinde as a sacred duty.   In the long chain of black
coats and top-hats, here and again is to be seen
a group of stalwart lasses, not alas ! in the old
picturesque costume—*that* in this half of the canton
is a thing of the past—yet in neat and good clothing.
But for the sabres and the distant Alps, I could fancy
myself in Cumberland, going to some open-air service
or great temperance demonstration.   Where the road
reaches the crest of a hill, we get a fine view of the
black, jagged, iron peaks of the snow-streaked Sentis,
round which clouds are beginning to gather.   At

another point, through a break in the hills, we look
down upon the plain of Thurgau, like one great
orchard, stretching away to the lake. Before us, on
the side of a steep hill, is our goal—the town or
village of Trogen. Towards it, along all converging
roads, an unbroken stream of Appenzellers is flowing.
No one of the male sex seems to be left at home in
the villages save a few old men. The very cows seem
interested in the unwonted thronging of the roads,
and forsake their placid grazing to come and have a
good look at us with their large intelligent eyes.
Arrived in Trogen, we are met by a Mr. Graf, of
whom I will speak presently, and, thanks to the good
company in which I find myself, I am invited to
lunch at the house of Dr. Huber, a *doctor juris*, and
one of the leading legal officials of the canton.
Perhaps, instead of lunch I should say breakfast, as it
was only ten a.m. Lunch or breakfast, it was very
welcome, and when it was finished we found that one
of the principal rooms at the Rathhaus, with two
windows looking right out upon the place of meeting,
had been reserved for us. This was a great comfort,
as the fatigue of standing so long in the crowd would
have been very great. When we reached our point of
vantage, the square below us was already crowded. It
is a large quadrangle of oblong shape, one end of
which is shut in by the church—a new building, which
would be handsome—for it is new, and looks clean,
spacious, and bright—if it were possible for a church to
be handsome that is built in a bastard classical style.
On one side of the square is the Rathhaus (town-
hall) in which we are, and the principal inn in the
place. Opposite to us are tall and very fine old
houses, said to belong to the patrician families of
Appenzell.

F

At the other end of the square, opposite the church, stands a fountain, with the "bear" of Appenzell mounted upon a column. At this end two roads debouch upon the square, the one from the west, the other from the east of the canton, and every moment fresh arrivals make their appearance. When densely packed, the square will hold 10,000 people, and it is estimated that 8,000 are now actually in it. Almost without exception they are men and voters. All are attired in the regulation chimney-pot hat, many of which the weather and a generation of Landsgemeinden have changed from their pristine blackness to a fine gold-coloured bronze.

Fifty years ago the grandfathers of the present legislators must have presented a much more picturesque appearance, attired as they were in blue swallow-tail coats, long red waistcoats and shorts, with cocked hats, and to such a costume the swords and sabres would have seemed more appropriate. One old patriarch is to be seen in the crowd, whose red waistcoat and faded blue swallow-tail tell of the past. But it is nearing eleven o'clock, the service in the church is ending, the organ peals out, and a sort of procession is formed to fetch the "Landammann" and the Regierungsrath (the Cabinet) from the Rathhaus. On a platform in front of the church a brass band is placed, a precentor takes his station in the midst, and the whole 8000 uncover and join in singing the old Appenzell hymn—a sort of ode to the Deity.

> "Alles Leben stroemt aus Dir
> Und durchwallt in tausend Baechen
> Alle Welten—Alle sprechen
> Deiner Haende Werk sind wir.

" Dass ich fuehle, dass ich bin,
Dass ich Dich Du Grosser! kenne
Dass ich froh Dich Vater nenne :
O, ich sinke vor Dir hin.

"Welch ein Trost, und unbegrenzt
Und unnennbar ist die Wonne,
Dass gleich Deiner milden Sonne
Mich dein Vateraug umglaenzt!

" Deiner Gegenwart Gefuehl
Sei mein Engel der mich leite,
Dass mein schwacher Fuss nicht gleite
Nicht sich irre von dem Ziel."

The tones of the grand old hymn, which, as sung by
the collective manhood of Appenzell, has a thrilling
effect, have hardly died away before the procession,
headed by two javelin men, whose spear-handles are
striped black and white (the cantonal colours), goes to
fetch the Regierungsrath. The javelin-men are arrayed
in white scarves ; behind them comes a piper blowing
away lustily, and then follows the brass band. The
Landammann wears a black mantle, like a clergyman's
surplice. The Landwaibel (beadle) and his brother-
official show to advantage in cocked hats and parti-
coloured mantles of black and white.

Landammann Hohl comes of no patrician stock ; he
has never received any but primary education ; he is
essentially a self-made man. Five years ago he was
first chosen by his sovereign, the people, to the highest
position in the state. A sixth term of office the Constitution does not allow. He is evidently a man of
decision—quick, and resolute. He steps well to the
front of the platform, and in a clear, resonant voice
delivers his valedictory address, which is also the
Throne Speech of the Lands-gemeinde. Of his admirable speech I will only venture upon a short *résumé*.

"Gentlemen, fellow-countrymen, and confederates, faithful and beloved," he begins. During his five years of office he had always delighted to stand in this, to every patriot, hallowed spot, and from the fulness of his heart to speak to his fellow-citizens. The times were troublous. The rash and reckless speculations, which during the last ten years had wrought so much mischief throughout all the world, had exercised a baleful influence even on Appenzell. Nature, too, had been unkind, and a succession of bad seasons had caused much suffering.

He referred to the olden times—times of simple habits and few wants, and spoke of the old patriarchal family life as of the root from which the former prosperity and happiness of the people of Appenzell sprang.

It was true that the present time offered much that was enjoyable and really good, of which their fathers knew, and could know, nothing; but if in gaining this we exchanged the desire to do our duty for a restless quest of enjoyment and amusement, our gain was really loss.

He spoke of the schools, and exhorted all con-nected with them to strive to see that the education of the children should harmoniously develope body and mind, and make them thoughtful, serious, and loyal citizens of the Fatherland. He then alluded to the financial statement, and to the questions upon which the people would have to decide that day, and con-cluded thus—"And now to our work. Let the feeling that we are all but one family be present with us in the exercise of our sovereign rights! Yes, may this day be a day of blessing for Appenzell-Ausser-rhoden, to which we, and even our children, and our children's children in the distant future may look back with satisfaction!"

He then handed back the great seal which he had held for five years to his sovereign—the people— and doffed the mantle of office. And now every head in the great company is uncovered, and a solemn hush pervades the throng. It is the moment set apart for silent prayer. And now the selection and voting-in of members of the government begins, to which nominations may be given by any one in the assembly, and accordingly name after name is called out from the body of the square, all of which the white-haired Rathschreiber notes down, and in turn they are voted upon. The voting is all by show of hand, and is repeated until all on the platform are satisfied on which side is the majority. It is not a little bewildering to a stranger, but seems to work uncommonly well. I am told that cases have arisen where the voting has been so close that it has been necessary to divide the people at the church-door and count them. Nothing of the kind occurred on the present occasion, and it must be far too cumbrous a plan to be often adopted.

Five times the vote was taken as to whether the resignation of Herr Sonderegger, a member of the government, should or should not be accepted. At length the authorities on the platform decide that the majority have said that Herr Sonderegger shall not be allowed to retire, and immediately the javelin-men, followed by the piper and the brass band, march down from the platform and through the crowd to find the man of the people's choice, and escort him with all honour to the platform. Herr Sonderegger, a hale and portly man, is just below our window in the crowd, and before the javelin-men can clear a way to him he has found his way unostentatiously and almost unperceived on to the platform ; and, as the first minister who has been re-elected, proceeds to conduct the business of the meeting. The rapidity with which the voting proceeds is really wonderful, nor is the satisfaction which it appears to give less remarkable. The other five old members of the government are re-chosen, and then a seventh has to be elected in place of the retiring Landammann. After many have been proposed, and the vote has been taken seven times, Herr Altheir, of Speicher, is selected. The javelin-men, the piper, and the brass band immediately go to seek him in the crowd, the people showing the way by holding their sabres above their heads and pointing out his whereabouts. He is quickly found and duly escorted to the platform with undoubted musical honours, on the principle of "thus shall it be done unto the man whom the king (people) delighteth to honour." Then came the selection of Landammann (Premier or President), and as every member of the Regierungsrath was in turn nominated, and at least one show of hands was taken on each, the voting was somewhat protracted. At length Herr Sonderegger was declared duly elected; the Landswaibel arrayed him in the mantle of office, and the common seal of the Republic was handed to him by the Rathschreiber.

The judges were then chosen in similar fashion. The members of the government, the Landammann, and the judges having now been chosen, the next business was to submit to the assembled manhood of Appenzell the proposed revision of laws.

This was done by the new Landammann, and was accepted by an imposing majority. There was evidently a strong difference of opinion as to the adoption of the article which forbids dancing on Sundays, and my view from the window would not allow me to say which side had the majority, as a forest of hands appeared both *for* and *against*. But when the officials declared that the article was carried there was no sign of discontent from the large minority, but, on the contrary, a good-humoured laugh ran through the crowd. The proposal for the establishment of a workhouse was also carried by a large majority.

At this point we were rejoined by Herr Züst-Brunnschweiler, who had been below in the crowd attending to his legislative duties. He looked pale and spent with his exertions, but was greatly delighted with the result. He said that he never remembered so satisfactory a Lands-gemeinde; on no previous occasion had all the proposals of the government been accepted. The dance article he regarded as of peculiar importance, as showing that the people of Appenzell were willing to appear to forego some of their freedom in the interest of public order, morality, and religion.

Now came the crowning solemnity of the day. The white-haired Rathschreiber, in clear and resonant voice, read over the terms, solemn to awfulness, of the oath of allegiance to the Fatherland, and administered it to the newly-chosen Landammann, who then tendered it to his assembled countrymen. The spectacle of the 8,000 men of Appenzell-Ausser-rhoden, with bared heads and outstretched right arms, taking the oath of fealty to their Fatherland was one never to be forgotten.

There was nothing theatrical about it: it was intensely real and almost sublime.

The Landammann now wished his countrymen all health and happiness, and the Lands-gemeinde of 1880 was a thing of the past. Nothing could exceed the earnestness and the simple dignity of the whole of the proceedings. The respect shown to the sovereign (the people) was exhibited by the " Landeswaibel" as he prefaced in stentorian voice every question put to the vote with "*Wenn es Ihnen gefaellt*" ("May it please you.") After visiting the council-room of the Rathhaus, where are hung the portraits of all the Landammanns from the time of the disruption of the two Appenzells, I was kindly included in the dinner-party at Dr. Huber's. A former Landammann of Appenzell-Ausser-rhoden is now the ambassador of the Swiss Confederation at the Court of Berlin; and, as was the case with Colonel Hammer, this post will probably lead to his some day being President of the Swiss Republic. It was interesting and very surprising to me that here, in an out-of-the-way place like Trogen, every one at the dinner-table either spoke, or at any rate understood, English. Among the company was Herr Graf who met us on our first arrival in Trogen. He has just returned home, after spending three years in London, solely because his parents are growing old and wish him to be near them. I felt very sorry for him ; in London he had formed a nice circle of friends among intellectual and literary people, and now he feels himself perfectly buried in Trogen. He is much more English than an Englishman ; English literature, English society, and English life are his *beau ideal*. The windows of the dining-room command a superb view over the green Appenzell hills, but Herr Graf would not admit that it was at all equal to the green of the English turf at Richmond or Hampton Court. The proceedings of the Lands-gemeinde, which began at 11 o'clock, were all over by 1.30, and from the windows of the room where we dined we could see the legislators in a long black chain, wending their way along the roads towards their homes. I am assured that there is but little drunkenness among them, and that, although in accordance with immemorial custom they all carry side-arms, it is unheard of for them to be used in any quarrel upon the evening of the day of meeting.

The Lands-gemeinde for Appenzell-Inner-rhoden was held the same day at Appenzell. In many respects it presented a great contrast to that I have described. The voting for Landammann was so close that heads had to be counted at the church door; whereupon the numbers that came out were 1,252 for Herr Son-deregger and 1,157 for Herr Streuli.

Curious that in both the Appenzell's a Sonderegger should be raised to the chief magistracy!

The punishment of death which, by the Constitution of 29th May, 1874, was abolished for the whole of Switzerland, was, in 1879, by a popular vote, again made optional for the individual cantons. Agreeably to this, the Lands-gemeinde of Appenzell-Inner-rhoden, by a very large majority, re-established it for murder, and arson attended by loss of life. It is noteworthy that it is only in some of the Catholic and pastoral cantons that the permission of the Central Government to re-introduce the death penalty has been acted on.

The beautiful national costume of the Appenzell-Inner-rhoden women is said to have shown to great advantage at this Lands-gemeinde.

CHAPTER VI.

ST. GALL.

IT seemed most suitable to insert the description of
the Lands-gemeinde at Trogen while we were in that
neighbourhood, but, with the reader's permission, we
will now go back ten months, from the end of April,
1880, to early in July, 1879.

Although the distance from Heiden to St. Gall is
only about nine miles, yet as you have first to descend
the cogged railway to Rorschach, and then to re-ascend
900 feet by railway to St. Gall, the journey takes nearly
two hours. The city which in the process of ages
arose around the cell of the holy Gallus, and which we
have now reached, is often called the Manchester of
Switzerland, but it has only 20,000 inhabitants, and has
no smoke. The sunny Uplands of the Canton of
Appenzell at St. Gall are dotted all over with bright
homesteads, the women of which busy themselves with
the preparation of embroidery, which they bring in to
the great dealers in the town of St. Gall, who distribute
it all over the civilised world. The United States are
among their best customers. When machinery was
first introduced into the trade, large fortunes were

rapidly acquired, and portions of these were spent with
no niggard hand in raising fine mansions and beau-
tifying the town with handsome public buildings and
parks.   There are few towns in Europe, of any
importance, situated so high above the sea level as
St. Gall, 2081 feet.   On Saturday, the 12th July, before
9 a.m., we found ourselves among the abbey buildings.
They have been repeatedly destroyed by fire, and the
present buildings are of little architectural interest.
The spacious abbey church was built in 1759 by the
Abbot, Cœlestin II., in the Rococo style, like the
abbey church at Einsiedeln.   It is richly, not to say
gaudily, painted and decorated, and by those who can
tolerate the style, would, I suppose, be considered
handsome.   Happily, although the casket has many
times been destroyed and restored with sad want of
taste, the jewels remain.

It is probably impossible for us to over-estimate the
debt that humanity owes to the monks who preserved
for us the treasures of sacred and secular literature
through àll the storms of the middle ages. Many monks
spent their whole lives in making careful copies of the
more valuable works.   When we remember that there
was no current round hand in those days, but that
each letter had to be painted in, we shall realise the
toil that was involved in multiplying manuscripts.
The monks rightly regarded them when written as
their chief treasures, and throughout the ravages of
the Huns, and the storms and troubles of the middle
ages, as well as when iconoclastic Reformers stormed
the abbey early in the sixteenth century, and French
sans culottes exemplified the doctrine of universal
brotherhood by unsparing plunder late in the eighteenth,
these priceless manuscripts were mostly saved.   Out
of a catalogue of manuscripts compiled in A.D. 823 as

being then in the possession of the abbey, no less than
400 are still extant. We were most courteously conducted through the library by a gentlemanly and
scholar-like priest, who devoted two hours to showing
us the manuscripts. Among the greatest literary
treasures is a copy of Virgil, believed to be the oldest
in existence. It is written in fine Roman capitals,
without division into words, or punctuation, and is
supposed to date from the third or fourth century.
More interesting even than this is the vocabulary
supposed to have been written and made use of by
the holy Gallus himself. It is pocket size, and was
intended to help him to acquire the language of those
to whom he came. From it we learn that the ante-
Carlovingian German was very like the Suabian and
Swiss dialects still spoken. From the Latin and German
words in parallel columns I take the following :—
" Columnæ "— " Sili " which is exactly what the Swiss
would still say for the German word " Saeule," a pillar ;
" Folium " is " Plat "—high German " Blatt," a leaf ;—
" Foliæ," " Laup "—high German " Laub," foliage.

Among the Greek manuscripts there is a copy of the
New Testament, dating from the end of the tenth
century, and a Psalter of the ninth century, the latter
of which is bound in an old Roman diptychon, on one
side of which are exquisitely carved ivory figures of
warriors and Bacchantes.

There are also several copies of the Gospels executed
in Ireland in the sixth and seventh centuries, and a
most interesting translation of the Bible into German
of the eleventh century, interlined with the Latin.
When the old monk is doubtful about the German
equivalent, he writes the Latin into the text and puts
the German in small letters above, thus :—(Filius Dei) with *Gottes* above *Filius* and *Kind* above *Dei*.

Rich however as the library is in very ancient

manuscripts of classical authors, even they are not so important as the unique collection of old German Chronicles, which are simply invaluable to the historian and philologist.

Very hard must the old monks have toiled copying out and gorgeously illuminating all these works. In the margins we find expressions of thankfulness that evening had at last come to end their labours; appeals to their patron saints to give them patience, or a desire for a bowl of wine or can of beer to sweeten the sour task; for monks were human and could be thirsty.

Well might a learned Benedictine monk say— "Quidquid apud antiquos eruditum ac scitu dignum et sapientiæ plenum; quidquid in consiliis sanctum; quidquid in libris sanctis divinum; quidquid in historiis firmum solidumque est: totum id per monachorum nostrorum manus ad haec usque tempora pervenit."

"Whatever was found among the ancients worthy to be taught, and to know, and full of wisdom; whatever is holy in the councils; whatever is divine in the Sacred Books; whatever is assured and trustworthy in history: the whole of this has come down to the present time, through the hands of our monks." Let us be grateful for all their labours have preserved to us.

Charlemagne, who, when he ascended the imperial throne in 770, said, "It is my will that in future the worship of God should be celebrated in a more worthy manner," gladly sought a short repose from his arduous campaigns and the cares of his world-empire in the seclusion of the Abbey of St. Gall. Here he did not think it unworthy of his dignity to attend the daily service, and himself to lead the singing and music. In this he compared himself to King David— not the only point of resemblance between the two monarchs. The unknown monk of St. Gall who wrote his life gives the following anecdote :—"After the Greeks had celebrated the morning service on the octave of the Theophany in the presence of the Emperor, they privately sang praises to God in their own language. Unknown to them, he was within hearing, and was so delighted with the sweetness of the hymns that he commanded his chaplains to eat nothing until they had handed to him these antiphons translated into Latin. The same ambassadors brought all manner of musical instruments and many other things with them. All these the workmen of the thoughtful Charles carefully examined, omitting nothing, and made others like them, especially that most excellent of all instruments which, by means of leather bellows filled with air, that blow in wonderful fashion through brazen pipes, produces now the roll of thunder by the power of its tones, and now by its sweetness the gentle strains of the lyre or the cymbal."

In 820 Abbot Gotzbert determined to rebuild the monastery, and happily his architect's plans, with all explanations, have come down to us. Among the many one-storied buildings stands conspicuous the church with two lofty towers, whence the watchman can give timely warning of the approach of wandering Huns or other prowling banditti. The abbot has a residence apart, with a private entrance to the church. Near him is a house for the reception of distinguished visitors, and another for more humble guests. The "refectorium," showing how the tables were to be placed and where the abbot was to sit, and the "dormitorium," with lavatories, are carefully planned ; so also are the cloisters, for the monks to perambulate in rainy weather. The graveyard is also a fruit garden, and the various trees are specified in Latin on the old plan,

as pear, plum, almond, medlar, and fig. There is a
hospital for the sick, with baths attached, and a little
chapel, and a garden specially devoted to the growth
of medicinal herbs, with the names given, as "salvia,"
"cumin," &c. Another garden is set apart for culi-
nary herbs and vegetables. The plan of the cellar
shows where each cask of wine or beer is to be ranged.
The bakery gives out 200 loaves of bread every day.
The workshop of the smiths and armourers is as far
as possible removed, for this important handicraft is
noisy. All round the settlement is a substantial wall,
for obvious reasons, which in addition to all the buildings above mentioned, encloses stalls for the cattle and
stables for the horses. All this was more than 1,000
years ago—about thirty-four generations back in the
dark ages! While upon the subject of the Monastery
of St. Gall, the old Latin hymns should not be forgotten
which were there composed, prominent among which is
the famous "Media vita in morte sumus." The monk
Notker, who, by his poetical and musical talent, was
one of the greatest ornaments of the abbey in the
ninth century, was one day walking in the direction of
Rorschach, when he reached the deep and gloomy
gorge of the Martinstobel. Workmen were at the
time busy throwing a bridge over the abyss, and, as he
saw them hanging as it were between heaven and
earth, the peril they were in so impressed him as to
become the motive of the hymn. Words and melody
were written together, the latter being indicated by a
species of accentuation above the words, which, in
process of time, developed into our musical notation.
The "Media vita" was sung all over Christendom; it
became a favourite battle-song among the Crusaders in
far-away Palestine; until, in the fifteenth and sixteenth
centuries, the inhabitants of the shores of the Rhine

attributing magical virtues to it, its use was forbidden by the Church.

While we had been pursuing our researches in the abbey library heavy rain had been falling. In the afternoon, however, it ceased, and we availed ourselves of the bright sunshine to climb the Freudenberg, a hill 643 feet above the city of St. Gall, and 2,724 feet above sea-level. Past the site of the cell of St. Wiborad, recluse and martyr, past the ancient and extensive fish-ponds of the abbey—now converted into swimming-baths for the citizens of St. Gall—we climb up a winding path through a pine wood. Behind us, glittering in the sun, lies the Boden See in its magnificent extent, and upon reaching the summit of the " Hill of Joy " a panorama of mountains meets our view. Far away to the south-west, faintly gleaming in the summer haze, are the summits of the Bernese Oberland. Glärnisch and Tödi are nearer, while the huge rugged mass of the Sentis rises in majesty right opposite to us from amid the green slopes and hills of Appenzell.

On Sunday, the 13th July, we found the large Roman Catholic church crowded with worshippers, and we afterwards listened to an eloquent discourse delivered to a large congregation in the handsome Protestant church. The following day, having an introduction to the firm of A. Göldi & Co., embroidery merchants, we walked out to the village of Bruggen, about a mile from St. Gall, where their offices occupy a fine mansion, formerly the residence of Mr. Göldi before he removed to London. The manufactory is some miles distant, and the firm has offices both in London and New York, England and the United States being their principal customers. Two young Englishmen have to do with the management here, and they kindly showed us all manner of beautiful embroidery, which had peculiar charms for the feminine eye. Some work which the firm had specially prepared for the Philadelphia Exhibition cost them nearly £4 per yard; and so extremely trying was it to the workman who made it, that they doubted if it would be possible to produce it again at any price. It has, however, more than repaid the firm for its cost, for they have pieces of it framed and exhibited as an advertisement in many of the cities of the United States. The young men complain that it is very lonely and out of the world here, but find a solace in wandering over the Sentis.

Our stay at St. Gall was slightly prolonged, and not rendered more agreeable, by a money *contre-temps*, which is perhaps worth recording, as showing that whenever the excellent Swiss postal arrangements break down, the Post Office is ready and willing to make amends. I was advised from Geneva of a remittance on the Saturday, the money to come in a registered letter which should have arrived at the same time as the advice. All possible enquiries and reclamations were made by me at the Post Office, but I was assured that nothing whatever had arrived for me; and at last, on Tuesday morning, afraid that the delay was owing to some culpable *laches* on the part of the senders, I telegraphed to them. It then appeared that the registered letter had been lying for three days at the Post Office of St. Gall, and had not been given to me in consequence of the stupidity of the clerk of whom I enquired. Under these circumstances it seemed only due to other travellers under similar circumstances to lodge a formal complaint with the postmaster, from whom, shortly after our arrival in Lindau, I received a full

G

and ample apology, and a remittance of the cost of my telegram.   He further added that it was his "duty to inform me that, according to the 119th Article of the Constitution of the Swiss Post Office, I was entitled to a compensation of 15 francs for the delay that had taken place, payable within ninety days."   Had I chosen to claim it, no doubt the clerk who was to blame would have had a little over a franc a week deducted from his wages during that time.

LINDAU

CHAPTER VII.

LINDAU.

Lindau—Tropical rain—The Suabian Venice—Our quarters—Ebel's description—History of Lindau—Grand-Duke of Tuscany—Gospels and "British Workman"—The "Spital"—Vaccination—A grand old warrior—The Colonel's history—Visit of the Kaiser to Lindau—The rose of Gorze—Bathing arrangements—Pleasant company.

On July 15th, as we travelled down to Rorschach, *en route* for Lindau, the rain poured down with a tropical violence worthy of St. Swithin's. We passed the night in our old quarters at the Gruener Baum, at Rorschach, and crossed the lake to Lindau between 11 and 12 o'clock on the 16th, by which time the sky had cleared, and as we approached the little island city, sometimes affectionately called by its inhabitants "the Suabian Venice," the sun shone out with great beauty. On one side of the entrance to the harbour of Lindau rises a handsome pharos, 100 feet high, and on the other a majestic lion of colossal size, the representative of Bavaria, serenely sitting upon his haunches on a stone pedestal, and for ever gazing out upon the lake. The lion weighs 50 tons, and is said to have been carved from a block of stone that weighed 100 tons.

The town of Lindau, with 5,000 inhabitants, of whom about one-half are Catholics, was originally built upon three little islands. The three are now substantially one, and united to the mainland by a

G 2

long wooden bridge, and also by a railway embankment 2,000 feet long.

The principal hotels are grouped around the harbour; they are embowered in greenery, creepers being trained all over them, and most of them have gardens full of flowers. Avenues of trees shade the main streets, and the squares are planted with chestnuts and plane-trees. We take up our quarters in a modest but comfortable little hostelry, the "Lindauer Hof," where the charge for board and lodging is four marks, or four shillings, a day. The front of our hotel is draped in a most luxuriant Virginian creeper, often called on the Continent "Canadian vine." In the evening, when the sun is no longer upon it, a rustic balcony beautified with a yellow jasmine and other flowering plants is an agreeable resort.

Old Schwab, when, in writing fifty-four years ago his admirable description of the Boden See and the Rhein, he came to that portion of his work which treats of Lindau, says, "descriptions of scenery by the same pen infallibly become monotonous." I fear my readers have already had too much reason to hold this view. I will therefore follow Schwab's example, and, instead of attempting a description myself, will translate a few lines from Ebel, who visited Lindau at the end of the last century. The view he describes is from the country house, on the mainland, of a Lindauer patrician with whom he was staying.

" The advantageous situation of the house secures most beautiful views over the lake and its shores. Through a telescope I saw from here quite plainly the towers of the abbey of St. Gall;* the cathedral of Constance was shrouded in grey mist; the little towns of Rheineck, Rorschach, and Arbon were most

* I should have thought this impossible.—S. J. C.

conspicuous among the hamlets which enliven the appearance of the Swiss shore from across the broad mirror of the lake.

" The clouds, no longer so heavy and black as in the morning, now floated in the higher regions of the air, and only hid the tops of the highest mountains. At length the sun broke through them, and I had the indescribable pleasure of seeing the mighty mountains of Appenzell. A terrible storm raged in this mountain region. Now and again the cloud-veil opened and revealed naked, staring walls of rock streaked with ice and snow, and then great rocky peaks rose high above the clouds. The impression made upon me by these huge and haughty masses of stone I am unable to describe. It was probably the more remarkable because the sea of mist which enveloped the whole only allowed particular points to be seen in momentary glimpses, and thus gave no strict limits to the imagination.

" My guide led me from the country house through smiling gardens to another point of view, in a vineyard, which, being higher, commanded a more extended view. The sun had at last established his mastery, and had scattered the clouds in the western heavens. Just as we climbed the hill he poured his rays out upon the wide landscape, which, like a blooming maiden, suddenly emerged from the shadow into glowing beauty. I threw myself upon the ground, and enjoyed, in long, slow draughts, the wonderful scenery around me."

Tradition assigns a Roman origin to Lindau, and a stone tablet upon the huge fragment of a wall, called the Heidenmauer, informs the traveller that at the time of Tiberius and Drusus a Roman castra was established on the island, This is more likely true than not, especially when we consider what an admirable

strategical position it forms; but definite history is
altogether wanting. Trustworthy mention of Lindau
we have first in the ninth century; in the eleventh it
was surrounded by walls, and in the thirteenth it was
constituted a free city of the empire.

Two Reichstags were held in Lindau; the first by
the Emperor Rudolph, the second in 1496, by
Maximilian the First. It was the effort of the latter
monarch to extend his authority and that of the
German courts over Switzerland that led to the
Suabian war (1496-1499), of which I have already
spoken in connexion with Appenzell. In this war
Lindau had to bear an important part, and to make
great sacrifices. This was the period of Lindau's
greatest prosperity. It was the centre of a great
trade; the haven was not large enough for the
shipping that resorted to it, and more than 1,400
carts and other vehicles were counted entering the
town to the weekly market on Saturday.

The Reformation was eagerly adopted by a majority
of the citizens of Lindau—"the impudent Lindauers,"
as the Count of Montfort called them at a meeting of
the nobility held at Ueberlingen, about 1531, to
endeavour to maintain and re-establish the old faith.

For a hundred years there was constant disquiet
between the adherents of the old faith and the new,
until in 1619 the Thirty Years' War broke out.

The Peasant War in the sixteenth century and the
Thirty Years' War in the seventeenth, exercised so
great an influence upon the inhabitants of the shores
of the Boden See, and especially upon the old imperial free cities that we are now visiting, that I
propose to treat of the two wars in subsequent chapters.
For twenty years out of the Thirty Years' War the
city of Lindau was occupied by an imperial garrison,

as much to overawe the Protestant inhabitants as
to hold Lindau for the Emperor against the Swedes.
The cost of the garrison to the town is estimated at
five million gulden, or say half-a-million sterling,
which at the then value of money must have been
an appalling sum for so small a place.

From this time onward Lindau had the misfortune
to be a fortress, from which circumstance it suffered
much in later wars. In the shuffling of the cards
consequent upon the breaking up by Napoleon of the
old German empire at the beginning of the present
century, Lindau was handed over to Austria in 1804,
and finally to Bavaria in 1806.

The Grand-Duke of Tuscany, since losing his dominions, has had the good taste to settle at Lindau,
or rather on a lovely estate on the mainland near to
the town. His handsome and well-horsed equipages,
with coachmen and couriers dressed as gorgeously as
English field-marshals, help to give animation to the
appearance of the little town. An English friend had
kindly placed at our disposal, for distribution, a large
number of Gospels in German, and of copies of the
Deutscher Arbeiter, a translation of one number, and
unfortunately of only one number, of the *British
Workman*.

This was a source of very great pleasure to us,
as old and young alike were delighted to receive them,
and it also enabled us, without intrusion, to visit many
institutions, hospitals, poor-houses, &c., in visiting
which we should otherwise have felt a degree of
delicacy. By great care in endeavouring to eliminate
everything in the least degree controversial, we hoped
to escape giving offence to the Catholics; but, as the
reader will see, this hope was only partially realised.

The old religious hatred seems to have quite died

out in Lindau.   The principal Catholic and Protestant churches stand close together, in a great square, and the bells summon the adherents of the two confessions to worship at the same hour.   On Sunday, July 20th, we went to the Protestant service, which was well attended, and where we heard a thoughtful sermon. In the afternoon we visited the " Spital " an ancient charitable foundation, for the benefit of a certain number of the aged poor as well as for sick persons. At first, we thought the lady superintendent, from her nun-like dress and the gold cross she wore upon her breast, was a Roman Catholic, and were doubtful how the offer of our little books would be received.   We were relieved, however, to find that she was a Lutheran deaconess.   She kindly conducted us through all the wards, and we had an opportunity of speaking to every one of the inmates, who accepted our little gifts with an eagerness little short of delight. An old man and an old woman who had met us outside in one of our rambles, claimed us at once as old acquaintances.   Everything in the establishment was exquisitely clean and neat, and there being no carpets, and the carefully planed wooden floors being painted a light brown, a wet cloth is all that is necessary to · maintain them in such a state that no one need scruple to eat his meals from off them were it necessary.   There was no one at the time in the small-pox wards, and the lady superintendent informed us that they rarely or never had Bavarian small-pox patients ; those suffering from this loathsome malady almost always come from Bregenz or other Austrian territory, *where vaccination is not compulsory.*   I present this fact for what it is worth, to those well-meaning philanthropists who regard resistance to the vaccination laws in England as a religious duty.

On the verandah adjoining that of our hotel, we had been much interested in observing a grand and somewhat gaunt-looking old gentleman of the Charles Napier type of face, with full flowing beard, simply attired in a cord hunting suit with metal buttons. His inseparable companion was a bright, intelligent boy of six, and together on the verandah they took their supper. I asked the little fellow if he could read, and, upon his replying in the affirmative, offered him a Gospel and a *Deutscher Arbeiter*. I ventured to ask the old gentleman about his "grandson," and found, to my surprise, that the lad was his son. Like ourselves, they had been travelling for eighteen months in Switzerland, and the old man and his little son had penetrated on foot almost every part of it, as well as of Savoy, and had even crossed several of the passes. The little fellow often walks eight hours a-day. His father told me that they rarely turned-in anywhere during the day's march, but just took a little bread and meat in their pockets. " No," said the bright little boy with great *naïveté* " Es kostet zu viel Geld." He then brought me the Gospel I had given him, to show me how much he had read that day, and added, " I am going to read just as much every day. " What are you going to become, my little man ? " said I, " with such a training, I should think a traveller." " No," said the boy proudly, " I shall be a soldier." " A soldier ! " I replied, " that's a bad trade." Here the father struck in : " We have all been soldiers for more than 300 years, and he must not disregard the traditions of the family." He then kindly handed me his card, from which I was a little startled to find that he was Von Z——, full colonel in the Prussian service. The family was originally Austrian, but as its members adopted the reformed faith very early in the

sixteenth century, they took refuge from persecution
in Brandenburg—there was no kingdom of Prussia
then—and ever since have been soldiers in the service
of that State.   Two members of the family fell in the
campaign of Jena, and two in the War of Liberation
in 1813.   The colonel's father received so dreadful a
wound upon the head at Leipzic, that he could never
again wear a helmet or military cap, so was compelled
to leave the army and received the appointment of
" forest-master."   He retained, however, his full
faculties both of body and mind until the age of
ninety-six, when he passed painlessly away.

" Those of us who do not remain upon the battle-
field always reach a great age," said the colonel.   He
was at the time of our meeting sixty-eight years of
age, fifty of which he had spent in the army.   He
served through the Baden Campaign in 1848, and
through the Danish, Austrian, and French campaigns.
He was wounded at Mars-la-Tour before Metz, and
on the spot had the Iron Cross sent him by the
present Emperor.   One of his sons fell at Königgrätz,
and two in the French War, one at Mars-la-Tour and
one before Orleans, and one was desperately wounded
at Gravelotte, but is now recovered and a major.   I
think the child now with him must be by a second
marriage since the war, and I gather that grief for the
death of the mother was the occasion of the wanderings of the old man and the boy.   To the little lad
the war-worn veteran is " father an' mither an' a'."
Whenever feasible they stay as at Lindau in private
lodgings, so that the boy's education may not be disturbed, to which the old gentleman devotes the whole
of every morning.

I subsequently visited the interesting couple in their
quarters—a simple suite of rooms, almost the only

ornaments of which were portraits of the Kaiser and
of Bismarck and Moltke. The boy showed me his
copy and exercise books with prattling glee, and the
old gentleman was good enough to show me his war
medals and orders, including the much-prized Iron
Cross. He gave me the very interesting information
that his old commander in so many wars, the Emperor
of Germany, was to pass through Lindau on the
morrow, the 21st July. Lindau was very bright and
gay to receive the old Kaiser, who passed through on
his way from Mainau (the summer residence of the
Grand-Duke of Baden) to the north. All the schools
had holiday, and, with few exceptions, the inhabitants
of Lindau were assembled round the harbour to do
honour to the Emperor. At length the fine steamboat
that bears his name, the " Kaiser Wilhelm" steamed
into the harbour. The King of Saxony, the Princess
Louisa of Prussia, the Grand-Duke of Tuscany, and
other grandees, were waiting to receive him, while
the Grand-Duke and Grand-Duchess of Baden, his
son-in-law and daughter, accompanied him thus far
on his journey. When I last saw him he was
returning from before Paris, in 1871, and just
stayed for half-an-hour at the Metz railway-station
on his journey to Berlin. Since then two attempts
had been made upon his life, and he had been
most cruelly wounded. One of his first wounds
was received in the attack upon Montmartre, in
1814, and his last at an assassin's hands in the
streets of Berlin, in 1878. Strange destiny! Yet
there he stands, straight and firm, upon the deck of
the steamer, with a smile upon his somewhat stern
features, as though he hardly felt the weight of his
eighty-three years. He is lame, however ; and, what
hitherto has not been usual, a carriage is in waiting to

take him to the railway-station. In former years it was his custom to walk. He seems in excellent spirits, and cordially returns the loyal greetings of his assembled subjects.

My readers will be in a better position to understand the enthusiasm his old soldiers feel for him after hearing the following story, told me by Colonel Z——, of his son, the one that was desperately wounded at Gravelotte :—

"The battle of Gravelotte had been fought and won ; but little knew young Captain von Z—— as to which army was victorious. On the morning after the fight he was lying desperately wounded on some straw in a barn in Gorze. A young French woman came to fetch some straw, and was horrified to find her barn full of wounded men. She addressed the handsome young officer ; but the paroxysm of the fever was too severe for him to talk much, so she went out and quickly returned with a beautiful white rose, which the wounded man faintly lifted to his face and then laid by his side. Soon after, the heavy tramp of horses was heard outside, and von Z—— cried to his servant, 'Frederick, quick ! thy musket ! the French !' The servant went to the door and speedily returned. 'It is not the French ; it is the King.' 'Quick, Frederick, take this rose and give it to the King from a badly wounded officer.' Away galloped the royal party. The war had come to an end, and Captain von Z—— was just able to move about upon crutches, when he went to see his King, now Emperor, who was always accessible to his wounded warriors. 'Majesty, I want work. I am of no use in the army at present, but I am a good penman : give me something to do.' 'Wait until you can walk about with only the assistance of a stick, and I will give you something to do.'"

When recovered to this point, the young man went again. The Emperor received him very kindly, made him sit down by his side, upon a sofa, and asked him how and when he had received his wounds? Upon hearing of Gorze, the Emperor said, "Gorze, there was something very interesting happened to me there," and spoke of receiving the rose. "I have tried my possible to find out who sent it to me, but hitherto without success." The young man's confusion betrayed him. "That you should have thought of me," said the Emperor, "and sent me that beautiful rose when you were lying between life and death, *I can and will never forget.*" A few days later the young man received an official letter making him a senior instead of a junior captain, which nearly doubled his pay, and he also received an appointment in the "Ministry of War," and at Christmas-time came a large package containing a sort of memorial painting showing the iron cross he had won, with his other decorations, and his sword. At the bottom was written "von deinem Wilhelm," and at the top of the frame was a white rose in silver, with the inscription "Die Rose von Gorze." It evidently gave the father much pleasure to tell this story of his son.

The charms of Lindau grow upon the traveller the longer he remains. Seen from the northern shore, the little island, densely packed with tall old-fashioned gabled and red-tiled houses, has a very attractive appearance. The old walls, against which the waters of the lake beat on all sides, are wonderfully preserved, and the bastions, once powerful to repel the foes of the good old city, are now planted with fine trees and laid out as promenades. Nothing can be more delightful at the close of a hot summer's day than a ramble along these shady bastions. Perhaps a strong south-west wind has sprung up, and sends rolling along the whole length of the lake, huge waves, worthy of the ocean itself, which break upon the bastions, and send showers of water and spray up among the trees.

Happily, several of the tall towers, whilom the strength of Lindau, remain to give it grace and beauty. Looked at from the northern shore, the precipices of the Sentis seem to rise immediately behind the wavy tree-tops, and the towers and spires of the city, and it is difficult to realise that, between, there intervenes the whole width of the lake, some seven miles, and as wide a tract of the Appenzell Uplands. The animated appearance of the harbour may be imagined from the fact that about thirty steamers enter and leave it daily, in addition to sailing craft and row-boats. The bathing arrangements in Lindau are as near perfection as they well can be. With similar erections to those at Rorschach for those who can afford $2\frac{1}{2}d.$, and a special establishment for ladies, there is also a separate free bathing place and shed for men, one for boys, and one for women and girls, as well as a swimming school for the soldiers in garrison. We had pleasant company at the Lindauer Hof. Captain H——, of the Würtemberg army, with his young and beautiful wife, were most amiable companions. Though only thirty-seven he had seen much service, having first come under fire in an engagement against the Prussian troops in 1866, and subsequently having served all through the campaign of 1870 under a Prussian general. It was pleasant to hear him say what lovable people the French were, and how he felt just like a son of the house in his quarters at Epernay, and looked forward to taking his wife to introduce her to his involuntary hosts of the now far distant war time. Her maiden

home was at Stuttgart, and she complained bitterly of
the ungenial climate of Ulm, on the Danube, where
they had been quartered throughout their married
life. A Saxon juris-consult, a friend of Captain H——,
was another pleasant member of our party. He had
not served during the war, but with a number of
college companions had taken lessons in elementary
surgery. and had volunteered to fetch the wounded
from under fire.

At Sedan, this hospital corps were ridden over by a
charge of cavalry, and only saved themselves and the
wounded under their charge by rapidly throwing themselves and their patients into a ditch. At a later hour
of the day three of these volunteer surgeons were
struck down by a shell.

One of the great charms of travel is that you
are constantly brought into contact with pleasant
people, and are led to take a more favourable
view of your race—the much maligned but kindly
race of men. But, alas! how seldom do you meet
agreeable acquaintances thus formed, a second time!
The old Colonel we quite hoped to meet again at
Constance or Ueberlingen, as he told me he intended
to come on on the first of August, unless it should fall
on a Sunday. "You prefer not to travel on Sunday?"
said I. "It is a principle with me not to do it," he
replied. "If necessary I do it, but do not like it.
No! on Sundays I feel the right thing to be to go to
church. The little fellow, too, can now join in and
enjoy the singing, which makes it very pleasant to me."
As all our friends insisted upon coming to the steamboat to see us off, we felt we were treated quite as
well as the German Kaiser, and have the pleasantest
recollection of our farewell to Lindau.

CHAPTER VIII.

THE PEASANT WAR ON THE BODEN SEE.

The Peasant War on the Boden See—Vadian and Kessler proclaim the Reformation in St. Gall and the Rhine-valley — The peasants downtrodden — Twelve articles of the Peasant League—Münzer—Heughlin Schappler—Argument of articles—Rising of the peasants—Truchsess von Waldburg—Suppression of the Insurrection.

THE sixteenth century had begun. Luther had burned the pope's bull outside the gates of Wittenberg. Charles V. had, when under twenty, succeeded to his splendid heritage, which comprised half the old world and the whole of the new. As early as 1518, a young citizen of St. Gall, of the name of Joachim von Watt or Vadian, who had studied medicine and taught philosophy at the University of Vienna, had returned to his native city, with the teachings of Luther in his head and heart, and the writings of the great Reformer in his pocket. Luther sent his books hot from the press to St. Gall and Zürich, and kept up an active correspondence with Vadian in the one city and Zwingli in the other. Johann Kessler, a sadler's apprentice, had listened to the lectures of Luther and Melancthon at Wittenberg, and in 1523 travelled from city to city, from village to village, and from hamlet to hamlet, along the shores of the Boden See, and up into the Rheinthal, everywhere proclaiming the new evangel. At Murg, on the lovely shores of the Wallensee, in this year a priest was celebrating mass at the altar, when a maiden approached it attired like a bride, and knelt before him. "Dost thou remember how we pledged our troth to one another at Zürich?" said the priest to her. "I do," she replied. "Then," said he, "if thou remainest in the same mind, I herewith take thee as my wife in marriage." Of this marriage he called upon the bystanders to be witnesses, partook of the sacrament himself, and handed it to the maiden.

The soil was ripe for the new seed, and as the down-trodden peasants of Southern Germany heard of spiritual freedom, they naturally felt how little of civil freedom they enjoyed. The peasant was a slave. The princes, the nobility, and the priests alike regarded their subject peasants as their property, over whose goods and person they possessed an indefeasible right. The clergy and nobility were so independent, that however benevolent a prince might be, or desirous of the happiness of his poorer subjects, he was almost powerless to .shelter them from the oppression of their feudal lords. The peasant had no seat at the Landtag, where the nobles, the ecclesiastics, and the representatives of the towns consulted as to the common weal. From the grace or pity of his lord he had but little to hope. I fear the age of chivalry was never so chivalrous as poets would have us believe; but at the time of which we write the feudal system was played out. It had served its purpose and had now become an unmitigated tyranny and system of cruel oppression. The nobles of the period are described as brave but brutal, and devoid of all culture. Thirsting for revenge for every insult, and towards their inferiors cruel despots, many, in addition, gave themselves up without reserve to the disgusting vice of drunkenness. The discovery of the new world had given a great stimulus to trade; the luxury of the courts increased at a dangerous rate. The little courts emulated the great in the fatal race of extravagance; the nobility emulated the little courts. In peace time the lot of the peasant was sufficiently sad, but in war it was far worse. In peace or in war he felt the truth of the old proverb which says, "the peasant pays for all." When no great war was on foot there were constant feuds between castle and castle, between princeling and princeling, which the central imperial government was far too weak to prevent. Hired soldiers and *landsknechts* were added to feudal levies to carry on these quarrels, and the peasant was the victim and his property was the spoil of all. Add to this the exactions of, in great part, a rapacious and shameless clergy, and it will readily be admitted that the cup of the poor German peasant was well-nigh full.

The doctrines of the Reformation served as a spark to explode the mine that had thus long been in course of preparation. On the other side of the lake was the Swiss Confederation, before whose serried pikes, and battle-axes, and *morgensterns* the flower of the imperial chivalry had more than once gone down in hopeless ruin. The German peasant felt that he was no less a man than his Swiss neighbour.

In the year 1525 appeared the famous twelve articles of the peasant-league, that served as a rallying cry for the insurgents against class tyranny all over Germany. These celebrated articles have been attributed to Thomas Münzer, and also to Johann Huegli, or Heuglin, who, two years later, was burned as a heretic at Meersburg. It is highly probable that they were written by a certain Christopher Schappler, who was born in St. Gall, and was a preacher at Memmingen, who it is satisfactory to know safely escaped from the subsequent search made for him by the Suabian league, and returned to the city of his birth, where he married and lived happily in the great love and esteem of his fellow citizens. These articles are singularly clear and moderate in tone, and, though they served as a rallying cry for the insurgent peasants, it is probable that the author had no intention of exciting to insurrection.

The articles maintain "that the peasants only desire to be governed according to God's word."

"Their humble request, which is also their will and opinion, is that every commune (Gemeinde) shall be allowed to choose its own pastor, who shall preach the pure and undefiled gospel; to him is due the tenth part of the corn, and what is beyond his needs belongs to the poor."

They complain of the custom "of treating them hitherto as serfs ('eigene Leute,' literally 'owned people'), which is indeed very pitiful, as Christ redeemed with his precious blood as well the shepherd as the highest in the land." It also seems to them "quite unsuitable and unbrotherly that no poor man should have the right to catch game, birds, or fish in flowing waters (in the rivers and streams), that the peasants should be obliged to permit, and that in silence, that the authorities should have the game, and so much of it to the great vexation and grievous injury of the peasants, and that the irrational animals should eat up the fruit of their toil."

They also reclaim for themselves the woods formerly owned by the different communes, but which had been appropriated by the nobles or clergy. They beg for a "gracious examination" into the terribly hard services they had to render, and that the various exactions in money and kind may be reduced to the scale of former times, and that more righteous punish-

ments may be inflicted, and not from hatred or favour
as heretofore. As did the Gracchi at Rome, they
demand that the fields that once belonged to whole
communes shall be restored, but if any of them have
been honestly purchased and have thus come into
other hands, they do not wish that the purchaser shall
be violently dispossessed, but that the matter shall be
arranged in friendly and brotherly fashion.

They are uncompromising in the demand that the
law by which in case of death the feudal lord demanded
a heavy tax before burial was permitted—a very cruel
form of succession-duty known as the "Todfall"—should
be abolished.

It is characteristic of the age, and very touching,
that this humble petition and cry of anguish of the
oppressed peasants, closes with an article to the effect
that if any of their demands can be proved to be
contrary to scripture, they are willing at once to
renounce such demand. The humility and moderation
of the twelve articles were not, however, practically
displayed by the peasants. All along the northern
shore of the Boden See they began to rise against
their oppressors. In 1523 the monastery of Weingarten complained that "the peasants, actually drunken
with the gospel," came in from all the villages to rob
the churches.

In the following year the great mass of the insurgent
peasants swept through Upper Suabia towards the
Boden See and Switzerland. The republics of Schaffhausen and Zürich, with prudent conservatism, warned
the wandering hordes not to cross their frontiers.
"We go about" they replied, "like the rooks in the
air, whither God's word, the Spirit, and our needs
lead us."

The peasants in Thurgau allowed their beards to

grow, and swore that they would never shave again until they were free men.

Early in the year 1525 the peasant serfs of the Abbot of Kempten rose against him, besieged him in his abbey, took him prisoner, and only liberated him at the price of a heavy ransom. The example was quickly followed by the peasantry in the Hegau, the Algau, and along the northern shores of the Boden See.

The most important body of revolted peasants numbered 18,000, and had established its camp at Laupheim, between Ulm and Biberach. The cities of the Suabian league were greatly alarmed. Their representatives met to take counsel at Ulm, and sent ambassadors to the peasants, who replied that they wished to injure no one, but only to have the gospel, and secure its enjoyment and the privileges it conferred upon all. The League replied with smooth words, but determined upon arming, and secured the aid of Georg Truchsess von Waldburg, whom they nominated generalissimo of their forces. Truchsess von Waldburg was a devout Catholic; his own peasants had risen against him, and his breast was full of rage and hatred.

He conducted the campaign with determination and skill—always taking the offensive, and attacking the peasants wherever he found them, without regard to the disproportion of numbers. This bold policy was successful. He attacked and dispersed them on the Danube, conquered the cities that they had occupied, and beheaded their leaders.

In spite, however, of this success, Truchsess von Waldburg found his own castles beleaguered by the peasants. Waldsee, in which was his best artillery, was surrounded, so also was Wolfegg, where were his wife and children.   A mutiny broke out among his foot soldiers, who naturally sympathized with their brother-peasants.   Radolfszell was for eight weeks besieged by the peasants, and the city of Ueberlingen—then, as now, the centre of Catholicism and conservatism—was threatened by them.   With consummate skill Truchsess triumphed over the difficulties in which he was placed, and the Bürgermeister of Ueberlingen, marching out at the head of the most trusty citizens, succeeded in inflicting a severe defeat upon the insurgents, and carried back into Ueberlingen 150 prisoners, who were beheaded in the principal square in one day by the public executioner.   The sword with which this terrible punishment was inflicted is now in the city museum at Ueberlingen.   The Emperor Charles V. was so pleased with the valour and the unsparing severity of the men of Ueberlingen, that he allowed the city to quarter a shield containing the lion of Hapsburg with a drawn sword, upon the breast of the imperial eagle which constituted the arms of Ueber-lingen.   The cause of the peasants was sullied by frightful atrocities, as was inevitable among hordes of rude and ignorant men without discipline, and who had been goaded to madness by oppression.

The repression on the part of the nobles and cities was bloody and cruel.   With the defeat of the insur-rection, the execution of its leaders, and the slaughter of many of its adherents, the yoke seemed more firmly fixed upon the peasant's neck than before.   But this was only in appearance.   The despised serfs had met their feudal lords in the open field, sometimes with advantage ; they had besieged them in their castles ; and, in spite of the ultimate success of the nobles, they had struck terror into their hearts.   The nobles began to realise that their bondsmen were, after all, men like themselves, and to entertain a feeling of respect for those they had learned to fear.

That this was a new sentiment is shown by the fact that even such a wild knight-errant as Ulrich von Hutten—half bandit, half reformer—whose whole life was a struggle for justice and recognition on behalf of the knights and petty nobility as against the greater nobles, ecclesiastics, and princes, never shows the least compassion for the wrongs of the peasants. He pitied them as little as would a soldier of Leonidas, a Helot, or a chivalrous southern planter of twenty years ago, his black groom.

The terrible sufferings entailed by the Peasants' War, and the blood therein shed, were not altogether in vain. The serfs struck a blow for freedom, and, though it failed, they had raised themselves in the scale of manhood by the effort, for—

> " Freedom's battle once begun,
> Bequeathed from bleeding sire to son,
> Though baffled oft is ever won."

CHAPTER IX.

BREGENZ.

BREGENZ is the capital of the Austrian Vorarlberg, and is beyond question the oldest city on the lake. It probably owed its origin to a Celtic race, for the Roman name, Brigantium, is merely a Latin adaptation of a Celtic name. On account of its strategical position, the Romans built a very strong castle here, on the site of which stands the greater part of old Bregenz. With the Romans Christianity came, but when the northern peoples overran the Roman empire, Bregenz was burned ; and, as before-mentioned, when Gallus and his companions reached Bregenz—in the beginning of the seventh century—they found Thor and Woden in possession of the ancient Christian chapel formerly dedicated to St. Aurelia. The fact that Bregenz was never a free city of the empire, but dependent upon some princely house—for many generations that of the De Montforts—is probably the reason that it never played the same important part in history as its sister cities of the lake.

Its siege by the men of Appenzell in the winter of 1408 has already been mentioned, together with the

BREGENZ.

heroism of the poor woman named Gutha or Judith. The night watchmen of Bregenz, in her honour, still cry at midnight, "Ehr' Gutha"—"Honour Gutha." In the Thirty Years' War General Wrangel and his Swedes took Bregenz after a lengthened siege. Of the two, I think Lindau is a more advantageous place than Bregenz at which to stay, and from which to make excursions upon the lake. The steamers only require twenty-five minutes between the two ports. Above the town rises the Gebhartsberg, where on a great rock stood a castle belonging to the house of Montfort, which was regarded as impregnable until Wrangel obtained possession of it and blew it up. On its ruins stand a little church and a modest inn, from the terrace of which one of the very finest views on the Boden See is seen. It comprises the whole extent of the lake, with the high Appenzell Alps, while immediately below the terrace, at a depth of six or eight hundred feet, foams the torrent of the Bregenzer Aach, over whose wide and rocky bed a long and quaint wooden-covered bridge leads to the village of Lauteraach. It may have been our fancy, but the people in Bregenz did not look to us so well-to-do and comfortable as the inhabitants of Lindau and of the Bavarian and Baden towns. There were more children without shoes or stockings, and looking unkempt and uncared for. There, as everywhere, our *Deutscher Arbeiter* and other little books seemed to give great delight to both old and young. I should mention that the walk to the Gebhartsberg can be easily managed in half-an-hour, and that almost the whole of the way up it is shaded by umbrageous trees, a very important consideration for visitors, if so blazing a sun is shining as there was on the 18th July, 1879.

The steamer takes two-and-a-half hours in making

the voyage from Lindau to Constance.   On the way
we pass, on the northern shore, Wasserburg, pic-
turesquely situated on a peninsula.   Its inhabitants
number 2,500.   The castle and church close together
form an interesting group as seen from the lake.   It is
in the centre of cornfields and vineyards, and is well
shaded with fruit trees.   In the latter half of the
eighth century, in the reign of Charlemagne, it is
mentioned as "Wazzarburuc."   It subsequently belonged to the Counts of Montfort, who sold it to the
Fuggers, from whom it passed to Austria, and finally
to Bavaria, in 1806.

Soon afterwards we leave the Bavarian shore, and,
entering Würtemberg territory, approach the palatial
castle, "Schloss Montfort."   On the site of this beautiful residence formerly stood a strong and frowning
castle named Argen, the origin of which tradition
assigns to the Romans.   When the present mansion
was built, the foundations were laid bare of two gigantic
towers, that may well have been of Roman workmanship.   Early in the fourteenth century Count
William of Montfort built a strong castle upon the
ruins of a much older one.   Burned down at a later
date, it rose, Phœnix-like, and is mentioned as a
fortress in 1556.   Through the cowardice of the commandant it was surrendered to the Swedes in 1647, for
which offence he was beheaded at Lindau.   In 1720
the fortifications were razed, and Count Ernest of
Montfort erected a princely castle upon the site.   When,
as one of the smaller results of the battle of Austerlitz,
it fell to Bavaria, in 1805, the ministry of finance of
that country sold it for less than £200 to be broken
up!   There was no delay in carrying this barbarous
decision into execution ; but before much impression
could be made upon its solid masonry, the fortune of

war took away the district from Bavaria and gave it to Würtemberg. King William immediately stopped the work of demolition, and commenced the present villa, which his son, King Charles, completed. It is now the residence of the Princess Louise of Prussia.

Hard by is Langenargen, which is also mentioned as early as 773. " It takes its name," says Vadian, " from that wild and untrustworthy stream the Arg, that here flows into the lake."

In 1629 almost all the inhabitants died of the plague, and in 1800 it was bombarded from the lake by the French. It now contains about 1400 inhabitants, and the view is at least equal to that from any point on the lake.

Very soon we reach " Friedrichs-hafen," formerly Buchhorn, and which first appears in the history of the eighth century under the name " Buachihorn." It was an early seat of the great Guelph family, to whom it belonged in the twelfth century.

In 1273 the Emperor Rudolph I. made Buchhorn a free city of the empire, which freedom it retained until 1802, when it was handed over to Bavaria, and in 1810 to Würtemberg. King Frederick was very fond of the neighbourhood, transformed the former cloister of Hofen—founded long before the tenth century—into a royal summer residence, and building a fine wide street between Hofen and Buchhorn, a distance of little more than a mile, named the two places, thus united, after himself — Friedrichs-hafen. He did much to improve the harbour in order to encourage the trade of the place with Switzerland and Italy, and the success of his efforts is shown by the fact that while Schwab in 1826 gives the population as 800, it now contains 2,500 inhabitants.

There is a very interesting story of the first Count of

Buchhorn, Ulrich by name, said to be historically true. Ulrich was descended from a brother of Hildegard, the consort of Charlemagne, and was married to a granddaughter of the Emperor Heinrich I., who was named Wendelgard. Their happiness was disturbed by an irruption of the terrible Huns—the same irruption described in " Ekkehard." Ulrich at the head of his subjects hastened to meet them : was, however, captured in battle, and universally believed to be slain. Poor Wendelgard, inconsolable for the death of her husband, took the vows of a nun, and entered a cloister. Every year, however, upon the anniversary of his death, she visited Buchhorn to pray in the church there and to distribute alms to the poor. For the third time she came upon this pious errand : she had finished her devotions and was leaving the church, when a ragged beggar stepped from the crowd and importunately demanded an alms. The countess granted him his request, but hardly had he taken the bounty from her hand when he sprang upon her, embraced and kissed her. Full of indignation and righteous anger she drew herself back, and her attendants were about to visit the unheard-of insult with condign punishment, when the beggar made himself known as Count Ulrich, so long believed to be dead. In spite of his misery and rags, the faithful woman recognised her long-lost lord, and threw herself into his arms. The rapture was momentary. Alas ! she was a nun, and, as such, lost to him for ever. The matter was referred to Bishop Solomon, of Constance, whose decision was worthy of his great namesake. He said that the vow that united the countess to her husband was older than that which had consigned her to a celibate life. Wendelgard returned to her husband, and lived with him in undisturbed happiness. In due time she bore her husband a son, whom his pious parents dedicated to God. The son became Abbot of Reichenau, and distinguished himself by his piety, learning, and administrative ability.

Of how the Swedes burned Hofen, and how they fared in Buchhorn during the Thirty Years' War, I may perhaps speak in a later chapter.

On the 20th June, 1879, as if to make amends for a long period of rainy weather, the sun shone out with great splendour, and we availed ourselves of the fine day to visit Friedrichs-hafen from Rorschach.

The sail is a very delightful one, and as we are less overshadowed by the nearer heights than upon the voyage to Lindau, the view is more extensive, Of this view I have elsewhere spoken. In little over an hour we steam into Friedrichs-hafen, which suffers by the almost inevitable comparison which the traveller makes between it and Lindau. The insular position of Lindau gives it a unique and singularly picturesque appearance, reminding the traveller some-what of Venice, but even more of St. Malo. In comparison with the Bavarian watering-place the appearance of Friedrichs-hafen is not striking, but what it loses in picturesqueness it gains in conve-venience, for, uncramped by water-sapped walls, it can spread itself out in every direction. Right and left of the town, along the shore of the lake, extend avenues of lofty shade-giving walnut-trees, and the town itself is completely surrounded by gardens—kitchen gardens if you will, but yet rendered beautiful and fragrant by great clumps of roses, honeysuckle, and syringa, to say nothing of all manner of old-fashioned flowers, such as red and white stocks, in the gayest profusion.

Taking the western avenue, a quarter of an hour's walk brings us to the entrance of the Schloss, the

former cloister of Hofen, and now the summer residence of the Royal Family of Würtemberg. Outside
the gardens there is a promenade, on an embankment
by the side of the lake, and along this we stroll,
enjoying the cool breeze and feasting upon the un-
equalled view. A brood of ten young downy yellow
ducklings take advantage of the bright sunshine to
make one of their first essays upon the lake. Their
caretaker (not an old hen, but a young woman,)
told us they were only four days old, yet they
had a shrewd notion of shifting for themselves, and
began to preen themselves like experienced old
birds. *Homo sapiens* is not so precocious. As His
Majesty King Karl of Würtemberg was to arrive
that very afternoon, we should hardly have in-
truded into the Schloss gardens had we not fortunately met at one of the side entrances a gentleman
whom we rightly guessed to be one of the royal pur-
veyors, and who encouraged us to enter. The Schloss
is too barn-like to be beautiful, but the ground seemed
to us on that hot summer day almost paradisiacal.
First we passed along an avenue of ancient and venerable chestnuts, and then into shaded walks which
extend all around the Schloss grounds, and which are
formed by training young beech trees over iron trellis-
work, so as to form an almost impenetrable shade from
the hot sun. The outside wall, which here separates
the gardens from the promenade on the embankment
by the lake, is pierced at intervals of about every
hundred feet, and an ornamental stone balcony is
thrown out, each furnished with a couple of garden
chairs, cosily inviting to a *tête-à-tête*. This walk leads
to a spacious pillared and partially-roofed court, built
out on to the lake, and provided with tables, chairs,
and curtains, and all other requisites for *al fresco* enter-

tainments. The view is what I have described from
the lake; but what I cannot describe is the exquisite
coolness—the hot rays of the sun being unable to penetrate into this sanctum, where, however, the cool breeze
from the water can freely enter with the murmurous
plash, plash of the blue waves, skimmed by swallows
or soared over by great sea-mews. Passing a splendid
silver poplar, we reached the stables, forming one side
of a large quadrangular courtyard. The horses, just
arrived for the season from Stuttgart, numbered thirty-
two, among which were some magnificent Arabs and
two long-tailed Russian steeds, which are favourites
with Queen Olga. The church is close to the castle,
from which there is a private entrance. There is a
fine portrait of Luther in stained glass in one of the
windows. The bank in front of the Schloss is entirely
planted with dwarf rose bushes—at the time of our
visit in full bloom. Many gardeners, both men and
women, were busy raking the gravel smooth. The
royal pair never tire of this sweet place, but always
pass the time of the great heat, from June to October,
here. The Queen was formerly well known in England as the Grand-Duchess Olga of Russia. What a
contrast is her lot, with her good husband and her contented, loyal, and loving people, to that of her brother,
the almost almighty Czar, who can nevertheless rarely
know what a moment's peace or content means. It is
true that Providence has denied this happy royal pair
the crowning blessing of children, but both the King
and Queen find great delight in the two sweet little
children of their widowed niece, Princess Olga. We
were sorry our steamer's early departure did not
permit us to see the arrival of His Majesty; but
by the time he was driving through his good city,
dressed out *en fête*, and along his stately avenue, we

were half-way across the lake.   Pursuing our way by
steamboat along the German shore of the lake, in a
westward direction, soon after leaving Friedrichs-
hafen we pass the last hamlet in Würtemberg territory, the village of Fischbach, also an ancient place,
for it is mentioned in the chronicles as far back as
early in the eighth century.   Near to it are extensive
remains of the lake-dwellers, which, until lately, were
regarded as the vestiges of an oak forest.   The
first towns on Baden territory are Immenstaad and
Hagnau—very old places, but presenting no special
object of interest to the traveller—and then the
steamer approaches Meersburg.

MEERSBURG.

CHAPTER X.

MEERSBURG.

WHETHER from the summit of the Pfänder, or the Gebhartsberg above Bregenz, from on the hill above Rorschach, or from any point that commands the full extent of the Boden See, the eye of the traveller is irresistibly drawn to a white spot on the Baden shore, which glitters again in the sunshine. This spot is the old town of Meersburg, which, although doubtless of much older date, is first mentioned in history as " Merspurc " in 1213.

In that year the Emperor Frederick II., after his coronation at Mainz, spent holy week at Constance and " Merspurc." The shore rises steeply, almost sheer from the lake, as we approach Meersburg, and as from the steamboat it appears even steeper than it really is, one is apt to wonder how it is possible for the little town to cling on to the side of the hill, up which it climbs to the old castles, which are firmly planted upon the rocks, and present a most imposing appearance.

There seems no good reason to doubt the truth of the tradition that the old castle owes it origin to King

Dagobert, in or about A.D. 628. It subsequently belonged to Charles Martel, the hammer of the Saracens, who, there is some reason to believe, resided here for a part his life, between A.D. 691 and 741. Then came the great house of the Hohenstaufen, under whom the characteristic civilisation of the middle ages attained its zenith, and who ruled in Germany from 1138 to 1254.

We have already mentioned the ill-starred Conradin of Suabia—the last of this great family. He was but eleven years old when he came to the home of his fathers on the Boden See, and is described as a wonderfully beautiful boy, most carefully educated, and possessed of a perfect mastery of the Latin language. He was a friend of literature and a Minnesänger, and some of his touching boyish love-songs have come down to us. It was from the Castle of Meersburg that he started for the Italian campaign, in which he hoped to win back the great inheritance of his race. History tells us how the bold and chivalrous effort failed, and how his rival, Charles of Anjou, caused the last of the illustrious house of Hohenstaufen to perish on a scaffold at Naples at the age of sixteen, in 1269.

As we dwell upon the tragic fate of Conradin it is impossible not to think of another youthful scion of another great imperial house, who, 610 years later, left the castle of his ancestors, also on the lake of Constance—Arenenberg—to seek fame and glory, name and distinction, that should enable him to carve his way to the imperial throne of France.

The young Conradin perished on the block at Naples; the young Napoleon in a skirmish in South Africa. Strange that there should be so much in common between the fate of the heir of the Hohenstaufen and the heir of the Bonapartes!

Upon the fall of Conradin the castle of Meersburg fell to the bishops of Constance, whose possession and residence it remained for more than 500 years.

In 1313 the Emperor Ludwig the Bavarian besieged Bishop Nicholas in the castle of Meersburg for fourteen weeks ; but so stout were its walls and so stout-hearted its defenders, that the Emperor, after unheard-of efforts, was compelled to raise the siege.

Among the besieged were a certain canon of Constance, a count of Toggenburg, who distinguished himself by his valour, and an experienced soldier named Jasso, who put archers and other soldiers on board ship and pursued the boats of the attacking force, against whom he raged like a lion. The old chronicler says, " he threw his net into the lake and caught them like fish."

The Meersburger sent out ships of war with which they captured the vessels bringing supplies to the Emperor's army, while they themselves were daily supplied with corn from friendly Constance.

On the occasion of the destruction of an old gateway of the town during the present century, great numbers of iron bolts were found imbedded in the oak beams— bolts that must have been thrown from the machines of Ludwig the Bavarian 500 years before.

The possessions of the bishopric of Constance fell to the Grand Duchy of Baden in 1806, and the old castle was made the seat of a provincial civil and criminal tribunal.

In 1836 this tribunal was removed by the authorities, and there was some talk of breaking up the ancient and now deserted castle. An antiquary and poet saved it from this sad fate. Joseph von Lassberg purchased the hoary old pile, and for nineteen years exercised a worthy hospitality in its ancient halls.   He loved men of letters almost as much as he loved his books and manuscripts; of the former of which the castle library contained 12,000, and of the latter 273.   Among these is one of the oldest manuscripts of the Nibelungen-lied.   His appearance was well suited to his abode, as he was a tall and handsome man with long flowing white beard.

A poet, Levin Schücking, who for years lived with him in the castle, writes—

> "Es schuettelt euch die Hand
> Ein grauer Rittersmann und spricht willkommen:
> Und fragt nach jeder Burg in eurem Land
> Und weiss Geschichten wie ihr nie vernommen."

"A gray old knight shakes you by the hand, and·bids you welcome, and asks about every castle in your land, of ·which he has stories to tell such as you have never heard."

In 1855, full of years and of such honours as he sought, in the enjoyment of the intimate friendship and affection of most of the authors and literary men of Germany, Joseph von Lassberg died.   Two of his daughters continued to occupy a couple of rooms in the old castle, but its ancient halls were tenantless.

At length, in 1877, the castle was sold for the incredibly small sum of 20,000 marks, or £1,000. The purchaser was the Ritter Mayer, of Mayerfels, a Tyrolese nobleman who had devoted a long life to the collection of ancient arms and antiquities of every description.   Hearing that the old castle of Meersburg was for sale, it occurred to him what an admirable local habitation it would make for his collection, then stored away in warehouses in Munich. Some forty or fifty railway wagons were necessary to bring the precious hoard, and at Lindau were

GATEWAYS OF THE NEW AND OLD CASTLES.

transferred bodily to the lake steamers, which are specially adapted for this traffic, and were so brought to Meersburg.

The cost of moving the collection is said to have amounted to two-thirds that of the freehold of the castle ; and the son-in-law of Herr von Mayerfels informed me that the absolutely necessary repairs to the masonry of the castle amounted to a similar sum.

The fitness of things seemed to demand that such a collection should have just such a setting as this venerable castle of thirteen centuries.

Of the details of the collection I have no space here to speak ; suffice it to say that it comprises arms of every age and nation ; a trophy of Chassepots, sabres, pistols, cuirassses, and helmets, from the French war of 1870-71 ; six hundred helmets, that once belonged to the famous Pappenheim Cuirassiers in the Thirty Years' War, and complete suits of Milan armour, some of them of the most exquisite and costly workmanship. These, as well as numerous executioners' swords and terrible instruments of torture, make the visitor rejoice that he lives in a better and more humane age.

The old castle of Dagobert is separated from the new Schloss by a deep trench cut in the solid rock in the fourteenth century, by Bishop Nicholas, who employed 400 miners on the task, and hoped to render the castle thereby impregnable. The gulf was spanned by a drawbridge, for which a permanent light wooden structure has now been substituted. The new castle was built for a palace by Bishop Anthony of Säckingen in 1750, in the prevailing fashion of the time, with the palace at Versailles as model. The celebrated Theodore of Dalberg was the last bishop who resided here, until the beginning of the century, when it passed to the Baden government, who have converted it into an institution for the deaf and dumb.   The intense heat which had been oppressing us was tempered by a severe thunderstorm as, on the 6th August, 1879, we approached by the lake the venerable old town.   Sheltering ourselves from the tremendous downpour of water in an ancient and massive building, which now serves as office and warehouse for the steamboats, as soon as the storm began to cease we climbed along the steep main street into the upper part of the town, and found a cool retreat in an upper room at the " Lion."   When the excellent and reforming Emperor of Germany, Joseph II., visited Meersburg, in 1777, the then Prince-bishop of Constance, Cardinal Roth, came to meet his imperial master and visitor, and invited him to take up his quarters in the palace.   The Emperor, whose simple tastes are well known, declined, upon the ground that he had already ordered rooms at the " Lion."   The Cardinal, an energetic and determined man, whose conservative soul loathed the · radical reforms in Church and State of the Emperor, bowed low, and, as he turned briskly away, said, " If that's the case, may God preserve your Majesty.   Yonder is the way to the ' Lion.' "

We had brought with us a large number of Gospels and *Deutsche Arbeiter* for the deaf and dumb pupils, and inquired with great anxiety as to the character of the director of the institution,   Right glad were we to hear that, though a Catholic and a Seminarist, he was not a priest.   One minute from the hotel brought us to the former episcopal palace.   The director received us very kindly, and when informed of the object of our visit, conducted us over the institution.   The spacious halls, noble apartments, and broad corridors, serve admirably for the purpose to which they are now devoted.   The carved and gilded panelling all remains as in the time of the bishops ; only the mirrors have been removed from the walls, as it was thought that such an excess of luxury might be prejudicial to the children.   There are at present about sixty boys and forty girls in the institution, and so excellent is their health that though, upon inquiry, a "sick room" was shown to us, we were informed that it had had no inmate for many months.   The children receive good meat-soup and meat once a day, and it is to the excellence of the dietary, more perhaps even than to the exceedingly healthy situation of the Castle of Meersburg, that the sanitary condition of the institution is to be attributed.   The fine walks in the neighbourhood and the baths in the lake have doubtless also something to do with it.   It was delightful to see the bright, happy look of these afflicted children, and to learn that most who pass through the institution are able to gain their own livelihood and become useful members of society.   It is interesting to know that the cost of each child for board, clothing, and instruction —for everything, in short, but the rent of the palace, which is granted free by the state—is £16 per annum. Some children contribute £12 per annum, some £4, and the very poor nothing.   It is open to both Catholics and Protestants, and the patience and devotion of the teachers seemed to us unbounded.   The director told me that if he had a teacher who did not appear to be fulfilling his duties as a labour of love, he told him gently that he had not found his vocation, and that he would meet with greater rewards in some other walk in life.   No sign language, *i.e.*, talking on the fingers, is allowed in the institution.   Instruction is entirely conveyed by teaching the children to watch the lips of their teacher, to read off what he says, and to imitate him.   This system involves infinitely more labour and patience in teaching, but once acquired, the pupil feels his deprivation of the sense of hearing comparatively little.   On the other hand, it appears to me that, even to the ablest pupils, this "reading off" is only possible where there is great distinctness of utterance on the part of the speaker; and though the director wore a beard, I noticed that the hair on the upper lip was carefully cut short, so as to allow the play of the mouth and lips to be clearly visible.   We were taken to each one of the nine classes, and to each I addressed a few words, the teacher repeating them very clearly and distinctly after me.   In one case they were asked why they could not "read off" (*ablesen*)—what I said —when they answered readily, "because of your beard and moustache hiding the motions of your mouth." The little books seemed to give great and general pleasure.

To the right of the Dagobert Castle and of the former episcopal palace stands another massive building, which, though presenting no architectural interest, yet helps to give to Meersburg its striking appearance of a mass of masonry set high above the lake upon a rock.   This is the former seminary for priests and now for teachers.

The Freiherr von Wessenberg, who performed the duties of bishop of Constance, though denied the title for nearly half-a-century, and who has stamped his name and personality more firmly upon the city of his labours than any other man except John Huss, took the deepest interest in this seminary; and his little shallop might every week be seen, even in the stormiest weather, approaching Meersburg on his weekly visitations to the students.

We must not leave Meersburg with its castles, its steep streets, and its queer old-world houses and squares, without mentioning its famous red wine, which from time immemorial has been considered the best grown upon the lake. The reader of "Ekkehard" will remember its effects upon the Chamberlain Spazzo. In the graveyard at Meersburg rest the remains of Joseph von Lassberg and of his gifted sister-in-law Annette von Droste-Huelshoff, who is regarded by Catholic Germans as their greatest poetess. Here also repose the remains of Dr. Mesmer, who has given his name to the science of animal magnetism.

CHAPTER XI.

UEBERLINGEN.

UPON leaving Meersburg we pass upon the northern
shore " Unter-Uhldingen,"—the nearest point on the
lake to the Castle of Heiligenberg,—Seefelden, and
Nussdorf. Great discoveries have been made in this
neighbourhood of the remains of the lake-dwellers,
from which it is evident that in pre-historic times there
must have been a large population living in houses
upon piles in this part of the lake. Just above Nussdorf is an imposing building, the church of New Birnau,
formerly a famous place of pilgrimage, and close to it
the former summer residence of the abbots of Salem.

As the steamer approaches Ueberlingen, we seem to
take leave of the nineteenth century, with its hurry
and bustle, and the thousand developments of modern
civilisation. The great iron horse has not found its
way to Ueberlingen, as it has to Lindau and Friedrichs-hafen, and the walls and picturesque towers
appear in perfect order, as though they might be
manned at a moment's warning should the bugle sound
from the church-tower to tell of the approach of the
Swedes or other foes.

UEBERLINGEN.

Ueberlingen has now 4,000 inhabitants, of whom 300 are Protestants. In the heat of summer it is much visited, principally by southern Germans, for the sake of the lake bathing. One of the great Roman roads passed over the site of Ueberlingen, and it is highly probable that there was a Roman settlement, or at any rate a fortification, here. The holy Gallus healed the daughter of Duke Gunzo here early in the seventh century.

Friedrich der Rothbart (Frederick Barbarossa), the greatest of the Hohenstaufen, visited Ueberlingen in 1155, and in 1397 it became a free city of the empire.

Early in the fourteenth century, along the shores of the Boden See, as alas! elsewhere, raged a terrible persecution of the Jews. Probably the same causes that render them now detested in the far East of Europe, in Morocco, and elsewhere, operated in the middle ages throughout all Europe. In Constance it was reported that a Christian had sold the sacred " Host" to the Jews, and a fanatical girl cried that the body of Christ was being terribly tortured by the Jews. Upon this the people, mad with superstition, rushed upon the first Jews they could find and butchered them with axes, as if they had been oxen. Twelve were burned alive and twelve thrown into the Rhine. Some leading citizens had the courage and the humanity to take pity on those that remained, and to assure their safety. It is a melancholy proof of the perverted conscience of the age that the historian of the period accuses these Christians in deed with having been bribed by the Jews, and adds that nothing ever prospered with them afterwards, but that Heaven punished their protection of the cursed race with an early death!

At Ueberlingen the mangled corpse of a boy who

had been lost by his parents, was found in a brook. The parents went wailing through the town, and charged the Jews with the crime. The nature of the wounds—their opening and bleeding afresh as the body was carried past the houses of the Jews—was considered ample evidence of their guilt. Under the pretence of saving them, the terrified Jews were advised to take refuge in a lofty stone house. The citizens had previously secretly filled a lower story with faggots, to which they now set fire. The agonised Jews fled from story to story, and some climbed on to the roof. In their fury and desperation they hurled down upon the mob below flaming beams, stones, knives, swords, anything they could lay hands upon. In vain! the whole house, into which 300 Jews had been enticed by the infamous faithlessness of the Christians, was a prey to the flames, and those who threw themselves out of the windows found the mob below quite as merciless as the fire.

It was inevitable that these constantly recurring and remorseless persecutions throughout the middle ages, should tend to make the Jews cowardly and to crush their spirit. It should, however, never be forgotten, for the credit of human nature and to the everlasting honour of the cruelly-persecuted race, that in spite of the timidity and cowardice ingrained into their national character by the oppression of ages, instances are not wanting in their history of sublime heroism and fidelity, in which they bore a magnificent testimony to a pure monotheism, and sealed that testimony with their blood.

At Constance, in the year 1349, during an outbreak of this furious hatred against the Jews, a Jew, who had been compelled to be baptized, set his own house on fire, and, taking his two children in his arms, cried out that he was determined to die as a pious Jew, and then perished in the flames. In the same city, in 1390, a Jew presented himself to the Burgomaster, fell before him on his knees, and besought that he might be burned alive, because he had sinned against his God in having renounced Judaism, and allowing himself to be seduced into being baptized. As he persisted in this request, he was publicly burned on the 28th September of that year. Jewish maidens of tender years threw themselves into the flames as they cried aloud the great confession of their faith :— "The Lord our God is one Lord."

Of the part taken by Ueberlingen in the Peasants' War I have already spoken. At the time of the Reformation it stood stoutly by the old faith, and when, in 1530, the bishop and canons were driven away from Constance, the refugees were received and welcomed with every mark of honour and respect at Ueberlingen.

During the Thirty Years' War, the city was closely invested and besieged by the Swedes under Gustavus Horn, in 1634. An old picture shows how the Swedes burned all the surrounding villages and cannonaded the town at close quarters. Fortunately for Ueberlingen its citizens for 100 years had been busy cutting through the soft free-stone an immense trench, which was but just completed when the Swedes came. Into this the citizens led the waters of the lake. Protected by this great moat, and strengthened by contingents from Lindau and Constance, and the peasants of the neighbourhood, who took refuge within the walls of the old town, they prepared to defend the city street by street, and at length beat back the northern foe. The trench extends all round the land-front of the city, and is now tastefully planted and converted into a charming promenade, where in the hottest days refreshing shade may be found.   In this contemporaneous painting of the siege, where besiegers and besieged look wonderfully close together according to our modern ideas of warfare, the men of Constance are represented coming in ships to their brothers of Ueberlingen.   When, a few hours after looking at this picture, we saw the magnificent new steamer, the " Kaiser Wilhelm," approach the landing with both its decks crowded with members of Sing, Schiess, and Turn-Vereine (Clubs for Singing, Shooting, and Gymnastics) from Constance, it seemed like history repeating itself in a happier era.

The welcome afforded by Ueberlingen to the Constance visitors was worthy of the traditional friendship of the two cities in old time.   Cannon thundered, cheers rent the air, and subsequently a solemn reception was held and a procession formed.

But to go back nearly 250 years.   What the Swedes could not effect, Conrad Wiederhold, the heroic commander of the Hohentwiel, accomplished to the great sorrow of Ueberlingen.   The same year that Gustavus Horn raised the siege (1634) he obtained possession of and plundered it, and again conquered it on the 30th January, 1643.   Of its subsequent fortunes, or rather misfortunes, until the end of the war, we shall speak later.   Not alone from its enemies had the good city suffered, but from the garrison of Bavarians and Spaniards who long held it.   What it suffered is but an illustration of what all Germany suffered from this dreadful scourge.   When at length the peace of Westphalia was signed, the number of the burghers of this proud old imperial city was reduced to 364, and of these there were hardly thirty to whom sufficient property remained upon which to live.

It was an intensely hot afternoon in late July, when

our steamboat approached the landing-place of the old imperial city, whose walls and towers rise imposingly from the water. We were fortunate in finding shelter from the heat, and accommodation in the "Lion," a rambling old-fashioned inn, close to the water, that has enjoyed a great reputation for more than fifty years. The charge here is 3 marks 30 pfennige (3s. 4d.), for bed and breakfast and the mid-day table d'hôte; supper is extra, and usually costs about a shilling, so that the cost of living is altogether a little higher than at Lindau. Our room is immediately over the lake, on to which it looks. The arm of the Boden See, here called the Ueber-lingen See, is about as wide as Lago Maggiore at Belgirate. At this time of the year it is gay with innumerable fishing and pleasure boats. Although so near to Switzerland, it is curious how entirely unlike our inn is to a Swiss hotel. It covers a great deal of ground, over which it seems to sprawl. Wide corridors and broad staircases seem to lead nowhither. The hotel buildings entirely surround one large courtyard, from which come whiffs, suggestive of stables rather than of "Araby the blest." Look out of another window, and you become aware of another court-yard, entirely shut in, in which grows a solitary and ancient apple-tree, the shade of which is most tempting in this tropical heat. There is a narrow strip of garden planted with shady trees between the front of the "Lion" and the lake, which is deep up to the brink, and a little bath-house belonging to the hotel is a delightful accessory to the garden. The charge for the use of the bath-house is one penny, and in this piping weather one is disposed to grudge the time one does not spend in it, or rather in the lake to which it leads. It is only in an old-world place like

Ueberlingen that one comes across a typical German inn of the olden time. We enjoyed our stay there, but it is fair to say, that in the matter of *cuisine*, as well as in cleanliness, the German hotels of this class are very inferior to their Swiss rivals.

Our stay in Ueberlingen coincided with a wave of heat, which probably rendered the ten days we spent there the hottest part of the summer of 1879. Throughout the day the thermometer ranged from eighty to ninety degrees in the shade, and the nights were hardly perceptibly cooler. In addition, the sun shone down with fiery rays from out a sky of brass. We found our best plan was to take our rambles in the town about six in the morning and after six in the evening. If the entire interval could have been spent in the water, with nothing more than the nose and mouth exposed, it would have been so much the better. The company in the hotel were exclusively Germans, mostly very quiet-going people, many of whom come here every year as regularly as their summer and only holiday comes round. An old Baroness from Thuringia was staying in the house, accompanied by her "Jungfer" or maid, who had lived with her forty-three years. There was something quaint and touching in the affection that evidently existed between mistress and maid.

To artists I strongly recommend Ueberlingen; and let them go soon, for there is a talk of taking a railway to the old city, in which case there is no telling how much of the quaint and old may go down to make way for the modern civiliser. Now, at every turn you come upon the loveliest bits of old architecture for the sketch-book—grand old towers, pieces of the city wall, and ancient gateways, to say nothing of the glorious Minster Church and the Rathhaus.

RATH-HAUS, UEBERLINGEN

For, after all, the great glory of Ueberlingen is its cathedral. Thither we returned time and again, and always with fresh delight. Its grand simplicity and perfect symmetry ought to soothe, and calm, and bring the mind into a fit mood for worship. Its foundation-stone was laid on May 13th, 1350, and it was built when Gothic art had reached its perfect development. Perhaps no higher praise can be given than to say that it is worthy to be classed with its sister churches at Strasburg and Freiburg-in-Breisgau. The five lofty aisles resting upon twenty-eight columns and eighty-one pillars, seem to have grown rather than to have been built, and fill the mind with a sense of vastness and of indefinite solemnity, such as the masterpieces of Gothic art alone produce. Nothing can exceed the variety of the ornamentation, yet the whole is pervaded by a strict unity of design. The high altar is a mass of gilding and of carving gorgeously coloured ; but of far more interest are two modern altars, carved and painted in exquisite taste. The one by a local sculptor and artist named Heberlé, representing Christ receiving and blessing the little children, cannot fail to be a joy to all sympathetic beholders as long as the Minster of Ueberlingen stands.

Near to the cathedral is the Rathhaus, dating from the early part of the fifteenth century, a most interesting building. The principal hall, the so-called Rathhaus-Saal, is little short of a miracle of mediæval art. Floor, slightly-arched roof, and side walls, are all of carved wood, and the whole with its decorations is intended to represent nothing less than the Holy Roman Empire, as it existed when the artist planned his work, between 1490 and 1494, when Maximilian had just ascended the imperial throne, Columbus was busy discovering

K

a new world, and Luther and Cortez were both
boys.

Forty-three shafts along the walls support forty-three
statuettes, each figure surmounted by a delicately
carved Gothic baldachin. These figures represent, and
are probably portraits of, the spiritual and temporal
electors of the empire : the margraves and counts, the
knights and representative peasants of Germany.
They are all most skilfully carved and coloured, and
now, at the end of 400 years, look as life-like and full
of expression as if they were portraits taken yesterday.
Between each figure, supported by some quaint
peasant or Moor, is the coat of arms of the respective
bishop or count. The hall is now regularly made use
of by the local courts ; when, however, they are not
sitting, it is a shady retreat, where the visitor may
escape from the too hot rays of the sun, and seated in
one of the carved chairs of state, can study the figures
instinct with life and character around him, and dream
that he is living at the end of the middle ages.

In addition to the public buildings are many private
dwellings of the old patrician families of Ueberlingen,
interesting from their architecture and associations.
As before mentioned, Ueberlingen is, and always has
been, intensely Catholic and conservative ; it is only
within the last few years that a Protestant church has
been established—regarded at the time as an unheard-
of and most dangerous innovation. The Gospels
and *Deutsche Arbeiter* had seemed to give such unfeigned pleasure in Lindau, Bregenz, and elsewhere,
that we were encouraged to distribute them in Ueberlingen also, where they were almost universally accepted
with apparent gratitude and delight.

One evening, when the sun was down, we found our
way to the City Orphanage, where we were cordially

UEBERLINGEN.
FROM THE UPPER TOWN

welcomed by the care-taker and his wife, who showed us over the institution. All the arrangements were very simple, but the children seemed as happy as possible, and we learned with satisfaction that they attended school with the other city children, as was also the case with the children in the orphanage at Heiden. This association with other children upon equal terms, helps to prevent the formation of a pauper class. The truly artistic illustrations of the *Deutsche Arbeiter* (German "*British Workman*") are an irresistible recommendation to almost every one, and great was the pleasure our books seemed to give. Encouraged by this, on the evening of a very hot Sunday I determined to visit the "Spital," which is at once a hospital and an asylum for the aged poor. It occupies a range of semi-conventual buildings near the city wall. I knew it to be under the care of nuns, so asked the lodge-porter for permission to speak with the lady-superior. A sister of mercy conducted me through long corridors to a central apartment, where the superior received me with frosty politeness. After explaining that there was nothing in the least degree controversial in what I wished to distribute, I presented her with copies, and asked her permission. These she would not accept, aud assured me, as far as the inmates were concerned, I might spare my trouble, as nothing of the kind was ever allowed. She, however, gave me the name of the Chancellor of the institution, and him I found in his beautiful home near the Bath hotel, and just outside the city wall, at the entrance of the public gardens. He received me very pleasantly, and, to my surprise, I found that he knew all about me and my doings during my stay at Ueberlingen. He had heard what long swims I was in the habit of taking. As to my request about the books; it was evident he

K 2

did not wish to refuse the patients in the hospital any
pleasure it was in his power to grant, but that he stood
in great fear of the priests. One matter he dwelt
upon, to which a liberal Roman Catholic priest had
before called my attention. The Gospels have upon
their covers, in conspicuous type, " Translated by Dr.
Martin Luther," If intended for distribution in
Roman Catholic Germany, hardly anything could be
more ill-advised. What would a Scotch minister, a
Low-church clergyman, or a Wesleyan preacher, say if
he found books were being disseminated among his
flock with the name of Ignatius Loyola, Socinus, or
Charles Bradlaugh upon the title-page ? Yet these
names are not so dreadful in orthodox English ears as
is the name of Luther among pious Roman Catholics.
This settled the question of the Gospels ; and, after a
pleasant chat with the Chancellor, it was arranged that
I was to call upon him at the office of the " Spital "
the following morning to receive his decision as to the
Deutsche Arbeiter, one of which I left for him to read.
Punctually at eight on Monday morning I waited upon
him at his office. He had read the *Deutsche Arbeiter*
through, and liked the letter-press as much as the
illustrations, which was saying a great deal. Personally, he said, he should have liked the poor people to
have the papers, but if he gave permission it would
infallibly lead to endless unpleasantness between him
and the priests. He then kindly took me all over the
institution, which was exquisitely clean, and the
arrangements for the comfort of the patients and old
people appeared excellent. The sister-superior hardly
seemed to know what to make of it when she saw me
being ceremoniously conducted round by the Chancellor; and when I greeted her and claimed her as an
old acquaintance, on the strength of our interview of

the previous evening, I doubt if she was greatly pleased. The almost total absence of anything like books or pictures in the wards was very striking; and remembering the pleasure the *Deutsche Arbeiter* had given in other places, I could not reconcile myself to the poor old sick men and women being deprived of it without one more effort on my part. So hearing that the parish priest was a good sort of man, I went straight from the "Spital" to try and find him. Unfortunately he was from home on a journey. His *locum tenens*, the Herr Beneficiary, proved to be a priest of decidedly *borné* intelligence. He knew all about me and my evil doings, and said "that the Church forbade the circulation of any translation of the Scriptures that was not authorised by the bishops, and that had not the requisite glosses and explanatory notes, and that he had warned the people from the altar, as was his duty, against receiving the Gospels at my hands." As to the *Deutsche Arbeiter*, "a gentleman who had examined it had assured him that it was intended to promote social democracy. Have you not been visited by the gendarmerie about it? If not, I can assure you that they have the matter in hand, and you may expect them at any moment." I replied, "The sooner the police come, the better I shall be pleased; and for any one to say that the *Deutsche Arbeiter* has a tendency to promote social democracy shows that he has not read a word of it;" and, with regard to those who found social democracy in that innocent sheet, the *British Workman*, I quoted that fine word which Schiller puts into the mouth of the dying Talbot in the "Jungfrau von Orleans":—

"Mit der Dummheit kaempfen
Götter selbst vergebens."
"Against stupidity the gods themselves fight in vain."

As a conclusion the Herr Beneficiary met my request
with a flat refusal, and we parted, I fear, without either
being greatly edified by the other.

Although glad to think that so many hundreds of
Gospels and *Deutsche Arbeiter* had been disseminated
among the homes of the good people of Ueberlingen,
as it is to be hoped they will diffuse some sweetness
and light, I am free to admit how much the priests
and the strict Catholics have to say on their side of
the question.   There is too much evidence tending to
show that in Germany while Catholicism is a religion·
binding the hearts and consciences and lives of its
adherents, Protestantism exerts little moral influence.
Let any one who doubts the truth of this examine
the statistics as to the morals respectively of Catholic
and Protestant Germany, as quoted from official documents by the Rev. S. Baring-Gould in his admirable
work, "Germany: Past and Present."   As a Protestant
of Protestants, I heartily wish that they could be
disproved or explained.   In the face of such facts,
however, it is not surprising that conscientious adherents of the old faith should regard Protestantism not
only as a heresy, but as opening the flood-gates
of irreligion and immorality.   Can it be wondered
at if, under these circumstances, they should reject
all Protestant publications upon the time-honoured
principle of—

" Timeo Danaos et dona ferentes " ?

Before leaving Ueberlingen I should mention that it
possesses a mineral spring, which, as far back as
1505, had a great reputation for the cure of certain
disorders.   The water now flows in a fountain in
the grounds of the " New Bath Hotel," a shady

and extensive garden adjoining the public park at one end of the old moat.

From Ueberlingen many interesting excursions may be made ; probably, however, we shall do best to continue our journey round the lake, halting awhile when we find places of interest.

CHAPTER XII.

GOLDBACH.

Goldbach — Heidenhöhlen—Sipplingen—Lachrymæ Petri—Sernatingen—Martyrdom of Heugling—Legend of Bodmann—The Ruins—Legend of Kargeck—
Mainau—Fair Maid of Bodmann—Visit to Mainau—The Schloss.

THE tiny village of Goldbach, with its ancient Gothic church, is the first object of interest on the northern shore after leaving Ueberlingen. It is quite sur- rounded by rocks, and is approached by land along a hollow way cut in the soft sandstone. In some places this roadway is twenty-four feet deep and only twelve feet wide, not altogether unlike the cutting through which George Stephenson carried the railway a part of the way between Liverpool and Manchester, before it was widened. This, however, is supposed to be the work of a Celtic people in pre-historic times, and is never likely to be widened.

Near to Goldbach are the celebrated Heidenhöhlen, a number of dwellings with living-rooms, kitchens, and cellars hewn in the soft sandstone which here rises sheer from the lake. Within the last few years the greater part of these interesting remains have been destroyed in the course of making a new road by the shore of the lake. The most striking was evidently once used as a church, and will hold about thirty people. Generation after generation of savants have discussed the question as to who dug out these dwellings, and for what purpose they were used. A modern investigator, Herr Oberstaats-anwalt Hager of Constance, after an elaborate description of the Heidenhöhlen and exhaustive discussion as to who built or hewed them, when and why, comes to the conclusion that they were originally the work of the early Celtic inhabitants of the shores of the lake ; that the Suevi supplanted the Celts, and in their turn occupied the caves. Then came the Romans, who greatly enlarged the caves, and gave them whatever pretensions they possess to architectural style. When the Roman empire broke up came the "Alemanni," and in the early Christian period no doubt they received the name Heiden-loecher or Heidenhöhlen (the holes or caves of the heathen), as so many Roman remains have been called in this neighbourhood—such as Heiden-Mauern, Heidenstrassen, Heiden-steine, Heiden-höhen, and, notably, the already-mentioned Heiden-mauer at Lindau. Scheffel, the author of " Ekkehard," makes the deposed Emperor Charles the Fat a resident in one of these dwellings, where he had taken refuge with one faithful attendant. Thither the Duchess Hadwig sends to him for advice upon the threatened invasion of the Huns, and thence he rides out with his trusty henchman, to appear, like Santiago in one of the Cid's battles, at the critical moment of the fight with the Huns, to spread dismay in their hearts, thus giving fresh hope and courage to the Christians, and then to find a hero's death. So much for romance : history tells us that the bulky Emperor finished his unhappy career in A.D. 888, while Dame Hadwig did not receive Latin lessons on the Hohentwiel from the monk Ekkehard until nearly a century later. Soon we pass the village of Sipplingen, formerly famous, or infamous, for its sour wine—said to be the worst grown upon the

lake.   It belonged to the sort called "Lachrymæ
Petri," because whoever drank of it went out and wept
bitterly.   It has now a very fair reputation among
connoisseurs of Boden See wines.

A little beyond Sipplingen, high upon a rock above
the lake, stand the ruins of Hohenfels, where, sometime
in the thirteenth century, lived and sang the Minnesänger Burkhard von Hohenfels, whose verses are
still highly appreciated by the lovers of the poetry
of the middle ages.

We now reach Ludwigs-hafen—formerly Sernatingen
—at the extreme western point of the Ueberlingen
See, and, indeed, of the whole Boden See.   Sernatingen played its part in the Peasants' War, and so
many of the leaders were here beheaded, that the old
chronicle relates how the executioner, George Teubler,
at length laid down his blunted sword, and said to the
Burgomaster Kessenring, of Ueberlingen,—"Sir, I am
now of opinion that I have done enough for to-day."
The priest of Sernatingen at this period, John
Heugling, was an enthusiastic adherent of the Reformation, and falling into the hands of the then bishop
of Constance, he was thrown into the dungeons of the
old castle at Meersburg, whence he was brought out
on the 10th of May, 1527, to be publicly burned.
His end was as saint-like and heroic as that of his
predecessor and master, Huss.   Like him he prayed
for his enemies, and continued to sing, "Gloria in
excelsis Deo! Te Deum laudamus!" until the rising
flames choked his voice.

Near to Ludwigs-hafen, but on the other side of the
Ueberlingen See, is the little market-town of Bodmann,
delightfully situated among vineyards and orchards,
with two old castles, one of which is a ruin standing upon hills which rise immediately above the

lake. The ruin is what remains of the old castle of
Bodmann : the castle upon the opposite hill is the
Frauenberg. Both belong to the Freiherr Bodmann,
of Bodmann, who now resides in a modern mansion
well placed in a park upon the lake. There is every
reason to believe that the Romans had a castle here,
and in the early part of the eighth century Bodmann
was a " Pfalz" (Palatium), a summer or pleasure residence of the Frank kings. As mentioned earlier in this
work, there is little doubt that it is from Bodmann that
the lake received its name of Boden See.

The family of Bodmann, of which the old chronicles
speak as early as the middle of the twelfth century,
was all but extinguished in tragical fashion in 1307.
A great festivity was being celebrated, and all the
members of the family, even to distant branches,
were assembled to do honour to the occasion. All
went merry as a marriage bell until late in the night,
when a terrible thunderstorm arose. Out of the
clouds descended a bolt of fire, so destructive and
dreadful that the castle was immediately in flames.
Escape was impossible for any one. The faithful
nurse knew that there was no hope for her, and
thought only of her charge. A happy inspiration seized her. A huge brazen cauldron stood in
the room. Into this she packed the hope of the
Bodmanns, tightly fastened in a great bundle of
clothes. Then out of the window and down the
castle wall she rolled it. Out of its brazen prison the
child was taken sound and unharmed by the crowd
who were assembled below. If any one doubt this
story, let him visit the present residence of the
Bodmanns, where the cauldron will be shown to him,
and he will be invited to take his stand inside it and
there drain a bumper of Bodmann wine to the health

of the Bodmann family, whose ancestor was thus so wonderfully preserved. Tradition says that this famous cauldron once passed out of the possession of the family, and that it was repurchased at the cost of the freehold of a farm. The legend of " The Fair Maid of Bodmann " we will reserve until we reach Mainau, with which island her sad story has most to do. Twice a week in the season a steamer plies direct from Ueberlingen to Bodmann, allowing its passengers three hours (from four to seven) to explore the neighbourhood. A stout awning on the steamer protects you from the summer sun, and the motion causes a delightful breeze from the water. The sail, which lasts twenty minutes, is very pleasant, as there is much to interest on both shores of the lake.

Arrived at Bodmann pier, three or four hundred yards have to be traversed under the blazing sun, and then we plunge into the deep shade of a beech-wood, which, by contrast with the sunshine, seems almost darkness. Through the wood a pathway zigzags so gently, that you hardly perceive the ascent you are making until, in half-an-hour, you reach the extensive ruins of the old castle of Bodmann, an immensely powerful keep with mighty donjon in the centre. On the topmost tower a pair of hawks have their eyrie, and they soar above our heads as we stand in a little belvedere of wood erected for the benefit of visitors. Very picturesque are the old ruins and the villages on the steep southern shore of the Ueberlingen See, which shore we now follow towards Mainau and Constance. Of these we need only mention one or two.

On a steep rock, high above the water, stand the ruins of the castle of Kargeck, said to have been destroyed during the Peasants' War. To these old

ruins there attaches a sad story. In the strong castle
of Kargeck, many hundred years ago, there lived a
stern old knight with an only and lovely daughter.
Though named Fortunata, she was not happy ; for she
loved the young knight of Hohenfels, whose castle
rose full in sight on the other side of the lake, and on
this attachment her father frowned. The young man
was forbidden access to Kargeck. But true love is
not easily overcome. When the nights were dark, a
light shone out bright and clear over the water from
the chamber of Fortunata, and the young knight of
Hohenfels, guided by its beacon-fire, swam boldly
across the lake to visit his lady-love. One night a
storm arose, and the bold swimmer had to battle for
his life with the waves. His heart was stout, his arms
were strong, and strong was the love that led him.
So long as the light from the keep of Kargeck could
be seen as he rose to the crest of the waves, he was
not afraid. Alas ! a wild gust of the storm extinguished the light, and in the darkness he succumbed
to the raging water around. With morning came a
calm, and the poor lady found the body of her beloved
knight on the shore just below her father's castle.
When the father saw his daughter sink heart-broken
into an early grave, he regretted, but too late, that he
had crossed her love. This is the Suabian version of
the old story of " Hero and Leander."

Following the shore, but now in an easterly
direction, we pass Dingelsdorf, an ancient and pic-
turesquely-situated village, exactly opposite to Ueberlingen, and reach the beautiful island of Mainau, now
the summer residence of the grand-ducal family
of Baden. When we first reached Ueberlingen
the Imperial flag of Germany could be plainly seen
floating proudly from the battlements of the old priory,

for, although the Kaiser had left two days before, the Empress still remained with her daughter. In a few days she also took her departure, and the grand-ducal family soon afterwards followed suit, when it became more convenient and suitable for strangers to visit the island. The steamboat takes about half-an-hour to make the voyage from Ueberlingen to Mainau, and but for stoppages the distance could be steamed in much less time. The island, which is about one-and-a-half miles in circumference, rises gently from the water on its western shore, until it reaches an elevation of 90ft. on its eastern limit, whence it goes down steeply to the lake. Upon this high ground the castle stands.

Originally an appanage of the Bodmann family, in the thirteenth century it passed into the possession of the Order of the Teutonic Knights, in whose hands it remained for more than 500 years, until in 1806, as one of the results of the Peace of Presburg, it was handed over to the Grand Duchy of Baden, and since 1853 has been the summer residence of the grand ducal family.

The legend as to how the island came into the possession of the Order may not be true, but is very beautiful.

On the shores of the Boden See, not far from Mainau, lived the lovely daughter of the knightly house of Bodmann, the rich heiress of many estates, among which was the island of Mainau. Among the noble families of the neighbourhood, none stood higher than that of the Knights of Langenstein.

A strong affection existed between young Hugo of Langenstein and the Lady of Bodmann. They were betrothed, and the day of their marriage had been fixed. But, alas! all Christendom was moving towards the East, to wrest from the cursed Paynim the tomb wherein the Lord Christ was laid.

The Abbey of Reichenau sent a contingent of its feudatories, and among these was the old Knight of Langenstein, the father of Hugo. But the old man's arm was grown too weak to wield his lance, and his frame too feeble to support the fatigues of the crusade.

Hugo, therefore, took his father's place, and with protestations of fidelity the lovers parted. Years passed, and of those who went joyfully and full of enthusiasm to fight the Saracens, a few returned, aged, sobered, and saddened, but many remained. Among these was Hugo of Langenstein. He had not been slain, but having been taken prisoner, was kept in cruel durance. If he will but renounce his faith his captors offer to throw open his prison-doors, but this he refuses to do.

Meanwhile the fair and wealthy Lady of Bodmann is surrounded by suitors, who in vain urge upon her that to sorrow for the dead is unavailing.

Years thus pass—he in his prison in Arabia, true to his faith, she in her ancestral hall, true to her love. At length, in a vision of the night, he is told that if he will forswear all earthly joy, and devote himself to God, his prison doors shall open. He consents, and vows that if escape is granted to him, while remaining a soldier he will become a monk. The opportunity of escape so wearily waited for, for long years, now quickly presents itself. On his own Boden See in former years he made the nightly heavens his study, and now by the help of the stars he is able to find his way through the desert, and when he reaches Egypt, he obtains passage in a ship leaving for Europe. At length, after long years of captivity, he sees again the blue waters of the Boden See. He dares not,

however, see again his faithful lady-love, but sends a
friend to her, to tell her of the vow he had taken, and
that he can never see her more—that he has joined the
German Order of monk-soldiers, and is away to fight
the heathen in Prussia.

All those long years the faithful lady has hoped
against hope for his return, and now she has not even
the satisfaction of mourning him dead; he lives, but
is lost to her. With a devotion worthy of the highest
type of womanhood, she writes to the Grand Master of
the Order of Teutonic Knights, offering to hand over
the island of Mainau to the Order for ever, upon
condition that Hugo of Langenstein be appointed
master at Mainau. And thus, says the legend, did
the island of Mainau come into the possession of the
German knights.

It is curious how the estimates of moral actions
change with the changing centuries. To the contem-
poraries of Hugo of Langenstein and the Fräulein of
Bodmann, the conduct of the knight and the lady would
probably appear equally praiseworthy: while to us,
standing upon the threshold of the twentieth century,
while the pure lustre of the lady's disinterested devotion seems all the brighter for the efflux of time,
nothing but large allowance for his distorted views of
religion prevents the man from appearing a brute or a
fool.

Of the fortunes of the island during the Thirty
Years' War I shall speak later.

The boat which leaves Ueberlingen at six in the
morning reaches Mainau at a little before seven. We
were the only passengers who landed, and so had the
island pretty much to ourselves. From the landing-
place a noble avenue of old lime-trees leads to
the tasteful gardens immediately surrounding the

Schloss, which stands at a considerable elevation above the lake. No one asked our business, and the charming grounds seemed as open to us as if they had been our own. There is a fine terrace in front of the castle, commanding a glorious view; and on the terrace are marble busts of some of the Roman emperors, conspicuous among which is that of Marcus Aurelius. Orange trees, laden with ripe fruit and white with blossom, fill the air with fragrance. A splendid clematis drapes the front of the house with its deep purple blossoms. Here, reclined in garden easy chairs under the deep shade of Virginia creepers and vines, we rested and read.

When the day was far enough advanced for us to be able to do it with propriety, about 9 a.m., we asked permission to see the Schloss, and were conducted over it by a pleasant and intelligent young woman. The rooms are simple, but are tastefully decorated and arranged. We saw them just as the Emperor and Empress and the Grand-Duke and Grand-Duchess had left them a few hours before. The room of the latter is adorned with two busts of her father, Kaiser Wilhelm, and with fine portraits of her three children.

The room used by the Grand-Duke and Grand-Duchess conjointly for writing, is a noble drawing-room with some fine family and battle-pieces on the walls, among which is a very spirited painting on a large scale of the Balaklava Charge. The rooms occupied by the Kaiser are small and simple, and he carries about with him the little camp bedstead upon which he invariably sleeps. Our conductress described him as singularly kind and affable; and the Grand-Duke and Grand-Duchess, she says, go round and speak pleasantly to every one when they arrive in the island. The Empress she describes as much more formal and

punctilious.   Some wreaths that lay on the pavement
of the church attached to the castle were placed there
by the Grand-Duchess and her daughter on the grave
of an old English nursery governess, who had for
many years been living in the grand-ducal castle at
Carlsruhe, past work and an invalid.   Upon her death,
a few weeks before our visit, her remains were brought
to Mainau, where her dust will mingle with that of the
old Teutonic knights who sleep in the vaults underneath the church.   The Hereditary Grand-Duke is so
well known at the Court of Windsor and in England
(and it is quite likely that he will soon be better
known), that it is hardly necessary to say that he
is a fine, handsome lad.   It was pleasant to hear
the enthusiastic praise bestowed upon him by his
dependents and future subjects.   He is also, we were
told, a prime favourite with the Emperor, his grandfather.   Nothing can exceed the kindness with which
the island of Mainau is thrown open to all comers,
even when the family are staying there; and this
gracious *bonhommie* has much to do with the affec-
tionate loyalty with which the reigning family are
regarded by their subjects.

Having regard to its situation and to the magnificent views it commands, there are few more
beautiful spots in all Germany than the island of
Mainau.

THE RHEINTHOR, CONSTANCE

CHAPTER XIII.

CONSTANCE.

Approach to Constance—Gottlieben—Kreuzlingen—First feud of Guelphs and Ghibellines — Frederick Barbarossa — His death — Believed to sleep — The Sicilian boy—Frederick II. demands admittance into Constance—Court at Basle—Walther von der Vogelweide—Death of Frederick II.

LEAVING Mainau, we round a promontory, beautifully wooded, and the old imperial city of Constance, with its majestic cathedral, comes into sight. The German shore of the arm of the lake on which it stands is dotted with stately mansions, and, as we approach the city, with charming villas bowered in trees. On a clear night the amphitheatre of lights surrounding the extremity of the lake gives the newcomer the impression of a much larger town than the little old-world city can claim to be, with its population of barely 10,000 inhabitants.

Perhaps, however, the finest approach to Constance is by the Rhine boat from Schaffhausen. As the river broadens out into the Unter or Zeller Zee, the flat, green island of Reichenau, rich in vineyards and hoar with legend, lies before the traveller. To his left rise the volcanic, ruin-crowned heights of the Hegau, which he might easily fancy to be tumuli raised over departed Titans. To his right are vine-clad and wooded slopes, with here and there a picturesque chateau or villa, as Salenstein or Arenenberg. Now the lake narrows again to a river. The fiery sun had

L 2

at last gone to rest as we approached Constance, on a perfectly beautiful day, after rain, in the late summer. We are passing the hoary, ivy-clad towers of the castle of Gottlieben, which, by an extraordinary coincidence was for a few days at once the prison of John Huss and of the unworthy Pope John XXIII before whom he had been arraigned. The old city lies immediately before us. Two or three picturesque towers remain of its former fortifications, and, high above all the buildings of the modern city, like a giant among pigmies, rises the cathedral against the pure blue sky. Though five-and-thirty miles away, the rocks of the Sentis rise sharp and clear, to all appearance, immediately behind. The emerald-green water is flowing swiftly past us; to our left is the thriving suburb of Petershausen; and now the descending funnel tells us that we are to pass under the handsome bridge which occupies the site of the wooden structure where, in 1548, the citizens—and notably the butcher lads—of Constance had a fierce encounter with 5000 picked Spanish soldiers sent against the city by Charles V., a great number of whom were slain and thrown into the Rhine, and the remainder beaten back. Having passed the bridge, the Boden See begins to broaden out before us, and leaving the public gardens upon our right, we enter the harbour and are at our landing-place.

In Constance the present and the past happily blend. Over against the ancient Concilium's-saal rises a handsome modern railway-station; and by the side of old hostelries, dating back full 500 years, and among narrow old streets, you come now and again upon open spaces tastefully planted and well kept up. It has, in fact, the quiet, contented, respectable air of an old cathedral city in southern England. Its principal suburb, Kreuzlingen, is in Swiss territory, and is so close that the two towns are really one, only distinguishable by the Swiss and German *douanes* on either side of the frontier. Constance is well provided with excellent hotels. For a prolonged residence, however, the visitor of simple tastes will find that Kreuzlingen has some decided advantages, one of which is cheapness. On the other hand, to have every little parcel examined and taxed at the frontier is not agreeable.

It will be wonderful if, under the new German protective tariff, Kreuzlingen does not become a hot-bed of smuggling.

" The first building of the city of Constance was the work of the grandchildren of Noah, no long time after the deluge." These are the words of the learned Benedictine, Father Gabriel Bucelin, of Weingarten Monastery, in his work " Constantia Rhenana."

If the good monk had authority for the above statement, there is no doubt that he was justified in adding as he does, "and it (Constance) can therefore boast a much earlier origin than any of what are regarded as the most ancient cities in German lands, such as Treves and Solothurn."

Without assigning to Constance, as Bucelin does, an immediate post-diluvian origin, there is no doubt that it is very old. In 1872 and 1873 in the process of excavating a new harbour, the remains of a considerable settlement of lake-dwellers were found, which there is no doubt Bucelin would have regarded as proof positive of his statement.

The camp which the Romans established at the point where the Rhine leaves the Boden See, is supposed to have been named Constantia after the Emperor Constantius Chlorus, early in the fourth

century.   This is, however, a pure conjecture, and it
may easily have received its name from some other
Roman man or woman, and there are not wanting
savants who maintain that the name is pure Celtic, and
simply means Water-town ; Co being Celtic for water,
and Stanz for town.

Be this as it may, there is no doubt that it was a
place of some importance in the sixth century, when it
became the seat of a bishopric.

Charlemagne and his consort Hildegarde, on their
journey to Rome in 800 to receive the imperial crown
of the Holy Roman empire, stayed some days in
Constance, where he summoned the monks of
Constance and of St. Gall to his presence, and granted
them valuable privileges.

A Reichstag was held in Constance in 1112, and in
1125 the first feud broke out here between the rival
families of the Guelphs and Ghibellines.

From 1152 to 1190, reigned in Germany the great
Emperor Frederick Barbarossa, the very flower of
German chivalry.   Shortly after coming to the throne,
he held a Reichstag in Constance from the 11th to
the 23rd of March, 1153.   He was then in the very
prime of early manhood—at the age of thirty-two—
and all the chroniclers concur in describing him as a
born ruler of men.   The commanding presence, the
noble features, the abundant yellow hair, the reddish
beard, the deep blue eyes, the ruddy and clear complexion, all proclaimed him a typical Suabian, a worthy
representative of the race that for 900 years had found
their home on the shores of the Boden See.

History describes him as the first in all martial
and athletic exercises, cheerful but temperate in the
knightly festivities which he loved, as a dauntless hero
and consummate general in war, but always regarding

peace as the end, to attain which war was only a means. He was severe towards his foes, but merciful towards those who yielded, full of dignified conde- scension towards his officers and servants, full of piety without affectation or hypocrisy, always willing to listen to counsel, but reserving the final decision for himself as became a king of men.

He had taken part in one crusade and had had much experience in both war and peace on this his first visit to Constance. He came determined to assert the imperial power, and to make all the different orders, the principalities, and powers, the cities, the knights, and the turbulent nobility, know that they had one master, and that the Kaiser was he. Probably no task could possibly have been more conducive to the well- being of the empire and the happiness of all his subjects. A strong central authority put a stop to the internecine feuds, which were waged by noble against noble, and prince against prince, whenever the imperial authority showed weakness. These feuds and disturbances, and the insecurity to life and property arising from them, caused constant misery to the citizens and peasants.

It was because Frederick Barbarossa sternly main- tained internal peace throughout the empire, and punished its disturbers, however high and mighty they might be, that up to within comparatively recent times the period of the rule of the house of Hohen- staufen has been looked back to in Germany as to a sort of golden age. This was in spite of the constant wars which he waged, which included no less than five campaigns in Italy.

He held Reichstags in Constance in 1155 and 1162, and as an aged man of sixty-three he, for the last time, held his court on the shores of the Boden See in 1183. This final visit was noteworthy as the occasion of the peace of Constance, signed on the 25th June, 1183, by which the Italian cities secured their local self-government, but undertook to swear fealty to the Emperor. Then followed a period of peace and great prosperity in Germany which was not disturbed until the conquest of Jerusalem by Saladin on the 3rd October, 1187, sent a thrill of pious horror through all Christendom. Then the peerless Knight and aged Emperor once more buckled on his armour, and with consummate skill and perfect discipline conducted a great German army on the third crusade, the same in which our Richard the Lion-hearted played so distinguished a part. Barbarossa was destined never again to see the blue waters of the Boden See. With youthful ardour the aged ruler was attempting to cross the rushing stream of the Saleph, the classical Calycadnus, when he was carried away and drowned near the spot where a cold bath in the Cydnus nearly cost Alexander the Great his life, just after the battle of the Granicus, fifteen hundred years before.

It was on the 10th June, 1190, that the greatest of the Hohenstaufen thus met his death; but his people would hardly credit it, and for centuries later the tradition lived among the German people that the great Emperor was not dead. They pictured him in a deep sleep resting in a cavern either in the Untersberg, near Salzburg, or in Kiffhaüser, in Thuringia. There he sat and slumbered, his noble head with its lofty forehead and flaxen hair resting on his arm, while the great red beard had grown through the stone table before him. From time to time he woke, and asked whether the ravens still hovered round the mountain. So soon as they were gone he would awake to bring salvation to Germany and a return of the golden age.

The grandson of Barbarossa, Frederick II., may be said to have secured the imperial crown at Constance. The strife between Guelphs and Ghibellines was raging keenly. Otto IV., the son of Henry the Lion, and the nephew of our Richard Cœur de Lion, the representative of the Guelphs, wore the imperial crown. Pope Innocent III. declared himself in favour of the representative of the Ghibellines, the grandson of Barbarossa, Frederick of Hohenstaufen, and in 1212 Frederick, then a boy of seventeen, made his way from Genoa to Pavia, and thence, after the greater part of his retinue had perished at the hands of the Milanese, to Cremona.

All the Alpine passes were held by Otto, who was most anxious to secure his hated rival, "the Sicilian boy" as he contemptuously called him. Almost alone, Frederick contrived to escape his pursuers. " Like the avalanche, that, hardly visible in the heights where it begins its course, suddenly grows, and crashing into the valley overthrows everything in its course ; so Frederick appeared, weak and alone, on the summit of the Alps. It was in vain that Otto held the Alpine passes." Baffling his pursuers by concealing himself in some remote high-lying valley, Frederick took his dangerous path, through the everlasting snows, by the Engadine and over the Wormser-joch, and so to where the foaming Albula hurries down to join the Rhine, to Chur. Here the first adherents gathered round the standard of the Hohenstaufen. He was warmly received by Bishop Arnold, of Chur, who did homage to him as German king, and entertained him and his little court in princely fashion. The warlike Abbot of St. Gall, Ulrich VI., hurried with trusty men-at-arms to Chur, and formed a body-guard for the young Kaiser. The nobles of Rhaetia came down from their castles and tendered him their swords. Abbot Ulrich's brother, Henry of Hohensax, left his fastness Forstegg, and emerged from his native woods at the head of his followers, to meet on his way and swell the onward march of the grandson of Barbarossa. Thus following the course of the Rhine, and like the Rhine receiving affluents as it advanced, the little band reached Altstädten. Here leaving the Rhine it plunged into the highlands of Appenzell, and so by mountain-paths to St. Gall. Thence, at the head of an ever-increasing array, Frederick came down to the lake, the shores of which had been the cradle of his race, and with shouts of triumph the little band approached Constance. But exultation was turned to dismay when messengers met the young chieftain with the alarming news that the great Guelph Kaiser Otto was close at hand. He was believed to be in Thuringia, busy prosecuting a war there, and his presence was as unexpected as it was undesired. As soon as he heard of the threatened approach of Frederick, he made forced marches towards the Boden See, and the smoke of his camp fires could be seen on the other side of the lake. With 200 knights in full panoply he had made his head-quarters at Ueberlingen. His cooks and quartermasters were already in Constance making ready for the reception of Otto's army.

What was the Boy-Kaiser to do? His followers numbered two thousand lances : beyond this he had no army. As in so many crises in the world's history, boldness carried the day. Frederick at once advanced to the gates of Constance, and demanded admittance. His demand was strongly supported by the energetic Abbot of St. Gall.

Bishop Conrad of Constance, who trembled for the consequences to himself, whatever his decision might be, wavered, and at length in consultation with the citizens, decided to open the gates to Frederick and sixty of his followers. A larger retinue was not permitted, lest the freedom of the city should be jeopardised. Three hours later the army of Otto approached from Ueberlingen and demanded admittance. It was too late. Those three hours changed the history of the world. Who can tell what would have been the fortunes of Christendom if Guelphs instead of Hapsburgs had for nearly six centuries worn the imperial crown of Germany? To return to the young Hohenstaufen,—Frederick lost no time, but leaving Constance hurried down the Rhine, everywhere receiving troops of adherents.

At Basle the bishops of Trent, Chur, Constance, and Basle, attended his court, as did the abbots of St. Gall and Reichenau, and the counts of Kyburg, Hapsburg, Freiburg, Homberg, and Rapperschwyl, besides almost all the lesser nobility of the neighbourhood.

Bavaria, Suabia, and Alsacè were quickly won for Frederick. Thus the avalanche that began its course among the snows of the Engadine, rolled seawards with the Rhine, while the Anti-Kaiser took flight through Breisgau, and only felt himself secure when he had reached his hereditary state of Brunswick.

In December Frederick II. was at Mainz; in January he received homage from the princes of the empire at Frankfort. After his consecration at Mainz he spent holy-week between Constance and Meersburg in 1213, and after conquering the imperial regalia at Trifels, in 1215, he appeared at a great gathering of the estates of the empire at the lake-city, which at such a critical moment had opened its gates to receive him. There, surrounded by the Suabian nobility, Frederick appeared wearing for the first time the imperial crown.

He was a strong man, and he found plenty of work to do. The empire was in a deplorable condition. The cruel war between the Guelphs and Ghibellines had wasted its resources and harried its people. The sweet Minnesänger, Walther von der Vogelweide, who lived in this troublous time, plaintively describes it—and his verses might well have been taken as watchword by the young Kaiser.

> " Die Sonne hat den Schein verkehret
>   Untreu den Samen aus geleeret
>   Allwaerts ueber Feld und Rain.
>   Der Vater bei dem Kind Untreue findet,
>   Der Bruder seinem Bruder lueget,
>   Die Geistlichkeit in Kutten trueget,
>   Statt Gott des Menschen Herz zu weihen
>   Gewalt siegt ob, des Rechtes Ansehen schwindet ;
>   Wohlauf ! hier frommt nicht muessig sein ! "

> " The sun has turned away his face :
>   Bad faith has poured out its vial to the dregs,
>   Scattering its evil seed in every field and furrow.
>   The father meets with treachery from his son,
>   Brother lies to brother,
>   The cassocked priests deceive,
>   Instead of turning men's hearts to God ;
>   Might alone rules, the force of right decays—
>   Up, then !   This is no time for sloth."

Frederick was not idle.   The empire was dissolving in chaos—out of this he brought some sort of cosmos. He showed the nobles that he was a true descendant of Barbarossa, and that they had again found a master. The building of new castles was forbidden, and all feuds were sternly repressed ; the public peace throughout the empire was once more established upon a secure basis.

This is not the place to go further into the history of this remarkable man and great sovereign, who for more than thirty years ruled Germany, and in many respects revived the glories of his grandfather's reign.

There is a striking parallel between his character and career and that of the first Plantagenet—Henry II. Like him, he was called, after a period of dreadful civil war, to bring order out of disorder in his distracted kingdom; like him, he ruled wisely and with a strong hand; like him, he was engaged in incessant struggles with the papacy; like him, he was constantly engaged in foreign wars, for Italy was to Germany what Normandy was to England, a *damnosa hæreditas*. Lastly, Frederick the Hohenstaufen, like Henry the Plantagenet, after a long and beneficent reign, died broken-hearted, because of the tragic fate of some and the undutiful behaviour of other of his sons, and the treachery of his most trusted adherents; with his last breath uttering these words, "Whom then can I trust, when my very bowels rage against me?"

The same year in which thus, in his fifty-sixth year, Frederick died (in 1250), a terrible conflagration—for the second time within seven years—laid Constance in ashes.

Rudolph of Hapsburg, the founder of the great family which, for nearly six hundred years gave emperors to Germany, and now rules in Austria, does not appear to have had much to do with Constance, nor is there any point of close contact between our city and world-history until we reach the most important event in its long and eventful history, the assembling of the great Church Council in 1415.

CHAPTER XIV.

THE COUNCIL OF CONSTANCE.

At the opening of the fifteenth century Christendom
was rent asunder by the pretensions and the contemporaneous reigns of two rival popes—Benedict XIII.
(Petrus de Luna) in Avignon, and Gregory XII.
(Angelo Coriario) in Spain.

The Council of Pisa, in 1409, did indeed depose
both these occupants of the Papal chair, and elected in
their stead Cardinal Petrus Philargi of Candia, who
assumed the name of Alexander V. In spite of their
having thus been deposed, Benedict and Gregory
continued calmly to exercise their papal functions
respectively in Avignon and Spain, as though they
were quite above the decisions of any church council.

As for Pope Alexander, within a twelvemonth of
his election he died suddenly, under circumstances of
great suspicion. It is characteristic of the age and of
the then state of the church that the man whom
common rumour named as his poisoner, the infamous
Balthazar Cossa, was elected to succeed him. The
new pope assumed the name of John XXIII.

So now poor Christendom was distracted by having

no less than three ostensible heads, and every day the anarchy, the corruption, and the scandalous disorders of the church became more and more intolerable.

John called another Council in Rome in the year 1412, and announced as one of its principal objects the reformation of the church. Probably with the connivance of the unworthy Pope, the roads leading to the Eternal City were occupied by the troops of King Ladislaus of Naples, and the church fathers were stopped and turned back. Nevertheless a few sittings were held, on the occasion of the first two of which tradition says an extraordinary appearance startled the assembled ecclesiastics. A gruesome owl flew out of a corner of the Lateran, and, with a hideous scream, fixed its glaring eyes full upon the Pope, so that the bishops whispered one to another, "under what a singular and questionable shape does the Holy Ghost here appear."

The Council solemnly condemned the two anti-popes and forty-five Articles of Wyckliffe as heretical, and when this stage of the proceedings had been reached it was unexpectedly broken up. King Ladislaus quarrelled with Pope John, and by a *coup de main* possessed himself of Rome.

The Pope and Cardinals were only too glad to secure their safety by a hurried flight, first to Florence and then to Bologna. Under these circumstances, John esteemed the calling of an œcumenical council as the only course open to him. The Emperor Sigismund was of the same opinion; and for this purpose he met the plenipotentiaries of the Pope at Lodi on the 30th October, 1413, when it was arranged that a universal church council should assemble on the 1st November, 1414.

There was great difficulty in persuading the Pope to

agree to the selection of the free German city of Constance for the place of meeting, as he knew that he
would have less influence there than the Kaiser. We
are fortunate in possessing a contemporary record of
the proceedings of the council in the Chronicle of
Ulrich of Reichenthal. Three important manuscripts
of this interesting Chronicle are known to be extant.
The earliest was executed by Albert Krintli, who died
in 1427, or nine years after the close of the council.
This received the active supervision of the author,
Reichenthal, and was adorned with illuminations in
1419. The second was prepared for the city archives by
the Rathschreiber (clerk to the city council), Johannes
Rastetter, in 1464, for which service he received
twenty florins. The third, called the Vienna Code,
dates from 1460. Reichenthal wrote in the language
of the age in which the council was held, the so-called
Mittel-hoch-deutsch, from which I translate the
extracts that follow.*

With a fair knowledge of German, Mittel-hoch-
deutsch is astonishingly easy to read after a little
practice. Any of my readers who may feel inclined
to try, can obtain Dr. Marmor's work for a few
pence. I dare not hope that I have succeeded in
retaining the quaintness of the original in my English
version. Before, however, we try to see what sort of
appearance old Ulrich von Reichenthal will make in an
English dress, it may be well to say a few words about
him. He is several times mentioned in the Chronicle,
and was evidently a man of importance at the time,
though he does not appear to have belonged to one of
the patrician families of Constance. He was, how-

---

* The copy I have used in preparing this work is "Das Conzil zu Constanz in
den Jahren, 1414-1418. Nach Ulrich von Reichenthals handschriftlicher Chronik
bearbeitet von J. Marmor, Constanz, Verlag von Otto Fritz."

ever a citizen, and lived in the house "zum guldinen Bracken," close to St. Stephen's Church. His father appears to have been town clerk in the year 1372.

As a good Catholic, and one who intensely delighted in all the pomp and parade of the lords temporal and spiritual, it is not to be wondered at that he is not always fair towards Huss and Jerome.

His ideas of numbers are vague and loose to the last degree. It is thanks to him that Constance has been credited with a population of 40,000 inhabitants throughout the middle ages, a number which it has been demonstrated could not possibly have existed within its walls. One illustration of the chronicler's untrustworthiness in this particular is cited by Marmor, and speaks volumes. The chronicle gravely states that upon the occasion of the Pope blessing the people there were often 150,000 persons assembled in the upper court of the cathedral, whereas, as a matter of fact, this court could not hold more than 5,000 or 6,000 at the very utmost.

There is every reason to believe that at the time of its greatest prosperity, Constance never had more than 10,000 inhabitants—about its present population. In spite of this want of accuracy, which was characteristic of the age, there is no reason to believe that the old chronicler purposely misrepresented anything, and his work presents a curious picture of life in the Middle Ages, in addition to its value as a history of a most important event.

Let us hear him first about the choice of a place where the Council should meet :—

"And meanwhile was there much talk on both sides—on the part of the Emperor as well as of the Pope,—'as to where the Concilium should be held.' And after all this talk, our lord the Roman King asked the lords who were about him if they knew of a town that lay

M

by a mountain, or close thereto, and that belonged to the Holy
Roman Empire. Now the noble Duke Ulrich of Teck was standing
near to him, who made answer, there was a town belonging to the
empire, that was called Kempten, and lay at the foot of the mountain
called the Ver. Against this, the lord Count Eberhart von Nellenburg,
Landgraf, who was also present, made answer, and said : True it was,
indeed, that Kempten was a city of the empire, but there was no suf-
ficiency of accommodation, nor was it possible to get food there for a
great company. But a day's journey from Kempten, perhaps a little
further, there lay a city where everything necessary was to be had,
which city was called Costentz, and belonged to the Roman Empire,
and lay on the Boden See, and close by the city ran the Rhine, and
even through it. This Boden See was eight miles long (German
miles), and as to breadth three miles wide, so that great ships could
sail upon it and bring all that was necessary and sail away again, when
that was desired. There also was a bishopric belonging to the archbishopric of Mainz. Besides, it was a well-built town, with abundance
of apartments and of stalls for the horses. And let it be known that lately,
and for a long time, the peasants of Appenzell, and some from Schwyz,
and the peasants that dwell in the mountains around, have made war
with great fierceness upon Costentz, and all the counts, barons, knights,
and men-at-arms, came to the help of the men of Costentz ; and the
same Duke of Teck and all his chivalry lay in this town. And if there
had been three times as many, there would still have been lodgment and
stabling enough. And also there came there that most serene prince,
our blessed ancestor, Ruprecht, with all his people, and lay in the city
for six weeks, and no one lacked anything, but everything necessary
was honourably provided. And whoever came to the war, had
lodging, food, and drink, fodder, hay, and straw, at the ordinary
market price, so that we all greatly wondered that we were thus able to
have everything so near at hand. And of fish and flesh there was
abundance, and, in addition, the town from old-time has been loyal
and faithful, and has never had war or trouble with the nobility, and
almost every day a court was held in it, and justice administered.

" Then our lord the Roman King turned to our Holy Father the
Pope, and said to him in Latin : ' As there is a bishopric in the city
of Costentz of which we hear so good a report, and as it belongs to
the empire, is your Holiness willing to go there ? '

" Then our Holy Father the Pope held a consultation with his lords
and asked their advice. They counselled him to accept the city as
it had so good a reputation, and no one had been known to come to
misfortune there.

"So he accepted Costentz as the place of meeting, and sent off that very same hour his 'explorators,' to spy out the land.

"Upon this, the well-born lord Count Eberhart of Nellenburg, sent word to Ulrich of Reichenthal, how things had gone at Lodi, and that the Council would be held (in Costentz,) and bade him arrange for fodder, hay, straw, and beds, and the message came before Christmas A. D. 1413.

"Now upon this, these 'explorators' arrived, and their servants with them, and wanted to spy out and examine the land and its surroundings, to see whether or no it were possible for the Council to be held there, and among them were two Italians * (Welschmen), who, however, could speak Latin, and they prayed Ulrich Reichenthal that he would ride with them into Thurgau to examine the land.

"These spoke and said, that the Council could not be held there because people would have to come there from all lands, for whom there would not be half lodgment enough.

"Herein, however, they spake not truly, for much room was left in the town. But many Hungarians lay at Petershausen; some preferred Paradies (now a favourite suburb of Constance); some Gottlieben, but not many, as you shall hear later.

"Then our Holy Father Pope John XXIII. sent out a 'bull' to all the archbishops commanding them to inform their bishops and suffragans of the calling of the Council, so that they might be ready to come to Costentz, and especially to the Archbishop of Mainz, under whose archbishopric Costentz lies, and to which it belongs, and whose superior he is. Now, therefore, Pope John prepared to travel to Costentz with his people. Now, be it known that when a Pope wishes to ride abroad, a covering such as I now describe is carried before him. A strong man-at-arms carries it, he riding upon a white horse, covered with a red cloth, sprinkled with gold, so that it is yellow and red. And it is carried as a shelter from the rain and the sun, so that he (the Pope) may be sheltered underneath it. And upon the covering is a golden angel holding a golden cross in the hand. The shelter spread out so wide as to cover forty square feet, as may be seen painted in the next plate (illustration). When the pope's 'bull' was sent out, and the archbishops had despatched their mandates to their bishops and suffragans, strict order was taken that no man should speak of it. Thus matters remained for eight

---

* Welsch—foreign, applied to Italians by the Germans throughout the Middle Ages, and even now used. The Anglo-Saxons called the Britons who took refuge in the western fastnesses of Britain welsch—foreign; hence Welsh and Wales.

weeks, so that nobody believed anything would come of it. But after eight weeks came many heralds and pipers, and many servants of the great lords, and took possession of the lodgings for their masters, and blazoned the arms of their lords upon the houses and the doors, and ordered fodder, hay, and straw. Then, three weeks before St. John Baptist's Day, A.D. 1414, came the Honourable Lord Herr Friedrich Grafnegger, of the Order of St. Benedict and Abbot of St. Gars, in the Hungarian land, and Bishop of Augsburg, and with him Count Eberhart of Nellenburg, and Herr Frischhans, of Bodmen, and now first arranged the right quarters for each. After they clearly understood what each lord needed, they placarded the inns and houses where each was to be. The notice did not, however, remain up; for when the lords rode in and took possession, then they took it down. For whoever came to an inn and found it good, there he remained; and, for all this, there was very great doubt felt as to whether the Council would be held or not, and this uncertainty continued until the third day before the Day of Our Lady, in the middle of August.

"On this day arrived Cardinal John Ostiensis, the Upper Arch-Chancellor of the Holy Roman Chair and of the Pope at Rome."

My readers cannot be expected to derive as much pleasure as did honest Ulrich Reichenthal from the endless entertainments, processions, festivals, jousts and tournaments, and solemn receptions of exalted temporal and spiritual personages, in the description of which he revels, and by which the Pope and Emperor showed their great anxiety for the reformation of the church. I will, therefore, endeavour not to tax my reader's patience too much, and will only give such extracts as seem specially worthy of translation.

The description of the Pope's journey is quaint :—

"Then came news every day as to how our Holy Father Pope John XXIII. was on the way, and was nearing Costentz, which was also true. And as he came on the Arlenberg, in the middle of the pass, near the cloister, his carriage fell over and lay in the snow—for much snow had fallen there. And, as he thus lay, there came to him his servants and courtiers (Churtisan), who followed his court, and said to him, 'Holy Father, how doth your Holiness?' Then answered he in Latin, 'I lie here in the name of the devil (Jacio hic in nomine diaboli).'

"When now he had got up again and had passed the cloister and come lower in the pass, there is a spot whence he could look down upon the Boden See and upon the land which separates Arlenberg from Lamparten, as it was before they learned German, and took possession of it. Now, when he saw this land and the Boden See, Bludenz and the mountains, it seemed to lie in a valley below him.

"Then spake the Pope in Latin :— 'Sic capiunt vulpes,' which in German means, 'Thus are foxes caught;' and the next day he came to Feldkirch, and the morrow afterwards to Rheineck, after that to Costentz. As we reckon from Christ's birth 1414 years, on St. Simon and St. Judas, on the evening of the Holy Twelve Apostles, on the seven-and-twentieth day, which was a Saturday, after lunch, between the twelfth hour and one, came the Most Holy Father Pope John XXIII. to Costentz, and first to God's house and the cloister of Kreuzlingen, just outside the city, and spent the night in the cloister, and presented the abbot of the cloister, who was named Erhart Lind, and belonged to Costentz, with a mitre (*inful*) and put it on him, that he and those that came after him might have and wear it for ever, though neither he nor any former abbot had ever used or possessed one.

"In the morning of Sunday, St. Simon and St. Judas Day, *after dinner*, in the eleventh hour, then was the Pope led with great honour from the cloister of Kreuzlingen to Costentz.

"To receive him came in procession all the prelates from around Costentz, the Abbot of Reichenau and other abbots, as many as dwelt within four (German) miles—to wit, the abbots of Kreuzlingen and Petershausen, all the deans and canons of St. Stephen's, St. John, and St. Paul, and all the clergy and religious orders; these came to meet him as far as Kreuzlingen. And they conducted him through Stadelhoven and through St. Paul's Street and the open spaces thereabouts into the cathedral, and sang 'Te Deum laudamus,' and rang all the bells for joy, and took him to the Pfalz (bishop's palace) where he was to lodge, and took his principal servants into the sacristy near the Pfalz, and with him came nine cardinals (who shall be named hereafter) in constant attendance upon him.

"And as to the procession that led him into the city, it was on this wise :—Our Holy Father Pope John XXIII. rode to the Kreuzlingen Thor upon a white horse covered with a red cloth spotted with gold, and he himself was clothed like a priest who stands at the altar, all in white, and wore a simple white mitre on his head, and over him was carried a golden cloth. This cloth was given him by the men of Costentz, and four citizens carried it on four poles. The first was Henry of Ulm, burgomaster that year; the second, Henry Schiltar; the third, Henry Ehinger, Amman (magistrate) to the city; and Hannes Hagen, Vogt (constable). And near him on foot walked on one side Count Bechtold of Ursin, a Roman, who came with him, holding the bridle on one side; and on the other side, Count Rudolf of Montfort, also holding the bridle; and thus they led him up to the cathedral, where they brought before him eight white horses, all in trappings of red cloth. And the eight had heavily-laden saddle-bags, and on the ninth was a silver-gilt chest with a 'monstrance,' in which was the Holy Sacrament, and this horse also was covered with a red cloth. On the red cloth stood two silver-gilt candelabra with burning tapers, and the horse had a bell hung round his neck; and behind came a man-at-arms on a very great horse. He held a stout staff in his hand and rested it on his saddle, and above the staff was a canopy made of cloth that was red and yellow, and the canopy was so broad that five horses could stand under it. And above the canopy was a golden button, and on the button was a golden angel who held a golden cross in his hand. Behind the canopy were the nine cardinals, all on their horses or mules, and all with their red mantles so long that they trailed upon the ground. And they all wore red caps and broad red hats on their heads, with long silken bands. And each one had a servant or page to hold the tail of his horse, that the robes might not be soiled. And whenever the cardinals rode about in the town, they wore their red hats; but when they went on foot they did not wear their hats, but great caps that were sewn to their mantles; and every cardinal was followed by a page, who carried the train of his mantle at least an ell and a-half behind. And while the Pope waited before the Kreuzlingen gateway, and the nine cardinals with him, then came the procession of all the clergy of Costentz, with all the holy relics, to meet him, and went in procession with the relics round the Pope and round the cardinals, and then turned into the gateway again and received the Pope's blessing. And when the priests with the cross and the relics had re-entered the city through the gateway, there came a priest on horseback clothed like an evangelist (one who read the Gospels in the cathedral), who wore a chorister's cap and had a staff in his hand and thereon a golden cross. This he carried before the Pope and the Holy Sacrament, and before him went slowly eight white horses in trappings and with saddle-bags. On the last rode the priest with the staff and the cross; after him came the horse with the Sacrament; then came our Holy Father the Pope, under the golden canopy, and with him—before him, beside him, and behind him—were the burning tapers of the guild and the burning tapers of the canons; then rode he who bore the canopy, and behind the canopy rode the cardinals, two and two, and behind them all their servants; and near the Pope rode a priest, who threw small coin among the crowd, so that the Pope might be the less thronged. And all together rode into the lower court and dismounted from their horses, and took the Pope's horse and his servants into the sacristy and the school. Then all went into the cathedral and sang 'Te Deum laudamus,' and rang all the bells; and this lasted until vespers. Then went the Pope on foot through the Chapel of St. Margaret into the bishop's palace. The cardinals rode each one home to his inn, and so remained Monday and Tuesday, so that every one who was a stranger might provide himself according to his need with food, fodder, and other necessaries.

   *   *   *   *   *   *   *   *

" Now, on the fourth day after that our Holy Father the Pope had ridden into Costentz—namely, on Wednesday—the town and citizens of Costentz presented our Holy Father the Pope with a great vessel of silver-gilt, which weighed five silver marks, and four laegelen (long casks) with Italian wine, and four great casks of wine of Alsace, and eight casks of wine of the country, each containing more than half a fuder, and forty sacks of oats. The presentation took place in the Upper Court, and Henry of Ulm carried the silver drinking-vessel, because he was Burgomaster, and he rode on horseback up to the Pfalz, and six citizens, members of the Council, also on horseback, came with him. And the Pope was on the balcony of the Pfalz, and sent an 'auditor' down to him. This auditor was named John Nass, and came from Bohemia; but he spoke German right well. He acted as interpreter, and told the Pope in Latin what the citizens of Costentz had given to him. Then they took the wine from the carts, and the sacks of corn from off the horses, and unloaded them into the Pfalz. Then the Pope thanked the citizens right warmly, whereupon the burgomaster and the councillors made answer that they always wished to do what was well-pleasing to his Holiness and his servants. Then the auditor took the silver vessel and gave it to the Pope; and the Pope sent the auditor back with a black-ribbed robe of silk, and presented it to the burgomaster, Henry of Ulm."

Thus far Ulrich of Reichenthal, but time would fail longer to accept his guidance. Indeed my readers may well be excused wondering if an ordinary life would suffice to master the history of the four years' Council if narrated with the wonderful fulness of detail of the above. As concisely therefore as may be, I will endeavour to tell the story of the Council.

In obedience to the summons of the Emperor and Pope came representatives from Italy, France, Germany, England, Sweden, Denmark, Poland, Hungary, and Constantinople, representatives of emperors, kings, princes, municipalities, churches, and universities.

Duke Frederick of Austria came with 300 mounted retainers; the legates of the two antipopes appeared to maintain the claims of their respective masters. The Greek Emperor sent two dukes as his representatives, the barbarous Russians, the Lithuanians and the Wallachians were all represented; the kings of unknown and almost mythical eastern lands, Mohammedan, and even heathen, sent lords in strange, gorgeous and fantastic garb to represent them in the great Church Council.

The little city seemed suddenly transformed into a stage, whereon players from all the world assembled to perform a great historical drama, which, in some of its phases, proved a comedy if not a farce, while in others it was a grim and awful tragedy.

According to the old chroniclers, the average number of strangers present during the two first years of the council was 80,000, and at one time this number grew to 150,000, with 30,000 horses. There are, however, excellent reasons for doubting these exceedingly liberal computations.

Johann von Müller, in his "History of Switzerland," says—" There was a rivalry between the princes and nobility of all Europe as to who should make the most splendid appearance, with retinue, horses, and arms, and to this end treasures that had been painfully collected by careful ancestors were freely poured out; the learned prepared themselves by dint of philosophical acuteness, learning, and eloquence to win fame throughout the whole Christian church. Many came as to a play, the like of which neither their fathers, nor even their remote ancestors, had witnessed.

"Europe waited in profound expectation; right-thinking men everywhere made solemn vows. They prepared themselves to assist in a serious reformation of the church; others came with subtle schemes to escape the reformation they dreaded; most came to enjoy every species of pleasure."

Duke Rudolph of Saxony, Marshal of the German Empire, instructed Gebhart Dacher to prepare an official list of strangers present at the Council. Dacher informed his master *inter alia* of the presence of 700 public women, and adds that he feared to inquire how many came secretly for purposes of intrigue, as he dreaded "lest he should be killed, and find out that which he would much rather not."

The zealous Catholic author of "Rund um den Boden See," Dr. Zingeler, protests against the use which has been made of the above melancholy picture of the morals of the age by Protestant writers, who are disposed to charge all this immorality to the score of the assembled ecclesiastics. However great the corruption of the church, it is only fair to remember that the laity of that age was not immaculate,—alas! has it ever been or will it ever be? and even had the ecclesiastics all been spotless the immense concourse of strangers would sufficiently account for the assembled vice.

The arrangements for the lodgment and victualling

of the enormous company appear to have left nothing
to be desired.   An official tariff of cost of food protected the visitors from imposition.   Pastrycooks took
carts through the streets arranged with cooking stoves,
which enabled them to serve up hot on the spot, fish,
flesh, and fowl.

One of the most distinguished scholars of the age,
who had done much to bring about the revival of Greek
letters in Europe, Emanuel Chrysoloras, was present
at the Council, and died before its close.   He was buried
in the Prediger-kloster.   He belonged to an old noble
family, and was born at Constantinople of a Roman
stock.   The Emperor John Palaeologus sent him as
ambassador to all the European courts to implore
assistance for the Greek empire in its agony.   When,
however, the Tartar Tamerlane defeated the Turks in
1402, and took captive their leader Bajazet, the danger
to Greece was for the moment removed, and Chrysoloras settled in Italy, and became a public teacher of
the old Greek literature, first in Venice, then in Florence,
later in Rome, and last in Pavia, where the most famous
scholars of the age were educated in his school.   Among
these were the Florentine Poggio and Peter Paul
Vergerius.

The following inscription may still be read, in Latin,
on a slab in a side chapel of the Prediger-kloster :—

" Emanuel Chrysoloras, Knight of Constantinople, of an old Roman
family, that came from Rome with the Emperor Constantine.

" This most learned, most prudent, and most excellent man, who
at the time of the general Church Council, died with the reputation
that of all men he had preserved his priestly character spotless and
worthy, was buried here on the 15th April, 1415.

" I, who once taught Latium to put away the confused language,
and to educate itself anew upon the art of ancient times ; I, who
brought to light the words of the great Demosthenes and the sweet
speech of Cicero ; I, by name known as Chrysoloras, having died

on this foreign strand, lie here and rest. Care for the Church Council brought me hither, when three popes troubled the world and the church with divisions. Rome begot my forefathers, but my being I owe to thee, beautiful Byzantium, and my ashes I entrust to the soil of Constantia.

"Where thou diest matters not, for all the world is equally near to the green fields of heaven, as to the abode of punishment."

The writer of this epitaph was the famous Æneas Sylvius, of the family of the Piccolomini, who was sometime secretary to the Emperor Frederick III., and subsequently wore the papal tiara as Pope Pius II.

We should make a great mistake if we did not realise that at the Council of Constance was assembled in addition to the less noble elements, all that Christendom could show of learning, virtue, and piety. Before the Council thus assembled was summoned to appear the famous Bohemian preacher, John Huss.

CHAPTER XV.

JOHN HUSS AND JEROME OF PRAGUE.

"JOHN HUSS."

" Every age, on him who strays
From its broad and beaten ways,
Pours its seven-fold vial.
Happy he whose inward ear
Angel comfortings can hear,
O'er the rabble's laughter ;
And while hatred's faggots burn,
Glimpses through the smoke discern,
Of the good hereafter."
—WHITTIER's *Barclay of Ury.*

Birth of Huss—Early studies—Helfert's Testimony—Kaiser Sigismund commands his attendance at the Council—His journey from Bohemia—Lodges in St. Pauls-Gasse—Cost of his living—Is arrested and thrown into a dungeon—Sigismund makes a public entry into Constance—His unworthy treatment of Huss—Sufferings of Huss in prison—Taken to Gottlieben—Brought before the Council—The brave Knight of Chlum—His last interview with Huss—Scene in the Cathedral when Huss was condemned—The blush of Sigismund —Taken out to be burned—Martyrdom—Cruel imprisonment of Jerome of Prague—Testimony of Poggio to the intrepidity of Jerome—"O sancta simplicitas !"—The Hussenstein.

JOHN HUSS was born in 1369, at the village of Husinec in Bohemia. He studied in Prague, and in 1393 was made Bachelor of Arts, in 1394 Bachelor of Theology, and in 1396 attained the dignity of Magister.

Helfert says, " Unanimous tradition and report picture to us John Huss as a man possessed of all those qualities, which are sure to secure the affection and confidence of individuals, and the sympathy and admiration of the public. His noble presence bore the mark of deep moral earnestness. A profound and catholic scholarship was happily united in him with an unsullied purity of life, upon which not even the malignity of his foes ever ventured to cast suspicion. With a sincere piety he combined a fiery zeal against abuses and corruptions of every kind. It was these mental and moral characteristics that secured for Huss universal respect and regard, though he very early displayed a strong leaning to innovations in the church. He was the darling of the Bohemian people, whom he addressed in their native tongue, and who eagerly listened to his powerful discourses, happily illustrated with familiar analogies, and clothed in words of simple eloquence. He was welcomed at the Bohemian court, where Queen Sophia, the second consort of Wenceslaus IV., chose him as her confessor, and revered him as a priest of unspotted character, and as a pious spiritual adviser. The Archbishop of Prague held him in high honour and regard, and willingly gave heed to the advice and recommendations of a man who never missed an opportunity of removing evils, of dispersing hurtful superstitions, and of promoting the introduction of wholesome reforms."

He rejected the transformation of the sacramental elements, the popular blind belief in the Pope and the saints, the power of absolution in a vicious priest, and the unconditional obedience towards earthly superiors; he condemned in the strongest terms the prevailing simony in the church, and declared the Holy Scriptures to be the only and sufficient rule of faith. In fact, to a very large extent, he adopted the views expounded by John Wycliffe at Lutterworth, thirty years before.

Pope Alexander V. had excommunicated him, and Pope John XXIII. branded him as a heretic.

The Emperor Sigismund commanded Huss to appear at the Council of Constance, and not only furnished him with a "safe conduct," but assured him of his assistance in securing a full hearing for his views. The "safe conduct" was of the fullest possible character, and assured and commanded the safety of Huss and his freedom to come and go, "we having taken him under our imperial protection, and under that of the Holy Roman Empire." In addition, the King Wenceslaus, and his brother the Emperor Sigismund, appointed three Bohemian noblemen to attend him—John of Chlum or Glumm, Henry of Echlum, and Wenceslaus of Duba.

He left Prague on the 11th October, 1414, and after a journey through Germany, of which interesting glimpses are given in his extant letters—reached Constance on the 2nd November.

The wooden springless chariot in which he made his entry into the city, is still to be seen in the interesting collection of curiosities preserved in the Rosgarten Museum at Constance.

John Huss took up his quarters in a small house in a street then called St. Pauls-Gasse, near to an ancient tower called the Schnetzthurm, which guarded the entrance to the city from the side of Kreuzlingen, and which still stands an interesting memorial of the past. At the end of the last century, probably in the reign of the enlightened Emperor Joseph II., a little tablet, with a medallion in stone of the Reformer, was let into the wall of the house ; and, since my first visit in the winter of 1877-8, his Bohemian compatriots have adorned the house with a fine medallion portrait, bearing a suitable inscription in Bohemian and German.

Relying upon the protection accorded him by the imperial safe-conduct, Huss seemed at first principally concerned as to how he and his companions were to obtain the means of subsistence until such time as the Council permitted him to depart. He writes at this time—" Living is very dear here ; a room with a bed costs more than half-a-Gulden (about a shilling) per week. I am greatly afraid that my funds will soon be exhausted. Please see my friends about this in Bohemia."

On the 28th of November, he was brought before the Council, and at the close of the audience he was arrested. " Now," said his enemies, " thou art in our power, we tell thee thou shalt not come out until thou hast paid the uttermost farthing." A week later he was thrown into the foul, damp, and stinking dungeons of the Prediger-kloster (now Insel Hotel). Shortly before, the Pope had said, " Even if Huss had slain my own brother, I would not suffer any harm to happen to him in Constance."

The Emperor Sigismund made his public entry into the city on the morning of Christmas Day, 1414, with all the pomp and splendour which Reichenthal so loves to chronicle.

The Bohemian nobles lost no time in appealing to the Emperor at once to set Huss at liberty in conformity with his safe-conduct. The result of this application is thus narrated by the eye-witness Reichenthal. " At this time our lord the king was very desirous to help him (Huss), and held that it would bring foul dishonour upon himself, if he allowed the free safe-conduct he had given thus to be broken.

" Then the learned answered him, it might and could

not be allowed with a shadow of right that a heretic, taken in his heresy, should have or hold a safe-conduct.

"When, therefore, our lord the king heard and considered this, he quietly allowed it."

The miserable dungeon in which Huss was confined is close to the refectorium in the Dominican or Prediger Convent. The refectorium is now the restaurant of the Insel Hotel, the handsome church of the monastery having been secularised into a magnificent dining-hall. The traveller upon rising from his luxurious *table d'hôte*, has only to take a few steps to see what sort of accommodation Huss received in his narrow cell. The stone to which he was chained—only I believe, however, at night—and the door with a little hole in it through which food could be passed to him, are preserved in the Rosgarten Museum. Here he suffered much from the wet and cold, but through the kindness of his guards, whom he won by his gentleness, he was able to write letters to his friends, and even short theological treatises. With touching quaintness he writes from his prison to his knightly friend and countryman John of Chlum:—"Do not allow the great expense (of his keep) to trouble you. If God should free the goose (Huss in Bohemian means goose) from his prison, he will not allow you to regret the expense. To-morrow it is eight weeks that the goose has been lying close to the dining-room."

The cold and wet of winter in his dreadful prison brought on an illness which threatened to rob the Council of its victim. He was therefore removed to a less severe imprisonment in the Franciscan Convent, and upon the flight of Pope John XXIII., of which more later, the papal guards were removed, and hope

GOTTLIEBEN.

revived in the heart of the Reformer. The Council, however, handed him over to the Bishop of Constance, who caused him to be conveyed to the strong castle of Gottlieben, where his feet were made fast in iron stocks, and at night his arm was fastened to an iron ring in the wall.

Twice he was brought before the Council in the dining-hall of the Franciscans, where he maintained his cause with profound scholarship, simple earnestness, and calm courage, against the long array of learned and distinguished men, of whom some were his accusers and some his judges. At the close of the second audience when, with great simplicity, he said, that, had he not chosen of his own free will to appear before the Council, it would have been easy for him to have found a safe asylum with some of the Bohemian nobles, his bitter antagonist Peter d'Ailly charged him with gross disrespect and impudence towards the Council. Then came forward the brave knight, John of Chlum, and with firm voice, said, " I am only one of the poorest and weakest of the nobles of Bohemia, but I .am confident I could defend Huss in my castle for a whole year against any force that could be brought against it : yes! even against the united might of both kings!" (The Emperor Sigismund and his brother King Wenceslaus). A dead silence followed this stout utterance.

Then the Emperor turned to Huss, and with threatening words demanded the recantation of his errors, and closed his speech by saying that if Huss obstinately continued in his errors, he, the Emperor, would with his own hands carry wood to form the faggot-heap on which to burn him.

After a night spent in the agonies of tooth-ache, Huss was brought in to a final audience ; but, though

N

he meekly asked for instruction if he were in error, and professed himself open to conviction, he was noisily and angrily commanded unconditionally to retract his heresies, and was taken back to his prison.

As a last effort the Emperor sent the Knight of Chlum to Huss to try and secure his recantation. The meeting between the honest and faithful soldier and his revered teacher is deeply touching as it rises up before us sharp and clear in spite of the intervening centuries. "Dear master," said the Knight to Huss, "if thou knowest thyself to be in the wrong, be not ashamed to give up thy opinions; if, however, thou feelest thyself to be innocent, I would encourage thee rather to endure the most dreadful agony than to deny that which thou art convinced is the truth."

With tears the holy man replied, that if he could be convinced of error out of the Holy Scriptures, he would gladly abjure his opinions, but otherwise not. Then he wrote the most touching letters of farewell to his friends, which he closed with the words, "Written in prison at the time that I hourly expect to be led out to death."

The fifteenth sitting of the Council was held in the cathedral on the 6th of July, 1415. Often, as I have sat in that grand old minster among a crowded congregation of devout worshippers I have tried to realise the scene that it must have presented on that great day, now 465 years ago. Along its, even then, venerable aisles were ranged powers and dominions, principalities, and supreme royalty itself; the highest dignitaries in church and state assembled from out all Christendom were there. Alone in that great assembly, upon a large stone slab which is still shown, stood the simple priest John Huss, alone in his conscious uprightness, alone in the presence of that great assembly and of his God.

There is a characteristic passage in Renan in which he deplores that a martyr's death should have prevented St. Paul from being in his old age *désillusionné*—from perceiving that all for which he had struggled and suffered was illusion, vision, and chimera. Well has it been for the martyrs for truth and conscience in every age that their faith has been stronger than that of M. Renan, and that they have felt it to be a reality, as Paul did, that when no man stood by them, but all forsook them, the Lord stood by them and strengthened them. It is natural for us to think of Huss as supported by a widely prevalent Protestant sentiment such as now exists in the world, but at that time no such sentiment had come into being. With many worldly, sensual, and cruel men, both among priests and laymen, assembled at the Council, there were also the best and wisest of their generation, and it was these who held that he was guilty of deadly sin. Against this consensus of the Christian world he had only to place his individual conviction of right and duty based upon the Scriptures. He was bitterly alone, and in his cold, dark, prison-cell, as well as now, standing before his judges, who were about to hand him over to a shameful and cruel death, the agonizing doubt may have come to him whether, after all, these men of learning and piety might not be right and he be wrong, A modern poet has said—

> "They are slaves who dare not be
> In the right with two or three."

But the choice spirits to whom the world owes most have often had to tread the winepress absolutely alone ; and who shall estimate the agony of this loneliness, compared with which the stake and even the rack are light torments ! Well do I remember the feelings with which, twenty-five years ago, I, for the first time,

looked upon Lessing's great painting of "Huss before
the Council of Constance." While looking upon it
the words descriptive of the proto-martyr came un-
bidden to my lips :—"And all that sat in the council,
looking stedfastly on him, saw his face as it had been
the face of an angel."

When the sentence had been read aloud to him,
Huss fell upon his knees and prayed very earnestly for
all his enemies, and especially that the exceeding great
sin of those who had borne false witness against him
might not be laid to their charge. It is melancholy
to know that this saint-like demeanour was greeted
with scornful laughter from all parts of the cathedral.

Then Huss fixed his eyes full upon Sigismund, and
reminded him of his imperial safe-conduct. The hot
blood mounted to the cheeks of the perjured Kaiser, so
that all present observed it. One hundred years later
this blush of shame saved the life of Luther. When
the youthful Emperor Charles V., was urged by his
clerical counsellors at Worms to disregard the safe-
conduct he had given to Luther, on the ground that no
faith was to be kept with heretics, he replied : "I
should not like to have to blush like Sigismund." It
is a melancholy instance of the perversion of conscience, that in his mature age, Charles never ceased
to reproach himself for this act of good faith.

The awful ceremony of degradation followed. He
was placed standing upon a high stool, so that all
present could see him, and seven bishops proceeded
to array him in priestly garments, and compelled him
to take the eucharistic cup in his hand. This they
then snatched from him, cursing him as the traitor
Judas. "But I" meekly replied he "have full confidence that I shall this day drink of this cup, which
you now take from me, in Christ's kingdom." As each

of the sacerdotal robes was taken from him a separate anathema was invoked on his head. At last the mark of the tonsure was rubbed out and a pointed paper cap painted with three devils, and with "Heresiarcha" written upon it, was set upon his head. "We commit thy soul to the devils in hell" said the bishops. But "I," replied Huss, "commend my spirit into the hands of my Redeemer."

He was thereupon handed over to the secular powers, with what I fear we must regard as the hypocritical wish on the part of the church authorities that the "king" (the Emperor Sigismund) should neither kill nor hurt him, but should keep him in life-long imprisonment. The Emperor showed how well he understood the meaning of this injunction by immediately rising and addressing Duke Louis of Bavaria, the Elector Palatine, in these words :—"Because we do not bear the sword in vain, but for the punishment of those that do evil, therefore, dear uncle, take this man John Huss and punish him as a heretic." A procession was soon formed ; the Pfalzgraf—Elector Palatine—with 800 soldiers leading the way, and the numerous city guard ; then followed a vast multitude with the spiritual and secular lords on horseback. Every step of the way to the place of martyrdom can be traced. It now leads past the handsome Protestant church, and through rather a pretty part of the town until you come to an ugly gasometer, where you turn down an avenue of poplars leading to a little spot enclosed with an iron railing, in which stands a huge boulder overgrown with ivy. In the fifteenth century this was a piece of waste ground where rubbish was shot.

With prayer and the singing of psalms he walked to his death. Smiling, he watched the burning of his books, confident that the truth contained in them could never perish. The executioner bound him to the stake first, by accident, with his face towards the east, but was ordered to undo him and place him with his face towards the west; for the heretic was never again to see God's sun. As he was fastened with a rusty chain to the stake he said, "Joyfully do I bear this chain. My Saviour bore much heavier bonds for the sinful human race."

Very touching is it that, spying his gaolers of the Dominican convent near to him in the crowd, he thus addressed them:—"Dear brothers! I render you heartfelt thanks for the many kindnesses shown to me by you during my long and painful imprisonment. You have been less my gaolers than my brothers; and I would have you to remember that I believe, and am fully confident, that I shall this day reign with that blessed Saviour for whose sake I am about to die." Well might the common people who were sufficiently near to him to hear his words say, "What this man may formerly have said or preached we know not; but nothing do we now hear from him but holy words."

The Elector-Palatine now rode forward and charged him, for the last time, to retract. Upon his refusal, the pile was lighted. In a voice loud and clear, so that it could be heard afar, the martyr cried, "Jesus Christ, the Son of the living God—Thou who didst suffer for us, have pity upon me."

The faggots had been mercifully intertwined with bands of straw, so that very quickly his voice was choked by the smoke, and then for ever hushed in death.

Within twelve months, on the 7th of June, 1416, on the very same spot of ground, Hieronymus, or Jerome of Prague, the friend and disciple of Huss, was also burned as a heretic. The character of Jerome was in many respects very unlike that of Huss. He came of a noble family, and his life in some respects was like that of a "knight-errant." With fiery eloquence and a scholarship which was the wonder of his adversaries, he preached the doctrines which his master Huss taught.

For 360 days this gentleman and scholar was confined in a dark and stinking dungeon, with very insufficient food, and where he could neither read nor even see. Nevertheless, when brought before the Council, he confounded his accusers by conducting his defence and citing his authorities with as much skill and aptitude as if he had had access to his books during the whole of his imprisonment. The prolonged agony, however, broke his spirit; and, after long confinement in this horrid hole, his hands and feet crossed and chained to a stake, so that he could neither sit nor yet hold his head erect, he consented to retract his opinions. In spite, however, of his recantation, he was led back again to his dungeon. This perfidy recalled him from his temporary weakness. On the 26th of May he was led before a sitting of the Council, held, as usual, in the cathedral. A fuller recantation was confidently expected from him; but, in place of it, he retracted his retractation, which, he said, rested upon his conscience as a terrible crime, which only physical weakness and the dread of a cruel death had wrung from him. With bold, brave words he praised his master Huss as a saint and martyr, and practically dared the Council to do its worst, concluding with the words, "I know you are determined to condemn me, although you have not proved me guilty of any error. So be it. My life is in your hands; but know that, after my death, I will leave behind me a thorn and gnawing worm in your hearts. I summon you before the judgment-seat of God, where, within one hundred years, you must all appear with me and render up your account."

His martyrdom is thus described by Poggio, a learned Florentine, who was present at the Council, and wrote thus to a friend at the time :—

"Arrived at the place of execution, he himself took off his clothes and fell on his knees before the stake. His naked body was then tied to it, first with wet cords and then with an iron chain. The faggots were thickly piled from his feet to his breast. The executioner was then about to apply the fire from behind. 'Come to the front,' cried Jerome. 'Light the fire in my face and before my eyes. Know that I am in nowise terrified thereat. Had I feared the fire, I should not have come to Constance.' Then he began to sing a song of praise, and sang it to the end with a clear voice, though by this time the flames leaped together high above his head. Had'st thou witnessed the heroic death of this man, thou would'st have acknowledged that without doubt this Hierony-mus belonged to the school of the wise.

"Mucius Scaevola did not hold his hand in the fire with greater constancy than Hieronymus allowed his body to be burned. The resignation with which Socrates drained his poison-bowl was not so great as was the joy with which this man hurried to the stake."

Another eye-witness, of the name of Dacher, who described the Council, simply remarks, in the intro-duction to his work, "Huss and Hieronymus were burned for celebrating the Lord's Supper *in the manner that Jesus Christ commanded*."

There is one incident, variously related by different chroniclers of Huss and of Jerome, which has always seemed to me one of the most touching within the whole range of martyrology. The confessor is bound to the stake, the executioner is about to light the pile, when an old peasant woman approaches with a faggot, anxious to further her salvation by assisting in the burning of a heretic. It causes no emotion of anger or indignation in the breast of the sufferer; but he admires the simple faith that prompts the cruel act, and gently says, "O sancta simplicitas." Those who sadly feel that they can no longer say "Shibboleth" as their fathers have said it, do not always possess the gentleness and humility of Huss, nor realise that the censure of good men who remain in the old paths may be animated by this "holy simplicity."

My readers may think that I have dwelt too long upon the sad and oft-told story of Huss and Jerome, but we are now treating of Constance, and the traveller, as he enters Constance, does not think of Barbarossa, or of his like-minded grandson of Hohenstaufen, or of Guelph, but "of the pale, thin man in mean attire" who witnessed a good confession outside the walls of the city, now 465 years ago.

Constance itself, too, though a Catholic city, recognises, as it were instinctively, wherein its true glory consists. Some, indeed, have alleged that glorying in Huss the old city glories in its shame. This, however, is absurd. Constance was no more responsible for the death of Huss than were the inhabitants of Smithfield for the martyr-fires that were lighted there, or than Oxford was for the deaths of Latimer and Ridley. It was the crime of Christendom, not of Constance.

A huge granite boulder, borne into the neighbourhood by a glacier untold centuries ago, has been placed by loving hands upon the spot where these two

brave and good men endured martyrdom.   On one
side is the simple inscription, " Johannes Huss, Juli 6,
1415"; and on the other, " Hieronymus von Prag,
Juni 7, 1416."   A luxuriant mantle of ivy half covers
the inscriptions; a simple iron railing surrounds the
sacred spot.   Let no visitor to Constance fail to spend
a few moments here, while he ponders how much
he individually owes to brave and true men, the
saviours of their race, who counted not their lives dear
unto themselves, and reckoned suffering and agony
and death as of small account, so that they might not
quench the truth in their breasts, but keep their consciences void of offence, as did on this spot John Huss
and Jerome of Prague.

CHAPTER XVI.

THE FLIGHT OF POPE JOHN XXIII.—ELECTION OF A NEW POPE AND CLOSE OF THE COUNCIL.

Pope John resigns—His flight—Energy of the Kaiser—Humiliation of Frederick of Austria—Condemnation of Pope John—Hoped-for reformation of the Church—Cardinal Zabarella—The Cardinals oppose reform—Election of a new Pope—The Conciliums-saal—How the Conclave was held—Martin V. is chosen—Enthronement of the new Pope—Results of the Council—The Kaiser in debt—Exeunt omnes—New wine must be put into new bottles.

IT seemed convenient to follow the trial of Huss and Jerome without a break until the tragic close, but in the order of time much of great interest to Christendom had happened while they were languishing in their dungeons.*

At the second sitting of the Council, on the 2nd March, 1415, it was decided that the best plan to restore peace to Christendom was for Pope John XXIII. to resign the papal chair, and then he, as well as the two antipopes, being now out of the way, for a new head of the Church to be chosen, to whom all might yield allegiance. The Patriarch of Antioch read the act of abdication, and John knelt before the altar and solemnly swore to accept it.

The Emperor rose, thanked the Pope in the name of the Council, fell upon his knees, laid aside his crown, and kissed the Pope's feet. In the name of the fathers of the Church, the Patriarch of Antioch thanked the

---

* In this description I have mostly followed Schwab.

Pope for his self-sacrifice for the good and peace of
the Church. Soon the cathedral rang with exulting
Te Deums, and until late in the night all the bells of the
city sent out joyful peals.

Very few days had, however, elapsed before the
bells were ringing anew. Now, however, they were
peals of alarm, for the Pope who had so solemnly
abdicated had fled, and no man knew whither. On
the 20th March, the secret confederate of the Pope,
Duke Frederick of Austria, held a splendid tourna-
ment just without the walls of the city, to which the
citizens as well as their guests thronged.

The immense throng watched with delight the
knightly prowess of the riders, conspicuous among
whom were the Duke of Austria and Count Cilly.
Meanwhile the Pope, in profound secrecy, clothed
himself as an imperial postboy, and, only attended
by a boy on horseback, mounted a miserable hack,
and rode through the city gates. Within an hour he
was at Ermattingen, where, refreshing himself with a
glass of wine at the priest's house, he took boat on the
Zeller See, and, before nightfall, had rowed down the
Rhine to Schaffhausen, a city which then belonged to
Duke Frederick, who, privily slipping away from the
festivities, which had so well answered their purpose,
joined the fugitive and perjured Pope the same
evening. The following day the alarming news was
known all over Constance. The universal terror was
indescribable. The consummation for which good
men had so long hoped, and prayed, and laboured—the
restoration of peace to distracted Christendom—had
seemed near at hand. The rival Popes having abdicated, it seemed possible to choose one who should
secure universal allegiance. All this bright prospect
was destroyed, like a house of cards before a hurricane,

by the flight of Pope John. Already hundreds of
Austrians and Italians pressed to the gates to leave
the city, and it seemed as if the Council, which had
commenced its sittings under such favourable auspices,
would break up in disorder, and leave the confusion of
Christendom worse confounded.

In this crisis, it is only bare justice to say that the
Emperor Sigismund acted with energy and decision.
He sent heralds throughout the city to pacify the
public mind. He himself visited all the money-
changers, so that the public credit might not suffer,
and went immediately to the principal Italian ecclesiastics and other representatives at the Council to
prevent their departure. This wise behaviour calmed
the minds of men, who had been lashed into fury at
the spectacle of the more or less secret departure
on foot, on horseback, and by boat on the lake, of
Austrians and others, who mostly chose the dead of
night or the early morning for their flight.

Duke Frederick was solemnly put under the ban of
the empire. Then in two sessions the Kaiser appeared
arrayed in his imperial robes and with the crown of
empire on his head. The necessary measures were
quickly taken, a large army was rapidly brought together
from the cities around the lake, and Sigismund assumed the command.

Within a few days the towns of Stein-on-the-Rhine,
Dussenhofen, Frauenfeld, and Schaffhausen, were conquered. Regardless of the peace that existed between
them and Austria, the Confederate Swiss, in alliance
with the Emperor, fell upon and occupied the Helvetic
possessions of Duke Frederick.

The Duke himself, in company with Pope John,
made his escape mid snow and storm into the fastnesses of the Black Forest; but, believing that further

resistance to the imperial will would only lead to utter ruin, the haughty duke voluntarily returned to Constance in the character of a humble suppliant for the Kaiser's mercy. The Emperor received him in the dining-hall of the Franciscan convent, where the most distinguished ecclesiastics, and especially the Italian representatives, were convened. Sigismund stood as far as possible from the entrance of the hall, when the fallen prince appeared led by the hand by Duke Louis of Bavaria, and Frederick of Hohenzollern, Burggraf of Nuremberg, who had just received the dignity of Elector of Brandenburg.*

Three times the suppliant kneeled before his of-fended sovereign.

"What is your request?" said the Emperor.

The Duke of Bavaria spoke for him, and commended him to the Kaiser's mercy, promising on his behalf, that he would give up the Pope on the latter's safety being assured. The Emperor then said, "Frederick, thou who art our princely vassal and that of the Holy Roman Empire, wilt thou hold to this?" ("Unser und des heiligen Reichs Fürst, Friedrich, will Er das halten?") The Duke replied "Yes, and I throw myself upon your majesty's mercy."

"We are sorry," said the Emperor, "that he has been guilty of this."

Then the Duke made over to the Emperor with oath, all his lordships from the Tyrol to Alsace, and did him homage until such time as it should please the Kaiser to restore them to him.

"Learn from this," said Sigismund to the assembled lords, "what a king of the Germans can do."

Shortly afterwards the fugitive Pope was given up to

* The ancestor of the royal house of Prussia, and the now imperial house of Germany.

the Council by his old friend Duke Frederick, and was kept close prisoner in a strong tower in Radolfszell.

In the twelfth session of the Council, Pope John XXIII., in the presence of the Emperor, and of all the princes and ecclesiastics, was tried as a fugitive, a breeder of discord in the church, a usurer and waster of the patrimony of St. Peter, and as one whose scandalous walk had grieved the church and the people of God. He was convicted, deposed, and handed over to the Emperor to be kept in safe ward. His first prison was the castle of Gottlieben, and there seems good reason to believe that for some days he was imprisoned there contemporaneously with his saintly victim Huss.

When the three existing Popes had been formally set on one side, earnest men hoped that the Council might at last proceed to the great object of its coming together—the reformation of the church. Even Cardinal Peter d'Ailly, the bitter foe of Huss, had preached a sermon on the day of St. Louis, in which he deplored in the strongest terms the corruption of the church, and denounced the luxury, the debauchery, the love of display, and the pride and avarice of the clergy.

The Emperor Sigismund and the German and English representatives urged in the strongest manner a reformation of the church before proceeding to elect a new Pope.

Cardinal Zabarella declared himself in favour of permitting the marriage of priests.

The mind fails to realise how different might have been the subsequent history of Christendom, if the reform of the church had thus been resolutely grappled with, one hundred years before Luther. But, as so often before and since, the prejudices and supposed interests of a great corporation (in this instance the church) proved too powerful to be overcome even by the most influential outside pressure. As the artificers of Ephesus rallied to the cry " Our craft is in danger," so the ecclesiastics were horrified at the idea of secular powers having anything to do with their reformation. The cardinals presented a solid phalanx of opposition, and on the 9th of September, 1417, at a sitting of the Council in the presence of Sigismund and the representatives of all the nations, they protested in the most energetic manner.

The Emperor, accompanied by the Patriarch of Antioch and many distinguished prelates, indignant at the conduct of these red-hatted " obstructives," rose and left the assembly, while the cardinals were in the midst of their protestations. Then arose from those who remained loud cries of, " It is right that the heretics should leave." The cardinals threatened to secede in a body from the Council, and insisted on reading through their protestations—though amidst a storm of opposition—at another session on the 12th September, they sitting together with their red hats pressed down on their foreheads, as a sign of their determination. Cardinal Zabarella was suffering from gout at the time, and was so excited by the discussion that in a fortnight he died.

It is not without a feeling of sorrow, if not of shame, that we read how the English were won over to the side of the cardinals, and the Emperor, finding himself deserted by all except the Germans, agreed to a compromise, by which the Pope was to be chosen *first*, and church reform was to be considered *afterwards*.

The election of the Pope was, therefore, proceeded with immediately. Twenty years before, in 1388, the city of Constance had erected a very fine market-hall, which stands to this day close to the railway station and to the harbour.   This building is wrongly called the Conciliums-Saal, for the meetings of the Council were all held in the cathedral.

The Market-hall, which up to the second floor is of sandstone—brought on the lake from Rorschach—and above of wood, was eminently suited for the purposes of the conclave.   Above the ground-floor, which was used for the storage and sampling of goods, is a very fine hall, supported by many oak columns, intended to be used as a banquet-hall on very solemn occasions, and during the great fairs for a display of the famous Constance linen, which up to quite recent times was well known in Italy as " tela di Costanza."

This fine old hall has recently been restored with great taste, and adorned with a series of paintings, illustrative of the history of Constance.   Among these are—" John Huss protesting before the Council in the Cathedral, 1415," " The martyrdom of Huss at Bruhl," " The coronation of Pope Martin V., 1417," " Victorious defence of the citizens of Constance during the Swedish siege, 1633," all by the court-painter Fritz Pecht, uncle to the artist who has illustrated this work. In this, at that time new, building, all necessary arrangements were made for the holding of the conclave, and Reichenthal fairly revels in a most elaborate description of how it was all managed.   For the first time for 400 years the conclave did not consist exclusively of cardinals to the number of thirty, but, in addition, of an equal number of archbishops, bishops, professors, and doctors chosen by the Council. For the accommodation of these sixty* electors, sixty

---

* Some authorities say that the number of electors who actually took part in the conclave was only fifty-three.

temporary apartments were prepared, each with a little
ante-room for a servant. All the windows of the
Kaufhaus and of all houses that looked upon it were
boarded up, and with sound of trumpet it was announced that no person should approach within a
specified distance of the building. The darkness of
the inside was lightened by two lanterns on each
floor, in which burned four great tapers. In addition,
each elector had tapers in his little room. Our
chronicler does not specify what means were taken to
secure proper ventilation, but on this question the
fifteenth century was not so precise as the nineteenth.

On the 8th of November, 1417, the electors entered
the conclave. The Emperor Sigismund received
them at the door, and conducted them one by
one to their apartments, charging them, conscien-
tiously to discharge their important duties. He
then left them, the door was locked, and the key
placed in the charge of the Grand Master of the
Knights of Rhodes, who, with two bishops and two
other representatives of the Council, kept watch and
ward, and minutely examined all food that was handed
in for the electors, to prevent the sending of any letter
from without, or any communication with the outer
world. For two days a white cloth hanging from the
Kaufhaus told the anxious citizens that the assembled
conclave had not yet made its choice. On the third day,
the 11th of November, St. Martin's day, Otto of Colonna,
a Roman, was chosen. The day suggested the name
he assumed of Martin V. The news was received
throughout the city with transports of delight. The
Emperor Sigismund hardly knew how to contain himself for joy, and to his shame forgot to exact from the
Pope what was due to his imperial authority—an oath

of fealty on the spot. Pope Martin now appeared, and accompanied by a multitude that could not be counted headed by the whole body of the clergy, the city council, and all the nobility, princes, cardinals, and bishops, proceeded with great pomp to the cathedral. Above the Pope, who was on horseback, a scarlet canopy was carried, and at his side walked humbly on foot, Sigismund, Kaiser of the Holy Roman Empire. The Pope was enthroned in the cathedral and received the adoration of the cardinals. On the 21st of November he was solemnly crowned. The courtyard of the bishop's palace, which was the scene of the ceremony, was splendidly decorated, and converted into an amphitheatre for the occasion. About one hundred of the most exalted ecclesiastics were present. The Pope took his seat upon a superb throne, richly hung with cloth of gold. While strains of triumphant music filled the air, three chosen cardinals flung themselves at the feet of the Pope; then one of them arose, and holding forth a wisp of flax at the end of a rod, he lighted it, and, addressing the Pope, said, "Sancte Pater, sic transit gloria mundi." Then the three cardinals and the Grand Master of the Knights of Rhodes, amid the clang of trumpets, and songs of praise, put the papal crown upon his head. A magnificent procession on horseback followed. First rode the clergy, knights, abbots, and cardinals, on fine horses, with handsome and uniform trappings —245 horsemen in all. Then rode Pope Martin in full canonicals, with the tiara on his head, in a white silk cassock, scarlet mantle, and slippers with a cross embroidered in gold on each. Holding his bridle on the right, walked the Emperor Sigismund, on his left the Elector of Brandenburg. Behind came a vast multitude. The procession rode to the Church of St.

O 2

Augustine, and then back to the palace, where the
Pontiff solemnly blessed the assembled crowd.

The hopes with which the election of Pope Martin
was hailed by good men, were not fulfilled. The
character of Pope Martin V. seemed the very opposite of that of Otto of Colonna. Councillor von
Windeck, a follower of the Emperor Sigismund, says
that from being the poorest and simplest of cardinals
he became the richest and most avaricious of Popes.

The reformation of the church seemed more distant
than ever ; every possible abuse received sanction from
Martin's pulpit rules. Stern repression was used
towards the Hussites, resulting in the dreadful Hus-
site wars, which so long scourged Germany. The
Greek ambassadors, who came to beg the aid of
Christendom against the terrible Turks, were sent
empty away. Pope John XXIII. was set at liberty,
and Frederick of Austria received some of his lands
back from the Emperor, but his ancestral land of
Aargau, wherein stood Hapsburg, the castle of his
fathers, passed away from the House of Austria for
ever, as did the whole of the Thurgau, both of which
joined the confederation of the Swiss Republics.

At the festival of Whitsuntide, 1418, Pope Martin
granted a general indulgence, and the next day, the
16th of May, with extraordinary pomp, he rode out of
Constance attended by all the magnates of church and
state. The Elector of Brandenburg departed on the
19th of May, and was speedily followed by the Emperor.
Sigismund found many difficulties in the way of his
departure. His followers were, many of them, heavily
in debt. His pride would not allow him to go without
them, and the most powerful prince in Christendom
had no ready money with which to settle the claims of
the citizens. He proposed, indeed, that they should

let his followers go, and charge their debts to his
account; but to this the citizens would in nowise
agree.   They replied that he himself had often told
them to let no one go until he had paid what he owed,
and the city councillors alleged that they feared what
the people would do to them if his followers left in their
debt.   The Emperor Sigismund proved himself quite
equal to the occasion.   He called together what was
practically a great meeting of his creditors in the
Kaufhaus (Conciliums-saal), where he. made a most
winning speech to the assembled citizens.   He des-
canted upon the great honour he had done to the city,
and spoke of how—now for so many years—he had
kept the Council there, to the great discontent and
jealousy of many other cities of the Holy Roman
Empire.   By so doing he had caused the name and
fame of Constance to be spread world-wide.   He
especially praised the common people, and thanked
them for their good behaviour, and for bearing so
much for the sake of peace from the numerous
strangers present at the Council.   He then said he
would gladly leave behind him the silver and gold
vessels belonging to his table, but that it would be a
great disgrace to him, the Emperor, to have his state
thus reduced, and he was sure they would not wish it.
He proposed, however, to leave silken cloths woven
with gold to the full value of the debts.   To this the
assembled citizens agreed, and old Reichenthal adds :—
"So he allowed the cloths to remain in Constance,
and they were packed in chests and locked up in the
Kaufhaus, where many of them still lie, and, likely
enough, will never be redeemed.   And this business
was the first misfortune, and the first occasion of
bad feeling, which happened to the citizens of
Constance."

This troublesome matter of the payment or arrangement of his bill at last happily settled, the Emperor left Constance on the 21st of May for Strasburg. The exodus now became universal, and in a few days Constance, which for nearly five years, from the winter of 1414 until Whitsuntide, 1418, had practically been the capital of Christendom, was deserted, and sank back into its normal condition of a somewhat insignificant city of the empire. As Schwab finely puts it, the Council had left no trace behind it save the ashes (Brandstätte) of two martyrs. Thus ended the greatest and most solemn council of the church that Western Christendom ever held. One good it certainly effected—namely, the healing of the sad division from which the Christian world was suffering. But how cruel and bitter must have been the disappointment of enlightened and good men throughout all Europe who had looked to the Council to put an end to crying scandals, and bring about a reformation, of the church.

When we think of the cruel wars which desolated Europe as a result of the great reformation of a century later, and of the sad division of Christendom which resulted therefrom, we are tempted bitterly to deplore the *vis inertiæ* which successfully resisted all reforming tendencies at the Council of Constance. It is probable, however, that, in the very nature of things, such a reform as was essential could not have originated among the princes of the church, but must have taken its rise in a revolutionary movement from below.

Who shall gauge, also, the full meaning of that profound saying, that "new wine must be put into new bottles"?

CHAPTER XVII.

THE HISTORY OF THE CITY OF CONSTANCE SUBSEQUENT TO THE PERIOD OF THE GREAT COUNCIL.

The history of the City of Constance subsequent to the period of the Great
  Council—The Reformation accepted by Constance—The Bishop expelled—
  Charles V. determines to punish Constance—Advance of a Spanish army—
  Fight on the Rhine bridge—Valour of the butcher-boys—The city at the
  mercy of Charles—Constance becomes Austrian—Kaiser Joseph II. visits the
  city—Genevese colony—General Dufour.

In a former portion of this work I have perhaps
sufficiently spoken of the Swiss and Suabian wars
which at intervals desolated the shores of the Boden
See from 1417 to 1499. I have also briefly alluded to
the spread of the Reformation, and to the outbreak of
the "Peasants' War" in these regions. In this place we
have only to do with the fortunes of Constance itself.

In 1529 the new religious movement showed itself
in a very questionable shape, in the iconoclastic fury
with which the churches and cloisters were stormed
and their contents destroyed or stolen by the mob.
The value of the spoil in the cathedral alone, was
estimated at 100,000 florins, and the body of the
holy Conrad was cast into the lake. Bishop Hugo, of
Landenberg, with his canons, took refuge in Ueberlingen.
The bishop sent Fritz von Anwil, a writer of hymns
still to be found in Protestant hymn-books, to represent
him at the religious discussion that was held at
Zürich with Faber. Constance declared itself in favour
of the views of Zwingli, and, together with Lindau,

Memmingen, and Strasburg, prepared, and sent to the Emperor Charles V. a confession of their faith. The Kaiser caused this confession to be replied to by Catholic divines, and demanded of the four cities an instant return to obedience. They, however, all joined the league of Schmalkalden, and signed the Augsburg confession in February, 1531. For twenty years Constance enjoyed its change of religion. The city council were all Protestants, and the children were educated in the new faith. Charles V. however now proved that he had the power as well as the will to crush the league of the Protestant princes and states by means of Spanish soldiers. As the victorious Kaiser advanced through southern Germany, city after city renounced the Schmalkalden league, and begged the imperial clemency. Constance would not, however, yield. At the head of the Zwinglian party stood the burgomaster Thomas Blarer, a man of strong religious convictions and of great determination and courage, and he and his like-minded brother Ambrosius encouraged the citizens in constancy to the new faith. When however the league was utterly crushed, and its beloved leaders, the Elector John Frederick of Saxony and Duke Philip of Hesse were taken prisoners and held in stern durance by their imperial master and Spanish conqueror, Constance felt that further resistance was vain. The magistracy sent an exceedingly humble letter to Charles on the 13th July, 1548, offering expiation for the city's previous contumacy, and begging that it might be allowed to retain the faith in which it had now lived for twenty years. The angry Kaiser vouchsafed no reply until the 5th August, when he simply sent word—" The Emperor sees clearly that with Constance no peaceful method will succeed; he will shortly take other measures." Before sending this message he had actually despatched 3,000 Spanish infantry and 4,000 cavalry, under the command of Colonel Alfonso Vives, to fall upon the devoted city. In vain the citizens appealed to Zürich for help. The dreaded Spaniards stealthily approached,—a portion of the army being sent through the forest which then surrounded Constance, in order to take the city unawares during divine service. Three members of the city-watch who heard the advancing troops were quickly seized and silenced ; and, noiselessly as a tiger about to spring upon its prey, the vanguard approached the walls. The first attack was directed against the suburb of Petershausen, which clustered around the further end of the Rhine bridge. The guard at this point observing something unusual hurried to the burgomaster at two in the morning. The city council was quickly assembled, and the alarm bells of the city rang to arms. The entrances to the city were quickly occupied by 200 citizens. It was full time. Already the half-dry moat was full of Spanish veterans who were climbing up the walls. The citizens brought their heavy artillery to bear, and at the very beginning of the fight the leader, Alfonso Vives, fell mortally hit. Alfonso's son also was severely wounded, and was carried back to Ueberlingen, together with the body of his father. A nephew of Alfonso died of his wounds at Radolfszell. But the Spaniards did not depend alone upon their attack from the land side. Eighteen ships crowded with soldiers approached from the lake, but when they attempted to land on the island where stood the half-ruined cloister of the Dominicans, the former prison of Huss—the present Insel Hotel—they were received by such a deadly rain of bullets that those of the assailants who remained alive quickly put the width of the lake between them and their foes. At last, however, the suburb of Petershausen was gained by the Spaniards, but further they could not advance : the citizens contested every foot of the bridge with desperate heroism. Fifty butcher-lads in solid phalanx held the bridge, and in vain did hundreds of Spaniards, though clad in steel, throw themselves upon them, until a portion of the bridge was broken down behind them, when they threw themselves into the Rhine and gained the Constance shore. One alone remained, as valiant as Horatius Coccles ; many Spaniards he had slain ; none could get near him, until two Spaniards getting under his sword tried to throw him to the ground. He had rendered yeoman's service to his native city, and now that his own position was desperate, he enclosed his two assailants in a deadly embrace, and buried them with himself in the surging Rhine below.

It is a pity that the name of this hero has not been preserved to us, to be enshrined with that of Horatius Coccles and Arnold of Winkelried. But, though the Spaniards had suffered terribly, the attack was not yet over. They contrived to repair the bridge. The portcullis of the city gate, at the bridge-head, had been rendered useless by traitors within the walls. Nevertheless, the Spaniards could not carry the gateway. The artillery on the towers and walls rained death upon the assailants. At last, even the proud and stubborn Spaniards were obliged to desist. To protect themselves from a pursuit by the enraged citizens, they burned the bridge with the bodies of their comrades, and retired in rage and fury, to wreak their vengeance upon the unoffending villagers of Allensbach. In the attack they had lost 500 men ; of the citizens there had fallen 111. It is usual to speak of this resistance as bootless heroism, because the bigot Charles was soon afterwards able to work his will with Constance; but the butcher-boys of Constance at least saved their city from the fate of many a Dutch town taken by Alva, and from that of Magdeburg at the hands of Tilly, and Drogheda at those of Cromwell in the next century. It is a fitting tribute to the self-sacrificing valour of these noble butcher-lads that it is commemorated in a fine fresco on the walls of the present Rathhaus.

No wonder that for a moment the citizens exulted in their victory and deliverance, but it was only for a moment. The little city stood quite alone, exposed to the fury of the master of two worlds, who at this period of his life seemed invincible. The Catholic party in the town counselled absolute submission, as the only way to save it from total destruction; and their view was naturally shared by the timid and the prudent. The city council was compelled to implore the intermediation of friendly princes and of the Swiss Confederation. Some thought there might be some hope if the city would dismiss its Swiss mercenaries, and receive back again the bishop and the cathedral-chapter. In their desperate circumstances the men of Constance were not in a position to bargain; so the ambassadors of the Swiss Confederation appeared before the Emperor and pleaded for the devoted town. He had only one word, "unconditional surrender." Then Ambrosius Blarer, eight Protestant ministers, and other leading men fled the city. Another attack on the part of the imperial forces seemed daily imminent. Even its enemies took pity on the unfortunate city. The Abbot of Weingarten, Count Frederick of Fürstenberg, and the Master of the Teutonic Knights at Mainau, met at Ueberlingen, and decided to intercede with the Emperor for Constance.

Meanwhile, the citizens turned to the Emperor's

brother, the Archduke Ferdinand of Austria, and undertook to give up their liberties as a free imperial town, and subject themselves entirely to the house of Austria, if he would turn away from them the Emperor's anger.   This offer was accepted, and on the 13th October, 1548, the city was handed over to the Austrian representative, Nicholas of Pollwil.

This was the end of the free city of Constance. She was now subject to the house of Austria, bound to accept her confession of faith from her lord, and in war and peace to serve him.   The city treasure, artillery, and archives, all had to be given up; the citizens were disarmed; the goods of those who had gone into exile were confiscated; the Protestant preachers, who until now had remained, were ordered to leave the city; the former nuns were immediately to return to the cloister or go into exile.

The high-minded burgomaster, Thomas Blarer, and almost the whole of the city council, left the city for ever.   Great changes were made in the city government, its constitution being made much more aristocratic.   The churches, monasteries, and convents were restored to their old possessors, and on the 11th May, 1551, the bishop made a solemn entry into the city at the head of eighty horsemen, again to enter upon the enjoyment of the cathedral and the bishop's palace, after twenty-one years' absence.

After a few years the Protestant powers of Germany applied to Ferdinand, asking that the evangelical worship might again be permitted in Constance, but he replied that the city had voluntarily submitted to his terms, and that he could make no change.   As a matter of fact, it is only within living memory that Protestant worship has been permitted in Constance, and the handsome new Protestant church built.   ·

In the year 1563, Ferdinand, now Emperor, was received amid the thunder of welcoming cannon, into what had become the Austrian town of Constance, where he spent three days, and inaugurated as mild a *régime* as was consistent with the deprivation of religious liberty, and what would now be called the destruction of the antonomy of the city.

It only remains to say a few words as to the subsequent history of Constance. Of the part it played during the Thirty Years' War, it will be best to speak in the chapter devoted to that subject.

In the war of the Spanish Succession, and in the Seven Years' War, Constance had to bear, like its neighbours, the burden of military occupation, but otherwise it did not suffer greatly from the military movements of the eighteenth century. Perhaps the most important event of the century to Constance, was the visit paid to it in 1777, by the young Emperor Joseph II. At that time the population had to a great extent died out, grass grew in the streets, and many of the inhabitants were so poor that they depended to a great extent for their subsistence upon the alms which were distributed at the various monasteries and religious houses, of which there were no less than forty-three in the decayed city.

The imperial radical-reformer came with his head and heart full of schemes to promote the happiness of his subjects, and he was not yet heart-broken by the deadly Conservative opposition, on which all his efforts were destined to be shipwrecked. He himself says that he found Constance a "neglected nest of priests" (verwahrlostes Pfaffennest).

As a first step to improvement, he suppressed several of the religious houses, among others the famous monastery of the Dominicans, now the Insel

Hotel.   A happy chance favoured his beneficent plans
for supplying what the city most needed, some trade
and manufacturing industry, without which it was impossible for it to rise from its decadence.

One hundred years ago, the Republic of Geneva
had an extremely aristocratic constitution from which
the immense majority of the inhabitants were entirely
shut out.   This unnatural state of things, especially
unnatural in a " Republic," led, as in old Rome, to
constant struggles between the Patricians who had the
power, and the Plebeians who had not.   In 1782, in
consequence of one of these troubles, the aristocratic
faction overwhelmed their radical rivals, and condemned
to exile nineteen of their leaders.   This led to a very
remarkable exodus : the friends of the exiled leaders
determined upon a bold experiment in industrial
colonisation.

To the number of some thousands, they emigrated
to the neighbourhood of Waterford, in Ireland, where
they founded the settlement of New Geneva, which
they hoped to make the rival of the parent city in the
valuable industries of watchmaking and the manufacture of jewelry.   The hopes of the settlers were
bitterly disappointed—why, it would be very interesting
to know—and they gladly accepted the offer of an
asylum in Constance, made to them by the enlightened
and philanthropic emperor.   To the 900 Genevese who
accepted his offer, was assigned the old Dominican
cloister, which they soon converted into a busy workshop, with the exception of the " winter-refectorium,'
which they turned into a Calvinistic church, presided
over by the eloquent Isaiah Gasc.

Among the names of these settlers is that of "Ami
Melly,"—no doubt an ancestor or relative of Mr. George
Melly, late M.P. for Stoke-upon-Trent,—and Benedict

Dufour, a young watchmaker, To the latter, on the 7th October, 1787, was born a son, who was named Henry, and was destined to become a great general, and hardly less famous for the wonderful map of Switzerland, which was carried out under his directions, and which cost him thirty years of unceasing toil, than for his ardent patriotism and military skill, by which, as generalissimo of the Swiss army, he in masterly fashion subdued the dangerous insurrection of the Sonderbund in 1847 and 1848.

The topmost summit of the Swiss Alps, the highest peak of Monte Rosa, bears the name of "Dufour-Spitz," as a sign of the gratitude of the Confederation to her foremost soldier and citizen, and it is only five years ago (1875) that all Switzerland was plunged into mourning by the death of this her greatest son.

There is no longer much trace left of the Genevese colony in. Constance. Many of the settlers doubtless returned to their mother city, where the rushing Rhone escapes from Lac Leman ; those that remained served as a good leaven, and the present comparative prosperity of Constance is partially, and indirectly, traceable to them. The wars of the French Revolution brought trouble to Constance, and, after many vicissitudes, the peace of Presburg assigned the ancient city to the Grand-Duchy of Baden. At that time the population had sunk to 4,000. In consequence of the development of the railway system, of which, from its position, Constance has become an important centre, Constance has, in recent years, made great strides forward, at least for a city of the old world, and its inhabitants now number about 10,000, probably at least as many as, the old chroniclers notwithstanding, were ever to be found living within its walls.

CHAPTER XVIII.

J. H. VON WESSENBERG.

> " Not vainly did old poets tell,
>   Nor vainly did old genius paint,
>   God's great and crowning miracle,
>   The hero and the saint.
> " For even in a faithless age
>   Can we our sainted ones discern,
>   And feel, while with them on the way,
>   Our hearts within us burn."
>
> —WHITTIER'S *Channing.*

CONSTANCE is emphatically the city of Huss. At every turn the traveller comes upon mementoes of the Bohemian martyr. But when you come to the end of the Huss Strasse you enter the Wessenberg Strasse, and soon you come to the Wessenberg Institute and the Wessenberg Gallery of Paintings; and if you spend the winter in Constance, you will probably attend a course of lectures also named after Wessenberg. The books I am now using in the preparation of this work are almost all from the Wessenberg Library. Who, then, was this man who has so effectually stamped his personality upon the city of

Constance, and secured for himself at any rate a local immortality?

Ignaz Heinrich Freiherr von Wessenberg was born on the 4th November, 1774, of a family for many generations distinguished by high virtues. His father was a conscientious statesman, his mother a woman of tender piety. Like Channing, whom he greatly resembled, and who was born only six years after him, he was "one of heaven's aborigines." All his letters show a youth highly endowed with mental, moral, and spiritual qualities, with a mind ever seeking more knowledge, and a heart always demanding and spending more love. His education was conducted in the ancestral castle of his father, on the right bank of the Rhine, in Baden. With a profound sense of religion, his parents impressed upon him the supreme importance of unwearying zeal in carrying out the duties of his calling, and self-sacrificing benevolence towards his fellow-men. An eye-witness mentions that it was a rule of the family never to miss the daily celebration of the mass.

After studying at Augsburg, and subsequently at Dillingen, where he came under the influence of that very saintly man, Professor, subsequently Bishop, Sailer, he spent several years in foreign travel. His rank and engaging personal qualities gave him access to the highest circles of society, and of all these advantages he availed himself to the full, while at the same time pursuing a vigorous course of study. From his youth up he had deliberately chosen the, to him, sacred calling of a priest, and to qualify himself for this position he felt that he could not possibly extend the range of his knowledge too widely. Upon one occasion, early in the present century, when visiting Vienna with a like-minded brother, they excited much interest in the mind of a successful minister and diplomatist. His feelings towards them were those of pity and commiseration. Poor young men, leading lives so simple and of such severe study! He assured them that they made a mistake, and it was quite unnecessary. "I never did it, and I have become a minister of state." When they told him that "they had not the slightest desire to become ministers of state, but that they did desire thoroughly to qualify themselves for their future vocation," he must have felt on what a different plane they were from that which he occupied. Wessenberg was made a sub-deacon and a member of the Cathedral-Chapter of Constance and Augsburg in 1801, and the notices in his letters and journals of the state of society in the old city when he first came to reside there, are interesting and curious. With quiet irony he mentions a leading professor whose principal claim to distinction lay in a series of essays against any relaxation of the celibacy of the clergy, but who himself had been married three times! Shortly after coming to Constance, the then Prince-Primate, Charles Theodore of Dalberg, appointed him his general-vicar and spiritual "Regierungs-President" for the bishopric of Constance.

When we remember that at this time the bishopric of Constance included a great part of Würtemberg, Baden, Bavaria, the Tyrol, and Switzerland, and possessed at the time of its greatest prosperity 350 cloisters, 1,760 parishes, and 17,000 priests and members of religious orders, we shall understand that young Wessenberg, anxious to do his duty and to reform all abuses, must have had his hands very full. The Bishop of Constance, in addition to his spiritual jurisdiction, ruled as temporal prince a territory of more than 400 square miles, with a population of more than 50,000 inhabitants. Napoleon put an end to Dalberg's temporal power in 1802, The young general-vicar showed himself so unwearied in the fulfilment of his onerous duties, and effected so many and such valuable reforms, that Dalberg, in the prospect of death, named him his coadjutor and successor. Had Wessenberg been an ambitious man, or had he been willing to yield a hair's breadth to the wishes of Rome, in spite of the disapproval of his conscience, he would, there is little doubt, have become successively Bishop of Constance, Archbishop of Freiburg, and Cardinal. But, though an earnest and zealous Catholic, Wessenberg detested the grasping spirit of the Roman Curiæ, and his whole life was a ceaseless struggle with the papacy. Therefore, though almost worshipped by the people of his diocese, and respected and supported by his sovereign the Grand-Duke of Baden, he was followed all his life with constant suspicion, misrepresentation, and persecution on the part of the Roman or ultramontane party, and after ruling the diocese with zeal and devotion as " Bisthums-verweser "—bishopric-administrator—for nearly thirty years, he passed the remainder of his long life, and died at last, as a simple canon.

I do not think my readers will grudge a few pages to the record of this beautiful life of ceaseless activity and self-devotion, which only terminated in 1860, after more than sixty years had been spent in Constance.

When Wessenberg entered upon his duties in Constance, he found much ignorance and indifference among the clergy. To remedy this and to inspire them with a new spirit, he felt to be his first duty. To this end he made great changes in the seminary at Meersburg. For many years the students counted upon a weekly visit at any rate from him, and however stormy the lake, his little barque was always to be seen rounding the promontory of the Loretto-wald at the appointed time. He was of opinion that a priest should not merely be thoroughly instructed in theology, church history, and the exposition of the Holy Scriptures, but in philosophy and natural science. He established reading societies among the clergy, so that they might see all the new books and keep themselves abreast of modern culture, and arranged for periodical conferences at which papers could be read upon any subjects relating to their calling, to be followed by a perfectly free discussion. He himself prepared an admirable paper upon the " Necessity, use, and most profitable arrangement of these conferences," and undertook the onerous and wearisome task of carefully reading through and criticising all papers sent in for the conferences in his diocese.

While striving after the intellectual development of his clergy, Wessenberg was even more concerned as to their moral growth, constantly reminding them that they were intended to be " the salt of the earth," and that it was their duty " in the midst of enervating luxury to give an example of abstemiousness and severe self-denial; as against narrow egotism, of beneficence and the renunciation of their own advantage ; and among the bewildering sophistries of sensuality, of the unadulterated pure truth of the mind, conversation, and conduct of the gospel." The reverent celebration of public worship received his earnest attention, and in March, 1809, he issued an order for the conduct of public worship, which is still followed ; and in order to make it possible for the public to take an active part in public worship, he soon afterwards published a Diocesan Book of Devotion with

Hymn Book, which immediately became a favourite among the Catholic population of Baden, and still maintains its place there. He also ordered, and I believe his example in this respect has since been universally followed in Catholic Germany, that throughout the whole of public worship, except alone the celebration of the Mass, no language but German should·be used. He condemned and did his utmost to suppress alleged miracles, exorcisms, and other superstitious developments, which at all times have a tendency to show themselves in the Catholic Church, and which of late have been so greatly fostered by an ignorant or interested priesthood.

The views and proceedings of Wessenberg, though they endeared him to all right-thinking men, were not likely to gain the approval of the Vatican. The Roman Curiæ were specially angry with him because of the great exertions he had made to induce the cantonal authorities in Lucerne—then a part of the diocese of Constance—to substitute a vigorous seminary for the education of priests, for a decayed monastery. They charged him with "disgracefully undermining the rights of the church, and treading under foot her power," and subsequently demanded his dismissal from the Prince-Primate in a brief of the 2nd November, 1814, absolutely commanding him "without delay to dismiss the notorious Wessenberg, as incontrovertible proofs were to hand of his erroneous teaching, his evil conduct, and his audacious opposition to the Chair of St. Peter, so that His Holiness could not longer endure him without great offence to the faithful, and without burdening his own conscience."

Dalberg manfully defended the "notorious man," and thought it consistent with his respect for the papal chair not even to mention the receipt of this brief— either to him or to the Cathedral-Chapter.

When Prince-Primate Dalberg died on the 10th February, 1817, the authorities at Rome refused to confirm his nomination of Wessenberg as his successor. Nothing remained for the Cathedral-Chapel to do but to proceed to elect a " Bisthums-verweser " (an administrator of the bishopric). Of course they chose Wessenberg, a choice which was immediately ratified by the sovereign of Baden. The Vatican refused however to sanction the election, and returned the insulting message to the Cathedral-Chapter that they must choose a " worthier and fitter man."

When the election of Wessenberg as " Bisthums-verweser " was rejected by the Curiæ, the Cathedral-Chapter followed the example of the late Prince-Primate, and bravely defended him.

The Pope then addressed a most flattering letter to the Grand-Duke Charles of Baden in which he begged his royal highness to assist him in shutting out Wes-senberg and securing the election of another, assuring him that it was not merely the well-being of the Catholic Church that was at stake, but also the well-being and the profit of the Grand-Duke's subjects, and even of his whole country. " What credit among the faithful," asks the Pope, " can a man maintain whom all good men abhor, whom they despise, and about whom they have certain and public proofs that he has not our approval ? In him, public tranquillity can so little find a support, that it is greatly to be feared that the minds of the Catholic population may be so excited by any protection extended to him, as to lead to a disturbance of the public peace."

The Grand-Duke of Baden had reason to hold

quite other opinions as to this "universally abhorred and despised man," and his reply to the letter of His Holiness was a very emphatic snub. Wessenberg, however, felt it due to himself and to the Cathedral-Chapter of Constance, to repair to Rome, there to answer all charges that could be brought against him. Of this step the grand-ducal government highly approved, charging the Curiæ to receive him with the respect due to so important a State, the population of which was to so large an extent Catholic.

It was well for Wessenberg that times and manners had greatly changed since—almost exactly 400 years before—Huss had repaired to Constance on a similar errand.

He reached Rome on the 18th July, 1817. How strange must have been the feelings of so loyal a Catholic as Wessenberg, thus for the first time approaching the Eternal City, his heart full of reverence for the authority of the church, yet feeling his conscience a higher law before which in the last resort everything must yield.

In spite of the powerful protection of the Baden government, he was received most ungraciously, The Pope, in a letter written by his secretary, Consalvi, expresses his extreme astonishment and sorrow that Wessenberg should continue to call himself Vicar to the Cathedral-Chapter, and to administer the bishopric in spite of the papal brief which rejected him, and then proceeds to charge Wessenberg with erroneous teaching, appending a long list of proofs. Among these are some which I think will not be without interest to English readers, even now, when more than two generations have passed away.

For instance, Wessenberg was charged with having

expressed a favourable opinion on a sermon, delivered by the ex-monk Hekelsmüller, and declared it consistent with the pure and wholesome teaching of the Gospel, although the sermon condemned the worship of the saints, pilgrimages, and the authority of the pope, and held the rosary up to ridicule.

Many of the writings circulated with his sanction among his clergy were severely condemned, especially a paper on the " German Church," and one entitled, " Grounds of Consolation for Mothers whose Children die without Baptism." He was also sharply blamed as having given great offence to all faithful souls in the administration of the bishopric, particularly in having curtailed the number of festivals to be observed, in having " done away with the regulations ordering only certain kinds of food to be eaten on Saturdays ; in having forbidden his clergy to apply to the Holy See for indulgences, privileged altars, &c., and for having attacked the exemptions and other just privileges of the religious orders." The Pope was specially displeased with him for the introduction of the vulgar tongue and other "vexatious abuses," into the liturgy and the conduct of public worship. His " contumacious be- haviour," the Pope alleged had been further shown by his relieving many monks and nuns from their religious vows, especially from that of chastity, and this in spite of many censures administered to him upon the subject, and especially by his continuing to act as general-vicar to the Cathedral-Chapter in defiance of the Pope's brief rejecting him.

To these charges Wessenberg sent an elaborate reply, the essence of which was that he was willing to make any personal sacrifice to satisfy the Holy See consistent with his duty to the clergy of the bishopric of Constance, to his government, and to the whole of Germany.

A reconciliation between the two parties was evidently impossible. So Wessenberg remained for the remainder of his long life a loyal Catholic, but a determined foe of the Ultramontane party.

He, however, showed his noble disinterestedness when, in 1822, it was decided ·to constitute Freiburg, in Baden, an archbishopric, and he was almost unanimously elected by the local ecclesiastical authorities to receive the high honour. His sovereign, the Grand-Duke Louis, informed him of his election in a letter which expressed the great satisfaction his Royal Highness felt at the choice. Wessenberg, however, now showed that they were no idle words, when he said that he was willing to make any personal sacrifice for the good of the church. He represented to the Grand-Duke that the extreme dislike the Vatican had to his person, and especially to his administration of the See of Constance, would probably only be increased by his accepting the archbishopric, and the peace of the church in Germany be thereby disturbed. He therefore respectfully and gratefully declined the election. Seldom has *nolo episcopari* been more worthily spoken.

I believe my readers will not blame me for translating a few passages from his farewell address to the clergy of the diocese over which he had presided for twenty-six years :—

"Far be from me the fancy that in my important post, in accordance with the requirements of the Apostle, I have really become all things to all men, and far be from all of us the thought that we have originated any good thing but what Christ has worked through us.

"Even if we succeeded in complying to the full with all the requirements of Christ, we should still remain unprofitable servants.

"What we are in God's eyes, that alone are we worth, and none of us more. He that glorieth, therefore, let him glory in the Lord. Meanwhile my conscience bears me witness that I have never sought any private interest in all the labours and conflicts of these many years, but always, as far as my limited powers and views would permit, the honour of Christ and the fruitful participation of His flock in the salvation of God.

"I feel also that I can call you all to witness, beloved fellow-servants of Christ, before Him who is judge of us all, whether I have not always shown that to give was more blessed than to receive; whether I have ever refused to make any sacrifice that the good of the brethren demanded; whether I have ever laid any other foundation than that laid by Christ the Crucified; whether your faithfulness in your calling and the good fruits of your activity have not ever been my highest joy and my crown of rejoicing? Whether any of you suffered in any way without my participating in your sorrow? Whether I have not unceasingly laboured that you all and the flocks committed to your charge might be like-minded, having the same love, being of one accord and one mind in Christ? . . . .

"Unforgetable are the love and the trust which under all circumstances you have constantly shown towards me. When my zeal and the earnestness of some of my warnings and admonitions displeased men, I was always strengthened by the consoling hope that He who sees our motives would not reject them. Now that with joyful heart I praise his infinite goodness for the increase that came of my, or much rather of your sowing, beloved brethren, I praise him none the less with a deeply humbled heart who led me through the fiery trial of misconception and unjust condemnation, by which the soul is purified and ennobled, while the applause of the world often only stains and ruins it. Who is worthy to be called a Christian who would not gladly suffer that Christ might be glorified? With the deepest prayers for you all and for your flocks, as members of the household of God, I retire from the position of shepherd until now entrusted to me. Always and everywhere these desires to serve you will animate me. In a cheerful consciousness of having faithfully discharged the duties of my office, with the apostle I commend you to God and to the word of His grace; to Him who has the power to lead you on unto perfection, and to grant you the inheritance of the saints in light.

"May all your names appear in the book of life! My hope is stedfast on your behalf, my brothers and friends, that you will show yourselves to be men in understanding, with the unspoiled spirit of children, watchful in your care of your flocks, immoveable in the faith, and full of love in all that you do.

"Your calling stands clearly before your souls; constantly, not alone

by your words, but by your lives, to fight against everything that is
evil in man, and you will always proclaim the kingdom of God with
success, because in your own hearts it is fruitful in faith, hope, and
love.

"You will not fail to see the finger of God visible in the signs of
the times that proclaim so clearly and distinctly that the letter killeth
unless the spirit of God gives it life; that with the sham righteousness of the Pharisee no one can enter the kingdom of God; that
God rejects all worship but that which is in spirit and in truth; that
only a spiritual second birth of mind and heart can save men
from ruin and make them children of God, and that it is just this
that condemns them, that after the light has appeared in the world
they love darkness more than the light."

He then affectionately commends to them their new
archbishop, and concludes :—

"May Christ dwell in us constantly!   May we entirely live to
Him!   May we always, walking in his love, be one body with Him!
Unweakened by all outward changes, may the holy bond continue
between us—'We in Christ and Christ in us.'

"The administrator of the Bishopric,

"IGNAZ HEINRICH FREIHERR VON WESSENBERG.

"Constance, 21st October, 1827."

Had he lived to witness the declaration of the
dogma of papal infallibility, it is humanly certain that
he would have thrown himself heart and soul into the
Old Catholic movement.

In addition to his strictly ecclesiastical duties, he
took a very active part in the proceedings of the
Representative Chambers of Baden, of which he was
originally a member *ex officio*, and later by election,
from 1819 to 1833.   In addition to participation in the
general debates, he brought forward motions on the
following subjects :—"On the pressing religious and
moral wants of the Catholic part of Baden."   "For
the establishment of an institution for the deaf and
dumb and the blind."   "The exemption of theological

students from military service." "The improvement of the national school system." "The establishment of technical schools." "The support by the State of old sick and reduced Protestant clergymen." "The erection of a seminary for Protestant teachers." "The abolition of lotteries and gaming tables." "The establishment of a Polytechnic School in Freiburg." "The establishment of a Seminary for Protestant pastors." "The Freedom of the Press." "The Responsibility of Ministers."

In merely reading over the list, the intelligent reader will realise the many-sidedness and liberal tone of Wessenberg's mind, as well as his incessant activity in promoting the well-being of his country. His speeches in favour of these various motions were characterised by the energy and warmth of heart which he threw into everything. In the course of the speech in which he brought forward his motion for the establishment of an asylum for the blind, he used the words :— " Recognise, feel the high value of the light of the eye, and then show the Giver thy gratitude for it, by holding out thy hand to thy brother to whom has been denied this inestimable gift. It is this that is the high merit of human society, that the misery of one becomes the object of the compassion and of the active sympathy of all."

He had the satisfaction not only to see his motion carried, but for many years to watch the successful and beneficent working both of the State Institution for the Blind and that for the Deaf and Dumb, the latter of which the reader will remember occupies what was once the Bishop's Palace at Meersburg.

Wessenberg's ideal was that of Dr. Arnold—a Christian Commonwealth—and to him his duties in the Chamber were just as sacred as those at the

Altar. The concluding stanza of a poem upon the funeral of a like-minded political friend runs as follows :—

> "O gib uns für das Wahre
> Und Rechte tiefen Sinn
> Das uns sich offenbare
> Schon deines Reichs Beginn."

"Oh give us such deep feeling for the true and right that the beginning of Thy kingdom may now already reveal itself to us."

Wessenberg's time would, one would have supposed, have been more than occupied by the incessant duties of a priest, of the administrator of a bishopric, and by his active political life. When, superadded to all these, we find carefully thought out works in many departments of human knowledge, we are as much puzzled by his versatile and amazing activity as we are by that of a Gladstone. I will not weary the reader by attempting to give a full list of his writings. They include three tragedies respectively on " Padilla, or the Last Fight for Freedom in Castille," " Christopher Columbus," and " Kaiser Frederick II., of Hohenstaufen ;" an epic poem on " Fénelon," whose character his own greatly resembled ; and, in all, seven volumes of epic and lyrical poems, which have run through many editions in Germany.

Among his prose writings may be mentioned—

" Christian Reflections in preparation for the Festival of the Lord's Resurrection."—*Constance*, 1827.

" The Power of Christianity in Hallowing the Heart and Conversation."—*Constance*, 1835.

" God and the World."—Two Parts. *Heidelberg*, 1857.

" Reflections on the most Important Events in the Development of Mankind."—*Aarau*, 1835.

" On the Moral Influence of the Theatre."—1825.

"On the Elementary Education of the People in the Eighteenth Century."—*Zürich*, 1814, and reprinted with additions—*Constance*, 1835.

"On the Education of the Artisan Classes generally, and in the Grand-Duchy of Baden in particular." —*Constance*, 1835.

"On Enthusiasm,"—*Heilbronn*, 1835.

"The Spirit of the Age."—*Zürich*, 1801.

"The Principal Epochs in the World's History before the Birth of Christ."—*Zürich*, 1804.

"Popular Life in Athens in the Age of Pericles." —*Zürich*, 1821.

"The Great Church Councils of the Fifteenth and Sixteenth Centuries."—Four volumes, *Constance*, 1840.

"The German Church, a Proposal for its New Foundation and Arrangement."—1815 (no place of publication mentioned).

Wessenberg had a great taste for art, and, in the course of his long life, made a very valuable collection of pictures, of his disposition of which I will speak later.

From his more serious studies he contrived to snatch time enough to publish—"Christian Pictures (Die christlichen Bilder)."—Two volumes, *Constance*, 1826, 1827—in which he treats at length of the history of Christian art, and illustrates it by a criticism of all the master-pieces of religious painting.

From early youth to extreme old age, through all his works, poetry and prose, one increasing purpose runs—to make men better and happier; to serve God by serving his fellow-men; as he himself has well expressed through the mouth of the great Hohenstaufen, in his national drama of Frederick II. :—

"O Gott so lang dein Odem mich belebt,
Streb ich auf's Ziel, wornach ich stets gestrebt

Auf die Entscheidung zielet all mein Trachten
Ob's endlich tagen soll, ob ewig nachten."

" Oh God! while thy breath quickens me,
I seek the goal which I have ever sought :
All my endeavour is to resolve the question
Whether the day at last shall dawn, or night remain for ever."*

I shall allow myself to translate a few passages from Wessenberg's writings, the better to illustrate the character of the man. The reader will often think that he is listening not to a Roman Catholic prelate, but to the Unitarian Channing, or the Quaker William Penn.

"In nothing is self-deception more dangerous than in the great concern of religion. The name of Christ without the spirit and the works of Christ is but as sounding brass. If any one calls himself a Christian and lives the life of an unbeliever, his name of Christian only serves to make the blasphemy of his walk and conversation the more culpable. Suppose, even, that he succeed in deceiving the whole world, how will this serve him in the end? for it is impossible for him to deceive the all-seeing Judge of evil and of good. How can any appearance of piety and righteousness help us before God if our deeds and our disposition accuse us to him? How can we expect that God will draw near to us with his blessing-giving grace if we by our conduct draw away from him? "— " Christliche Betrachtung," No. 14.

" By fasting is to be understood abstinence—the breaking off of sensual indulgence. But this abstinence—this breaking off—has only then any value before God when it is our intention by it to make ourselves stronger for the fight of virtue, and to render more easy to us the victory over our lusts. But just for this very reason, because the value of fasting consists alone in strengthening the spirit against sensuous temptations, God rejects all fasting by which our sensual nature is not tamed, by which our will is not practised in self-denial, by which our spirit does not gain power and readiness to withstand sensual temptations. Therefore Jesus rejects all fasting

* I have to apologize to my readers for my dismally prosaic translations of German poetry; all who have any knowledge of German will easily make better ones for themselves.

that has for its object to appear before men pious and God-fearing. Then only will thy fasting be agreeable to God when thy heart is free from sin and pure and open 'to all good influences. It is sheer hypocrisy, on the other hand, outwardly to fast while inwardly cherishing any sinful disposition. True fasting must show itself by its fruits, by changing hate into love, discord into peace, anger into gentleness, harshness into kindness, imperiousness into meekness, luxurious indulgence into temperance, and the employment of what is thereby spared, in the relief of those in want and in clothing the naked.

* * * * * * *

" Let us so fast that, with a good conscience before the Father who seeth in secret we may say,—We were in the habit of slandering and backbiting our neighbour, but we do it no longer. There were among us many fault-finders; now every one thinks the other better than himself, and we reprove the erring brother with humility when alone with him. We were in the habit when annoyed of using oaths; but we have overcome this habit. We were formerly given to excess: now we enjoy the gifts of God with thankfulness to the Giver and with moderation. Formerly we placed a silly confidence in super-stitious things; but this we have now exchanged for a child-like trust in the wise, fatherly goodness of our God. Formerly we were only concerned about ways and means to make ourselves rich; now we have restored what we formerly obtained by fraud or sharp practice, and so employ what substance we have that our needy brethren may have a share therein, and praise God for our bounty. Formerly the sight of our neighbour's prosperity excited envy in our breasts, and his suffering and misery we treated with callous indif- ference; now we rejoice with those that do rejoice and mourn with those who mourn, and heartfelt is our sympathy with one another in sorrow and in joy. The peace of our marriages was formerly disturbed by jealousy, unchastity, and unfaithfulness: from this time forth there shall be no more of all this; but husbands and wives shall be according to Christ's command—one body and one soul."

* * * * * * *

Under the heading " How a Christian should regard suffering" he writes :—

" The apparent discords in creation, the many hardships that are inextricably bound up with the earthly destinies of our race, become all clear to us when we, as childlike, willing scholars, recognise in them the fatherly, warning voice of God, that calls us to the discharge of our duties from lukewarmness and indifference, and to awake from the deadly sleep of sinful habits, from lacklove indifference to the wants of our fellow-men, and from all those beguiling dreams with which the vain spirit of the world chases from our hearts the thought of a better life. Then, instead of complaining of them, we recognise the troubles and difficulties of this life as messengers from God to bring us nearer to his everlasting kingdom. The great of the earth should learn in the school of misfortune to turn to that God whom they cannot forget and remain unpunished. Humbler men will feel themselves impelled by the sufferings of the present time to strive after the enduring inheritance which the Lord has promised to those who love him, and for his sake obey those who are set over them. The oppressed Christian will see in his enemies protecting spirits for his tottering innocence, and ministers of Providence for the trial of his virtue, and he will answer hate with love. According to the expression of the apostle, he will look forward with confidence to being raised up in due time, as the rich man may look forward with trembling to a coming humiliation. But even he, in order that he may not pass away like a flower of the field, will surely resolve, by beneficent support of his starving brother, to enrich himself with good works. In the same way the luxurious and effeminate man may be held back from sin by want and bodily suffering in order that he may devote the rest of his earthly life, not to the lusts of the flesh, but to the will of God, which alone can satisfy a heart created alone for him. As gold is purified from all dross only by fire, so suffering cleanses our souls and renders them more open to virtue and more pleasing to God. We who, with such levity, are often, in thought, word, and deed, unfaithful to the eternally faithful friend of men—Jesus Christ—need disappointments and adversity to bring us to Golgotha, there in deepest contrition and with tears of penitence to embrace the cross on which the Son of God offered himself as a sacrifice that not one of us might be lost."— " Die Kraft des Christenthums" ("The Power of Christianity.")

The public life and the views of Wessenberg drew down upon him, as we have seen, determined opposition and bitter persecution ; but no opponent ever ventured to say a word against his private life. It was manifest to all men that it was the life of a saint— the path of the just, shining more and more unto the perfect day. His was an eminently happy life. There

Q

was no department of human thought, feeling, or activity that was not full of interest for him ; and, having no family of his own, he felt that every man, woman, and child in his diocese were members of his family.

He was more disposed to be a disciple of the Porch than of the Garden. In his work " God and the World," he says :—

"The conscience of every one not sunk to the level of the beasts (nicht ganz verthierten), tells him that sensuous enjoyment is not the highest good of man, and experience confirms this truth." And in another place :—"Without pain, real joy would be almost an impossibility to men ; but without joy, we should want one of the most powerful aids both to the development of bodily health and of spiritual power and activity."

His stoicism was the tender loving philosophy of a Plutarch or a Marcus Aurelius ; or rather, it was the doctrine of the Porch brightened and glorified by the light of the cross, which changes proud indifference to suffering into deepest sympathy, and for the callous insensibility of the philosopher gives us the resignation and self-sacrifice of the saint.

His own habits were exceedingly simple. Let any visitor, after inspecting the choice pictures which he collected, and which now form the Wessenberg Gallery at Constance, ask to be shown his private room, which served at once for sleeping room and study, and which remains just as he left it. It contains a deal table, a camp bedstead, also of deal, a large wooden chair without cushions, a crucifix, and a few family portraits ; this is all. He only took one frugal meal daily, and in the evening, as long as he was in health, contented himself with a little fruit, a piece of bread, and a glass of wine. If he had not lived thus simply, he would not have possessed the necessary means for his inexhaustible charity. He was, however, very fond of drawing around him a select social circle, in which his cheerfulness and innocent mirth were conspicuous,

True happiness, he recognised, could only be found in the idea of perfection—in God.

"The one good that can give and does give to man full satisfaction, is spiritual moral perfection, or, what is the same thing, becoming like God: in other words an agreement and union with God in heart and life.

"Man only attains to his highest good through the love of God, of which every real and true affection is an outflowing and reflexion. It is not what a man has that makes him happy, but what he is, and the highest good to which he can possibly attain is to become like God. He who trusts in God is never forsaken or alone; he whose will is conformed to the divine will, always stands upon a rock."

Those who witnessed his celebrations of the mass, say, that there was a radiance and glow upon his face while engaged in those—to him—sacred offices.

He was just as particular in his private devotions. When his strength was gone, in his last illness, he had the morning and evening prayers daily read to him, which he silently followed with the most touching devotion.

Of his private benevolence I cannot do better than allow Priest Kotz to speak, in the funeral sermon he delivered above Wessenberg's grave.

"The poor, the needy, and the suffering, of all conditions and classes, from far and near, but especially those of our city, reverenced in him their warmest friend and benefactor. Who shall estimate their number, much less recall their names, during more than sixty years?

And he gave not only small but important sums, so that his left hand did not know what his right hand had done. He consistently acted upon the principle 'What ye do unto the least of these my brethren, ye do it unto me.'"

We have seen how active he was in the establishment

of asylums for the blind and the deaf and dumb in the Grand-Duchy of Baden. In 1833, at his suggestion, the members of the Upper Chamber gave the whole of their allowance to these two asylums, so that the interest of the capital sum might be applied to the purchase of tools, instruments, and materials for work, for pupils leaving those institutions. But, if all the inhabitants of Constance belonged to his family, he had a more intimate circle still, for whom he cherished a peculiar affection. This circle consisted of morally neglected and orphan girls. In August, 1879, when walking the short half-mile from the city of Constance to our lodgings at Kreuzlingen, taking a different road from the usual one, I came upon a large house surrounded by a good-sized garden, then glorious with roses of many colours and other summer flowers. Noticing a number of young girls about the place, I made inquiries, and learned that it was the "Wessenberg Rettungshaus." The name of Wessenberg was then quite strange to me, but the "housemother" gave me permission to distribute Gospels and *Deutsche Arbeiter* among the inmates, and told me it was open to both Protestants and Catholics. The founder, she said, by a special clause in his will, forbade that the management should ever come into the hands of the Jesuits. The institution now contains thirty-six girls. This asylum he established out of his private means, and during life supported it, and it was one of his greatest pleasures to visit it and see how the inmates were progressing. When about to die its future well-being was very near his heart, and he requested his sovereign, the Grand-Duke of · Baden, to purchase for 20,000 florins his picture-gallery, to be used for the public, and with this sum he endowed the institution. With this exception I believe, the city of his love became his heir.

One thing, and one thing only, he felt that he had to do before he died. He had often observed how the Jesuits reported death-bed recantations from those who during their life-time had esteemed it their duty to oppose the papacy. To prevent anything of this kind, when, in his eighty-sixth year, he felt the touch of mortal weakness, he summoned his most intimate friends around his bed, and assured them that he died in the principles in which he had lived.

As long as consciousness remained he discoursed with his friends upon the mysteries of life, of death, of judgment, and of the world to come. The last rays of the setting sun were lighting up the cathedral towers, opposite to his window, on the 9th of August, 1860, as he smiled farewell to those around him, and then closed his eyes for ever.

The solemn bells of the Münster soon told the inhabitants of Constance of the loss they had sustained.

> "Where is the victory of the grave?
> What dust upon the Spirit lies?
> God keeps the sacred life He gave,
> The Prophet never dies."

CHAPTER XIX.

CONSTANCE IN SUMMER.

My experience of Constance in summer was limited to a few days, while our winter stay at Kreuzlingen extended from December to May.

Constance is only too well supplied with hotels. In addition to a number of commercial inns, the old Dominican convent, of which so much mention has been made in connection with the history of Huss, and also with that of General Dufour, has been in recent times converted into a magnificent and luxurious hotel, named—from the island upon which it stands, and which is laid out in beautiful grounds—the Insel Hotel.

Visitors of an economical turn will find first-class accommodation at a cheaper rate at the comfortable Hotel Halm, close to the station.

Constance by no means escaped the speculative mania which wrought such dreadful ruin throughout Germany, when, after the triumphant war with France, every one seemed to act on the belief that he had the hard-won milliards in his pocket.

Constance was again to become a "Weltstadt," and as if to accommodate such an influx of visitors as might be expected if another council were to be held there, a splendid palace was run up on the German shore of the lake near Petershausen, with I know not how many entertaining and sleeping-rooms, which was called the "Constanzer-hof." This huge hotel has proved a total failure, and besides involving many of the early shareholders in ruin, is still a great drain upon the ratepayers, who are finding out with reference to their beautiful city, the truth of the French proverb, "Il faut souffrir pour être beau."

If the visitor have very simple tastes he cannot do better than follow our example, and drive or walk for about half a mile from the railway station, across the frontier, into Switzerland. Here, stretching along the shore of the lake, is the clean and well-built town of Kreuzlingen, consisting principally of handsome villa residences on either side of the high road, each standing in a good-sized garden, which in summer is gay with many-coloured flowers. The road for the whole distance from Constance to the abbey-buildings of Kreuzlingen is planted with trees, boulevard-fashion, and, as there are no high walls or other obstructions, the eye ranges at will over the blue waters of the lake, or over the highly cultivated hilly slopes of Thurgau, where the monotony of the culture of corn and wine is relieved by innumerable fruit-trees. We chose the "Pension Helvetia," about half-way between Constance and the Abbey of Kreuzlingen. The hotel is pleasantly situated in a large garden, and a grove of fine trees close beside it affords a delicious shade to visitors in the heat of summer, while a refreshing breeze can usually be counted upon from the lake. The hostelry, the lower story of which is about 200 years old, is not without a history.

Upon its site, and the ground around, stood the old Abbey of Kreuzlingen, founded about the year 1125, by Bishop Ulrich of Constance, at the very commencement of the feud between the Guelphs and Ghibellines. During the Swedish siege of Constance, in the Thirty Years' War, the old buildings were burned down, and, when peace was re-established, the monks very wisely decided upon a site upon higher ground, about as far again from Constance, for the new abbey. Far and wide around, stretching down to the lake, were vineyards belonging to the monks, and in order to create a ready retail market for their wine, the abbot caused what was then called the " Schöpfhaus " (*schöpfen*—to draw water) to be built, where for several generations thirsty travellers were able to get draughts, long and deep, of the red wine of the lake-shore, at what we should now think an astonishingly cheap rate.

"Other times, other manners!"—the monks are gone, and a seminary for the teachers of Thurgau occupies their deserted halls ; but the Schöpfhaus, now Hotel Helvetia, still stands, although its ample grounds, once reaching down to the lake-side, have been greatly curtailed, and the groves that adorned them destroyed, by two lines of railway which here enter Constance. Here visitors are entertained in the summer months at the rate of five francs per diem, while even lower terms are accepted in the winter.

Mine host of the Hotel Helvetia, having been advised of our coming, sent down a carriage for ourselves and a cart for our luggage—neither of which ever appeared in the bill. Heavy thunderstorms had cleared the air, and relieved the oppressive heat of the few previous days ; and, satisfied as we had been with our German inn at Ueberlingen, the exquisite cleanliness of a Swiss household was nevertheless an

agreeable change to us. The view from our room, which
looked away from the lake, was shut in by the high
ground of Thurgau and the more distant Hegau.
The most conspicuous object in the near distance was
the modern castle of Kastell, in a most commanding
position on the edge of a high wooded ridge, and with
lofty towers and battlements, without which we
English think the designation " castle" inaccurate.
Although the present building is modern, the ruins of
the old castle still remain. It was built by Gebhart, of
Zähringen, far back in the middle ages, and was
destroyed in 1128 by the Bishop of Constance in
one of the early Guelph feuds. Somewhat further
away upon the same woody ridge, a little white
spot is visible among the trees. This is the Château
of Arenenberg. The Swiss National line of railway
takes you in a few minutes almost from the door of
Helvetia to the little village of Mannenbach, beautifully situated on the shores of the Unter See. Thence
a rather steep walk of ten minutes brings you to the
Château of Arenenberg. When we visited it, it was
a glorious summer day, after drenching rain, and the
sun fairly blazed down upon us. For the greater part
of the way we had, happily, considerable shade from
walnut and other trees, for our umbrellas were a very
imperfect protection. Do any of my readers know
what a " Bremse" is ? If they do not they are happy
in their ignorance. If they do, they will not wonder
at Juno selecting a gad-fly wherewith to torment her
rival,—for *bremsen* are gad-flies, but such gad-flies!
I am sure I have seen many the size of hornets.
Something in a gingham umbrella seems to attract
them, for some forty of them sit on the inside of one's
umbrella as solemn as judges. Suddenly you feel a
sharp prick through your glove or light coat, and,

though you usually slay the wretch, for he cannot quickly withdraw his mandibles, revenge is small consolation, when, after two or three days the bite gets hard, swells, and irritates you. Barring the heat and the gad-flies, the walk to Arenenberg is a lovely one. Here in this charming villa—for Arenenberg is as little like our English ideas of a "castle" as any building well can be—Hortense, the daughter of Josephine, and ex-Queen of Holland, made her home, retiring to it upon the fall of the First Empire, to economise and to educate her two sons. In this Château, from 1818 until the death of his mother in 1837, lived Louis Napoleon Bonaparte, studying his profession as an officer in the Swiss artillery, and revolving his destiny. Thence, in 1836, he repaired to Strasburg to attempt the *coup-de-main* at which all the world laughed. From America, whither the government of Louis Philippe had magnanimously sent him, he returned to Arenenberg to stand beside the death-bed of his mother. Then it was that Louis Philippe, unmindful of the safe asylum which forty-five years before Switzerland had accorded to himself, haughtily demanded that the young Napoleon should be expelled from Swiss territory. A French *corps d'armée* was actually massed on the Swiss frontier, and as the Republic was determined to defend her independence to the last, nothing could have averted a war, had not the prince determined not to bring such a calamity upon his brave hosts, and voluntarily left the soil of Switzerland. When the Second Empire, with its glory, guilt, and shame, had passed away, and Napoleon III. had died, like his uncle, an exile, his widow and the young Prince Imperial formed the habit of spending a couple of months each autumn at Arenenberg. Just twelve months before our visit

CHÂTEAU OF ARENENBERG,
THE RESIDENCE OF QUEEN HORTENSE

they were there as usual.   Though no castle, Arenenberg is a beautiful villa in extensive grounds, including
a grove of magnificent beech and other forest trees.
Standing some two or three hundred feet above the
level of the lake, it looks over the water and the island
of Reichenau to the plain of the Hegau, dotted over
with picturesque old towns and ruin-crowned heights.
Vineyards slope down from the Château to the lake.
The garden was sweet with summer flowers, noticeably, petunias and bignonias in lavish profusion.   The
steward—a simple but intelligent Swiss—conducted
us through the principal apartments.   In the first
room we enter is a fine life-size portrait of the Prince
Imperial at the age of seventeen, by Lefèvre.   The
very image of his mother, he stands there a handsome
intelligent lad, with a premature thoughtfulness in his
face.   Within the last two or three years, our guide
told us, he had grown wonderfully like his father.
Near to this portrait, the surpassing loveliness of
Fluelen on the Vierwaldstätter See is rendered by the
genius of Calamé, as only his pencil could do it.   In
the principal apartments there are some interesting
portraits of Queen Hortense, in one of which the
great likeness to her son, Napoleon III., is strikingly
apparent.

On a large canvas is a fine painting of the late
emperor, as a young man, leading his horse through
the snow up a steep path to the Arenenberg.   A
marble bust, from a mask taken after death, gives us
the well-known face, with long waxed moustachios and
deep-set, brooding eyes, so familiar to most middle-
aged Englishmen.   Ticking away quietly, as if it had
not seen the fall, the resurrection, and the deeper fall
of a mighty dynasty, is a silver-gilt timepiece that
Napoleon I. had with him at Longwood, in St.

Helena.   Very striking is a marble bust of the Duke
of Reichstadt (Napoleon II.), beautiful as Apollo;
while a painting represents the founder of the dynasty,
with sword drawn and eyes flashing fire, as he led the
troops of the Republic he was so soon to betray, across
the bridge at Arcola.

Two handsome cabinets in the same suite of rooms,
have a strange history.   They were wedding presents
from the municipality of Paris to Marie Antoinette.
The room in which Queen Hortense died remains in
every particular just as it was, except that the field-
bedstead which Napoleon III. carried with him on his
campaigns, and which he had at Sedan, has been
brought into the room and placed by the side of that
on which his mother died.   In the little chapel attached
to the Château is a kneeling figure of the queen in
marble, with the inscription,—"À la reine Hortense son
fils Napoleon III."   In spite of the loveliness of the
scenery, enhanced by the glorious summer day, the
shadow of death seemed to rest upon the residence of
this doomed family.   When we spoke of the poor
prince to an old man whom we met in the grounds, he
burst into tears, and exclaimed, " I dare not speak of
it.   I cannot bear it."   He had known Napoleon III.
from the time he was young Prince Louis Bonaparte,
and spoke of the Château with its many visitors as
having been the life of the neighbourhood, finding
employment for a number of people, and disbursing
money on all sides ; "and now it is all dead—dead."
With a saddened feeling we walked under the stately
elms and down to the landing of the village of Mannenbach, near to which the reader will remember the
wretched Pope John XXIII. took boat after his
sudden flight from the Council at Constance.   Here
we are sheltered from the sun's fierce rays by trees

planted in the garden of the village-inn, which stretches down to the lake. On the very top of a hill, a little to the right of Arenenberg, stands the picturesque old castle of Salenstein, dating back at any rate to the thirteenth century. Louis Napoleon was a citizen of the commune of Salenstein.

In five minutes the steamboat took us across to the island of Reichenau. The little island is principally devoted to the vine, but there are a few walnut and other fruit trees which afforded us a little shade in our short walk of a mile to the northern side of the island, where stands the old abbey church founded by St. Pirminius in 724. In some places, too, the tall and densely-planted vines afforded us most welcome shade from the slanting rays of the evening sun. A stone cross near the southern landing-place serves as a pious memorial to the two Reichenauers who fell in the great war of 1870-71. The island of Reichenau is about three miles long by something less than two miles broad, and supports about 1,500 inhabitants, all of whom are Catholics. Its history is singularly interesting. Above the little town of Berlingen, over against Reichenau, there still stands the castle of Sandeck. In this castle, so far away back as A.D. 724, there lived the Frank governor (Landvogt) of the district, Sintlas, to whom belonged our island, then called Sintlas-au. The Landvogt invited the holy Pirminius to come and settle near him upon the lake, so that the saint might use his influence there and prevent "the people falling back into heathen customs, error, and unbelief," which they seemed but too likely to do, as their faith and morals were far from satisfactory. Pirminius came, and the Landvogt asked him where a house of prayer should be built for him ? The missionary pointed to the island that lay before

them. Sintlas cried with horror and disgust, "Not
so, my lord and father, for this island is a nest, abode,
and home of vipers, serpents, and other noisome and
doleful creatures, and no man has ever ventured to
make his home there." "Has not Christ" replied
Pirminius "given power to his elect to tread upon
adders and baselisks, and to trample upon lions and
dragons?" So he persevered with his request, and the
legend says that, as soon as he had landed on the island
with his companions, in the name of God he drove out
all the snakes and vermin. Then with his forty brethren
he proceeded to clear the dense jungle with which the
island was covered, and to drain the swamps, so that
in a short time, as the monkish chronicle tells, there
was a pleasant and suitable place for human habitation,
where formerly had only been "thickets and holes for
monstrous lizards and snakes." It is delightful to think
of the change accomplished by these resolute and God-
fearing men, but the exodus of the noxious and unclean
beasts must be somewhat exaggerated in a crude painting in the abbey church. It represents the building
of the monastery while the lake all around the island is
being lashed into fury by hosts of strange and monstrous creatures making their escape. So successful
were the monks in their cultivation of the island, and
so richly was the monastery endowed by the neighbouring princes and nobles, that it received the name
of "Augia dives," or the "rich pasture," which it still
bears in "Reichenau." The army of the monastery was
larger than that of many princes, and many a knight
had to summon his followers to arms at the command
of the Abbot of Reichenau.

In literary activity throughout the ninth century the
monks of Reichenau rivalled their brethren of St. Gall,
and a catalogue prepared by Reginbert, librarian of the

Abbey in 854, shows the astonishing number of works which the monks had written out or collected. Among the most celebrated of the holy and learned men which Reichenau has produced may be named Hatto (836), Reginbert (846), Walafried Strabo (849), and especially Hermann the Lame, who died in 1054. He was one of fourteen children borne by Hildrude to her husband, the powerful Count Wolfrad of Vehringen, and, being lame from his birth, seemed marked out by nature for the cloister. Having studied at St. Gall, he became a monk at Reichenau, where for the rest of his life he presided over the monastery school, and was rightly regarded as the most learned man of his age. He is the author of the famous hymn "Salve Regina," and of other hymns and poems. The important influence which Reichenau exercised upon the religious and secular life of the middle ages is sufficiently indicated by the fact that out of it came no fewer than eighteen archbishops, sixty bishops, and twenty-nine abbots. The reader of Scheffel's "Ekkehard" will remember how the monks of Reichenau with sorrowful hearts decided to leave their monastery, and take refuge on the Hohentwiel, upon the approach of the Hunnish horde, and the ludicrous adventures of the insane monk who insisted upon remaining to receive these strange guests.

With the thirteenth century its fame as a nursery of piety and learning began to decline, and in 1540 Charles V. handed it over to the bishopric of Constance. There are now three parishes in the island, to each of which a priest is attached—Oberzell, Niederzell, and Mittelzell.

The sail back to Constance was delightful, the sun having gone down and the Alps coming sharply into view. At Ermatingen the officers of the 114th

Regiment, quartered in Constance, came on board on their return from a visit to Arenenberg. They were fine-looking, war-worn veterans, and the medals and decorations on their breasts showed in how many campaigns they had taken part. Among these the coveted Iron Cross for valour was very noticeable. With them was a certain General Obernitz, come to attend the military manœuvres, and to whom they all showed great deference.

The centre of interest in Constance itself is, of course, the cathedral, the crypt of which dates from the sixth or seventh century. In the tenth century Bishop Conrad, the Guelph, added greatly to the church-building. He visited the Holy Sepulchre at Jerusalem, and proceeded to build an exact copy within the crypt of the cathedral. This idea was more perfectly carried out in the twelfth or thirteenth century. It is a twelve-cornered chapel, richly orna-mented with early Gothic figures. A space outside the entrance to this chapel, then under the open sky, Bishop Conrad chose for his own place of sepulture. A handsome chapel now covers his tomb, the head of the saint being preserved in a gilded reliquary richly adorned with reliefs representing scenes from the life of the holy man. The reliquary is a gift of the late King George of Hanover. In a niche above his grave is to be seen a silver statue of Conrad, repre-sented seated as a teacher of the church. It will be interesting to Englishmen to know that this statue is the gift of our gracious sovereign Queen Victoria. Both she and the King of Hanover were desirous of thus showing their recognition of St. Conrad as a distinguished member of the family of Guelph. In the choir lies buried Robert Hall, Bishop of Salisbury, one of the English representatives at the Council.

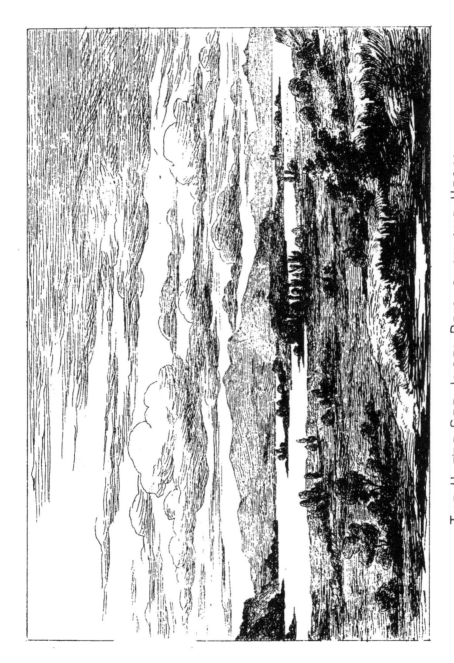

The Unter See, Insel Reichenau, and Hegau.

Another excursion which we made during our summer stay near Constance was to the Hohentwiel. To the west of the Unter or Zeller See stretches the fertile plain of the Höhgau, or Hegau, from which rise many bold, steep volcanic hills, almost all of which were once crowned by strong castles. From these heights some of the great ruling families of the world took their names—as the Hohenstaufen and the Hohenzollern. Among these ruin-crowned peaks, the most striking in appearance and the most interesting by reason of its history, is the Hohentwiel. Often have I stood close to our hostelry at Kreuzlingen, and watched the westering sun as he went down behind the Hegau, causing the Hohentwiel and his congeners to stand out in bold relief. Although so near, in order to reach the Hohentwiel from Kreuzlingen, parts of no less than three countries have to be traversed. First we must needs enter the Grand-Duchy of Baden in order to take the train at Constance, which, in little more than an hour, lands us at Singen, above which arises, almost sheer, the Hohentwiel. The huge rock rises 1,200 ft. above the plain, being 2,200 ft. above sea-level. It is about one and a-half to two miles in actual distance from the railway-station at Singen; and when we have walked about half-way, a sign-board informs us that we have left the territory of the Grand-Duchy of Baden and have entered the kingdom of Würtemberg. Soon afterwards we reach a typical German country inn, large, straggling, and bare-looking. In front of the doorway stands an ancient and umbrageous lime tree, around the trunk of which pigs are rooting and grunting, and geese are strutting and craning their long necks at the sight of visitors. This is the Maierhof, where the visitor to the Hohentwiel can take his dinner, or other refreshment, on a

R

verandah commanding an extensive view of the plain below. Here we met some pleasant Germans from Offenburg, in the Rhine valley, a place always interesting to me as that from which, in September, 1870, I reached the trenches before Strasburg during the bombardment. At that time I had noticed with great interest, in the market-place of Offenburg, a statue to Sir Francis Drake, the base of which is all festooned with artistically-designed wreaths of the potato plant. An inscription sets him forth as the introducer of the potato into Europe, and the consequent benefactor of untold millions. Our Offenburg acquaintances now told us that there is a popular German song ("Volkslied") in honour of Sir Francis Drake and of the potato. This is the more curious, as children in England are always taught that the introduction of the potato was due to Drake's great contemporary, Sir Walter Raleigh.

The visitors' book at the Maierhof is not without interest, though its greatest and most fitting ornament—a poem above the signature of Scheffel, the author of " Ekkehard,"—has been ruthlessly torn out by a Roman Catholic priest. Our little waiting maid charitably expressed the opinion that "he must have been out of his mind.'

Before leaving our inn, and asking the good offices of the old Würtemberg soldier, now the solitary custodian and guard of this once impregnable fortress, let us inquire what claims the history and associations of this mass of ruins have upon our interest. Its legendary name, " Duellum," old Latin for "bellum" (war), points to its once having been a Roman fortress; but recent discoveries carry its history far further back into the past even than that. Strange to say, on its summit, beneath the *débris* left by those who have occupied it in succession for nearly 2000 years, have been found, within the last few years, remains of the stone-period precisely similar to those which have been found in such abundance around the lake-dwellings in the lake below, thus showing that our pre-historic ancestors were alive to the importance of this natural fortress. There is good reason to believe that when Attila, "the scourge of God," swept over Europe with his Huns, in A.D. 451, he destroyed what the Romans had erected. The Alemanni, the East Goths, and the Franks succeeded one another in its possession until, in 806, it became the property of Charlemagne's son Pepin; and a monastery was founded on the summit of the rock between 814 and 840.

We now approach the period which, to all Germans and to many Englishmen, has been made to live again, in connection with the Hohentwiel, by the genius of Scheffel.

The astonishing popularity of his romance "Ekkehard," throughout Germany · cannot, I think, be accounted for, except by acknowledging its great and crowning merit of making the men and women of the far-away tenth century seem as real to us as those we now meet in the street, or on the market-place.

It will interest many of the readers of "Ekkehard" to hear that the greater part of what he relates is historically true, though great liberties are taken by our author, both with the names of the actors in his story, and with the period of their activity. A century or two earlier or later is nothing to Scheffel, if the change facilitates the development of his plot.

In the early part of the first half of the tenth century, the Huns carried devastation with fire and sword through all the region of the Boden See, and on the 1st May, 925, they appeared before the Abbey of St. Gall. The monks, armed with clubs, shields, and bows and arrows, withdrew themselves, their warlike abbot Engelhard in armour of proof at their head, to a strong fortification which they had hastily thrown up on the River Sitter, when first threatened by the Hunnish invasion. A half-witted monk, named Heinbald, alone remained to receive these strange visitors, he being out of humour because, as he alleged, the prior had failed to give him the necessary leather for shoes in which to flee. Either because he amused them, or because like many rude peoples they regarded the insane as peculiarly under the protection of the Gods, the rude Hunnish horsemen spared his life. They gorged themselves with raw flesh and made themselves drunk with the wine found in the cellars of the monastery. Two, attracted by the gilded statue of the holy Gallus, which stood on one of the towers, attempted to climb up to it, but fell down and were killed. They called upon their Gods, and compelled Heinbald to cry with them. They were just upon the point of murdering their interpreter, a priest whom they had captured, when some. scouts they had sent out brought word that the monks were standing armed in the stronghold on the Sitter. The whole band, in great alarm, then made for the shore of the lake, setting a few farms on fire to light them through the night, and they disappeared down the Rhine as quickly as they had come. The only victim of their rage was the pious recluse, Wiborad, who had refused to leave her walled-up cell. In the hope of finding treasure the Huns penetrated into it, and in their disappointment at not finding anything, ran her through with their lances. .

They laid waste the whole neighbourhood of Constance, but could not take the city itself. Reichenau, whither the literary treasures of St. Gall had been removed, was strongly occupied by armed men, who brought all the boats and ships on the little lake to the island. The Huns, not liking the appearance of matters, passed by Reichenau, ravaging the shores of the mainland as they passed.

Engelhard and his monks returned to their monastery of St. Gall. One Hun had remained behind, who demanded baptism, and married a Suabian maiden. The whole region around the Boden See lay waste and desolate after the Hunnish incursion, with villages and farms burned and destroyed, and just at this juncture the ruler of the whole of Suabia, Duke Burkhard, died.

The whole of this history Scheffel transfers from St. Gall to Reichenau, and makes it happen fifty years later, or about 980, in order that it might come within the life-story of the heroine of his romance, the Duchess Hadwig.

Duchess Hadwig was the daughter of the Duke of Bavaria, and was married to Burkhard II., who, after a considerable *interregnum*, had succeeded his father, Burkhard I. During his reign the empire of Germany was terribly harassed by the Huns and it was owing to the terror they inspired, that walled cities began to appear at this time in South Germany. Altstädten, Rheinau, Stein-on-the-Rhine, Constance, and probably Arbon and Bischofszell, received now their walls, and the Abbot of St. Gall caused a trench to be dug around the dwellings that had congregated themselves about the monastery, and also built a wall with forty-three towers, thus giving a beginning to the city of St. Gall.

The great Emperor Otto, however, defeated the

Huns in a decisive battle on the Lechfeld in 955, with a slaughter of one hundred thousand men, after which Europe suffered but little from them. At this battle Burkhard II. commanded the 7th and 8th Corps, composed exclusively of Alemanni. After a warlike and eventful life, Burkhard II. died in 973, in the same year as Otto.

The Salic law absolutely forbade that women should rule, and on the death of her husband, Hadwig was not formally appointed reigning Duchess; but her cousin, Otto II., conferred upon her the control of the great monasteries in Southern Germany, and as he did not appoint another duke in succession to her husband, she was left as his representative and viceroy in Suabia, over which she ruled with manly vigour from her castle on the Hohentwiel. Without doubt she was one of the most remarkable women Germany has ever produced, with as great a genius for government as Catherine II. of Russia, or our own Queen Elizabeth. Daughter of the Duke of Bavaria, and niece of the emperor Otto I., she was sought in marriage by, and formally betrothed, while a very young girl, to the grandson of the Byzantine emperor, Constantine Porphyrogenneta, who, under the name of Constantine, afterwards ascended the throne of the Eastern Empire. A eunuch was sent as ambassador from the Byzantine Court, who was also to instruct the princess in the Greek language. The high-spirited German girl, however, loathed the match, and when a Greek painter arrived to prepare a portrait of the future empress for the court at Constantinople, she made such terrible grimaces as completely to *nonplus* the poor painter. The marriage was broken off, and Hadwig devoted herself to serious studies, acquainted herself with the masterpieces of Greek and Latin literature, and eventually married the grey-haired and war-worn veteran Burkhard II., who,.when he died, bequeathed a great estate to her, and the lordship in the duchy. For five years she ruled with great energy, wisdom, and skill as the emperor's vicegerent in South Germany; in 978 a grandson of the Emperor Otto I., also named Otto, was appointed Duke of Alemannia, and subsequently of Bavaria, but Hadwig continued to reside on the Hohentwiel, and at her death in 993 bequeathed her great possessions to the monastery on the Hohentwiel, in which she had always taken great interest, to that of Petershausen, and to other cloisters.

In the exercise of her authority over the monasteries she on one occasion paid a visit to St. Gall. The porter of the monastery was a young monk who, according to contemporaneous reports, was endowed by nature with extraordinary personal charms, and was greatly distinguished as a scholar. His name was Ekkehard, and him she demanded as teacher from the abbot, and took him back with her to the Hohentwiel. Under his guidance she prosecuted with unremitting zeal the study of the classics; but until Scheffel published his romance, no breath of slander ever sullied her fair fame.

We have seen the liberties Scheffel has taken with history in making Dame Hadwig's *régime* coincident with a Hunnish invasion that took place fifty years before. It remains to mention that poor Charles the Fat, who had been lying in his tomb at Reichenau since 888, is made by Scheffel to ride on to the battle-field with the Huns at the critical moment, and achieve victory just as he expires from fatigue and the weight of his armour. This battle is purely imaginary, and its date is fixed about 980, or a century after the death of the Emperor Charles, to suit the exigencies of the story.

The crowning blemish of Scheffel's work—and it appears to me equally a sin against morals and against history—is that he represents the relation of Dame Hadwig to her Latin master to have been not as all history affirms, a pure and noble one, but as prompted, on the part of the Duchess, by amorous longings. It is true that Scheffel does not affirm that there was any actual intrigue, but he represents the beautiful duchess as making love to the young priest until he is all on fire and beside himself with. her charms, when she crushes his hopes in a moment, and remorselessly hands him over a prisoner to his bitter foes. This is absolute fiction, and, as I think, very unworthy fiction.

. History tells us, on the contrary, that the severe discipline with which Dame Hadwig ruled her duchy she by no means relaxed towards her favourite instructor in the classics. On one occasion she had him whipped upon his pallet of straw; and it was only upon his pitiful entreaties that she refrained from further punishing him by shaving his head smooth, and thus obliterating the tonsure. Shortly after the death of Duchess Hadwig, the monks presented a petition to the emperor, Henry the Pious, alleging that the climate of the top of the Hohentwiel was really too severe, and requesting that they might remove to a more genial station. Their request was granted, and they settled at Stein-on-the-Rhine.

Throughout the whole of the Middle Ages the Hohentwiel remained a place of arms of first-class importance; and when the Thirty Years' War broke out, early in the seventeenth century, it was the most powerful fortress in Southern Germany, and belonged

to the Protestant state of Würtemberg. A man of
the Cromwell type, Conrad Widerhold, was appointed
commandant, and for fifteen years he held the fortress
for the Protestant cause amid raging foes all around.
Twice they climbed the mountain and forced their way
into the outer court of the castle; but each time they
were driven out with terrible loss. Widerhold was the
terror of Catholic Germany, as he and his garrison
only subsisted by levying contributions far and near.
The abbeys around Constance and in the valley of the
Upper Danube knew the terror of his name; and he
even succeeded where the Swedes had failed, and
obtained possession of Ueberlingen, as the citizens
have good reason to remember to their cost. At
the end of the war he had the satisfaction of handing
over the Hohentwiel to his sovereign as an unconquered maiden fortress. But what open enemies
could not do, a false friend accomplished. One
hundred and fifty years later, when France was at
peace with Würtemberg, a French army under
Vandamme passed under the Hohentwiel and demanded its surrender. The commandant was old
and feeble (many believe him to have been bribed),
his officers were mostly invalided, and they allowed
themselves to be cajoled or intimidated into giving
up the unconquered fortress, under a solemn engagement that it should be given back to Würtemberg
intact at the close of the war between France and
Austria. First-Consul Bonaparte was not, however,
a man to be turned from his purpose by any such
trifle as a solemn promise; and he at once sent special
orders that the fortress was to be dismantled and
destroyed. For six months (from October, 1800,
until March, 1801) the French engineers mined and
blew up, leaving the Hohentwiel the ruin we now

find it.   The results of this atrocious bad faith on
the part of Napoleon are not to be regretted.   The
improvements in artillery would have deprived it of all
value as a fortress, and the traveller and lover of the
picturesque could ill afford to exchange the grand
old ruin that now crowns the height for a useless
castle or possibly admirable model prison.

The rock still continues to belong to Protestant
Würtemberg, though surrounded on all sides by the
Grand-Duchy of Baden, which in this district is
Roman Catholic.   But all this while the old Würtemberg pensioner, sole warder of the Hohentwiel,
is waiting to conduct us over it, and I fear lest my
readers may be as tired as he with this long excursus
into the past.   A stony pathway leads under a precipitous side of the rock to the long archways or
tunnels which conduct into the *enceinte* of the ruins.
Their extent is so great that they give the impression
of some ruined and deserted city.   Enormous blocks of
masonry, torn and rent, and often hurled *en masse* from
their original position, show what the fortress must
once have been ; and although the destroying French
engineers did their worst, it is wonderful how much
remains of tower and keep, and of spacious halls and
casemates for the soldiers, while what may be called
the donjon-tower still rises strong and almost intact
from the rock.   The upper fortress had no walls—they
were unnecessary ; not even a chamois could climb
the precipices by which it is surrounded.   It is very interesting to trace where the cloister stood which subsequently became barracks ; also the ancient castle of
Dame Hadwig, which is quite clearly to be distinguished from the enormous accretions of later centuries.
From the old courtyard of the tenth century there is a
picturesque view of the volcanic peaks, each with its

THE HOHENTWIEL,

ruin rich in story; Staufen, Stoffeln, Howen, Mägdeberg, and Neuhöwen.   The vast *enceinte* is now thickly grown over with young trees ; what once were court-yards are now lovely meadows, bright with such flowers as golden-rod, Canterbury bells, and gentian, while the ruins themselves are everywhere festooned and buried by most luxuriant masses of white clematis—at the time of our visit, in the early part of August, in full blossom.   Our guide informed us that in the early morning all the Oberland mountains had been visible as well as those of the Vorarlberg, but now, in the after-noon, a summer mist obscured the distant region.   In really clear weather the view of the Alps from the Hohentwiel is one of the most extensive conceivable, probably even finer than that from Chaumont, above Neuchâtel, and equal to the very wonderful view from the summit of the Ballon d'Alsace, the highest peak of the Vosges.   It includes the whole range of Alps, from the Sentis to Mont Blanc.   It was once my great privilege, in March, 1871, in perfectly clear frosty weather to behold the marvellous mountain panorama from the Ballon d'Alsace, but I have not been so fortunate from the Hohentwiel, though I have visited it often—in the spring as well as summer.   I am dis-posed to think that the days on which a perfect view may be obtained from it are but few every year.   On the occasion of our summer visit the Hohe Sentis loomed up shadowy and vast, and the gigantic forms of Glärnisch and Tödi were just distinguishable in the clouds, but this was the whole of our mountain view. The view immediately around and beneath will, how-ever, always repay the visitor.   The ruin-crowned volcanic peaks of the Hegau present different but always striking pictures, as seen from different points of view in the ruins.   A thousand feet below us, and apparently so absolutely at our feet that from the battlements we might drop a stone into it, meanders the little river Aach, through fields golden with ripe grain or green with the vine. Once more, and for the last time, to refer to " Ekkehard;" the reader of Scheffel's work will remember that it was by the side of the Aach that poor little Audifax watched and waited through the bitter cold winter gloamings until his perseverance was rewarded by capturing an otter, from the fur of which he made a Christmas present for Hadumoth.

A forest, many hundred acres in extent, lies between us and the Unter See. It is the forest of the Hohentwiel, and, like the fortress, belongs to the kingdom of Würtemberg, though surrounded on all sides by Baden territory. Among the hills to the south-west, the Rhine is flowing towards the cataract of Schaffhausen. To the east rises the old town of Radolfszell, and beyond, like a green gem upon the bosom of the lake, is the island of Reichenau, with the great minster of Constance rising beyond.

One Sunday afternoon during our summer visit to Kreuzlingen we walked about a mile-and-a-half into Thurgau to visit a small reformatory for boys. The house is clean, and is beautifully situated among the orchards, woods, and meadows belonging to the institution. There is no attempt at show about the place ; the furniture is all of deal, and very little of that ; not a carpet of any kind in the whole house. The clothes of the boys are rough and scanty, though probably quite enough for comfort during the hot weather. The superintendent or " Hausvater" was not much better clothed than the boys. Most of these latter were enjoying their Sunday afternoon gathering wild raspberries in the woods, but the " Hausvater" summoned those within call to receive the "gospels" and *Deutsche Arbeiter*, which seemed to give great pleasure ; and the absentees were not forgotten. The "Hausvater" then showed us specimens of their work. Their proficiency was truly astonishing, and led to humiliating comparisons. These unkempt, barefooted urchins, some of whom had been sent here for arson, and other serious crimes, write a beautiful hand, and can show specimens of neat and accurate book-keeping.

Is not this typical of the instruction and culture rapidly permeating all ranks, which, while they sweeten life, cannot of themselves remove poverty or raise the possessor in the social scale, seeing that all will be equally well educated ? Surely this, if anything, will teach us how foolish and wicked is the social brand attached to the practice of the mechanical arts. All "educated' people cannot be crammed into already over-crowded professions, and the radical changes now taking place in the distribution of goods and manufactures, are fast destroying the sorry refuge of retail shopkeeping. In the more enlightened and manly age which we must hope will succeed ours, a man will not, because his mind is stored with knowledge, and his nature refined by study, think it shame to earn his bread by making a pair of good shoes or a well-cut coat, nor will good and wise men of any class regard those engaged in the humblest mechanical arts as unworthy of their society and intercourse merely because of their occupation.

Attached to the hostelry at Kreuzlingen is a large hall, used for balls, dramatic entertainments, and the like. During our visit in August, 1879, there came one morning no fewer than six wagons full of children from Bischofszell to dine and spend the day. It seems it was a festival given to them by subscription once every three years.   As there were children among them, as well as teachers, of both confessions, both the Protestant pastor and the Roman Catholic priest were of the company, but no jarring strife of creeds marred the harmony of the proceedings, and no objection was raised on the part of any to our contributing our mite in the shape of the little books, which were gladly accepted by the hundred children.

COURT-YARD OF THE STADT KANZLEI,
CONSTANCE

CHAPTER XX.

WINTER AT CONSTANCE.

WE left Constance on the 13th August under so blazing a sun that even the motion of the steamboat and a thick awning failed wholly to protect us from his rays. We returned from the mountains on the 13th December, with a view to going into winter-quarters, after the fashion of Julius Cæsar and all old-world commanders.

The cold had already been intense in the mountains and in Zürich, through which we passed on our way. An open sledge was sent to meet us at the Kreuzlingen station by our hosts at the Helvetia, and we quickly glided over the snow to our inn.

Let me say at the outset that our experience in the winter of 1879-80 would not justify me in recommending any one to winter at Constance. It was, no doubt, an exceptionally severe winter, and the intense frost caused the shores of the lake to be constantly enveloped in dense vapour, through which the sun's rays in vain attempted to penetrate. In normal winters there is more sunshine, but, except in seasons of quite exceptional mildness, I am disposed to think that there is much fog, as may reasonably be expected near so large a sheet of water. The fog did not, however, extend far from the lake throughout the severest frost. Heiden and Trogen enjoyed bright sunshine almost every day, while we, a few miles away, and 2,000 feet nearer the sea-level, were immersed in an impenetrable and deadly-cold vapour-bath.

Our quarters consisted of a sitting-room about twenty feet long by fifteen feet wide, with two small bed-rooms opening out of it. One large German stove was designed to heat the three. As, for some time after our arrival the outside temperature remained at about 5° Fahrenheit, the stove was hardly adequate to its duties, and, until its construction was slightly altered, we often found that in spite of double windows we could not raise the temperature above 50° Fahrenheit, which was too cold for the children. If a stove is sufficiently heated, and care be taken always to keep a can of water on it, the warmth diffused is very agreeable.

Our regular company at dinner consisted of a retired Swiss judge, a venerable old gentleman of seventy-four, always addressed as Herr President; a cultivated German gentleman about sixty, who proved to be a contributor to the *Frankfurter Zeitung*, holding very advanced democratic, if not socialistic, opinions, with a pleasant young wife; a German who, after spending years abroad at Constantinople and Buenos Ayres, where his commercial rides used to take him to the borders of Patagonia, has settled down as a manufacturer of sacks and bagging at Constance and Kreuzlingen; and a well preserved little old gentleman, an old bachelor of more than three score and ten, originally from Hamburg, who, after spending many years of his life in the Brazils, has now for a score of years spent his summer in the Engadine and his winters at Constance. As an illustration of the social economy of this part of Switzerland, it may be interesting to mention that our host and hostess own the hotel, with its grounds, besides several vineyards. Their only son, a fresh-faced, merry lad of twenty, will inherit this property in course of time. Meanwhile, he has spent some considerable time in an hotel in Geneva, and, more recently, in the kitchen of Monsieur Grèvy, the President of the French Republic. At present he is at home, acting as *chef de cuisine* for his parents; and when he has completed his military service in the Swiss cavalry, he contemplates spending a year in London and another in Rome, so that he may add English and Italian to the languages of which he is already master — German and French, and extend his knowledge of the business of hotel-keeping

His education and prospects, however, far from causing him to despise his condition and calling, make him, it seems to me, take pride in his uniform of snow-white cap and tunic. The idea that his calling involves any social inferiority to that of a lawyer, a doctor, or a professor, has never, I think, occurred to him. When out of uniform, he wears as good broadcloth as his late master, President Grèvy himself. Take another illustration of how universal education and social equality work in Switzerland. Our table companion the Swiss judge, or Herr President, has never been married, but has for many years lived in the family of a carpenter, in each member of which he takes the deepest interest, especially in one of the sons, whom he has trained to the law, and who, to the great delight of the old man, has just been appointed, at the age of twenty-five, professor of criminal law at the University of Zürich.   If my memory serves me aright, one of our English Lord Chancellors was the son of a barber ; but with us, such an advancement would involve his stepping out of and forsaking the class from which he had risen.   Here in Switzerland this is unnecessary.   I met this young man upon the ice with his sister, a blooming girl, who acts as secretary to the Herr President, and found him modest and intelligent.

The principal drawback to our comfort at the Helvetia was that the little old-fashioned Speise-saal opened out of and was practically one room with the Gast-stube, or apartment open to the public, where the small shopkeeper, or artisan, or travelling pedlar, came in to get his glass of wine. Yet it was wonderful how well behaved all comers were.   The universal patronage of the Virginian weed against which our sapient monarch James I. fulminated his counterblast, alas ! in vain, was, however, very disagreeable to us, as there was no escape from its acrid fumes except by taking refuge in our own apartments.   Well might my younger daughter, aged three, call it " naughty tobag !"   Close below the grounds of Hotel Helvetia is a shallow bay of the lake, which early in the season was frozen over.   Here an enterprising contractor from Constance, who in the summer follows the calling of a gondolier, and keeps many boats for hire, maintains a fine sheet of ice in good order by sweeping and watering.   An hour's exercise upon skates of a morning was always agree-able, however dense the fog.   My sole companion was usually a local doctor, who truly said he could be as easily fetched from the ice as from his study.   On

Sundays and holidays, happily for the contractor, his ice was crowded.

It was a question with us parents, how, far away from country and friends, we could best keep Christmas, so that our two little girls, aged five and three, might have most enjoyment. Happily, Wessenberg's asylum for neglected girls came to our minds, which, although within the German frontier, is only five minutes' walk distant from Hotel Helvetia. A Christmas-tree and presents are provided by subscription for the inmates. The "lady-superintendent," or Haus-mutter, of the establishment kindly arranged that the hour for the lighting of the Christmas-tree should be five, to suit the convenience of our little ones; and, though the evening was bitterly cold, with the thermometer standing about 9° Fahrenheit, we muffled them up in heaps of wraps, put them upon a little hand-sledge, and drew them over the hard snow to the Orphanage.

We found the lights already burning upon the gift-hung pine sapling which served as Christmas-tree, and which was placed at one end of the long dormitory, cleared out for the occasion. The girls, twenty-six in number, were very neatly dressed, and were grouped around the piano, which stood close to the Christmas-tree. They sang some appropriate hymns, and sang them very well. Then followed recitations, delivered with great spirit, after which one of the elder girls stepped forward and delivered a set speech, evidently very carefully prepared and learned off by heart, in which those who had contributed towards the expenses of the entertainment were warmly thanked. A young worn-looking man now rose, and delivered a very eloquent and liberal address upon the meaning of Christmas, and the lessons it had for us. Dr. W—— my frequent companion on the ice, who is a member of the committee of management and honorary physician to the Orphanage, informed me that the orator was formerly a Roman Catholic priest, but is now an Old Catholic. I think the founder of the Orphanage, the saintly Wessenberg, would have been quite satisfied with the Christmas celebration.

As we were breakfasting in the "Gast Zimmer" on the 29th December, the children cried out "Why, father, look ! there are people holding up umbrellas"—a sight they had certainly not seen for two months. It was true, and though at first the rain froze as it fell, the change, which most had ardently desired, had really come with the close of the old year.

The owner of the skating ground on the shore of the lake was decidedly dejected, though sanguine that the thaw would be but transient. "Such a pity," he said, "after all my labour and outlay," and the more so as the level of the lake having considerably fallen, if the ice once melted the water would flow away leaving his rink high and dry. During the night of the 28th December, the thermometer was as low as 7°, but on the 29th it rose to 37° Fahrenheit. It was in the storm connected with this sudden thaw, that occurred the awful catastrophe of the fall of the Tay Bridge. A heavy downpour of rain helped to clear away the great masses of snow, and the New Year, 1880, was born amid a tremendous hurricane of wind and rain.

For two months we had seen nothing but the dazzling white vesture of snow everywhere, and now we could appreciate the joy with which Noah saw the green grass reappearing. Delightful, too, it was to be able to open our windows and feel a warm and spring-like air instead of the piercing cold that had so long reigned.

The morning of January 2nd, 1880, dawned warm and genial, and with a clear blue sky. After several days' confinement to the house, the children were delighted to get out, and at 9.30 a.m. we were walking towards Constance. Looking through the rails into a garden, the children held up their hands, and cried, "What lovely grass!" So beautiful are the common sights of nature, and we realise their beauty when we have been long deprived of them. It is pleasant to think of the increasing efforts made to provide a day in the country for the poor London children, so that they too, at least once a year, may be able to cry "What lovely grass!"

Our little girl, Nelly, age five, thinks that the light grey clouds that streak the blue sky are like "angel's hair." Everything in the softened aspect of nature is a source of keen enjoyment to them both, and their elders become young again in watching their delight.

By the "Concilium's Saal," we pass into the grounds, recently recovered from the lake, and laid out as a public park by the city authorities. Looking east we have the harbour, and the pharos, and beyond, rising behind the nearer hills, the scarred and snowy top of the Hohe Sentis. Then, making a circuit round the Insel Hotel, we cross the handsome iron bridge, which has taken the place of the wooden structure, where the butcher boys of Constance did battle against the Spanish veterans of the bigot Charles. Along the parapet on either side, the bridge is adorned by statues of great men belonging to the histories of Constance and of Baden, and is ingeniously arranged to serve at once for the railway, as a carriage road, and for foot passengers. Under it the blue waters of the lake hurry away towards the Unter See and the distant ocean.

On the far side of the bridge there is a fine promenade and "Rotten Row" by the side of the lake, which skirts the grounds of the palatial "Constanzer Hof," always closed in winter. Not only the Sentis but the seven Churfürsten, the Scesa Plana and many of the Vorarlberg Alps, stand out grandly in the distance. It is so warm that we are glad to sit down on a seat by the lake-side, while the children amuse themselves by throwing pebbles into the clear blue water. A trifling incident which here happened I may perhaps recall, as it pleasantly illustrates the good side of a class of men often accused of overbearing rudeness. While we were walking along the pathway underneath the trees, a Prussian officer in uniform passed us at full gallop along the "Rotten Row," and for a moment startled the children. Returning quickly, he rode up to me, and with a military salute, said, "I am very sorry if I have frightened the children; I was in full gallop before I noticed them, and though I tried to check my horse I had not time."

The thaw proved of but short continuance : a few days of open weather, just sufficient to melt the snow, and then back came the frost with increased severity. The peasants were much alarmed at this change. As long as deep snow is upon the ground they are without fear either for their seed or their fruit-trees, however great may be the cold ; but it is quite otherwise when the ground is bare and no kindly mantle of snow takes off the sharp edge of the frost.

During the snow, too, every species of vehicle was put upon runners—from farmer's carts to mail-coaches. The postmen and shopboys took out their parcels upon tall hand-sledges that they could push along.

For nearly two months or, reckoning the two months' frost previous to the short thaw, for four months we seldom had the thermometer at night higher than 16° and, at least on two occasions, it went down to the zero of Fahrenheit.

It is a trite enough observation that the world is small, but a curious illustration of its truth was given me one morning, upon going down, as usual, for a "constitutional" skate. My usual companion, the doctor, was not on the ground ; but in his stead were two young men, who talked French, and one of whom told me he came from Geneva. I asked him if he was acquainted with the distinguished scholar, Monsieur Rilliet de Candolle, to whom the kindness of a friend had given me an introduction when I was staying in the beautiful little city beside Lake Leman. "Oh, yes!" he replied, "he is my uncle." The other lad then came up and said that his friend was sure from my accent I was English, and that he was a compatriot and from Suffolk. Formerly I had a large circle of acquaintance in Ipswich, and I mentioned one name to him, the late Allen Ransome, of agricultural implement fame. "He was my grandfather," replied the lad, "and I bear his name." They were studying German with a clergyman in the neighbourhood.

The huge mass of the Boden See, which, with its arm the Ueberlinger See, and its little neighbouring dependent, the Zeller or Unter See, covers a superficial area of more than two hundred square miles, constantly seemed to work and boil with the intense cold, and the vapour it continually threw off completely obscured the sun to us, with occasional happy intervals, and made the rime lie, or more properly, stand out upon the trees and on its shores from three to six inches. After

an hour spent in the open air, one's beard was a mass
of icicles, and I have seen the hoar-frost standing out
on the hair of the countrywomen, who, even in such
bitter cold, often go out without any covering for the
head.   Upon returning from an hour's skating, not
only were my beard and moustache a mass of ice, but
a black Astrakan-fur cap became quite white, and
flakes of hoar-frost formed all down the texture of my
top coat.

It was early in January that I first heard of there
being superb ice on the Zeller See at Allensbach.   The
reader will remember that it was this village upon
which the Spanish soldiery wreaked their vengeance
after their unsuccessful attack upon Constance in the
sixteenth century.   Previous to the thaw the ice had
been deep in snow.   The railway takes you to Allensbach in ten minutes.   In two minutes more you are
upon the ice, slipping-on your skates.   I say advisedly
slipping them on, for in nothing has modern civilisation
made greater strides than in the improvement and
simplification of skates.   In my younger days the boring
of a huge hole in the heels of the boots, to the said
boots' destruction, and the tightening of a multitude of
straps, was a long and most painful process.   Oh, the
agony in fingers and toes on those dark mornings, a
quarter of a century ago, when the enthusiasm of
youth took my brother and me out on to some frozen
brick-ponds at five A.M., and the cold steel of the
skates almost burnt our hands like hot iron, as we painfully endeavoured to fasten the skates on to recalcitrant
boots!   Those days are passed.   You now touch a
spring, or turn a screw, and without any boring of
holes or any straps whatever, your skate is as fast to
your boot as your boot is to your foot—aye, and a
great deal faster!   From Allensbach to the island of

Reichenau the distance is about a mile, and the islanders for the past month have had a road across the ice, marked by fir-trees placed every few yards, so that the way may be plain at night and in foggy weather. Now, however delightful it may be, and undoubtedly is, to shoot along and seem almost to fly over the smooth surface of (for the most part) virgin ice, the time arrives, and with many of us very quickly, when Nature, by an unmistakable sensation in the feet, demands repose. Nothing can then be more luxurious than to recline at full length upon the ice.

At first I was struck by what appeared to be an extraordinary traffic upon the lake. In every direction carts seemed to be traversing the great frozen plain; upon closer investigation, however, these objects proved to be fishing-stations. The fisherman is provided with a screen of wood and straw about three feet high, which he can push before him upon runners to the spot where he desires to pursue his piscatorial avocation. He also has with him a pole-axe and a long conical tub, in which fluids are usually carried on the back in this country, a dish of bait, and a small tub for the fish. Arrived at a spot upon the frozen lake which experience has taught him to be a favourite haunt of the fish, he proceeds to cut with his pole-axe a round hole, about eighteen inches in diameter, in the ice. He then fixes his shelter over the hole in such a way as to protect himself on three sides from the wind, and drawing off his big boots with the skates attached, lays them beside him, and proceeds to bestow his legs as comfortably as may be in the long pail, which is padded and stuffed with straw. His line, twenty or thirty feet long, is then sunk through the hole, and he patiently waits for a bite, often remaining thus for many hours. When he leaves for the night, he turns the straw shelter over the hole, to mark the spot, and, as far as possible, to prevent the water from freezing, and thus to spare himself labour in opening the hole afresh when he next comes. When, for any reason, the shelter is not left, the round disc of ice taken from the hole is often left standing upright beside it, where it freezes to the ice underneath, and is a conspicuous mark. Where there are many of these near together, they have a curious effect, as if "turn the trencher" had been played upon a large scale. The fishing-stations were scattered over a great part of the lake, but were mostly in groups, each separate fisherman being about fifty yards from his fellows. I visited a dozen or more, and, sitting down to rest, had a chat with each. They were all doing pretty well, their spoil consisting for the most part of small perch, but some had secured one or two fine "Felchen"—the "Férat" of the Lake of Geneva—a delicate fish belonging to the trout family. Upon subsequent skating visits I took these solitary fishermen upon the great frozen expanse some little books, the receipt of which seemed equally to surprise and please them. And here, if I may be allowed, I would say a word upon the subject of tract distribution. It is often held up to sovereign contempt as the most offensive form of Pharisaic impertinence—and, unfortunately, it often is Pharisaic impertinence. If a fine lady or gentleman stiffly thrust a tract at some poorer neighbour or stranger with an expression and manner which say as plainly as any words, "Stand apart, I am holier than thou," "so holy, in fact, that I am willing to poke a tract at thee, hoping that it may possibly save thee from an awful destiny," it is an offensive impertinence. But a man or woman, endowed by Providence with some leisure, means and culture, who has not become a convert to the fashionable materialistic philosophy, but who believes that the highest philosophy the world has yet seen is to be found in the teaching and life of Jesus of Nazareth, and who desires above all things to imitate His example, by regarding and treating all men and women as brothers and sisters, such a one desires in some practical way to show his Christian interest. What is he to do? If rich as Crœsus he could not give money to every one, and if he could and did, it would only pauperise. By some small sacrifice of money or time, or both, he can, however, provide himself with little books calculated to humanise and Christianize, and to promote "sweetness and light" among the poor and neglected whom he may meet either at home or abroad. He meets them upon common ground, as a fellow-traveller in a world of mystery "between the two immensities," and he gives them what may help them in the fight of virtue, or cheer them mid privation and sorrow. What can any one object to in this? Even a benevolent Agnostic or Atheist can only cry, with a smile of deepest melancholy, "Alas, for the amiable delusion, for the dreamings which would be glorious if not so absurd, of these poor creatures of a day!" In Roman Catholic countries I think it very desirable, of course, to disseminate nothing calculated to wound or offend.

To return to the ice;—most of the fishermen to whom I talked were boys or young men, but one elderly man told me he had five children at home, and gave me some excellent practical advice as to how I was to reach Radolfszell. He said that I had better avoid the north shore, where there were many streams which flowed into the lake and rendered the ice unsafe. There is a wonderful charm in the surface of a frozen lake, where solitude is, to a certain extent, tempered by association with the "kindly race of men," even if they be but poor fishermen, each sitting at his fishing-hole. A glance at the map will show that Radolfszell stands at the base of a narrow promontory which separates this end of the lake into two bays. In my ignorance I took the northern one, more especially as I was doubtful of the strength of the ice nearer to the current of the Rhine. But I am no longer alone upon the ice ; a troop of school-boys come sweeping along upon skates from Markelfingen, which I mistake for Radolfszell, and a wild duck urges its peculiar flight above me. The water is no longer deep ; I can see the water plants at the bottom, and even an occasional fish, through the six inches of pure ice. Landing at Markelfingen I find out my mistake. The fields near the lake are strewed with a peculiar manure ; it proves to be the husks of grapes from which the wine has been expressed. A delicate fresh-water shell, about the size of a periwinkle, is very frequent in the marshy grass. I take to the ice again, which shows black under the dull sky, and is perfectly smooth, and quickly approach the old town of Radolfs-zell, originally a hermit's cell in the twelfth century. A poor frog frozen into the ice among the reeds near the shore, shows that the frost is not good for all lake-dwellers.

On my second visit to the lake, a few days later, without loss of time I made straight from Allensbach to Radolfszell, keeping to the south of the promontory. The distance, which may be six miles, is easily run in an hour, with plenty of time for rests and social inter-course with the fishermen. There, while enjoying at the

"Sonne" a modest libation of the mild and delicious golden wine of Baden, I met some gentlemen from Berlingen, on the Swiss side, who had just skated straight across, unaware that the ice had been declared to be unsafe there by no less an authority than the "Fischermeister" at Reichenau, an official of whom more anon, and that the passage at that point had been forbidden. They were intending to return by Itznang and Horn, and so to cross the Rhine near Steckborn, where the ice was reported strong, and they invited me to accompany them, informing me that I could catch a train at Steckborn or Berlingen that would take me to Kreuzlingen almost as quickly as the train from Allensbach would take me to Constance. I bargained for a little grace in case I found myself unable to keep up with them, as I had no wish to find myself at nightfall alone upon the pathless ice, and uncertain as to how much of it was to be trusted. The distance, including the circumnavigation of the promontory of Horn, is about nine miles. The afternoon was superb: though a pretty constant visitor to the lake during the remaining month of frost I never saw such another. The sun shone brightly from a perfectly blue sky: it was 4.30 P.M. when we took to the deep-green ice, which was so smooth that skating seemed no exertion whatever, but was like flying. Soon the sun set behind the fantastic peaks of the Hegau, the Hohentwiel, Hohenstoffeln, Mägdeberg, and all the other volcanic heights, which showed a deep purple in his departing rays. The broad expanse of ice was purple too. As we sped along with race-horse swiftness, the ice groaned, and cracked, and thundered ominously underneath; but my experienced companions assured me this was a healthy sign, being merely the result of the shrinking of the ice with the increasing cold of the evening.*

Around the "Horn" the ice had frozen in waves, and as we dared not pull up, for fear of the night overtaking us, we went bumping over the ice as if it had been a ploughed field, not without one or two awkward falls. To a stranger it was rather alarming to see open water close to us in the gloaming, but my companions evidently knew what they were about, and as the · daylight faded away and the stars came out in majesty from the empyrean, we reached Steckborn, on the other side of the Rhine, in safety.

It is characteristic of the excellence of the telegraphic system of Switzerland that finding my train on this side would bring me home a quarter of an hour later than the train on the German side of the lake, I was able to prevent anxiety to my wife by sending her a telegram at a cost of sixpence. One of my companions on the ice proved to be the landlord of the hotel at Steckborn, where I waited until the starting of the train. His history curiously illustrates a phase of the social life of the Swiss. A toddling little girl of perhaps two years old came into the "Gast-stube"— *the* public room in country inns, in winter warmed by a great porcelain stove—to greet her father on his return. I asked if she had begun to talk? "Yes,

---

* It is worthy of remark that water at the temperature of freezing is almost, if not absolutely, the only substance that expands with cold. If it did not, but contracted, as according to the rule of analogy one would expect, ice would of course be heavier than water, and would sink to the bottom. Water being a bad conductor of heat, the heat of summer would not suffice to melt the ice formed at the bottom of the lakes and rivers in winter. Each year the frozen mass would increase, and probably all animated nature would gradually be involved in the fatal embrace of an ever-extending cold. Curiously enough it is only at a little above freezing point that water expands with cold ; below freezing the ice contracts again, as shown by the crackings and thunderings to which I have alluded.

a few words of French," he replied. "French," I exclaimed, "the people don't talk French here, do they? Are you a Frenchman?" He came from Neuchâtel, it seems, and the only daughter of the proprietor of the inn at Steckborn, of which he had now become master, was sent by her parents to his parents at Neuchâtel to learn French. There she not only acquired the French language but a husband, and the young Neuchâtel lad found a wife, with the "Wirthschaft" of the "Krone" at Steckborn as dowry.

In every Swiss paper you may see advertisements from parents in German Switzerland wishing to exchange a child for a year or two with parents in French Switzerland, so that he may learn French, or *vice versâ*. These exchanges frequently lead to inter-marriages, and this is one of the ways in which the inhabitants of the little congeries of republics, of race and origin so dissimilar, are being welded into one people.

The very next day after this excursion a poor carpenter of Horn, although he had just been warned by the Reichenau Fischermeister that it was unsafe to attempt the passage to Berlingen upon the ice, actually pushed a hand-sledge with some goods he was transporting, right into the open water, where he was drowned. Thanks to the admirable arrangements and regulations as to the traffic on the frozen lake, of which I shall speak later, this was the only accident—if it be fair to call it accident, for it was practically a suicide—that occurred during the whole of that long winter on the Unter See, when the only feasible communication between Reichenau and either mainland was over the ice.

To the delight of the poor peasants, but to my

selfish sorrow, a pretty heavy fall of snow had taken place before my next visit, and though the innkeepers at Radolfszell and Allensbach had a broad causeway swept clear between the two places, I could no longer wander at will over the wide expanse, or pay little visits to my friends, the fishermen, without painfully floundering through the snow. With the continuance of the frost, however, what had been open water froze, and from Mannenbach to Steckborn the ice was pretty good, though the fog was generally so heavy, especially at night, that the ice became covered with rough blossoms of rime as large and thick as dahlias, very beautiful to look at, but almost more obstructive to the skater than snow. During the following month, in spite of the obstacles of snow, and rime, and fog, I continued to traverse the Unter· See in almost every direction. Once, starting from Mannenbach, I followed a very indifferent track through the snow down the Rhine, from Steckborn across to Wangen, in Baden, and then on to Mammern, on the Swiss shore. A very favourite route was to Mannenbach, on the Swiss shore, by train, thence along a track followed by cart-sledges across the lake to Reichenau, and then on foot across the island. What a change since the summer! The frost was so intense on the island that all the vines were killed that had not been carefully laid along the ground—a serious business in an island almost entirely planted with vines. Arrived at the northern shore of the island, there was a fairly good track across to Allensbach, in Germany, though latterly it was so much cut up and injured by the constant traffic of carts and horses, as well as sledges, as to be little adapted for skaters. Not being a scientific skater, I find little enjoyment in pursuing the amusement in a confined space. The charm to me is to have a practically unlimited space over which to roam; here to round an island, there to catch sight of a castle haunted by romantic or tragic associations; now to pass a monastic pile, secularized and turned into an engine manufactory; or to meet a huge load of hay moving like a great elephant across the snowy waste. Under most circumstances, compensations are to be found, and the fact that the lake was covered with snow with only certain well-defined routes upon it, was not without its advantages. In the dense fog that too often hangs upon the lake, even with a compass the skater may easily lose himself on the wide frozen expanse; while on the swept causeway, even in the middle of the lake, and with the fog so heavy as to prevent his seeing more than a few yards, he is as safe as if upon a high-road on land.

Nothing can exceed the charm of these solitary glidings, though of an evening there was a sense of loneliness in traversing the lake, and especially when lying down to rest for a few minutes. Though in a profuse perspiration from the exercise, my beard and hair would be full of ice, and my cap and coat quite white with hoar-frost. Everything was indistinct in the mist, and nothing was to be heard save the strange mysterious grumblings and moanings of the ice and the water underneath. In the course of my wanderings I found out an old-fashioned little inn near to Allensbach, "Das Untere Haus." I was tired and hungry upon my first visit, and the people themselves seemed astonished to see such an embodiment of winter entering the warm upper room. Its warmth was produced by a large china stove, filling up a corner of the room and extending on two sides. In the warm embrasure thus formed sat an old man—mine host. After he had assisted me to rid myself of the ice that clogged my hair and beard, and to wipe the hoar-frost from my clothes, he told me that he was seventy-six years old, that he was born in the house, had lived there all his life, and that it could not be long before he should die there. Never in his life had there been such a winter except that of 1829-30, when the Boden See was frozen over. How shall I give an impression to my readers of the fare they gave me there? Household bread and home-made cheese, and sparkling "*most*," a beverage made from the juice of pears and apples mixed. Did ever emperor enjoy such a feast? I trow not. Compared with it I think the nectar and ambrosia of the dwellers in Olympus must have been poor and savourless, for I never heard of their going skating, And the cost! For a litre of this delicious beverage, and a hungry man's allowance of bread and cheese the charge was sixpence. The old man's conversation was very interesting to me. Though such a hermit, he was a great reader in his way, and held original opinions about men and things. Though a Catholic, he expressed great approval of a religious book I had left with him on one of my visits, and, with calm trust, he seemed to be waiting, in the warm embrasure in the house in which he was born, for the summons to his last long journey. On the occasion of my last visit I told him I did not expect to come again, as I hoped to be able to skate the whole length of the Boden See as far as Bregenz. I was touched with the earnestness with which he warned me to be careful. "They don't understand ice at all upon the Boden See. Here we have the 'Fischermeister,' who is paid to look after the ice, and warn people off if it is unsafe, but there is no one to do this on the Boden See. Many a one goes joyously on to the ice, and little thinks his last hour has struck." The good old man had too good grounds for his fears. The freezing of the Boden See cost no less than twenty-five lives, and that within a fortnight; while on the Unter See, thanks to good management, as we have seen, only one life was lost, and that through reckless disobedience.

CHAPTER XXI.

THE FROZEN BODEN SEE.

READERS of German literature will remember a favourite poem in collections—" Der Reiter und der Boden See,"—" The Rider and the Boden See,"—which describes a horseman in winter riding south, through the Suabian hills, intending to take ship for Switzerland when he should reach the lake of Constance. Over hill and dale he wearily pushes his tired steed, until the hills are all left behind, and the snow stretches away around him in the evening gloaming, like the sand of the desert. City and village he has left far behind—not a house, not a tree, not a rock is to be seen. Many miles he rides over this dreary plain. The wild cry of the snow-goose and the call of the water-hen are the only sounds that reach his ear. He meets no traveller to direct him aright on his way, but ever onwards he trots on the snow, soft as velvet. When will he hear the roar of the water? when see the lake glittering before him? But now he sees lights in the distance, and trees show through the fog, and hills shut in the horizon. · His horse's hoofs strike fire from stones over which he is riding, and dogs bark at the stranger. "You are welcome at the window, my little maid. Pray tell me how far it may be to the lake?" The maiden stares at the horseman in astonishment. "The lake! the lake lies behind thee, and if I did not know that it was covered with ice, I should have said that thou hadst just landed from the boat." The stranger shudders and breathes hard. "There! behind, on the level plain, that's where I rode!" The maiden throws up her arms, and cries, "Good God! it was over the lake thou didst ride." The villagers, old and young, assemble around him, and congratulate him upon what they regard as a miraculous feat. They press him to share their humble repast near the warm stove; but the shock has been too great for him, and he sinks dead from his horse.

I owe an apology to Schwab for this bald and prosaic epitome of his spirited poem : for the poem was written by Gustave Schwab, to whom, more than to any one else, I have been indebted in the preparation of this work.

It is curious that when he wrote it the lake had not been frozen since 1695, or for about 130 years, so that the awe and astonishment of him who crossed and those who witnessed the marvel, might well be nearly as great as if, we will say, he had found to his amazement that he had ridden across the straits of Dover. Schwab lived to see the lake again frozen over in 1830, an event which he celebrated by another poem, called the " Spectre on the Boden See."

When it is remembered that in places the lake is nearly 1000 ft. deep, with an average depth of 300 ft., and that its area is nearly 200 English square miles, no wonder will be felt that in ordinary winters it does not freeze. In the warm days of August, September, and October, 1879, the temperature of the water of the lake at Ueberlingen was as high as 77° Fahrenheit, and on the 2nd November it was so warm in the public gardens of that city that many coloured butterflies were seen disporting themselves around the late-blooming autumn flowers. On the 3rd November came snow, followed by ice on the 4th, and in the middle of December and the middle of January the barometer stood extraordinarily high, while the thermometer registered only about 2° above the zero of Fahrenheit, a very unusual cold in a place which the good Badensers are pleased to call the " Suabian Genoa," or " German Nice." The few days' thaw to which I have alluded, had no perceptible influence upon the cooling of the water, which may be said to have gone on continuously from the 3rd November, 1879 to the 17th February, 1880, or for 106 days. As has been already mentioned, warmth expands almost all substances while cold contracts them. Water in cooling from 212° to about 40°, loses one twenty-second part of its volume. But from 40° to 32°, in the most exceptional and wonderful manner, it expands, and when at 32° it turns to ice its specific gravity becomes lighter than that of water by one-fourteenth part, which is the reason that the ice remains on the surface. But as the temperature of the ice sinks below 32° it immediately begins again to contract. With increasing temperature it again expands, becomes shivered and brittle, turns to water at 32°, from which point to 40° it contracts, while above 40° it again expands, according to what, as we have already remarked, is almost a universal law. On the 2nd of November, 1879, the temperature of the water of the lake at Ueberlingen was 59° Fahrenheit; the cold of the following days cooled the surface of the water, which thereby became denser and heavier, and consequently sank to the bottom, and sent up in its place a volume of warm water from the bottom, in its turn to cool and sink. This process continued until the water at the bottom was cooled down to about 40°, at which point it attains its maximum density, when no further sinking of the surface-water was possible. It is manifest that the shallower any body of water is, the sooner the whole mass cools; the deeper it is, the longer time it takes for the water on the surface to come to the freezing point. This is the reason that the shallow Unter See freezes almost every year, while the Boden See, which is almost ten times as deep, has during the past 1,000 years frozen only twenty-eight times.

Early in December, the Unter See was covered with a thick coating of ice, and this was also the case in the shallows along the shores of the Boden See, as at Kreuzlingen, where, in consequence of the fall of the level of the lake, and the disappearance of the ice from the upper reach during the temporary thaw, the skating contractor was obliged to remove his refreshment hut bodily some hundred yards nearer to the lake, where he laid out and kept in order a more extensive rink than the first. Already in December there was capital skating between Lindau and Bregenz. The main volume of the lake continued to move and work unceasingly until the 27th January, when the process of cooling, above described, was complete, and the water became perfectly still. Since the 20th the water had been down at freezing point, while the temperature of the air was often only two or three degrees above zero. The freezing of the main body of the lake began at three o'clock on the afternoon

of the 27th January, under a bright sun, and with
the thermometer as high as 19° in the shade.   For the
next few days a dense fog hung over the lake, while
a death-like calm proclaimed that its stormy waters
were at length motionless in the stern embrace of the
frost.   On the 3rd February all the steamboats from
Constance had to cease running, as the ice broke the
paddles.   A Würtemberg steamer tried to make the
voyage from Langenargen to Lindau, but stuck fast
in the ice mid-way, and was only got home with great
difficulty.   The steamboats from Romanshorn to Lindau,
and from Rorschach to Lindau, were obliged to cease
running the same day—the 3rd February—while the
enormously powerful camel steamboats, which carry
whole railway trains from Friedrichs-hafen to Romanshorn, and which, by crushing through the ice, had
hitherto kept a way open between the German and the
Swiss ports, were obliged to cease running on the 8th.

From the 5th to the 10th of February the whole of
the vast expanse of the Boden See was frozen over,
and to such a thickness as to make it everywhere
passable.   Until the 9th of February the ice continued
to increase in thickness.   From that date, however,
even when many degrees of frost were shown by
the thermometer in the air, the ice diminished ; and on
the afternoon of February 27th, with the thermometer
at about 36°, while the sun was shining, and a
pretty stiff wind blowing from the west, the last
ice-fields of the Ueberlinger See broke away between
Nussdorf and Uhldingen, and soon disappeared.   It
required the full fury of an equinoctial storm on
the 4th of March finally to break up and clear away
the ice between Bregenz and Lindau and from the
Unter See.   According to observations taken by
B. Brehm, of Ueberlingen, the thickness of the ice on

the 6th of February was 88 millimetres; on the 7th, 95; on the 8th, 110; on the 9th, 120; and on the 10th, with the thermometer in the air at 36°, again at 110. Thus the maximum thickness of the ice was nearly five inches.*

The records of the freezing of the Boden See in former generations are very complete, and a few particulars will, I hope, be interesting to my readers.†
An old chronicle, speaking of the winter of 1571, says: "Upon a deep snow, during a profound calm, followed such cold that on the 3rd of January the Boden See was frozen from Lindau to Bregenz, and the next day the Bregenzers went on the ice to Lindau to market. On the 1st of February the whole lake froze, so that the ice was used as a road from Romishorn (Romanshorn) to Buchhorn (now Friedrichs-hafen), as well as from Constance. The Bregenzers danced upon the ice at Carnival, and struck sparks against the ice as they stepped. One man rode on horseback on the ice from Bregenz to Ueberlingen" (nearly the entire length of the lake—the prototype of Schwab's Reiter).

The freezing of the lake was formerly taken advantage of for obtaining measurements of its length and breadth.

In the year 1695 a schoolmaster of Altnau, near Constance, took all his boys for a walk over the ice to Langenargen, where they were feasted by the Count of Oetingen. It is interesting to note the much greater frequency of frosts sufficiently severe to freeze

---

* I am indebted for all the facts, given above, which did not come under my personal observation, to a brochure entitled "Der Boden See ist zugefroren im Winter, 1880," von Anton Metz. Ueberlingen.

† The Boden See was frozen over in the years 895, 928, 1074, 1076, 1077, 1108, 1217, 1227, 1277, 1323, 1325, 1378, 1379, 1383, 1409, 1431, 1435, 1437, 1460, 1465, 1466, 1479, 1497, 1512, 1552, 1560, 1564, 1565, 1571, 1573, 1695, 1829–30.

the lake, throughout the Middle Ages than in later times.   The eighteenth century is the only one since a record has been kept, in which the lake was not at least once frozen over.   Very full particulars of the freezing in 1830 have come down to us, and most aged people remember it well.   Our landlord at the "Helvetia" remembers being driven across to Meersburg in a sledge with his father and mother, and the latter's satisfaction and thankfulness when they all reached home safely after their unusual excursion.

The cold lasted from the 29th of December, 1829, for nearly two months.   Thus the frost did not last nearly so long as in 1879-80, but was much more intense.   In the beginning of January the Rhine was frozen over at many places; and in the early days of February 22° to 24° of cold were registered by Reaumur's thermometer, equal to 17½° to 22° below the zero of Fahrenheit.   The weather was generally cloudy in the morning, at night clear, and towards mid-day there was sunshine.   By the 3rd of February it was reported from all points that the lake was frozen over, and many of the inhabitants of its shores ventured across.   The first venturesome explorers obtained certificates from the local authorities of the places to which they crossed, some of which are still preserved in family archives.   Very soon hundreds availed themselves of the unwonted opportunity.   On the 7th of February, a Sunday, no fewer than 200 sledges were counted on the ice at Rorschach, and the whole lake was crowded alike by young and old—dancing, sledging, walking, running, and a few skating.   Old people who remember the time seemed greatly struck with the difference in the matter of skating between 1830 and 1880.   Then it was quite a rare sight—now one of the most common.   From Kreuzlingen to Hagnau a

Madonna was carried in procession across the ice, to be returned to Swiss ground when the lake should again be frozen over. Many, however, felt very uncomfortable as they crossed the frozen surface, and, as it cracked and groaned, thought their last hour was come. On the night of the 7th-8th of February the Föhn (hot south wind) blew unexpectedly, and brought with it a thaw, to the great relief of the inhabitants of the shores of the lake, who were suffering from want of water, as most of the wells and streams were frozen, and almost all the flour-mills had been brought to a stand-still. On the lake itself the Föhn only melted the little snow upon the surface, and, as a frost immediately set in again, the lake became as smooth as a mirror. With the increasing cold the want of the corn usually brought across the lake from Germany was keenly felt in Switzerland; for, be it remembered, at that time there were no railways. In order to reopen communications and procure the necessary corn, a canal through the ice was commenced at Rorschach on Saturday, the 13th of February. It was 24 ft. wide, and had to be cut through ice eight inches thick, and the first day it was carried a distance of 8,100 ft. The work was vigorously prosecuted on Sunday, the 14th, as well from the German as from the Swiss shore ; and as a dense mist hung over the frozen surface, the two parties worked towards one another guided only by the compass, exactly as the engineers of the St. Gotthard have recently been obliged to work. On the 15th, the Swiss party of 128 men reached the middle of the lake, and at three in the afternoon the firing of cannon and mortars told that the connection had been made, and that the canal was completed. On the 17th of February a naturalist travelled over the ice from Rorschach to Lindau in a sledge provided with sails. On the 18th a thaw set in; but the frost did not fully break up until the 25th. Until the 22nd, wanderers continued to traverse the ice; but after that date the higher temperature and the many canals that were cut to facilitate navigation rendered it dangerous. Interesting narratives are still preserved of extraordinary adventures of wanderers upon the ice; but, so far as I can learn, there was but little loss of life in 1830 as compared with 1880.

It is not a little remarkable that the lake should have been frozen over again under very similar circumstances after an interval of exactly fifty years, for the 7th of February, both in 1830 and 1880, was almost the height of the frost. It seemed as if the Boden See had determined to keep an icy jubilee.

In both years the poor water-fowl had a bad time of it. As the streams and marshes froze they took refuge near the greater sheets of water. The Lake of Zürich, as might have been expected, from its smaller size, was frozen over long before the Boden See, and on Sunday, February 1st, 1880, it is estimated that no fewer than 50,000 pleasure-seekers in all were upon its surface, and from 20,000 to 30,000 at one time. I visited Zürich on the 3rd, and at once noticed that of the hundreds of gulls usually to be seen skimming the surface of the lake, and in the winter coming in great flights to be fed at the bridge, which spans the Limmat just where it leaves the lake, not one was to be seen. They migrated, there is little doubt, in a body to Constance, where, even at the coldest, there was a considerable expanse of open water where the Rhine leaves the lake. Here they assembled in hundreds, which in ordinary seasons is quite unusual. Great numbers of wild ducks betook themselves to the mouths of the principal affluents of the lake—indeed to wherever they could find a little open water. Many were found frozen upon the ice, and others, less able to run or fly than to swim, were caught upon its surface by the villagers. Twenty little Divers arrived opposite to Ueberlingen about the middle of December. The water of this part of the lake swarms with little fish in winter. At first the little birds took refuge under the bottoms of the bathing-houses, now left high and dry by the receding water, where most of them were caught. For four that remained, the Customs officers stationed at the steamboat landing kept a little space of open water, and it was a very pretty sight to see the birds plunging through the hole, swimming around underneath the transparent covering of ice, until they had caught a fish, when they brought their prey up through the hole and swallowed it at the feet of the spectators. One of these adventurous divers, not being able to find his way back from his excursion under the ice, was drowned beneath the fatal crystal ceiling.

The contractor of the Skating Rink at Kreuzlingen deserted what had for months been the object of so much care to him, and brought his hut, with refreshments, and skates, and chair-sledges, down on to the immense sheet of virgin ice. Upon my remarking that if he took to sweeping and watering *that* rink he would have his hands full, he said, "God Almighty has made us a rink now, and it will do without my care."

For thousands and thousands of acres along the Kreuzlingen shore the water is very shallow, so that with a little care there was practically no risk. Every morning for about a week I had a run of ten or fifteen miles upon skates, and upon one occasion pushed my wife and eldest daughter in a chair-sledge a good many miles over the frozen surface—an experience which during the lifetime of either is very unlikely to happen again. The ice was in perfect condition,—to skate upon it was like flying. No exertion seemed necessary: compared with this ethereal motion a gallop is a fatigue. At Constance, several fatal cases of drowning arose from the skaters in the fog venturing too near to the open water, where the Rhine escapes from the lake. On the afternoon of Sunday, February 8th, two skaters were thus drowned, and in the evening cries of agony were heard proceeding from the lake (doubtless from a drowning man) but in the fog and darkness it was impossible for the slightest help to be rendered. It is curious how much easier it is to preach prudence than to practise it. On the 16th February, I relieved my mind to the skating contractor about the folly of attempting to cross the lake at the risk of your life, when you could have as many miles as you chose of perfectly smooth ice along the shore. The contractor said in spite of all this he should like to cross, as it was very unlikely the opportunity would occur again during our lifetime. We agreed that the next morning we would take a boat upon runners between us, and so get across to the St. Loretto Chapel, thus crossing the arm of the lake upon which Constance stands. As, however, we were both upon skates, we took a little run just to examine the route for our next morning's excursion. Upon reaching the point we had fixed upon as our limit, a skater appeared from the other side and reported "all safe." Our wise resolutions were forgotten, the boat was despised, and in less than five minutes we had crossed the mile-wide arm of the lake. It is, doubtless, exceedingly foolish, but human nature is so constituted that the knowledge that the mirror-like surface upon which you are skimming separates you from a profound abyss, and that a fall might have very awkward consequences, gives a wonderful zest to the wild delight of skimming the frozen azure. Had we waited until the following day, I do not think that our projected excursion would have come off, even with the assistance of the boat ; for the temperature rose, and in proportion the ice became untrustworthy and unsafe. Between the 7th and the 16th, the lake was crossed in almost every direction, and in many places, roads across the ice were staked out by the authorities; for it must not be forgotten that to the inhabitants of many of the towns and villages it was not a mere question of amusement, but the ice was, in fact, the only means of communication with their neighbours. Thus, for example, the little town of Meersburg, usually within little more than half-an-hour by steamboat from Constance, when once the lake was frozen, and the ice was yet not strong enough to bear safely, was practically placed at as great a distance from the city, of which it may be regarded as a suburb, as Paris 400 miles away.

The records of some of the passages that were made on Saturday and Sunday, the 7th and 8th of February, compare in hardship with, and exceed in peril, many arctic adventures. Take, for example, the experience of a party of peasants and fishermen belonging to Altnau, on the Swiss side, who determined to see safely home eight German visitors from Hagnau, in the Grand-Duchy of Baden. I give the story in the words of one of the party :—

"There were eight men in all, six from Altnau and two from Kessweil (both places on the southern or Swiss side of the lake), who accompanied home the eight men from Hagnau. When we started at 10.30 in the morning we found ourselves surrounded by a dense fog. One of us was provided with a compass, and, acting as leader, led the way; not, however, in a straight line, for our leader carefully avoided every place that seemed at all suspicious. Soon the dangerous place was passed, where yesterday the men of Hagnau were ferried across" (this was an opening in the ice very near the Swiss shore, where, by their cries, the Germans had attracted the attention of some Swiss boatmen). "For a couple of hours we proceeded like this without any accident. Strange thoughts came into our minds as we thus marched over the surface of the lake where we had so often battled with wind and waves. All, however, went well, and we were still far out upon the lake when we heard the fog-bells of Hagnau. Now we came to some open water which seemed to extend the whole length of the lake. Our leader tried hard to cross, but found it impracticable. At last we found a spot where the water was narrower, and where, by putting the ladders we had with us across, we one after another succeeded in reaching the solid ice, and soon after the German shore. This was about two o'clock, the crossing having taken three hours and a-half."

Here they were received with great rejoicing and large hospitality. They dared not return the same way, but kept along the shore to Ueberlingen, where they crossed and returned home by Constance. Happily this journey did not have a tragic end. Too many did; for twenty-five lives were lost by drowning, while there were many very narrow escapes.

At first sight anything more imbecile cannot be imagined than to risk your life by crossing a lake of unknown depth in a fog and upon a thin sheet of ice. It is a game at which you are very likely to lose your life, and cannot possibly gain anything. On the other hand, it should be borne in mind that the Boden See, is to the dwellers on its shores, what the ocean is to those who live on the sea-coast. They have been accustomed to gain a great part of their living by fishing in and navigating its waters. They have battled with its storms and rejoiced when the sunshine played upon its smooth blue mirror. The tradition lives among them that now and again, with intervals sometimes of many generations, its surface is frozen over; and in the archives of the various lake-cities are records of those who were bold enough to cross upon the ice. The ambition to be as bold as their fathers fires them, and the enshrinement of the names of those who make the hazardous crossing in the local archives, and their publication in the newspapers, act as an unhealthy stimulus.

A singular phenomenon was observed at Utweil, on the Swiss shore. On the morning of the 8th of February, about 9 a.m., with a temperature of 20° Fahrenheit, and during a perfect calm, great fields of ice in the middle of the lake separated themselves from the main body, and came crushing in upon the Swiss shore. The ice-floe forced itself under the sheet of ice near the shore, or piled itself up in a huge wall, which snapped like twigs the piles and beams of the landing-places for steamers and ships.

For several days after the thaw set in, the ice on the Kreuzlingen shore continued to bear, and I was able to try a curious experiment upon it. In the ice, mostly near the shore, though often in water from ten to twenty feet deep, were to be observed numbers of great white spots, from a foot to two or three yards in diameter. These spots are formed by an accretion of marsh gas (carburetted hydrogen) underneath the surface of the ice, and the ice is usually thinner at such places. If you now bore a hole with your Alpen-stock (or, better still, with a pointed hammer) in the centre of the spot, and an assistant instantly applies a lighted candle, the marsh gas will ignite, and in some cases the jet of flame will rise four or five feet.

On the afternoon of February 17th the sun shone out brightly, and the temperature was like that of our English June. We took advantage of the genial change to take a drive towards Romanshorn. A great part of the lake lay at our feet, the surface

U

apparently about equally divided between ice and water, as the hot Föhn that had been blowing for the previous twenty-four hours had a good deal broken up the ice. The appearance of the lake was not singular solely from the vast ice-fields which covered so large a part of its surface, but also from its stillness, which seemed preternatural. Not a boat, a ship, or a steamboat could be seen as far as the eye could reach; and this solitude and stillness were not even relieved by the presence of skaters. Beyond the water, however, were the glorious Vorarlberg Alps, of which and of the Sentis we had a superb view while we enjoyed the balmy air and the warm sunshine. So soon as the thaw commenced, one or more of the imprisoned steamers in Constance harbour went out about noon, and crushed as far as possible into the solid ice. At length, on the 19th of February, after several lovely spring days, with a temperature of 50° Fahrenheit in the shade, and plenty of warm sunshine, a steamer succeeded in forcing its way through the ice to Meersburg. Almost all the inhabitants were down upon the pier to welcome its arrival ; for, there being no railways near, these poor people had been almost shut off from the rest of the world for the sixteen days during which the ice had stopped the navigation. Soon afterwards the ice entirely broke up, and huge fields went floating down the Rhine, crushing themselves to fragments against the buttresses of the Rhine bridge. The 21st of February was a most lovely summer's day, the lake being of that wonderful blue which one associates with the Mediterranean or Lake Leman. That afternoon my wife and I rowed in a little boat across the Constance arm of the lake, exactly in the track over which I had skated only five days before. Then it was a solid sheet of ice : now not a trace of ice was to be seen, but the blue water curled itself up in tempestuous waves. Constance is a delightful station for boating ; but, with all its delights, how toilsome is rowing compared with skating ! It is the difference between skimming through the air like a swallow, and with toil and labour pushing your house along, or carrying it like a snail.

I had fancied that the high temperature and hot sun must have long since made the ice on the Unter See unsuitable for skating, and did not visit it again until the 28th of February, when there was a slight return of frost, and I took a train down to Allensbach before nine in the morning. There was a good deal of water here near the shore ; but at my old station, *Das Untere Haus*, the ice was accessible, and in spite of eleven days' hot weather, was very strong and thick, and I had a pleasant run of about three-quarters of an hour ; but what a change from the appearance of the frozen plain on my previous visits ! Always formerly, the ice was dotted all over with the stations of fishermen ; great lumbering wains with two, three, or four horses were drawing across it mountainous loads of hay or faggots ; skaters and pedestrians, travellers on horse and on foot, gave animation and life to the scene ; now upon the great sheet of ice, whitened by the frost of the previous night, not a cart, not a fisherman's shelter, not a skater, nor wayfarer, nor living creature of any kind was to be seen. Even the row of fir saplings that marked the route from Allensbach to Reichenau had been pulled up and removed. The solitude was weird and uncanny. Just before leaving the ice I noticed half-a-dozen men leaving the island of Reichenau with a boat upon runners between them ; and when I reached the Allensbach station I there met the Fischermeister from Reichenau, who had come in charge of the boat and the mails from Reichenau. We were old acquaintances, and he greeted me heartily, saying, " I saw you in the distance skating upon the ice near Das Untere Haus, and knew at once that it was no Reichenauer or Allensbacher. The ice is still good and strong near Das Untere Haus and in some other parts of the lake; but it is treacherous, and in some places dangerous, and since last night I have forbidden all traffic upon it. The communication is kept up, and the mails are carried to Reichenau, but only by men who take with them the ice-boat (*eis-schiff*) or safety-boat (*noth-schiff*)," as the boat upon runners of which I spoke is indifferently called. "Any one from this time going upon the ice without the boat will be punished." He told me further that, up to the previous day, all through the ten days' thaw, the ice had been everything that a skater could desire. My ignorance had not been bliss. I had fancied the ice soft and rotten, and had waited for the first fresh frost. The post of the Fischermeister had been one of great responsibility all through the nearly four months' frost. It was his duty to keep a constant watch upon the ice, and to issue the necessary regulations for safe traffic upon it. Thanks in great measure to his energy and skill, no loss of life occurred save that mentioned of the joiner who, contrary to his express orders, had persisted in attempting to push his way across from Horn to Berlingen.

When the first accidents occurred upon the frozen Boden See the authorities at Constance requested the services of the Fischermeister; for by that time the Unter See was so hard-frozen that his presence there could be spared. He came and issued what he

regarded as necessary orders ; but the inhabitants of
the various states around the Boden See were very
different from the docile islanders of Reichenau, and
he could exercise no authority over them. As he
concisely expressed it to me, " They disregarded my
orders. Every one did just as he chose—and the
freezing of the Boden See has cost twenty-five lives "

CHAPTER XXII.

CONSTANCE IN THE SPRING.

Constance in the Spring—Apple and pear trees in bloom—Rowing—Professor
Kinkel—Grumble about insufficient ventilation—Theatre—Storms—Stein-
upon-the-Rhine — Hohenklingen — Schachzabelbuch — Abbot David von
Winkelsheim—The Hall of the Frescoes in the Abbey of St. George—
The cells of the monks.

For months a large pear-tree just under our window
at Kreuzlingen presented a picture of singular beauty
in consequence of the rime, which stood out two or
three inches from every branch and twig. When a
high wind arose, the hoar-frost lay in heaps under
every tree as if it were a considerable fall of snow.
Two months later the pear-trees were again almost
as white, but now with blossom.

Nowhere is spring more beautiful than in the
Canton of Thurgau, and at this time of the year the
drives, to places easily accessible from Kreuzlingen,
are lovely in the extreme. Warmed by the rays of
the sun, which already in March are very hot, the
grass springs up green and bright, and very soon
the meadows are yellow with innumerable cowslips
and oxlips. The banks are full of sweet violets,
and every little stream is gorgeous with marsh-
marigold and the golden balls of the globe flower.
The woods are budding into life and exhibiting in
exquisite variety their vernal tints, while the ground

below them is carpeted with wood anemones and wood sorrel, with its delicate green leaves and exquisitely veined blossoms. At every turn you get new views, each fairer than the last, of the blue lake below you. Each of the myriads of pear-trees, with which the whole Canton of Thurgau is dotted, is a pillar of white, relieved by the young green of the leaves, and is in itself a picture of exquisite beauty. Perhaps, if there is anything in nature more beautiful than a pear-tree in full blossom, it is an apple-tree, and when the pear bloom begins to fall, the apple-trees begin to open their exquisitely-rounded pink blossoms. This is the season *par excellence* for boating upon the lake. The sun's rays are powerful, but what the French call " *le fond de l'air* " is cold, and the warmth resulting from the exercise of rowing is pleasant. Nothing can be more delightful than to row past the country seats, the gardens, and parks, on the promontory of St. Loretto, and watch nature bursting everywhere into fresh life and beauty ; and more beautiful even than the parks and gardens is the forest which serves as background to them.

We neglected to provide ourselves with letters of introduction, and had but little social intercourse at Constance. In the spring, however, we were fortunate enough to make the acquaintance of a most amiable family, that of Dr. S——, a physician in large practice in all the country-side, a man of considerable culture, and of scientific and literary tastes. He resides near to the Constanzerhof, in the suburb of pretty villas extending towards the Loretto-wood, and his large and beautiful garden, running down to the lake and commanding a superb view, was a source of constant pleasure to our children. The culture and refinement of this happy home, and the pleasure of little visits, easily made by rowing across the lake, greatly added to the enjoyment of our stay at Kreuzlingen.

Every fortnight, during the winter, lectures were delivered at the Wessenberg Institute which were always well attended—in fact, they were inconveniently crowded.

I hope the good people of Constance will excuse a characteristic British grumble. Some of the lectures were excellent. Very interesting was it especially to see the distinguished poet and author—perhaps even better known as a lecturer and political exile—Dr. Gottfried Kinkel, now of the Zürich University, but for many years a resident in London—received here in Constance as an honoured guest. Thirty-two years ago, this eminent, and eminently loveable man, took part in the Baden insurrection, and falling into the hands of the Prussians, was sentenced to death by a court-martial. The subject of his lectures was the history of the Assyrian monarchy, and all the thousands of Dr. Kinkel's old pupils in many lands need not be told that it was made very interesting. But to my grumble. The room in which the lectures are held is a well-proportioned square hall, adorned with busts of the Emperor, the Crown Prince, Bismarck, and Moltke, and well lighted with gas. The lectures are always crowded with the *beau monde* of Constance. What preparations are made for due ventilation? First, care is taken that there shall be no possible outlet or hole of any kind in the ceiling; then all the windows—double windows, remember—are carefully fastened. Lest any of that deadly compound, fresh air, should by any chance find its way through the two walls of glass into the room thus hermetically sealed, inside the inner window curtains are drawn. The room is then packed and brilliantly lighted and great care is taken that the doors shall be religiously closed as soon as the audience have taken their places. Now, whatever may be the case with Germans, Englishmen cannot live without a certain moderate supply of oxygen; and, however interesting the subject or brilliant the lecturer, I soon found my thoughts wandering away from it and him to a vivid realisation of the sufferings of my countrymen a century ago in the Black Hole of Calcutta. Suffocation seems imminent, the veins swell on one's forehead, and one begins to speculate upon what an odd exit from the world it would be, to be asphyxiated in a lecture-hall in Constance. The ladies to whom—by what I am Goth enough to regard as an over-strained courtesy—are assigned *all* the seats in the middle of the hall, fan themselves and look blooming and happy; the gentlemen—who are relegated to the sides of the hall, most having to stand the whole of the time—seem profoundly absorbed in the subject of the lecture; you would suppose any atmospheric aliment for the lungs of either ladies or gentlemen quite unnecessary. The Doctor, who was so frequently my companion on the ice, and other gentlemen to whom I made forcible protests, listened very politely to what I had to say, said something about the ladies taking cold if the windows were open, and evidently regarded my desire for fresh air as one of those inexplicable and whimsical crotchets to which Englishmen are so much given.

The Theatre at Constance, which was formerly a Jesuit college, is a large hall of oblong shape, peculiarly arranged, but well-suited for its purpose. A very good company performed, and I am sorry now that the weather and other circumstances prevented me from going more than once or twice during the season. I believe, however, that although only

moderately patronised, some capital plays were well put
upon the boards, and that, as in many small provincial
towns in Germany, the theatre is without sensation or
extravagance, a healthful recreation, and a means of
intellectual and moral culture.   It is particularly
to be hoped that this is the case in Constance, for
the saintly Wessenberg believed that this was the
mission of the drama, and laboured here to make it
such.

The spring was not all sunshine : had it been so we
should have missed much that was grand and picturesque.   In a cloudless sky, away to the east a
storm would gather, somewhere on the skirts of the
Sentis, and towards sunset the whole heaven over
the lake became an intense blue black, deeper than
the deepest indigo.   Then would burst the storm,
and cover the road and choke the gutters with
pear blossoms.   Often a few days of heavy rain would
follow.

Among the excursions I took at this time was one
to Stein-upon-the-Rhine, a curious old town, now
belonging to the canton of Schaffhausen.   It stands
on the Rhine, about fifteen miles below Constance,
just where the lake, a continuation of the Unter See,
finally contracts into the limits of a river channel.
An old wooden bridge here spans its waters.   The
monks of the monastery on the Hohentwiel besought
Henry the Pious that they might be removed from
that cold and ungenial situation.   This request was
granted, and they were transplanted to this lovely
and sheltered spot on the Rhine, where, among green
pastures, vineyards, and fruit trees, they and their
successors lived in peace and prosperity for many
centuries.   Above the picturesque old town (once
doubtless a Roman settlement), and on the summit

STEIN·ON·THE·RHINE,
WITH THE CASTLE OF HOHEN-KLINGEN

of a hill now clothed with vines, towers the old castle of Hohenklingen, built by the lords of Klingen, to which family belonged the martyr-recluse Wiborad, slain by the Huns at St. Gall in 925.

The monastery of St. George had been transplanted from the Hohentwiel and richly endowed in 1005, and the family of Hohenklingen, as Lords Protectors (Schirmherren) of Stein, and of the monastery of St. George, in 1336 built their new castle above the town. For five hundred years the monastery flourished, and in the thirteenth and fourteenth centuries displayed considerable literary activity, the only relics however of which that have come down safely through the troubles of the Middle Ages being a very beautiful copy of the Gospels, now in the Hermitage at St. Petersburg, and a curious work called the "Schachzabelbuch," written by the monk Conrad of Ammenhausen. This work is a description of, and an allegorical disquisition on, the game of chess. The moves are all described, and each piece is compared with the corresponding rank in real life—as, the king, the queen, the knight, the judge, the landvogt, and the different trades, which he likens to the pawns. He gives plenty of good advice to both poor and rich, and, while he reproves the tradespeople for their increasing dishonesty, he warns the landvogts that they may one day become poor, and recommends to the nobility a virtuous life. Conrad, though a monk, was also an accomplished man of the world, and had travelled much, not only in Germany, but in Lombardy, Provence, and France, and his work is embellished by many quotations from Cicero, Seneca, Valerius Maximus, and Boethius. It is curious that in spite of all this scholarship and knowledge of the world, he should speak of the wars of the Guelphs and Ghibelines (*Gelffen und*

Gibeling) as belonging to ancient Roman history. He meant, of course, the struggles between Marius and Sulla.

When the Reformation came, a certain David von Winkelsheim was abbot. He was a mighty hunter and great friend of art, and was for many years constantly engaged in rebuilding and adorning the monastery. He was, however, an utter heathen of the Leo X. type, and nothing could be more scandalous than life in the monastery of St. George during his art-loving *régime*. From out the old abbey came Erasmus Schmidt, the reformer of Stein, who became subsequently a canon of Zürich Cathedral, and a great friend of Zwingli, but who continued to be called "Pfarrer von Stein" until the year 1528. By his preaching and personal influence he greatly helped on the Reformation in his native city. Hard by, at Burg, lived the famous orator, Hans Oechslin, another friend of Zwingli, from the days when they were both at Einsiedeln together; he also laboured by word and deed to further the Reformation.

Stein, sometime a free city of the empire, was then under the protection and control of Zürich, and it and the abbey followed the fortunes and changes of the city upon which they were dependent. Constant quarrels took place between the citizens and Abbot David, and at last, in 1524, the latter, wearied by the struggle, agreed to hand over the abbey to Zürich, on condition that a sufficient income should be reserved for him and as many of his monks as did not "wive" (*weibeten*). On the part of the Cathedral-Chapter at Zürich, a caretaker was appointed of the name of Conrad Luchsinger, whom the monks were bound to obey, and who seems to have maintained a severe discipline, and to have kept a specially sharp watch on the doings of Abbot David. This soon became intolerable to the Abbot, and he contrived secretly to convey the principal valuables out of the abbey into a boat on the Rhine by means of rope-ladders; and, with a number of monks of his own way of thinking, made his escape to Radolfszell, where he revoked the agreement he had made with Zürich, maintained that he was still Abbot, and sought the help of the Catholic Powers to reinstate him. Death, however, cut short his endeavours on the 10th November, 1526, and he lies buried in the Church of Radolfszell, the last actual abbot of the Monastery of St. George at Stein. From this time until the French Revolution, the property of the abbey was administered by officials from Zürich, who three times a year came for a fortnight to the abbey, and there exercised the lordship formerly pertaining to the abbots.

Thanks to its affiliation to the powerful Protestant republic of Zürich, the town of Stein and its abbey buildings passed unscathed through the storms and wars of the three succeeding centuries.

On the 28th of August, 1633, the Swedish army, under Field-Marshal Horn, passed under its walls; but the Swedes came as friends, and neither city nor monastery suffered from their presence. Even the French revolutionary armies of one hundred and sixty years later did very little mischief; and now the old abbey buildings have been purchased by a retired Protestant clergyman from Schaffhausen, and have been converted to the uses of a modern dwelling-house. The abbey buildings are very interesting, as showing how a monastery of about twenty monks was accommodated throughout the Middle Ages. Some part of the building dates from the eleventh century; but by far the greater portion bears the impress of the architectural activity of Abbot David of Winkelsheim, in the early years of the sixteenth century.   The whole was so solidly built that it looks as strong and as fit for use as when erected.   The " Hall of the Frescoes," a room 26 ft. by 19 ft., of irregular shape, is unique of its kind.   It was probably used as the refectorium by the monks during the summer months, and a very nice summer dining-room it must have been, with its windows looking down upon the Rhine, which flows immediately beneath, and away to the green Swiss hills beyond.   The carving of the beams and roof is most elaborate, in a late Gothic style, while the frescoes with which the whole of the walls are adorned, and which are as fresh and sharp as when Abbot David caused them to be painted, show the influence of the Renaissance.   The subjects are not in the least degree ecclesiastical, or even Christian. They comprise the building of Rome, the founding of Carthage, the boy Hannibal swearing eternal hatred to Rome, the taking of Carthage by the Romans and of Saguntum by the Carthaginians.   The actors and fighters, however, in these scenes and battles are neither Romans nor Carthaginians, but nobles, knights, and Lanzknechts, such as the artist saw around him in southern Germany.   Carthage is represented exactly as an imperial German city, with moat and drawbridge, over which the Carthaginians, or rather the German soldiers who represent them, are fleeing after an unsuccessful sortie.   In the taking of Saguntum the warriors are armed with halberds, great two-handed swords, and even with fire-arms, while the cavalry have helmet and crest, armour with coat of arms, lances, and long swords.   The besieged defend themselves with crossbows, firelocks, and stones, while in the background some are seen throwing the women and children on to the funeral pile, where their valuables are already burning. Altogether these pictures are wonderfully quaint and life-like, and give a most realistic notion of how battles and sieges were conducted towards the end of the Middle Ages.

A part of two sides of the room is covered with a most elaborate representation of the fair at Zursach. A stream flows past the town. To the left is the horse-market with the dealers. Near at hand is a sick man in the hospital, while beggars in most miserable rags are imploring alms, and a girl is being led away in the charge of a market official. Bowls and other games are being played, while a number of youths and maidens are vigorously dancing to the sound of drum and fife. All the fun of the fair is represented by the painter without reticence or sparing of its coarser incidents; and he shows that human nature was much the same in Suabia in 1550 as in England in the time of Hogarth, or now in 1880.

The "cells" where the monks slept are really fine large rooms, such as most of us would now regard as very eligible sleeping apartments. The rough, unpainted, and unplaned oak pillars and beams that support this part of the building show no signs of decay, and there seems no reason why they should not be in as good a state of preservation when ten more generations shall have passed away.

Stein now numbers about twelve hundred inhabitants, and is still confined within its old walls. As you walk through its streets you meet hardly a soul, and might almost fancy it plague-stricken. There are some very curious painted houses, similar to those at Schaffhausen; and as seen from the hill-side above, on the way to Hohenklingen, the old town, with its walls and towers grouped around the abbey buildings, makes a very pretty picture.   Past it, through the valley, winds the Rhine, reflecting in its brilliant green waters the pastures and fruit-trees by which it flows, as well as the old monastic buildings of the Abbey of St. George.

CHAPTER XXIII.

THE THIRTY YEARS' WAR ON THE BODEN SEE.

The Thirty Years' War on the Boden See—Historians of the War—Schiller—
Motley — Its outbreak at Prague — Battles of Lützen and Nördlingen —
Devastation wrought throughout Germany—On the Boden See, Ueberlingen is
the head quarters of the Catholics, Lindau of the Protestants—Wallenstein's
army—Pestilence—War Commissaries—The Kaiser remonstrates with Wallenstein—Fresh troops and fresh exactions—The Swedes under Horn—Besiege
Constance and Ueberlingen—Conrad Widerhold at the Hohentwiel—Takes
Ueberlingen by surprise—Is himself besieged—The Swedes take Bregenz and
besiege Lindau—Diary of Sebastian Bürster, Monk of Salem—Condition of
the Abbey at the beginning of the war—Strange portent in the sky—Abundant
vintage—The Abbey and the fortune of war—Swedes come to burn Salem—
Death of Gustavus Adolphus—Troubles of the Monks—A relieving army—
Apostrophe to the Kaiser—Nördlingen—Plague of field-mice—Caterpillars—
Pestilence—Starvation and misery—Vicissitudes of the War—The Abbey
almost deserted—Sudden close of old Bürster's Diary—*Requiescat in pace.*

OF transcendent interest, not only to the historical
student, but to every lover of freedom, is the record of
the great struggle which lasted for eighty years, from
its first inception at Alva's Council of Blood in the
Netherlands in 1568, until the tardy negotiators at
length gave peace to an exhausted world at Münster
and Osnabrück in 1648. With the intuition of a true
poet, Schiller saw this and gave to the world his great
histories of the Revolt in the Netherlands and of the
Thirty Years' War.

In 1814, nine years after Schiller's early death, was
born in far-away Boston, a boy destined to make this
great theme the labour of his life, John Lothrop
Motley, the eminent historian.* The old world owes

---

* "I had not first made up my mind to write a history and then cast about to take
up a subject. *My subject had taken me up, drawn me on, and absorbed me into itself.*
It was necessary for me, it seemed, to write this book."—Extract from letter from
John Lothrop Motley to William Amory.—Dated Rome, February 26, 1859.

a deep debt of gratitude to the new, for the soul-thrilling picture which the genius and untiring industry of Motley have given us, of the former part of this eventful period. Death, alas! called the artist away before he could give to the world a portrait of Gustavus Adolphus as a companion picture to that of the earlier hero, William the Silent.

When we think of the stupendous nature of the task, and the varied qualifications requisite for its competent execution, we are tempted almost to despair of the mantle of Motley falling upon any one capable of worthily completing his great work.

It would, indeed, be presumptuous and out of place for me to do more than briefly indicate how the rolling war-cloud that desolated Germany affected the cities and shores of the Boden See.

It may be convenient for the reader to remember that the Thirty Years' War commenced on the 23rd May, 1618, when the indignant Protestant representatives of Bohemia threw the three Imperial Catholic Councillors out of the windows of the Council Chamber of the Castle at Prague. At the end of eleven years Protestant Germany lay crushed and broken at the feet of the Emperor Ferdinand, who had to thank, for this success, the excellent General Tilly and the splendid adventurer Wallenstein. When the Protestant cause seemed well-nigh hopeless, Gustavus Adolphus landed in Pomerania, on the 24th June, 1630. Before his enthusiasm and extraordinary military genius, the Catholic powers arrayed their armies in vain. For two years his campaign was little else than a triumphal procession through Germany, until, on the 6th November, 1632, the "stainless hero of the north" fell, at the age of thirty-eight, on the field of Lützen ; a desperate and long-doubtful battle, which ended in the defeat of the Imperialists under Wallenstein.

The Swedish king had maintained the severest discipline in his army ; but, after his death, the Swedes practised upon the inhabitants of the countries where the war raged, cruelties as great as any that had been perpetrated by their opponents.

Two years after Lützen, the Swedes suffered a complete overthrow at Nördlingen (6th September, 1634), and so the war dragged on its dreadful course with alternating success to either party, until, in 1648, the peace of Westphalia brought it to a close.

The war reduced the population of Germany by one-half. Villages and even towns were left without a single inhabitant. Whole districts, once in a high state of cultivation, were reduced to deserts, over which packs of wolves roamed and sought their prey. Augsburg once had a population of 90,000 ; at the close of the war, there remained only 6,000 to wander through its broad grass-grown streets. The trade of the Free Cities of the Empire was ruined,—the spirit of the German people was crushed and broken. Art disappeared, and the mental activity which characterised the epoch of the Reformation, gave place to the torpor resulting from physical exhaustion. The material and intellectual development of Germany was thrown back by at least a century. Of all this misery, Suabia and the region of the Boden See had its full share.

In February, 1619, the Bishop of Constance called together, at Ueberlingen, the Catholic leaders of the neighbourhood and told them that their enemies had in contemplation nothing less than the total extirpation of Catholicism. They proceeded to collect supplies and to levy troops. Lindau was the head-quarters of the Protestant party, under the leadership of the Count of

Solms; its fortifications were put in good order; the important passes in the neighbourhood of Bregenz were occupied; ambassadors were sent to the leading Protestant powers, and intimate relations were entered into with other cities in the Algau and with the Swiss Protestant Cantons.   Constance was in great terror lest Count Ernest of Mansfeld should take the city by a *coup de main*, and, as a matter of fact, some of the freebooters of the dreaded Protestant leader did show themselves in the neighbourhood, where they lived at free quarters, and from which they seemed in no hurry to depart.   The Emperor, having no troops to spare with which to drive away these marauders, gave permission to the peasantry to murder them wherever they found them.   Later, for years, a large number of Imperial troops were quartered in every city, hamlet, and village, along the shores of the Boden See.   The citizens were greatly impoverished by constant contributions for the support of these protectors, but worse was to come.

In March, 1627, the alarming news arrived that the "land-waster" Wallenstein intended to bring a strong army into Suabia.   This was by no means welcome news even to the Catholics.

Count Egon of Fürstenberg thus aptly described Wallenstein, Duke of Friedland: "he goes about everywhere, where there are still cities and nobles from whom something can be taken, and with him the word is—'*sic volo, sic jubeo, stat pro ratione voluntas.*'" The whole of Suabia was soon full of Imperial troops, nominally friends, but friends from whom the inhabitants might well pray to be saved.   The Croats conducted themselves as if in an enemy's country, set the villages on fire, and openly drank "*in sanitatem diaboli.*" With them came a terrible pestilence.   In

1628, two thousand of the inhabitants of Lindau perished by the plague. In 1629, a strong Imperial garrison took up its quarters in the little island-city, and remained there for twenty years. This "friendly" occupation is estimated to have cost Lindau five million gulden, an enormous sum that might well bring the much-tried citizens almost to despair. In the whole of the Hegau the soldiery did exactly what they chose, stole all the horses, unroofed the houses, and threw men and women out of their beds; in many places even the Catholic churches were not spared; the sacred elements were desecrated and thrown on to dung-hills.

The avarice of the War Commissaries added to the burdens of the unfortunate people; and, curiously enough, the greater number of those harpies (who, in levying moneys to maintain the cause of Catholicism, did not forget their own interests), were not Catholics. In view of this circumstance the people cried out, in bitter jest—"This year God has turned Calvinist."

Colonel Wolf Rudolf von Ossa, the Imperial War-Commissary at Memmingen, was by no means a bad sort of man. He saw through the plans of Wallenstein, and detested them. When Friedland despatched his confessor, an Italian Carmelite monk, on a mission to Italy, the emissary came to Ossa for a passport, and the Colonel took the opportunity of asking him, why Wallenstein continued to quarter so large an army in Suabia. "In order to ruin the country," was the laconic reply of the monk. "Why?" demanded Ossa. "In order to carry out his designs," answered the other. From this moment Ossa saw clearly that the ruin of Southern Germany, and the consequent enfeeblement of the Emperor, was intended to subserve the boundless ambition of Wallenstein.

To Ossa, then, the local authorities turned, and begged for a redress of the terrible grievances under which the land groaned. He replied that he deeply sympathised with the misery of the people, whose total ruin seemed inevitable, more especially as the Generalissimo purposed to increase the army by 2,000 men, but he himself was under authority and must act according to orders. The conduct of the worthy colonel reminds one a little of that of the Walrus towards the oysters in the story. The Suabians also were in danger of being eaten; Colonel Ossa assured them of his profound sympathy, but did not omit to accept very substantial gratuities from them. They then sent an embassy to the Kaiser, detailing their wrongs. He expressed his grief for Suabia, but professed himself powerless to help, and declared that he had no desire to oppress his people with his army, but only to protect them. He showed his sincerity by ordering the army to be disbanded in the following September, but this order was never carried out. Two years later the Kaiser wrote to Wallenstein, Duke of Friedland (nominally his servant, but really his imperious master), about the oppression of his Suabian subjects. This was on the 13th March, 1633. Wallenstein replied from Gitschin, on the 19th of the same month, in a very off-hand manner, that he had several times written to the Freiherr von Anhalt on the subject, but that he now purposed going himself to Memmingen at Easter personally to inquire into the matter. He really ordered Ossa to prepare to receive *his court*, and to have one thousand horses in readiness; but instead of coming, he sent ten more regiments into Upper Suabia. The impudent idol of the soldiery sought to quiet the Kaiser by telling him that he contemplated removing his armies altogether from these lands, and within two years, with their help, *to secure Constantinople for His Majesty*. The misery of the inhabitants reached such a pass that even Colonel Ossa and Count Wolf von Mansfeld (an Imperial general, though a relation of the great Protestant champion) were on the point of resigning. Meanwhile, the miserable people could hear the thunder of the cannon of the Swiss Protestant cantons, from the other side of the lake, and to the secret joy of the Protestant cities, many-tongued rumour brought the news of the victorious advance of the Swedes under their heroic king. The commandant of the Imperial garrison in Lindau, Captain Hans von Treitschnall, noticed the ill-concealed joy of the citizens, and, fearing that they might rise against him, sent pressing demands for reinforcements. They came, and with them, under the guise of army chaplains, to the terror of the inhabitants, came the Jesuits. News came also that thirty thousand Spaniards were about to march through Suabia, many of whom would pass through Lindau. Two thousand Italian Banditti were also on their way under the Duke of Mirandola. These wretches openly announced that they were ready to put any enemy of his Imperial Majesty " to sleep"—a citizen for a ducat, a burgomaster for one hundred ducats, and a prince for a thousand ducats.

These curious facts, which we owe to the industry of Schwab, who disinterred them from unpublished and rare manuscripts, throw a flood of light upon the well-known conversation between the Emperor Ferdinand and Wallenstein,* when the latter said he could not afford to maintain any army of 20,000 men, but for

---

* May I refer the reader, interested in the career of this magnificent but heartless charlatan, to Schiller's great drama of "Wallenstein," as well as to his history of the "Thirty Years' War"?

one of 50,000 he would provide without troubling His Majesty.

On the 16th April, 1632, appeared the first Swedes, under Major-General Patrick Ruthven—whose nationality ought not, one would think, to be open to much question. The citizens at Ravensburg, near the Boden See, received them with open arms. It was, however, only a scouting party, and the Imperialists were soon again masters of the district. Whichever party was successful the inhabitants suffered : as an old chronicler says—" It was an ocean of misery and distress."

In August, 1633, Field-Marshal Gustavus Horn, at the head of a Swedish army, determined, if possible to take Constance. He came from Ulm, and decided to reach Constance by way of Stein, crossing the Rhine at the bridge at that place; and from Stockach he wrote to the city of Stein, demanding permission to take his army across the bridge there. The City Council were in a sore predicament; they prayed for delay, so that they might communicate with Zürich; but while they yet deliberated, a Swedish colonel tapped at the door of the council-chamber, and demanded a quick decision. Under such circumstances only one answer was possible. The traditions of the great king still lived in the Swedish army. The Swiss Confederation, also, was so strong and warlike, that the most powerful states dreaded to give it cause of offence. Horn violated Swiss neutrality by his march through Thurgau, but he conducted it with such exemplary and perfect discipline, that the inhabitants along the road taken by the Swedes, had not the slightest ground for complaint. No one in Constance had the faintest idea of the approaching danger until Swedish horsemen were descried from the walls. The bishop, in abject terror, collected all his valuables, including the treasures of the Abbey of Reichenau, a costly emerald, and a silver image of St. Mark, alone valued at 350,000 thalers, put them hastily on board ship, and tried to escape to Lindau. Before, however, the anchor could be weighed, the Swedes were there and secured the rich booty, though the bishop himself contrived to escape to Lindau on another vessel. Horn commenced the siege in regular form on the 8th September. Eighty-five years before, the citizens of Constance, full of enthusiasm for the Protestant cause, beat off their Catholic assailants. Three generations of Austrian rule had changed all this; now, ceaseless Masses were said for help against the Swedish Protestants, and boys and women helped the men to prepare a desperate resistance.

For several weeks the citizens were exposed to a heavy bombardment, mines were dug and exploded, and a practicable breach was made in the walls.

The Catholic cantons were, however, very angry at the violation of Swiss neutrality, and the Protestant cantons seemed not altogether indisposed to make common cause with them; a great Imperial army, consisting of Germans, Italians, and Spaniards, was rapidly approaching to the relief of Constance; Horn was compelled to raise the siege.

In the following year, 1634, Horn again appeared in the Boden See, and long besieged Ueberlingen. It was on this occason that the citizens led the waters of the lake into the city-moat, and prepared to resist, street by street. They were, however, brought at last to the point of capitulating, but the peasants from the neighbourhood, who had taken refuge within the walls of the city, and who were filled with frenzied hatred of the Swedes, would not hear of it. Their courage was at last rewarded by seeing the besiegers retire. The Swedes, however, remained intrenched at Radolfszell and Buchhorn (Friedrichshafen) at which latter place four ships of war were ready to be launched, and one war galley, with twenty-two guns, to which the Swedes gave the name of their Queen, " Christina." Although the Imperial garrisons of Bregenz, Lindau, Ueberlingen, and Constance, made great efforts, and even besieged Radolfszell both by land and water, they found it impossible to drive out the Swedes, until the total defeat of the Protestant army under Bernard of Weimar and Horn at Nördlingen, on the 16th August, 1634, changed the entire complexion of affairs, and within a month there was hardly a Swede to be found in the neighbourhood of the Boden See.

It was at this moment, when the Protestant cause seemed hopelessly lost, that the command of the Würtemberg fortress on the Hohentwiel was committed to Conrad Widerhold. He was then in his thirty-seventh year, and had been a man of war from his youth, having served as Reiter in the army of the Hanseatic League at the age of seventeen. Later he had learned the art of handling heavy artillery in the service of the Venetian Republic, and had perfected his military education by visiting, in various capacities, England, France, Spain, Portugal, Italy, and even Barbary. All his military science, and his natural firmness of character, were now to be put to the proof. With his small garrison of Würtembergers and Swedes he was completely surrounded by foes ; for the Hegau, and indeed the whole of Würtemberg and Suabia, was in the hands of the Imperialists. Like an eagle, however, he kept watch from his eyrie on the rocky Hohentwiel, ready to swoop down upon his enemies whenever they should expose a weak point. The same year that he assumed the command (1634) he distinguished himself by a brilliant feat of arms. The citizens of Ueberlingen were beginning to breathe freely, believing that they had seen the last of the Swedes and their other foes. They knew, however, that trains of provisions and munitions passed near their city from the heretical city of Ulm. To surprise and secure these, 550 armed men left Ueberlingen. In some way Widerhold obtained information of this attack, and the captors of the munition train found themselves surrounded by the dreaded garrison of the Hohentwiel: 350 Ueberlingers were slain, and 200 carried away prisoners to the Hohentwiel. Disguising his men in the clothes of the Ueberlingers, Widerhold presented himself at the gates of Ueberlingen, where his men were taken for the party who had gone out to plunder the munition-wagons, and were admitted. They quickly struck down the sentries and made themselves masters of the town, which, being unable to hold it in the face of the Imperialist armies surrounding it on all sides, they plundered and evacuated, retiring with the booty and cannon to the Hohentwiel. The Imperialist General Vizthum determined to make an end of Widerhold, and, collecting an army of several thousands, in September, 1635, he advanced to the attack. The storming party actually succeeded in entering the outer court of the fortress, whence, however, they were hurled back with terrible slaughter and chased down the hill. A second time, in 1639, the Imperialists succeeded in forcing their way into the outer court, and a second time were they driven out with loss. Meanwhile Duke Eberhard of Würtemberg was anxious to spare his subjects by assuming a neutral position, and the Bavarians who occupied Würtemberg insisted that if he really desired this, before he could expect any mercy from them he must suppress the hornet's nest on the Hohentwiel, which was the scourge and terror of the whole of Catholic Suabia. Duke Eberhard, in no condition to resist, wrote twice to Widerhold to command him to yield up the fortress. The veteran commander was well aware that his sovereign was not a free agent, and on the principle, as an old chronicler puts it, that "no answer in some cases is a good answer," sent no word back. For a third time the Duke wrote, and this time in his own hand. "If thou, Widerhold, really wishest to remain loyal to us, and to save thy fealty, honour, and good name, thou wilt no longer delay to obey our command and yield the fortress." But even to this command Widerhold paid no manner of attention.

The learned Burgomaster of Ueberlingen, J. H. von Pflummern, gazed up at this "robbers' nest" on the rock, and in sadness of heart and astonishment wrote—"The siege of Hohentwiel bids fair to outdo that of Troy."

In the month of September, 1640, the Bavarians in their turn raised the siege, which had cost them 1,500 men. In the following year a Spanish army-corps, under Don Frederico Enriquez, which numbered seven thousand infantry, besides cavalry, was no more successful. Widerhold made an attempt, which nearly proved successful, to take Constance by a *coup de main;* and, assured by his freebooters of the negligence of the warders of Ueberlingen (which they proved by bringing back with them to the Hohentwiel a piece of the outer of the three city gates, which they had cut out in the night without being observed), he marched his little army down to Ueberlingen, and took it by surprise in the night of the 30th of January, 1643. Poor Ueberlingen was immediately occupied by a French garrison, under the Vicomte de Corval, on behalf of the allied Swedes and French; but its sufferings were not over, for the following year it was besieged by the Imperialists under the Bavarian General Mercy; and only after 700 of the garrison had fallen, and starvation and pestilence had more than decimated the inhabitants, while all the towers on the walls had been shot down, and a breach thirty yards wide had been made in the city-wall, would Corval agree to a capitulation.

Well might worthy Burgomaster von Pflummern, in the bitterness of his heart, exclaim that it were better to be "cum Ovidio in Ponto" than at such a time to be Bürgermeister of Ueberlingen.

In 1646 the Swedes, 10,000 strong, under Marshall Wrangel, appeared again on the Boden See, and, after desperate fighting, took Bregenz; and on the 3rd of January, 1647, they advanced upon Lindau. A sword of fire had been seen hanging in the heavens at night over the unhappy city, and the unfortunate inhabitants had, as far as was possible, sent their wives and children into Switzerland for safety. Then began a terrific bombardment which lasted for weeks; and on the 14th, within three hours, 350 flaming balls fell into the town. Strange to say, though many houses, including the churches, were greatly injured, the town did not catch fire, no citizen was killed, and only one old woman, a stranger in the town, lost her life, being struck by a shell.*

* This will not surprise any one who has observed how little loss of life is usually suffered during a bombardment. Of this I had ocular demonstration in 1871. There was hardly a house not struck by shells in Thionville, Longwy, and the other fortified towns, into which the Germans threw hundreds of thousands of shells, yet it was an exceedingly rare thing for any of the inhabitants to be hit.

Not only was the land ravaged by constant fighting, but both sides maintained considerable fleets on the lake, which for three years became the scene of a bloody naval warfare.

The Swedes were unable to take Lindau, but took and occupied Mainau until the end of the war.

At length came the general armistice, followed by the peace of Westphalia. No sooner was the armistice proclaimed, then, as if by a charm, the appearance of the lake changed, the war-fleets disappeared from its surface, or were converted into the peaceful means of intercommunication and commerce. The commandants of the whilom hostile armies now crossed the lake to visit and banquet with one another.

But it is noticeable that it was the poor citizens and peasants who always suffered most from the hostilities. The soldiers always had a certain respect and consideration for one another as following the same trade. Of the sufferings of the inhabitants, a few extracts from a contemporary record will give some idea to my readers. These extracts I translate from the diary of a certain Sebastian Bürster, a monk belonging to the monastery of Salem, near to Ueberlingen. The manuscript was edited and published by Dr. Friedrich von Weech in 1875, and I am indebted to the learned Xavier Ullensberger, of Ueberlingen, for my being able to lay it before my readers.

We learn from the diary that he was born at Neufrach, a village south-east of Salem, and that as early as 1610 he was an inmate of the monastery, in the economy of which he filled the important position of "Brodkeller" (bread-steward) and distributor of alms. Many times he had to flee with his companions, and in 1646 he speaks of himself as one of the oldest of the monks.   His testimony distinctly shows that, although the hostile Swedes were by no means gentle in their treatment of the convent, they were not nearly so much dreaded by its inmates as were the natural protectors and champions of the Catholic church, the soldiers of the empire.

It is evident also that there was a long-standing quarrel between the Abbey of Salem and the neighbouring city—intensely Catholic as it was—of Ueberlingen, for the good monk shows throughout his pages a bitter *animus* against it.   He is also very severe against the Imperialist commanders, believing that they were much fonder of living upon the fat of the land and oppressing the poor Suabians than of fighting.   Honest Bürster has a keen eye for the signs of the weather as well as for the signs of the times, and, as was proper to a personage in his position, is deeply interested in the success of the crops, both of corn and wine, especially of those that belong to the Abbey.   The crabbed old German in which he writes is, I confess, almost more difficult to me than the earlier *Mittel-hoch-deutsch* of Ulrich of Reichenthal, although Reichenthal's chronicle was written more than two hundred years earlier.   His monastic Latin, cropping up here and there in the old German, is very racy.

We will commence our excerpts with two or three which illustrate the condition of affairs before the Thirty Years' War broke out, but when both Protestants and Catholics were making ready for the struggle. The "League" referred to in the first entry, was an association of Catholic nobles and others at Ueberlingen, to resist any attack on the part of the Protestants.

" December 29, 1614.—On this day *reverendissimus*

dominus Petrus Müller, fell asleep in God, *cujus anima requiescat in pace, amen.* Within the twelve years of his government of the abbey, he contributed 180,000, and some hundreds besides, of Gulden to the League, and towards the Hungarian war against the common enemy, those bloodhounds (*bluodhund* in his old German) the Turks. All this, however, was nothing, and mere child's play when compared with what our present prelate, *reverendissimus dominus* Thomas expended in building, and the indescribable costs of the wearisome war against the Swedes, through which he, the Lord Abbot, and all his subjects were reduced to the utmost poverty, and were utterly spoiled and ruined, *qua de re leges et perleges sequentia.*"

Our "gracious Lord Abbot Thomas" evidently had a great taste for architecture, and appears to have nearly rebuilt the abbey from cellar to roof.

In 1618-19 the first troops passed through Salem, on their way from the Netherlands to Bohemia, and our monkish traveller writes:—"At that time our cloister was still in good *esse;* we could keep plenty for ourselves, and at the same time send out to all the houses in the hamlets around, where the soldiers were lodged, ample supplies of fodder and provender, and enough of fish, fowl, and flesh, and other *condimenta*, so that with good discipline it need not have cost our subjects anything, as everything was provided by and sent out from the cloister. At that time the ways of war were new, strange, and unusual to us, but since then we have had to learn to accustom ourselves to them, as shall be plainly demonstrated in the course of this my narrative. Not only had we to receive friendly forces in passing, but to suffer the quartering upon us, and that for long, of both friends and foes."

Bürster shared in the almost universal belief in the marvellous and the supernatural peculiar to the age in which he wrote, yet there is much shrewdness perceptible in the following passage :—"4th February, 1630. — In the evening, from eight until midnight, so strange a portent appeared in the sky, as never before was heard of. Indeed, had I not seen it myself, I could not have conceived it possible, nor believed it had I been told. It was, however, visible far and wide, and men's hearts are filled with fear and wonder as to what it portends. The whole heaven was yellow and fiery red, especially towards the east, over Heiligenberg, as if the glow arose from a terrific conflagration. Then we saw the fiery clouds pass backwards and forwards in the sky, just as two great camps or strong armies would manœuvre against and attack one another, and all was bathed in blood. Everything relating to an engagement and great pitched battle was perfectly plain before our eyes. All the arms with which they attacked one another—the spears, the pikes, the fire-locks, even the flash and smoke of the muskets and artillery, as well as the marching and counter-marching, the advance and retreat of the hostile hosts—were plainly visible. What this should portend puzzles us all, though some, indeed, pretend it is only a *metheorum*."

The vintage of 1630 was so extraordinarily abundant, and the quality of the wine was so excellent, that the vineyards yielded double the usual quantity, and it was impossible to find casks enough for the new wine. With regard to this abundance, the good monk sorrowfully adds, "*vide disparitatem sequentium annorum.*" In order to have casks wherein to bestow this "noble and good wine," the poor growth of the previous two years was given away to any who liked

Y

to fetch it; indeed, in many places it was thrown away. Elsewhere, any one who would bring a cask, received a cask full of wine in exchange.

"1631.—On New Year's Day of this year, it was reported that at Milan there appeared, and was seen by many, a *Principe de Mammona*, in the shape of a very handsome huntsman, clothed in green, in a very fine coach, drawn by six black horses. His *officium* was to promote dire mischief, and especially to scatter abroad the poisonous seeds of pestilence throughout the empire."

The wonderful harvest and vintage of 1631, exceeded in abundance even those of the previous year, and Bürster makes especial mention that the wheat was being cut on the 23rd July, and that there was such abundance of wine, that all the reapers and harvesters received as much as ever they chose, not only when they came to eat in the cloister, but also taken out to them in the fields. This was done because of the abundant promise of the vineyards, and in order that there might be casks enough to receive the new vintage.

The good monk adds, " God pity us that we should have so much wine that we cannot keep it all. It was, indeed, a merry hay and wheat harvest." He then speaks of tremendous thunderstorms at Sipplingen and elsewhere, with hailstones " the size of hen's eggs," and then follows a passage which I think I must give in its entirety, as it forms, with the humorous picture of plenty that follows it, a pleasing contrast to the lugubrious descriptions of outrage, rapine, and war, of which the principal part of his narrative consists :—

" September 24th, 1631. To-day there was such wild weather upon the lake, that many sailing upon it thought they must infallibly go to the bottom. With this was thunder. This, however, was nothing compared with the weather at and around Ulm, where was such a storm that the wives of the burghers, who had gone for a walk outside the city walls and were overtaken by it, had damage done to their furs to the amount of two thousand florins. *Relatio ab homine laudato et fide digno.* At the castle of Gunzburg, too, all the windows were beaten in.

"*Nota :* The furs must indeed have been valuable, and not many of the women folk can have remained at home in the city ; perhaps only the old women remained, and being obliged to let the young ones go for a walk, allowed them to wear their furs as well, and this led to so unheard-of a bath of furs !

"September 26th.—Item. The vintage began at Meersburg and Hagnau, and on the 30th at Nussdorf and Ueberlingen. ·

"*Mirum in modum, miranda et mirabilia vera tamen jam scribam.*"

He then dilates upon the extraordinary abundance of the vintage, and proceeds :—" Most wonderful it has been to see, here at Salem, such a fetching and carrying, as much going out as coming in, that it looked like Schloraffenland [probably an allusion to some well-known popular story] ; it is true, however, that the roast pigs with knives stuck in with which to eat them, were not forthcoming. The decision was almost arrived at, that in order to make room for the new wine, the old should just be allowed to run, but instead of this, huge tubs-full were put outside the little gate of the cloister towards Schweindorf, that whosoever would might help himself, both those of the neighbourhood and strangers from the mountains. Never in my lifetime have I seen so many children's cradles used as casks, rigged up upon hurdles, carts, and barrows of all sorts. I should not have believed it possible to find so many, if the whole world had been searched for them. The cellar-door was always open, and all the cloister servants went as often as they chose with barrels and tubs and every imaginable vessel, in which they stowed away the wine in their rooms and workshops. Besides this, for more than half-a-year before, all the people employed about the cloister, as well as the reapers and harvesters during the hay and wheat harvest, had as much wine as they could drink, so that we might have empty casks enough against the vintage.

"*Nota :* However fast the wine came in, this and the previous year, it went out faster in 1633, down the throats of the men-at-arms and the Imperial *soldatesca,* of whom, in consequence of the attempt upon Constance of the Swedish army under Gustavus Horn, more than 30,000 (or, with followers, 100,000) persons were moving backwards and forwards in this neighbourhood, while in the cloister itself more than 4,000 troopers were quartered."

On the 16th November, 1631, on the motion of the Bishop of Constance, a meeting was held at Ravensburg of the leading local Catholic magnates, and it was agreed that the fifth man among their subjects should be called out for local defence ; not that it was possible to make head against the main army of the Swedes, but to keep in check any predatory bands in search of plunder and black-mail. Two-thirds of these levies were armed as musketeers, each of whom was supplied with two pounds of powder, four pounds of lead, and ample fuse, the remaining third being armed as "pichieri" or pikemen.

"On the 6th and 7th January, 1632, came the

Colonel Ossa, everywhere better known than liked, with his body-guard and two companies of troopers, who passed the night at Salem, on their way to Ravensburg from Alsace; and on the 17th, Count Egon von Fürstenberg, from Würtemberg, with his cohort of two or three hundred horsemen, with whom he did little enough, and did not fight the foe as he could and ought to have done. He was too fond of money, and flattery, and easy times, and so left the opportunity to strike a blow unimproved, for which may God forgive him if He will."

On the 23rd March, Count Wolf of Mansfeld came and passed the night at Salem, with twenty-five horsemen and thirty-six dragoons, but observed such perfect discipline that no one would have known any one was there; "no drum, no shouting, no firing, not even a trumpeter, all in good discipline, *quod rara avis.*"

" On April 6th, in Holy Week, six hundred horsemen appeared in the villages around Salem, and gave our poor subjects *hebdomadam pænitentiæ*, and those with whom the Confessor had been too mild and easy, had the matter of penance made good by the soldiers with blows, thumps, and whacks, and were *rigide* absolved by the same.

"Anything in the nature of penance that these neglected to inflict, the poor people received in full from 170 horsemen and 100 foot soldiers who were sent by Ossa, and so God pity the poor peasants for their miserable Passion Week.

"April 26th, 1632, matters became serious. A great troop of Swedes were despatched from Ravensburg to burn the cloister and leave it in ashes.

" It was about five in the evening, and we were just sitting down to supper when the alarm came. As

many of us as could, made haste to escape, and as I
mounted close to the hostelry, I saw the Swedes ride in
by the lower gateway, and they reached the cloister in
time to take prisoners eight or nine monks who were just
getting into horse-litters. The Swedes told them to
mount into the litters, and then sent them under guard
to Ravensburg, where they held them as prisoners for
a ransom of 6000 thalers. When, however, the
Colonel of this troop, before executing his mission to
burn the Abbey, entered the church, and saw the
beautiful, heroic, majestic fretted vault, and the high
altar, as he himself confessed, he was seized with such
horror, repentance, terror, and trembling, that as he
stood before the high altar, *ante gradum*, he was so
terrified that he believed the altar would fall upon him,
so that he neither would nor could set his men to the
work he had been ordered to carry out. I have no
doubt this wonderful preservation was due to the
mediation and special protection of our most beloved
and for ever blessed Virgin, Patroness, and Protectress
the Mother of God, to whom this great miracle must
be ascribed, in that she spread her mantle over the
dear house of God (the Abbey), and especially over
the beautiful church, and saved them from being
burned." Bürster goes on to say that as the Swedish
Colonel would have been hanged if, after being sent
upon such a mission, he had not burned something, he
set fire to the village of Neuffra on his way back to
Ravensburg, and burned down twenty-six houses,
carrying off seventy-five head of horses and cattle.
"Our head gardener was pierced to death near the
smithy, and three persons were burned," he adds,
without any comment.

"On the 28th of April the ransom of 6000 thalers
was paid, and our monks were set at liberty. As they

were confidently assured—and that often—that if the
money was not forthcoming they would be hanged,
the time must have seemed long to them until the
money arrived."

On the 3rd of May the cloister received a visit
from the Swedish general Bruschardt, with thirty
dragoons, and great was the terror of the poor
monks. He, however, only came to fix the monthly
contribution of the Abbey at 1000 thalers, which
money was sent in to the Swedish head-quarters at
Ravensburg the next day.

The entries to the end of the year 1632 are of a
similar character to the above. On the 11th of July
he mentions that the Swedes made a reconnaissance
before Ueberlingen, where, however, they were received with a heavy fire from the upper gate, which
killed many of the assailants, among them "a young
duke of Weimar, whom with other dead officers they
put into a sack and carried to Ulm."

The Swedish requisitions continued very heavy all
the year; but, as matters seemed to have quieted
down, all the members of the monastery had returned
home to Salem by September 1, 1632, when the
cloister was suddenly surrounded by Swedes, and
neither ingress nor egress was permitted. "There
we were all together in the fruit-garden, while troopers
watched the gates. Laughter was scarce among us,
and all joy departed, and nothing lay before our
eyes but *memoria mortis*, so many of us began to
confess one another." The raid ended, however,
simply in a new exaction, and the same evening
the good monks for the third time took flight from
the Abbey.

Perhaps the greatest event of the century is concisely related in the following short entry :—" On the

17th of November it is reported that the Swedish King fell before Leipzig, and lost his life there."*

" 1633·—Item.   13th January, about four in the evening, the town of Kämpten was taken by storm, and for four hours the soldiers hacked and slew every one they met, so that afterwards it was found that there were 500 souls missing.   Then these Lutheran Kämpter themselves set the town on fire, for they preferred to perish in the flames and be burned rather than to be hacked to pieces.   Then the imperial soldiers proclaimed by sound of trumpet that they would give quarter to all who remained, if only they would assist in putting out the fire—otherwise the whole town must have been burned."

On the 18th of January he mentions, without comment, that the Imperialists slaughtered 800 Würtemberg peasants, and on the 25th, "*in conversione Pauli*," 4000 Swedes from Mämmingen were destroyed by the Imperialists, being driven into the river Iller.

On the 21st of February, before proceeding to enumerate other acts of violence, he says, "A state of war and trying to get the better of one another, with quartering of troops, sorties, reconnaissances, plundering, man-catching, and hacking, hewing, and slaughtering, has become the rule throughout the whole country-side.

" 27th February.   *Dominica Oculi*.† Colonel the Count of Rüdtberg came here with his staff and three companies to remain until the 11th of March. For these I was obliged (we must remember the good monk was bread-steward) to have white bread, kneaded with milk and baked with butter.   Besides the staff of

---

* At Lützen, on the 16th of November.

† I give the good monk's Latin as he wrote it, and leave all responsibility as to its quality with him.

Count Rüdtberg and the three companies for whose food and lodgment we had to care, we were not relieved from constant marching and counter-marching, and finding quarters in our hamlets and villages for an endless succession of troops, which causes our subjects terrible loss in horses, cattle, pigs, sheep, fruits, corn, and oats; thus the Croats sacked and burned two houses at Meilhoffen. Indeed, in some respects our friends treat us worse than do our foes. Grievous comparison! Wherever they come they are absolute masters. They use wine as if it were water—as if the wine-presses ran with wine day and night, year in, year out. They never thank any one for anything, but always demand more. They hold constant Carnival while we fast; and I greatly fear that worse, longer, and severer fasts are yet to come."

On the 13th of July he tells of Imperial regiments, beaten by the Swedes, passing by Salem, eating up everything in the villages, so that the poor peasants came crowding around the cloister-gates for alms, which he (Bürster) was obliged to refuse, as it was with the utmost difficulty he could find sustenance for the monks. Starvation stared the peasants in the face, from which they were only saved by the approaching harvest. Sadly the good monk adds, "Alas! this was only the beginning of sorrows!"

On the 7th of August the feast of harvest-home was held in the cloister, and the festivities were prolonged far into the night. Suddenly, at four in the morning, the monastery was set upon by 150 Swedes. Bürster says the Swedes brought with them a locksmith who had often been hospitably treated in the convent, and who evinced his gratitude by showing the plunderers how to get what they wanted, and by taking the locks off the doors for them. With drawn swords and cocked pistols the Swedish marauders went about their work, and, after killing and wounding six or eight people, they got clear away with thirty of the convent horses. At six o'clock, when the people of the convent were fully awake, the marauders returned to complete their work and carry away some fine stalled oxen that had escaped them on their first visit. The monks, however, now took heart of grace, made a barricade in front of the gateway, sounded the alarm-bell, and received the Swedes with a brisk fire, driving them off, and then pursuing them, with the men who had come to help upon hearing the alarm-bell. The good monk regrets that this was not done before the robbers got away with their first spoil, and especially that the pursuit was not more vigorously conducted, in which case he is sure the whole of the Swedes might have been slain and the booty recovered.

On the 15th of August the monks held a muster of 400 well-found musketeers of Salem and 150 badly-furnished peasants from Heiligenberg, armed only with boar-spears, halberds, badger-forks, and clubs. The monks gave them each a loaf and a good drink, and dismissed them, encouraging them to be prompt in appearing at the sound of the alarm-bell. All this helped little, for, on hearing that Field-Marshal Horn, and Duke Bernhard, of Weimar, were on their way into the neighbourhood at the head of a great Swedish army, the monks decided that further resistance was useless, and took refuge in Ueberlingen.

Then follows a description of the siege of Constance, of which I have already spoken; and on the 30th of September Bürster tells of the relieving army under the "*Ducis de Feria*;" but the good monk shall speak for himself:—"In all there must have been 100,000 persons, and in the cloister alone 4,080

troopers were lodged until the 5th of October. All
the villages, all the hamlets, all places of every kind
were full of troops. One would have thought that no
one was left anywhere else in the world, but that all
mankind was gathered around Salem. How will it
then appear at the Day of Judgment! I have often
thought that they must have grown and crept out of
the ground like the cockchafers in May. *Ach lieber
Gott*, how wondrous fine, well-dressed, and well-armed
was this host! and how much good they might have
done! They could have eaten up the Swedes, or
drowned them in the lake, but for foul play and
treachery. This, however, was the last thing they
thought of doing; for Wallenstein had forbidden them
to fight. Of this I was assured by Rittmeister Gol-
linidsch and many others. What a state the cloister
was in, with the 4,080 troopers, and as many horses, it
is impossible to describe. What sorrow and shame,
what squandering and waste! is neither to be written
nor told. Out of the bakehouse, out of the kitchen,
and out of all the cellars, at all hours of the day and
night, there was such a constant fetching of bread,
meat, and wine as no one could imagine, much less
describe. All vessels, clean and unclean, were pressed
into the service—anything, in fact, that would hold
wine—tubs and bowls, jugs and ewers and pans,
shoes, boots, and hats, sow-troughs, dog-troughs,
cow-troughs, fire-buckets, *in summa summarum salvo
honore*, pots and pans of every degree. The kindly
fruits of the earth, they took wherever they could find
them—not only out of the barns and storehouses, but
they knocked them down from the trees, and chose
the finest. They even strewed them under the horses'
feet, and in the court-yard, good hay and straw lay half
as high as a man, and as soon as ever they were a

little soiled, 'Away with them!' was the word, 'and let fresh be pulled down.' The whole cloister soon had the appearance of a *Cloaca*, slaughter-house, or den of thieves and murderers; and the stench was everywhere so abominable, that you would have thought it impossible for any one to live in any part of the monastery. Yet all this was as nothing—mere child's play, and a shadow of what was to come later, in 1643. On the 11th of October, Wallenstein, or the Friedländer, for once did something good in Silesia— to wit, destroyed forty companies of the enemy, conquered thirty-three standards, and took prisoners old General Thurn and Taubadell; for which reason the garrisons of Constance, Ueberlingen, and Reichenau fired salvos of artillery for joy."

Bürster closes his observations for the year 1633 with the following entry :—

"31st December.—Much trouble at the end and close of the year, and particularly in the month of December. In consequence of the great scarcity, I have had to give money to many of our people to buy coarse meal, so that they might bake some bread for their children for Christmas, who would otherwise have died of hunger. On all sides already a great many people have died, partly of hunger and grief, and partly of famine-fever and other pestilence. I have also been very busy because of the wretched way in which the war is being conducted. God pity us! with a constant useless marching to and fro of troops, ruining the country and its people, and nowhere attacking the enemy, as they might do with good effect; my pen refuses to record such worse than worthless work, so I will leave it until next year. O Kaiser! Kaiser! what blind eyes, stopped-up ears, and heavy palsied arms and hands must thou have, that thou wilt neither see nor hear, nor yet at least comprehend, how treacherously they deal with thee, and how falsely they serve thee under the rose (*underm hüetlin*, under the little hat).

"*Solutio :* The beer has worked at last, and the froth has come to the top, for, as will be related, Wallenstein or Friedland (*der Wahlsteiner oder Früdlender*) has been struck down, and the other ringleaders found out and dismissed."

The descriptions given of the bootless siege of Constance by the Swedes, raised late in the autumn of 1633, and of how Ueberlingen was taken by surprise by Widerhold, are quaint and very spirited, but my space will not permit me to dwell upon them.

Great is the good monk's rejoicing at the decisive victory over the Swedes at Nördlingen, which seemed, for the moment, as if it would end the war. Alas! in 1634 the war had only half run its dreadful course, and in April, 1635, he gives the following narrative, typical of what the poor Suabians had to suffer from the soldiers sent by the Emperor to protect them—soldiers now become utterly brutalised by the protracted hostilities.

"On the 10th of April, the parish priest of Leudtkürch, Magister Jacobus Rueff, was so badly handled by the Justinger troopers, now lying in the neighbourhood, that he very shortly died. They gave him some blows with a pointed hammer, and made a great hole in the nape of his neck.

"On the 26th of April, some troopers belonging to five or six troops of General Mercy, after having behaved shamefully and beyond all measure at Weingarten, *sicuti colligi poterit ex sequentibus*, detailed twenty troopers from each company to fall upon the hamlet of Owingen, the inhabitants of which had

given them no manner of offence. This then these
miscreants did, on a pitch-dark night, between ten and
eleven, just as the poor peasants were laid down in
their first rest and sleep. They gave out that they
were from the Hohentwiel—so as to throw the blame
of their evil ·deeds upon the enemy—broke in all
doors, stormed the church, spared nothing, only not
taking the poor people's lives and not setting the
village on fire. Of the other infamies of that night
it is not fit that I should write. (The good monk *does
write*, however ; alas! our last quarter of the nineteenth century has seen just such atrocities in
Bulgaria). The Swedes could hardly have behaved
as badly ; and present and in command of these
scoundrels and ravishers, was Oberst-Wachtmeister
(sergeant-major) Bell."

In this year (1635) unseasonable cold prevented the
fruits of the earth from ripening. Bürster says he
has not made many notes this year, as he spent the
greater part of it in the cloisters in Würtemberg, for
God Almighty had been pleased to bring upon them
at once his three ̇ scourges of war, famine, and
pestilence.

A most severe frost at Whitsuntide ruined the vines
for the year, and did incalculable damage to the crops.
Then came *a plague of field-mice*, and ate up almost
all that was left.

"Then in the autumn came pestilence, and such a
pestilence as I suppose was never before seen, at any
rate in Germany, a pestilence of which the inhabitants
of whole villages died ; in many communes or villages
with 200 or 300 citizens or peasants, now there remain
hardly ten or twenty, or at most thirty, *et sic in com-
paratione de minore ad maius et de maiore ad minus.*
If I were only to go through this district, and tell

of the mortality of each village, I should not be believed, while in reality I should be within the truth.

"The land also has fallen out of cultivation and become a jungle of weeds and brushwood, and all furrows and landmarks have been overgrown and lost; and as no one is left in many of the villages and hamlets, there is good store of dispute, as to the possession of the land, laid up for time to come. But to return to the field-mice : all the fields and meadows were full of them, and they made great store-houses for themselves in hollows of the ground, so that I myself have seen the peasants go out with spades and sacks to dig out and carry home what the mice had collected, often getting several bushels out of one hole —peas and other fruits, of which I have seen many sacks full, that had been taken from the mice. They were the most wonderful creatures, these mice, of all possible colours, and some, as I have heard, quite white, especially the larger ones, with short tails— larger than moles. All the fields and meadows were so traversed in every direction by their runs and pas- sages, that no grass would grow, to say nothing of corn or other fruits, for the mice gnawed and bit away the roots.

"It was a great wonder that God Almighty, in punishment for our sins, should send these creatures; no one knew how they grew or whence they came, and just as suddenly as they came, they disappeared; for in one day came a thunderstorm and downpour of rain, and flooded the fields and meadows to that degree that the mice were all drowned and perished."

The mice were followed by a plague of caterpillars, "White beasties as long and thick as one's finger, with brown heads at either end; with these all the fields were full. They also devoured the roots in the ground, especially of the oats, so that you might see a field, showing bright yellow, and seeming to promise abundance, and when you came to it, you found only husks on the ears, and if you gave the stalks a pull, up they came, because the root was bitten through.

" Holy David had the choice of three evils—war, pestilence, or famine; but upon us, all three have come at once, and thus sadly ends the year 1635."

Three times at least in the year 1636 was the cloister besieged by wandering bands of famishing troops, for the soldiers as well as the peasants were almost dying of hunger. These attacks were either beaten or bought off.

And now all discipline being at an end, and the whole country-side being given up to a ferocious and brutal soldiery, the peasants subject to the Monastery of Salem dared no longer remain in their villages, " but came with wife and child, cattle, horses, pigs, and whatever else was left to them, into the cloister, so that the court-yards, the hospital, the justice chambers, the house for the women, the mason's house, the weigh-house, the barns, the garrets, the stables and stalls, and even the little house over the great gateway, *in summa*, every hole and corner were as full as they could be crammed, all through the grim (*grümb*) cold winter (when many of the poor people were frozen), right through the summer and into the autumn of 1636. Terrible were the sufferings of these poor people from cold, frost, and hunger. I did all I could, and caused bread to be baked of acorn meal, for I ground up acorns, hemp-seed, lentils, dried carrots, and even the bark of trees, all together, but with all this, I could not give them enough. The dogs and cats were not safe from these famishing people, and, what was a more revolting diet, they greedily scrambled for the carcases of any cattle or horses, even of those that had died of loathsome diseases. The children would stand like dogs, up to the middle in pig's wash, and if they could fish out a peas-cod, a crust of bread, or a carrot, they thought themselves happy. Snails they ate unroasted and unboiled; also any young birds they could catch, even beetles and cockchafers, anything, in fact, with which they could still the cravings of hunger. At last came the spring, and they found in the young grass and the shoots on the trees a little relief. We, as their superiors, were most anxious to help them, but we were in evil case ourselves, and often in want of bread."

Happily, after the severe winter came a very early and warm spring, so that *"in medio Aprilis"* was more like *"in medio vel fine Maii,"* with the promise of a good fruitful year; for which the much-tried monk thanks God, as he hopes that the poor people, who are still alive, though without bread, may yet be able to exist on the green stuff now abundantly sprouting forth. It seems the previous autumn the oak forests yielded an unusually abundant crop of acorns; and, as the pigs had to a large extent been stolen or driven off, the acorns served as a last resource for the starving villagers, which seemed to the pious monk a special providential arrangement. Already, in the middle of April, the grass was ready for a first mowing; the tulips, hyacinths, and narcissus were in full bloom in the garden; the rose-trees were covered with leaves and flower-buds; and before the end of the month the cherries were half-formed upon the trees. "Then in the autumn, thank God, to the great joy of the poor, hungry people, there was much fruit. Many people say such a crop was never before heard of. In our orchard there were thrice as many props as there were trees. Some trees required as many as ten to twenty props ; and, in spite of this, great branches were broken right off with the weight of the fruit, and smaller trees were completely pulled down by it. This summer more fruit was spoiled and wasted from there being so few people left to gather it, than the whole crop of an ordinary summer. This abundance was a real godsend to the poor."

The following passage will remind the reader of Schiller of the famous lines from " Wallenstein's Lager," where the " Kapuziner " says :—

" Und das Römische Reich—dass Gott erbarm
Sollte jetzt heissen Römisch Arm."

" And the riches of the Roman empire, which may God pity,
Should now be called the poverty of the empire."

The point of the sentence lies in " Reich " meaning both " empire " and " rich," thus standing in antithesis to " Arm " (poor).

To return to Bürster's last entry for 1636 :—

" ' Reddite quae sunt Caesaris Caesari et quae
Dei sunt Deo.'

" Dear reader, the empire has belonged to the Kaiser, and has always been obedient to him, and yielded as much tribute to him as was reasonable, or even possible. Now, however, the gospel words read backwards, and, in place of *In illo tempore* the empire (Reich), it is now, God pity us, the lack-all *(Arm, poor).* If, then, instead of being a rich empire *(Reich),* it has become a lack-everything *(Arm),* it no longer owes anything to the Kaiser, for he has no gospel for it *ergo facti sumus liberi.*

"Now for so many years, ever since 1618, the empire has been laid waste by endless armies, regiments, and soldiers, and now whatever remains and has been spared to us by the enemy *in annum præsentem*, is wasted, spoiled, and utterly ruined by our *friends*. O Kaiser, Kaiser! dost thou wake or sleep? O that thou wouldst really wake up, look around thee, and see the signs of the times, and how thou art being led to thy ruin, so that, of all thy many lands and peoples, some might still remain to thee. O Germania, Germania! O my country, my country! how art thou laid waste and brought to naught, and there is no eye to pity! O pious Emperor, little dost thou know how evil are thy counsellors and how traitorous are thy servants!"

1637.—Early in 1637 the subjects of the monastery again left their villages and came to the Abbey for protection. Small as was the protection the monks could give them, without it one would think they must really have been exterminated. All this year, imperial troops were constantly quartered on the Abbey, and endless contributions and exactions had to be paid. On one occasion, by a ruse, a roving band of soldiers — friends, remember — got inside the Abbey-buildings, and expressed their intention of driving away all the cattle, pigs, &c., belonging to the poor peasants who had taken refuge there. "You should just have heard the cries and lamentations of our wretched subjects, when they understood that their ruin was thus to be consummated." Ultimately, a sum of money, which the monks had to borrow, was accepted in place of the property of their miserable subjects. The freebooters now evidently thought that they had carried matters too far with a friendly convent; so, having as a last enormity—on the plea that the ready money was not forthcoming—taken two yoke of oxen and all the milch cows and sold them, they set a watch around the Abbey walls, and forbade the monks, or any of them, to go out, lest they should make complaint of the soldiers' conduct.   The monks thought to overawe the soldiery by marching in procession and demanding egress ; but no, they were all sent back.   " However, that same evening, the 24th of March, just as it was growing dark, we found out a secret place of which they knew nothing, nor were they ever able to discover it.   Just as towards evening the bats come forth from behind walls and boards, so we came forth, crept out, and succeeded in reaching Constance, and this without being observed by their watch, though they had strengthened it all round the Abbey."   In Constance all the monks remained until the 27th of May. On the 26th of October Bürster makes mention of the neighbourly kindness of the citizens of Pfullendorf. The monks, having been robbed, as related, of their oxen and horses, knew not how to prepare their land for the autumn sowing ; then came the Burgomaster of Pfullendorf and all the principal citizens, with thirteen ploughs, to the help of the monks.   These occasional touches of friendliness and human kindness are a great relief to the dismal narrative.   By December of this year (1637) wolves had become so common, that it was no longer safe to walk alone along the shore between Meersburg and Ueberlingen.

1638.—"Again an untranquil year," says the good monk ; "for on the 13th of February again *seniores et aegroti* left Salem and retired to Ueberlingen, because of the near approach of Duke Bernard of Weimar with his army."

The oxen and mules which the monks had purchased to replace those carried off were again looted.

Still, on the 23rd of May, Bürster and some of the other "older" monks returned to Salem to celebrate Whitsuntide, at which festival, on the 30th of May, they had already ripe cherries; indeed, the heat of the summer was so unusual and severe that all the people in the monastery were troubled with continuous headache, giddiness, and fever.

"June 15.—On the 15th of June we were obliged to flee again; *in summa*, this year there was nothing but starting and running, by day and by night, with such terror and fear as cannot be written or told. Not a bit could we eat or a drop drink in peace, neither could we rest nor sleep for a quarter of an hour at a time, for fear of the Hohentwieler. Only the younger monks ventured outside the walls. The old and sick remained indoors."

On the 12th of October he mentions an act of revenge on the part of the misused peasants, which shows the pass to which matters had now come. It seems thirty imperial troopers, roaming through the district, no doubt requisitioning and pillaging wherever they went, passed the night at Altenbeyren. The villagers of Zustorff fell upon them at midnight, and butchered twenty-eight of them as they lay, two only escaping to tell the tale. The peasants then fortified their village, and prepared to resist assailants from what quarter soever they might come, and their example was followed by other villages.

At Christmas, 1638, the weather was so warm that Bürster says you might with comfort bathe in the lake.

The years 1639 and 1640, to the events of which the good monk devotes many pages, present the same melancholy and somewhat monotonous picture of robbery, pillage, and murder, and a war which seemed equally endless and aimless. "*Abeunt et redeunt ecce,*" says Bürster, in the summer of 1639, and the sentence aptly describes the whole period. He makes the remark that during the whole of 1639 he did not taste a cherry, and the grapes were a total failure—not a single properly-ripened grape to be seen in the vineyards of the Abbey. Contrasting this with the abundance of former years, he says, " What a falling off and inequality! Almighty God has done it, who acts as it pleases Him, and true it is that we have deserved it. *Sit nomen ejus benedictum.* Had we had abundance of the best wine, with such guests as were with us we should not have had the drinking of it."

In 1641 the Abbey of Salem found itself compelled to make terms with Conrad Widerhold at Hohentwiel, and to send him a regular contribution, as the monks could not defend themselves against his raids, and the imperialists failed to defend them.

In this year, Bürster mentions that a serf of the convent, convicted of repeated thefts, was sentenced to death, and was to have been executed at Ueberlingen. The Abbot, however, used his influence in favour of the poor wretch, and his sentence was commuted to lying three years in irons.

About September, 1641, he mentions " that six troopers from the garrison at Radolfszell, not meaning plunder, asked permission to pass the night in a farm belonging to the Abbey of Salem, called Bachopten. The peasants in the neighbourhood had been recently frightfully harried by the *soldatesca*, and they now surrounded the barn were these six lay, and, although they were quite innocent, their request for quarter was not listened to, but one after the other they were fetched out of the barn and slaughtered as if they had been oxen. On the 13th of September, 1641, ten priests and *Conventuale*, were sent away from Salem to Switzerland and Bavaria, and as seventeen had already gone, our convent was so weakened, that we could no longer celebrate divine service *in choro*, and it was given up altogether, as there now only remained in the convent a few brothers or *conversi*, together with four or five who were old and sick, and had no longer any voice."

In October, 1641, " His princely Grace the Bishop of Constance," called a great meeting of the authorities of all the cities and abbeys belonging to the bishopric, to take measures to destroy the Hohentwiel. As we know, this effort was not successful, but it is characteristic of the war and the times, that while the despoiled Abbey of Salem had to contribute largely to this effort, which reduced the garrison of Hohentwiel to the greatest straits, no sooner was the siege raised, than the monks were obliged to pay up the arrears of their agreed contribution to the garrison they had just been doing their best to destroy.

In 1642, August 20th, *in festo St. Bernardi*, the good monk deplores the dilapidated condition of the Abbey. Only five monks remained in residence, of whom he was one; the others, mostly old and sick, had taken refuge in Ueberlingen, Würtemberg, and Switzerland. He says they formed a procession as well as they could, with cross and banners, and marched round the church singing the joyful hymn, " Rejoice, Maria, thou queen of heaven, rejoice," but their hearts were sad, and they wept more than they sang. Three parish priests from the neighbouring villages assisted them, else they could hardly have got through the service. " And when I thought in how stately fashion we were wont to celebrate this great festival, and contrasted it with the present poor and pitiful celebration, and the wretched singing, my eyes ran over, and I could not check my tears."

On the 30th of January, 1643, Ueberlingen was taken by a *coup-de-main* by Widerhold, and worthy old Bürster empties the vials of his wrath upon the authorities of the unfortunate city, to whose negligence alone he charges this great misfortune. Not content with several pages of denunciation of their folly, in a style which sometimes reminds one of the Apocalyptic song of triumph over Babylon, and sometimes of Butler's " Hudibras," he devotes a poem of about two hundred lines, full of fierce irony, to a " Panegyric of the great deeds of the Citizens of Ueberlingen, in everlasting remembrance, and to the honour and glory, of the said City." All the monks now left Salem except two *patres bursarii*. The French commander of Ueberlingen, with the courtesy of his nation, gave those who · left a safe-conduct to Constance, and offered to convey them in one of his ships, if the garrison of Constance would undertake to let it come back in safety.

The villages all round the Cloister were in ruins, so that the inhabitants came and took up their abode in the Abbey, where they would have all died of hunger, but for the assistance the *patres bursarii* were able to give them.

The Abbey itself was little more than a shell, for the armies that now, one after the other, occupied it, tore down all the interior woodwork. Wainscoting, doors, tables, &c., were torn down and either burned or otherwise made use of by them, so that from the ground-floor you could see right up to the inside of the roof. The crops of rye and barley were trodden under foot, and the vineyards utterly laid waste.

During the first half of 1644, Ueberlingen, now in the hands of the French, was besieged by the Bavarians, by whom Salem, with all the surrounding country was occupied. After its surrender, on the 12th of May, it was hoped that an arrangement would be made between the Imperialists and the unconquerable garrison of the Hohentwiel, and some of the monks, including Bürster, appear to have returned to the Abbey; but the arrangement falling through, Salem and the other monasteries and cities of the district, were obliged to continue sending their contributions to Widerhold.

In 1646 came the Swedes again, under Field-Marshal Wrangell, by whom Salem was frequently occupied. A Swedish lieutenant-colonel is especially commemorated, as having a remarkably keen scent for plunder. He always carried a little hammer in his pocket, with which he tested all suspicious-looking places in the inner walls, and wherever they gave a hollow sound, he had them broken into and examined. In this way he succeeded in finding some brass candelabra, that had been walled up, and thus preserved from freebooters for many years.

The last entry in the diary is of the date 23rd April, 1647, in which Bürster says that, although most of their people were away in foreign lands, they found it necessary " to send away eleven or twelve more, so that there now only remained in the cloister, beside some *conversi*, Pater Balthasar Hornstein Prior, Pater Raimundus Bucheler, Pater Ambrosius Humler, *et ego.*"

I fear that, without the context, these extracts may have grown wearisome, but they give a graphic picture of what life on the Boden See must have been during those terrible years of war.

From the sudden close of the diary, it is to be feared that the now aged Sebastian Bürster did not live to see the much-longed-for peace. Let us hope that, after his long and troubled life, he rests happily in the peace of God.

CHAPTER XXIV.

THE INHABITANTS OF THE WATERS OF THE BODEN SEE.[*]

The inhabitants of the waters of the Boden See—The ocean much richer in
living organisms than the lakes—Fresh-water fish, mussels, &c., originally
came from the ocean—How did they come?—Water-fleas—Their propagation
—Nature's post-carriers—The Felchen—Its variations in the different lakes—
A pirate of the lake—The "White-fish"—The "Nasen"—The Tench—The
Pike—The Wels—The Salmon-trout—Might not a fish-ladder be made for
the salmon to pass the Falls of the Rhine?—Migration of eels—The Kilch
or Kropf-felchen—Only lives in the depths of the lake.

In the course of this work I have had much to say
about the human inhabitants of the shores of the
Boden See, from the period of the early lake-dwellers
to the present time. My work would, however, be
very incomplete if I failed to say something of the
myriads of denizens of the pure azure depths of the
lake itself. To me this would have been impossible
but for the learned and interesting work of Dr. Weismann's alluded to in the foot-note.

While of late years great efforts have been made—
as in the voyage of the "Challenger"—to explore the
mysteries of the abysses of the ocean, and to find out
what living creatures they at once contain and conceal,
but little attention has been devoted to the zoology of
the great masses of fresh water. This is not to be

---

[*] A great portion of this chapter is little more than a very short *précis* of a
learned and deeply interesting paper by Dr. August Weismann, Professor of the
University of Freiburg (Baden), on "Das Thierleben im Bodensee," published
in the seventh volume of the "Schriften des Vereins für Geschichte des Bodensee's und seiner Umgebung."

wondered at. Animal life in the ocean is infinitely richer and more varied than in the largest body of fresh water. So far as our present knowledge extends, there are not only numerous families, but even whole classes of animal life, represented in the ocean by hundreds and thousands of different families, which are altogether wanting in fresh water. The comparative paucity of animal organisms in fresh water as compared with the ocean, is accounted for by the undoubted fact that salt water affords much more abundant and more varied food in the immense number and variety of sea-plants. Another reason, according to Dr. Weismann, is that the ocean may fairly be regarded as the birthplace of all the animal and vegetable life which has since spread itself over the land and in the watercourses that flow through the land. When the dry land arose bald and naked into the air, the ocean already swarmed with animal organisms, from the very lowest forms of life to creeping things and fishes. And since the beginning of life in the depths of ocean—who shall say how many æons of æons ago ?—it has never ceased : there has not even been any break, or solution of continuity. It is true that, in the course of the physical history of our earth, what was once sea has often become land ; but never, there is reason to believe, so suddenly as to destroy the whole of the animal life within it. There was always time for the living creatures to emigrate into other parts of the ocean. And as in process of time—almost infinite—special forms of life were unable to resist the change of circumstances to which they were subjected, out of them new forms arose. No wonder, therefore, that the ocean teems with its myriad forms of life. Quite otherwise was it with the basins of fresh water. They changed so often, and, comparatively speaking, so quickly—one disappearing before another was formed near it— that almost every time animal life had to start afresh. Thus we know that at the end of the Tertiary Period, in the place where now the lower part of the Boden See lies, there was already a lake. The numerous fossil-remains, found in the quarries at Oeningen, give us a tolerably exact picture of the animal life of that lake. There are not only the shells of mussels and snails, but also a great mass of delicate and easily destructible creatures. We know quite a number of insects which peopled the neighbourhood of the Oeninger See, some living in the air or on the land, and some—as the larvæ of dragon-flies—in the water. Yet it is impossible that the animal life of this lake could have been directly transplanted into the Boden See; for between the disappearance of the Oeninger See and the formation of the Boden See, long periods of time must have elapsed, during which the whole valley was dry ground. And thus it was in most similar cases. It is a probability, nearly amounting to a certainty that the animal life of the lakes came almost exclusively from the ocean, in most cases not immediately, but by means of the rivers that united lake and sea. These served as halting-places and stations for acclimatisation, where the dwellers in the ocean might, in the course of generations, become fitted for habitation in the fresh-water lakes. Some lakes have, so to speak, separated themselves from the ocean. In such we find a much richer fauna. Thus the Caspian Sea has a real ocean fauna. A great number of the mussels, snails, worms, and crabs which are found there are true sea animals. There are also much smaller lakes that betray the fact that they were once a part of the ocean, by the sea animals which live in their depths, and which could not

have found their way up the rivers.   Thus, in the lake
of Garda a small sea crab is found, as is also the case
in some of the Norwegian lakes.   The Boden See was,
however, formed long after the ocean had withdrawn
to a great distance.   Only such emigrants from the
ocean could, therefore, people its waters as were able
to find their way either by swimming or creeping up
the rivers.   To these belong fish, snails, mussels,
and worms.   We find, however, that the Boden See
and similarly-situated lakes are peopled with a dense
population of living organisms that could not possibly
have found their way up stream.   The question then
arises, Where did they come from, and how did they
come ?*

In reply to this question, Dr. Weismann first shows
how many animals found their way into the lake by
means of the river; animals for which such wandering
would at first sight seem impossible.   For instance, take
the various kinds of mussels.   How could these
creatures, who can only slowly drag themselves along
the bottom of streams, ascend the whole length of a
rapid river like the Rhine ?   The reply is *that they do;*
that a tolerably large, beautifully-formed sea-mussel,
(*Dreissena polymorphia*) is known to have found its way
in the course of the last few centuries, from the brackish
waters of the delta of the Rhine, to above Mannheim,
up the Main and its tributary the Regnitz, and into the
Main and Danube canal.   So far the adventurous and
travelled mussel has only been observed in the harbour

* I must again remind my readers that all I am attempting to give, or that the
plan of my book will allow, is a very short abstract of Dr. Weismann's paper.   I
strongly recommend any who have the opportunity to read it in full in the
original.   Doubtless the learned author would inform any applicant whether it
is published in a more convenient form than in the huge folios of the Proceedings
of the Society for the History of the Boden See, where I have consulted it.
Address—Dr. August Weismann, Professor in Freiburg, in Breisgau.

where the canal opens into the Danube, but there is nothing now to prevent the continuance of its journey to the far east of Europe.

The professor humorously says that these journeys are not to be regarded as entirely pedestrian tours. The young mussels fasten themselves on to fish, and thus make the journey up stream with the greatest convenience, while their elders often attach themselves with their so-called Byssus-threads to the keels of ships, and if occasionally there should be a steamer amongst these, it may fairly be said that the mussels are marching with the spirit of the age, and making use of the power of steam as one of their means of transport.

But while the presence of fish, and even of mussels and some water-snails, may be thus accounted for, there remains a vast population of small organisms that, to a large extent, supply the needful nourishment for all the rest, to whom such immigration is simply impossible.

The whole race of water-fleas—shrimp-like creatures, none of them exceeding two millimetres in length, and most much smaller—which people the depths of the lake in countless millions, could not possibly have made head against the current of the Rhine, nor can they live except in clear untroubled water. These crystal-clear, almost transparent crustaceans, as well as many worms, snails, and infusoria, could not possibly have found their way from the sea by the rivers.

Dr. Weismann is of opinion that all these various races must have come from other lakes, where in long ages they had been developed, but they came not as individuals but as germs or eggs. He supports this opinion by a reference to the manner of the propagation of water-fleas. All these creatures have two sorts of eggs: thin-shelled, delicate, so-called summer eggs, and thick-shelled, tough winter eggs. The first are produced throughout the whole summer, and develope themselves immediately, in the breeding pouch which is placed in the water-flea's back. This pouch is not merely a protection to the young, but has been recently discovered to have another most important function. It is, in fact, filled with a nourishing fluid, on which the young live until their full development, and without which the eggs are far too small ever to become water-fleas. This propagation, by means of the summer eggs, is unsexual, and proceeds with a rapidity that is perfectly marvellous. Ramdohr, an observer who wrote at the beginning of this century, says :—

"Before the young have reached half their natural size, the breeding pouch is full of eggs, which, at the end of about forty-eight hours, swim away, as living young, to give place to another mass of eggs, which in their turn, after a similar period, give place to a third, and they to a fourth, and so on." Ramdohr computes "that a single individual that begins to produce eggs on the 1st of May, by the end of June will have produced a progeny of 1,291,370,075, the greater number of which will live and promise a still larger population for the coming months."

If, however, the summer eggs secure the rapid increase of the race, the winter eggs are a provision that it shall not die out. If, in the late autumn, a fine net is drawn along the surface of a pond, amongst much besides, will be found, sticking to the meshes of the net, minute brown and black bodies. These are the winter eggs of water-fleas, a great number of which float upon the surface of the water, while others sink to the bottom and remain there. They lie inside a horny capsule, called Ephippium, and possess a wonderful power of resistance against all possible injury. They can be dried up or even frozen without losing their vitality. Among zoologists a favourite method of procuring these and similar creatures from distant regions, is to have a little dry mud sent through the post, which is plunged into water upon arrival. The winter eggs that have been dried up in it develope into young, and soon the whole aquarium swarms with water-fleas from Hungary, Turkey, or Egypt. As the Post Office can thus secure the artificial emigration of any given species, to London for instance, so nature has post-carriers enough who take charge of such eggs.

A single duck, seeking food in a swamp, will carry away with it, attached to its feathers, hundreds of these eggs, which it will transport to the next swamp it visits, and thus, principally by means of birds of passage in the autumn, every lake as it is formed or becomes fit for organic life after, for example, a glacier epoch, is quickly stocked with the little crab-like creatures. Only in this way can the wonderfully wide dissemination of these tiny crustaceans, and of the lower forms of animal life in fresh water generally, be accounted for.

Leptodora hyalina, a water-flea, much like a shrimp but much smaller, that lives in countless myriads in the Boden See, is found in all the Swiss lakes, in the Lago Maggiore, the lakes of Bohemia, Denmark, and Sweden, and in at least one lake in Southern Russia. This would be an impossibility if the *leptodora* had been developed in the Boden See and could not get out of it.

It may, however, be asked, Have no new sorts developed themselves in the Boden See? The conditions of life are different from those in the sea, or in rivers, or even in other lakes—have the emigrants

A A

adapted themselves to these new conditions ?   Dr.
Weismann replies that such changes have taken place,
as may most clearly be seen in the case of the fishes.   In
the Boden See are found many kinds of fish that are
also found in the other Swiss lakes, and in those of
the Bavarian Highlands.   For example, the "Felchen,"
(French " Férat,") abound in all lakes on the northern
slope of the Alps.   But the Felchen is not exactly
the same in all these lakes, and the fish of the different
lakes are distinguishable by certain small and, in themselves, unimportant variations.   This, however, simply
shows that since the time when they journeyed up the
rivers their form has, to a small extent, changed, and
be it observed, in each lake in slightly different
fashion.   In the Scandinavian lakes, Felchen are
also found, which show a slightly greater variation
from those in the Swiss lakes than the Felchen in
each of these do from one another.   In the Italian
lakes no Felchen whatever are found, which would
seem to show that these fish originally wandered, both
into the Swiss and Scandinavian lakes, from the seas
that wash the shores of both Germany and Scandi-
navia, and at a time before there was any fall of the
Rhine at Schaffhausen.   Naturalists seem pretty
certain as to the family of sea-fish from which the
Felchen are descended.

I dare not follow Dr. Weismann in the further
elaboration of this most interesting subject, but before
for a moment dwelling upon the various kinds of fish
to be found in the Boden See, I will venture to quote
the conclusion of his paper :—

" It seems very immaterial that streams and rivers with their water
should also carry mud and dirt into the lake, but it is exactly upon
this circumstance that the existence of the greater part of the inhabitants of the lake depends.   For with the gravel, mud, and sand

the water brings an extraordinary quantity of organic matter, excretions, and remains of animal and vegetable life of every possible description, mostly no longer recognisable, but resolved into the finest particles. If we had it in our power to prevent this constant influx of dead organic matter, in a short time, not only would the whole of the lower crustaceans die out, but also most of the fishes. Most of the latter live entirely upon these little crabs, and the others upon fish that consume them. Thus the dead organic matter that is washed into the lake is anew transformed into life; it supplies food, and consequently existence, to a whole army of low organisms, which in their turn supply food, and consequently being, to creatures higher in the scale of life—to fishes. Nor is the circle yet complete, for on the fish live in their turn higher organisms, birds and fish-otters, and to some degree also the highest organism of all—man.

*　　　*　　　*　　　*　　　*　　　*

" If this constant mutual destruction, this everlasting victory of brute force over weakness, seem to us depressing and discouraging, let us remember how well this view was recently combated by Carl Ernst von Bär, when he maintained that there was some consolation in bearing in mind that even what seems mere food for other organisms, itself lives for a time and enjoys its existence."

Any one taking his stand upon the shore of the lake and looking into the blue-green water, will usually not have long to wait before he sees plenty of fish; generally, whole shoals of silver-bright little white fish are to be seen playing among the stones and seeking their food, which consists of the organic matter to which we have already referred, and also of the little worms to be found near the stones. Very often this innocent occupation is disturbed, and that in a very unpleasant manner. In a moment one of the worst pirates of the lake is in their midst. This is no other that the common perch, called in the Boden See, Aegle (*Perca Fluviatilis*), very easily recognisable by his zebra-like coat of black and white stripes. He comes with all the spines of his dorsal fin erect, and in wildest haste the little fishes struggle each to be first in escaping from his devouring presence; often in their desperate efforts, dozens at a time leap clean out of the water, and propel themselves for quite a distance above the surface—real fresh-water flying fish—giving us a good idea how the flying fish of the tropic seas, with their large wing-like fins may have developed out of ordinary fish.

These two sorts, the "white fish" and the perch, represent the two classes that we find in fresh water as well as in the sea, as indeed throughout all animated nature—the class that lives upon plants or dead organic matter, and the class that lives by preying upon its kind.   Among fish, however, there are in reality very few that live entirely upon plants ; almost all vary their vegetable diet upon occasion ; even that most innocent-looking fish, the carp, in addition to the water plants upon which he browses, consumes quite a quantity of worms and of the *larvæ* of insects. It would be more correct, therefore, to speak of great and little robbers among fish.   Both are largely represented in the Boden See.

In speaking of "white fish" a special family was intended, the *Leuciscus alburnus*, called in the lake, "Laube" and "Uckeley," a slender little fish, with a beautiful sea-green back and silver-bright sides.   The name "white-fish" belongs however, to a whole race, including many families.   For example, there is a fish frequently to be seen close to the shore, not only of the Boden See, but of the other Swiss lakes, vulgarly called "Nasen" (noses), from its very prominent snout. This fish is commonly more than a foot long, and to the uninitiated would seem an eligible spoil for the fisherman.   It is, however, regarded with great contempt on account of the tastelessness of its flesh.

Nearly related to the "white-fish" is the narrow high-backed Bley (*Abramis Brama*), the mud-loving, smooth, slippery tench (*Tinca vulgaris*), the great family of the carps and many others, all of which abound in the Boden See.

Among true fish of prey, besides the perch, there is largely represented in the Boden See the fresh-water shark, the pike, whose popularity is shown not only by so habitual an appearance at *table d'hôte*, that Englishmen, at any rate, are disposed to think it possible to have too much even of a good thing, but also by his giving his name to numberless hotels. Hardly a town of importance around the Boden See but what has among its inns one " Zum Hecht," or called by the French equivalent " Hotel du Brochet." But even this terrible robber and slaughterer, which occasionally reaches a weight of fifty to sixty pounds, is not the largest representative of the fish of prey in the Boden See.

Near to where the Rhine flows into the lake, and also occasionally where it flows out, there is taken by the fishermen, the huge broad-mouthed Wels (*Silurus glanis*), a fish which sometimes attains to a length of five feet, and to a weight of several hundreds of pounds But the whole family of the *salmonidæ* are fish of prey, and as food for man, the members of this family are the most important of all the lake fishes. The magnificent salmon-trout, which in and around the Boden See bears nearly a dozen aliases, often reaches a weight of from 15 lbs. to 20 lbs.. It inhabits the deeper parts of the lake, which it leaves only in the autumn at spawning time. Like all members of the salmon family, the salmon-trout does not deposit its spawn in lakes or in the sea, but in flowing water. It ascends the Rhine and the Aach, near Bregenz, in order to deposit its spawn far up near the sources of these rivers, away in Montafun in the Prättigau, and in the valleys of the Vorder and the Hinter Rhine. When it has hidden its spawn under stones and water-plants, in level sheltered spots, it immediately returns to the lake. The wanderings of the true salmon are much more familiar to us than are those of its fresh-water congeners. The salmon proper is in reality a sea fish, that only leaves the salt-water and wanders up towards the sources of rivers in order to deposit its spawn in safe and sheltered spots. No salmon are found in the Boden See, for the falls of the Rhine present an obstacle which even those mighty leapers cannot get over. I believe that we in England have much to learn from foreigners in the matter of the rearing and utilising of fresh-water fish; but I think if the dwellers in Rhine-land were to seek the advice of Mr. Frank Buckland, he would tell them how they might construct a fish-ladder, by which the Falls of the Rhine might be overcome, and the true salmon, the king of all fish from the angler's and the epicure's point of view, might find its way not only into the Boden See, but into all the Swiss lakes that discharge into the Rhine, and thence up rivers and streams into the very recesses of the Alps. If salmon-fishing were added to the charms of scenery, what country would be able to compete with Switzerland, for travellers seeking not only scenery but a noble sport? As, however, the inhabitants of the shores of the Rhine below Schaffhausen are not likely to be very anxious to stock the Swiss lakes and rivers with salmon, and as it would be difficult to reconcile conflicting claims and interests in the construction of such a fish-ladder, the owners of salmon fisheries in England, Ireland, Scotland, Norway and elsewhere, may regard the threatened competition with equanimity.

What the lor lly salmon cannot accomplish is, however, effected by the snake-like silvery eel. Unlike the salmon, the eel spawns in the sea, and as soon as the young are conscious of independent life, they commence their long journey, sometimes of nearly a thousand miles, until they reach some stream, lake, or swamp, where they make their home. No obstacle seems insuperable to these immense armies of little eels. Rapids and water-falls they overcome in the most astonishing manner. These eel migrations have been watched and described by many observers. In immense numbers, closely packed, they appear at the mouth of such rivers as the Rhine, the Rhone, or the Elbe. Here they divide into two columns, which ascend the stream on each side, often visible from a distance as broad dark bands. At the mouth of every affluent stream a detachment breaks away from the main column in order to ascend it in like manner, and thus in the end all the tributary streams, and all the lakes, tarns, and ponds connected with them, become peopled with eels. When they come to rapids and waterfalls, they cannot, by means of mighty springs, leap - over them as the salmon can and does, up smaller cataracts, but they make a circuit and so turn positions which they find it impossible to carry by direct assault. They have been seen to make their way past a waterfall by taking to the rocks at the side, and climbing or gliding along them until the summit of the fall was reached. The tiny creatures, not more than an inch or two long, have been observed gliding like little snakes through the damp moss on the rocks. Thousands perish or fall back again into the water, but some succeed in effecting their object, and reach the water above the fall.

The reader of Yarrell's " Fishes," will remember

how that distinguished naturalist relates the story of a gentleman who was particularly anxious to stock his fish-ponds with eels, but in spite of repeatedly putting them into the ponds, he could never find any trace of them, much less of their expected and desired progeny.   At length the mystery was explained.   These ponds were about half-a-mile distant from a running stream, and one clear moonlight night either the gentleman or one of his gamekeepers was walking between the stream and the ponds.   Suddenly he observed something gleaming at his feet in the grass, and upon examination he found the last colony of eels he had had put into the ponds, literally making tracks for the running water, in a long silvery procession.

This has never been actually observed at the Falls of the Rhine, but the presence of eels in the Unter See and Boden See would seem to point to their getting past the Rapids and Falls of Schaffhausen, exactly as the navigation used to be managed by taking the goods ashore and dragging them overland to the top of the fall—a process which gave rise to the name *Schaff*hausen.

There is one other very important family of fish in the Boden See, which, so far as I know, has no representative in our English lakes and waters.   This is the "Felchen" already referred to, the "Férat" of the lake of Geneva.   The Felchen is closely allied to the salmon family, but while the salmon and trout are armed with tremendous teeth, the mouth of the Felchen has no teeth whatever.   They do not eat other fish, but live on the larvæ of insects, and principally upon the tiny, almost microscopic, crab-like creatures, alluded to in the early part of this chapter, with which the stomach of the Felchen is almost always found to be full.

In the Boden See there are three varieties of this fish, of which the blue Felchen is the best known. When young it is known by the name of " Gang-fisch " and is regarded as a very great delicacy; now-a-days, indeed, these little fish bring an almost fabulous price. In former times they appear to have swarmed in the lake in incredible numbers. In an old Chronicle of Constance it is related that in the year 1534, in one draught of a net no fewer than 46,000 Gang-fisch were taken, and similar stories are to be found in the Chronicles of Lindau.

More interesting is the much rarer " Kilch," or " Kropf-felchen," to obtain which is very difficult. This fish lives only in very deep water, and, indeed, has its *habitat* at the very bottom of the Boden See, as deep down as 900 feet. As we always find the structure of an animal admirably suited to the conditions of its existence, so, in the case of the Kropf-felchen, its structure is exactly adapted to the depths in which it lives, and alone can live.

A Kropf-felchen never comes willingly to the surface; if caught and brought to the surface from its native depths it dies almost immediately. This arises from the fact of its possessing a swim-bladder. All fish do not possess this organ; in those that do, it serves as a so-called hydrostatic apparatus, which makes it possible for the fish to render himself by turns and as he chooses, heavier or lighter.

The swim-bladder is filled with air, and the fish can at will contract or expand it, and thus sink or rise at pleasure. But this convenient and useful organ may prove very dangerous to its possessor. This arises from the fact that the pressure of the water in the depths is much greater than near the surface. In fishes which live at great depths, the air in the swim-bladder is under great pressure, and, consequently, highly condensed. It is calculated that with every ten metres of depth the pressure increases to the extent of an atmosphere. A fish that lives at a depth of 200 metres is under a pressure equal to twenty atmospheres, and the air in his swim-bladder is, as a consequence, exceedingly condensed. Now if such a fish be forcibly pulled up to the surface, the air in the swim-bladder expands more and more as the pressure becomes less, and in the case of the Kilch of the Atten See, which are weaker and more delicately built than their relations of the Boden See, the bladder at last explodes and blows the fish to pieces with a report. This does not happen with the " Kilch " of the Boden See, but the bladder forms a large swelling or crop on the fish which gives it the name of the Kropf-felchen. The pressure on the other organs is, moreover, so great that the fish quickly dies.

If he escaped with his life he would never again be able to seek his haunts in the abysses of the lake, for by the forcible expansion of the swim-bladder its muscles become paralysed and are never again in a condition to contract it. Without the agency of man it sometimes happens that a Kropf-felchen through his own want of care, and quite against his will, comes up to the surface. This occurs whenever the fish rises so high as no longer to be able to control the expansion of the air in his swim-bladder. If he does not instantly, by means of his fins, strike down again into the depths, he is lost beyond recall, the swim-bladder expands ever more and more, and his upward course does not stop until he reaches the surface in a dying state. This, probably, explains how it is that these deep-water fish are occasionally found dead upon the surface of the lake.

CHAPTER XXV.

THE RHEINTHAL, THE PRÄTTIGAU, SEEWIS.

The Rheinthal—Liechtenstein—Landquart—Valley of the Prättigau—Village of
Seewis—Chur—Graubünden (Grisons)—Cathedral of Chur—Its roof, wood
carvings, and ancient manuscripts—Pyx of the seventh century—Chur captured by the French.

I WILL now ask my readers to bid farewell to the
Boden See, and, leaving it where the Rhine enters it,
to ascend the valley of that river until the turbulent
Landquart comes rushing into it from out a narrow
and majestic gorge. After all, we are not travelling
far away from the Boden See. One of the most
conspicuous mountains seen from the Boden See is
the Scesa Plana, a huge wall of rock which effectually
shelters the fertile valley of the Prättigau from the
north and east.

In the spring of 1879 I consulted my friend Dr.
Kinkel, of Zürich, as to a quiet Alpine station
suitable for little children during the summer, and
he recommended Seewis, in the Prättigau. Until
then I had never heard of the valley of the Prättigau,
much less of the village of Seewis. I imagine many
of my countrymen are equally ignorant; and yet
assuredly this beautiful valley is well worth knowing.
In the first instance my wife and I went merely on a
"prospecting excursion," to use the language of gold-
diggers. This was in June, 1879. The train, at a

leisurely pace, takes about three hours from Rorschach on the Boden See to the station of Landquart, situated just where the river of that name enters the Rhine, and near to where the gorge of the Landquart serves as entrance to the valley of the Prättigau, and gives the most convenient access to the health-resort of Davos, of late years so much frequented by consumptive patients. The Rhine valley is one of great richness and beauty, and is hemmed in by mountains of surpassing grandeur. There is a certain likeness between it and the valley of the Rhone before that impetuous stream falls into Lake Leman; but there are also striking differences. There the valley and the accessible hill-sides are mostly devoted to the vine and to Indian corn. Here, also, are vineyards, and the tender young maize is springing; but the bulk of the land is in grass, and as we passed along, the whole available population was hay-making, rejoicing in a fine day and a good hay crop. The mountains are densely clothed with forest, from out of whose deep dark green peep exquisite fresh pastures. On jutting crags stand the ruins of turreted castles, often commanding the whole width of the valley. These were the cradles of many noble houses. For some little distance the Rhine is the frontier between Switzerland and Austria. Afterwards, to the left of the Rhine as you ascend, lies the independent little state and principality of Liechtenstein, which stands towards Austria in somewhat the same relation as the states of Southern Germany stand towards Prussia. Happily, however, the little state has no army and no compulsory military service. During the war of 1866 it possessed an army, and supplied a contingent to the Austrian forces; but when peace was made after Königgrätz, the tiny state was entirely overlooked by

The Gebhardsberg and the Rheinthal.

the diplomatists who had to arrange the details of the treaty ; and consequently no peace was made between Prussia and Liechtenstein, and therefore, in a technical sense, they are still at war. The princes of Liechtenstein have played a great part in the military history of Austria, and art lovers will remember the priceless collection of pictures in the Palace Liechtenstein at Vienna. When the then Prince Liechtenstein was building this palace, about one hundred years since, he sent for stones for the foundation from the picturesque ruin in the Rhine valley, which was the original seat of his ancestors. A few miles before reaching Landquart, the railway passes fashionable Ragatz, whose stately hotels are built just at the entrance of the gloomy gorge of the Tamina, at the head of which have stood for many centuries the convent-like buildings of the Pfäffer Baths. Hither, at the advice of Zwingli, came the prematurely worn-out Ulrich von Hutten to try the virtue of the hot baths, alas ! in vain.

Arrived at Landquart, we took an *einspänner* (it exactly realised the idea of a one-horse " shay ") to reach what was to us a complete *terra incognita*—the village of Seewis, whither we found no diligence ran. The first part of our road follows the perfectly flat valley formed by the alluvial deposits of the Landquart, and now grown over by dwarf forest and scrub. Then the road enters a tremendous gorge, through which the milk-white river fiercely pours. Above, on either side, to a height of nearly two thousand feet, tower perpendicular and overhanging rocks. There is only just room for the river and road, and in the winter the latter is not free from danger, as great masses of earth get loosened from above and come crashing down, while avalanches are of frequent occurrence. Here at the narrowest point, with the Clus-höhe rising on one side and the

Valzeina-Haupt on the other, are the ruins of a fortification which formerly commanded the pass. I cannot
call to mind anything finer than this gorge, either on
the Simplon or the St. Gotthard. When it is once
passed, the valley of the Prättigau opens out. It is
magnificently wooded and very fertile; but the un-
tameable Landquart, with its floods and ever-shifting
course, devastates it as it passes through. About four
miles from Landquart, at a village called Pardisla, a
zigzag ascent commences, by means of which carriages
can reach Seewis. The village of Seewis nestles on
the southern slope of the Vilan, Bovilan, or Augusten-
berg, a mountain which belongs to the Rhaetikon
chain of the Rhaetian Alps, and rises to a height of
7,900 ft. above sea-level. The village looks down into
the valley of the Landquart and away to the lofty
peaks of Piz Bija and the Quosanna. Although it is
3,000 ft. above the sea, maize and hemp flourish, and
the village is completely embowered in fruit-trees—
apple, pear, cherry, and plum, which attain almost to
the dimensions of the forest-trees of less favoured
climes. Extending to a much greater height up the
mountain are forests of beech, sycamore, oak, ash, and
maple, which are succeeded by great pine woods.

There are three hotels in the village—the hotel
" Scesa Plana," which formerly had a great reputation
among mountaineers; the very modest " Pension
Walser," with accommodation little superior to that
of a country-inn; and the " Kurhaus," the appearance
of which, as well as that of its host and hostess,
greatly pleased us. Here, then, we took up our
quarters; and the experience of two successive
seasons has only strengthened our first favourable
impression.

In 1863 the larger half of the village of Seewis was

destroyed by a terrible conflagration, and the burned houses have been replaced by large, white, spacious and comfortable, but prosaic-looking, buildings, each in its own garden, by the side of regular streets ; while the portion of the village spared by the flames consists of old wooden chalets mahogany-coloured with age, presenting every charm to the lover of the picturesque, but, in point of cleanliness and comfort, very inferior to their common-place neighbours. Happily, the interesting old church, with its lofty taper spire, was saved from the flames. Not so fortunate was the old Schloss, the ancestral seat of the famous family of Salis-Seewis, to which the fire did great injury. Quaint and curious must the old Castle have been, with its Herren-Saal and Frauen-Saal, and its Hercules-Saal and Brutus-Saal, the two latter being decorated entirely with scenes painted from the lives of the two heroes. It was full also of art treasures and curiosities, brought by a former lord of the castle, a Salis, who for many years had been in the service of the Venetian Republic. A curious illustration of the wealth of the former lords of the Schloss was given at the time of the conflagration. The day after the fire, one of the then proprietors was walking through the courtyard, with a peasant of the name of Lietha, who is still alive, and ·from whom I have the story. Among other *débris* that had fallen from the Castle-tower was the metal-ball from the base of the flag-staff. The heat had burst it, and Lietha, who picked it up, found it to be full of Spanish doubloons, together with four square gold coins, one of which had been melted by the heat.

The ruins were purchased by the Commune ·of Seewis, who forthwith proceeded to rebuild it in an eminently practical and substantial manner. It is, however, to be regretted that the old Schloss has thus been converted into a villanously ugly building, which looks like a cross between a lunatic-asylum and a jail. It serves as town-hall, where the members of the Commune meet and deliberate; as school-house; post and telegraph office; and as residence for the family of the schoolmaster, who is also post-master; the manse for the clergyman of the village occupies the upper story; and I do not know to how many other public uses it is put. What was once the courtyard now serves as a pen for the sheep and goats of the village, upon their return from the nearer Alpine pastures.

The village is protected, from the north and east, by the enormous rocky wall of the Scesa Plana—10,000 feet high,—and is singularly free from wind, so that the climate, in spite of its elevation, is mild and equable. Numberless streams keep the air fresh and the herbage green, even in the height of summer. Probably, if Sir Henry Thompson came this way, he would confine himself to his favourite beverage, cold tea; but the fear of typhoid poisoning must indeed be over-mastering to enable any one to resist the temptation of the cold, clear, sparkling water, which here perpetually bubbles up, fresh from the mountain-spring. Of the scenery I will speak later, only remark-ing here that, in all my experience of Switzerland, I have never met with such a combination of rich vegetation with grand and wild mountain scenery. The rich pastures all around are studded over with clumps of forest and with numerous isolated fruit-trees, so that an Englishman might easily fancy himself to be walking in some vast park. On raising his eyes, however, peak upon peak, and Alp upon Alp, would remind him that he is not in his native land. Some of the mountains are smooth and green; others clothed with pines to their summits ; others rocky, savage, and bare ; while the loftiest of all are crowned and glistening with everlasting snows.

How shall I describe the profusion of flowers upon the occasion of our first visit in June ? In many places the nearer hill-sides were blue with a labiate plant, with whorls of salvia-like corollas of a corn-flower, blue in colour. The golden balls of the globe-flower abundantly dotted the green grass near the running waters, while the columbine, lupin, bugloss, pansy, rock-cistus and sweet woodruff, filled the pastures with beauty and the air with fragrance. Like a sunflower in miniature, the sturdy *Arnica Montana* reared his deep-yellow head, and here and there a gentian could be seen. A little earlier the fields had been white, and the air sweet with narcissus. These glories are but transient ; the upland flora can be seen in perfection only in May and June, though there are always some flowers to be found from the time when the snow melts until it once again wraps the Alpine pastures in its pure white mantle. The air at night seemed at once balmy and bracing, if such a combination be possible; it was neither too hot nor too cold, but so soft and light as to render respiration a delight. The result of our visit was that we decided upon Seewis for our summer quarters. Returning to Rorschach the next day, we made a *détour* in order to visit Chur.

Chur—familiar to every visitor to the Engadine and Davos, as well as to all who cross the Splügen into Italy—hardly perhaps, of itself, receives the attention which it merits. Lying, indeed, as it does, at the bottom of a hollow, and surrounded on all sides by mountains, it is in summer such an oven that the first and often only desire of the traveller is to get out of it as soon as possible. Yet Chur has many claims to attention, the first of which is that it is the capital of the Republic of Graubünden.

Graubünden, or the Grisons, is at once the largest and the least densely populated of the republics belonging to the Swiss Confederation.   It contains nearly 3,000 square miles, with less than 100,000 inhabitants.   The exceeding sparseness of the population occasions no wonder when we remember that the whole canton is in the region of the high Alps, which intersect it in every direction like a net, and that more than a tenth part of its entire area, or no less than 300 square miles, is covered with glaciers.

About 40,000 of the inhabitants, or considerably less than half, are Roman Catholics.   Its small population, which, as I have just mentioned, numbers less than 100,000, shows a great variety in race and language. About 36,000 speak German, 42,000 Romansch, and 12,000 Italian.   The present pastor of Seewis, for the first three years after his ordination, was stationed in an Italian Commune and preached in Italian; for fourteen years he was in a Romansch Commune and preached in Romansch; and now he is in Seewis where he preaches in German—and very good German too.   In Graubünden, be it observed, where, to the major portion of the inhabitants German is a foreign language, only acquired at school, very fair German is spoken, whereas the dialects which obtain almost everywhere else in German Switzerland, however interesting to a philologist, are singularly unintelligible to the ordinary German student.   The principal employment of the inhabitants is the rearing of cattle, of which the canton possesses 80,000, or nearly one to every man, woman, and child.

Graubünden has with propriety been called the Swiss Thibet.   Under its classic name of Rhaetia, up to the

Treaty of Verdun, in A.D. 843, it belonged politically to Italy; from that date it formed a part of Germany. Its ecclesiastical relationship with Milan was at the same time dissolved, and it was united to the see of Mayence. From the thirteenth century, loosely attached to the German empire, the inhabitants of the valleys of Graubünden were cruelly oppressed by numberless feudal lords, the ruins of whose castles, crowning hundreds of heights, now give an additional charm to the scenery of the canton. Against these oppressors the people rose, and in 1396 the "Gotteshaus-bund" (the league of God's house) was formed; in 1424 followed the "Grauerbund" (the Grey league), from which the canton subsequently took its name; and in 1436 the "Zehngerichten-bund" (or league of the Ten Jurisdictions). In 1471 these three leagues united; shortly afterwards they became associated with the Swiss Confederation, and in 1803 Graubünden became an independent canton.

In the latter days of the Roman empire Chur was a very important station, as commanding the Splügen pass, and was known as Curia Rhaetorum. Some Roman towers in good preservation still tell of the former occupation of Chur by the masters of the world. The centre of all interest in Chur is, however, the Cathedral, which, though externally most unattractive, is an epitome in stone of the last twenty centuries.

It was John the Baptist's Day, and as service was proceeding when we entered the venerable building, we took our seats with the assembled worshippers. After our journey in the bright sunshine, rest in the cool church was doubly welcome, while the last anthem pealed down the aisle. Soon, however, the service closed, the priests, magnificently robed, left the chancel and the congregation dispersed. The sacristan then came to us and offered to conduct us round the Cathedral.

For hundreds of years Chur was a Roman stronghold, and where now stands the episcopal residence was the camp or *Castra*; of this, two towers, having been built into the subsequent edifice, have remained all through the Middle Ages down to the present time. In one corner of the Castra was a square temple with an altar to Mars, and when at last, in the fifth century, Christianity triumphed over paganism, the old temple was turned into a Christian church, and formed the nucleus of the Cathedral. Not being able to obtain the ground they required, the builders of the fifth century had to make the nave crooked in order to avail themselves of the temple for the choir. Three hundred years later Bishop Tello completed the church in Romanesque style, and in the side-aisles are some curious Saracenic arches, which lead antiquarians to suppose that their architect had been among the Moors in Spain. At that time there lived and ruled in the Prättigau a certain terrible scoundrel named Roderick, Count of the Landquart. The gorge of the Clus can easily be held by a handful of men against all comers, and from his impregnable fastness in the Prättigau, Roderick came out to rob and pillage and levy black-mail. He seems to have entertained a hearty abhorrence of bishops, and the special object of his hatred was the bishop of Chur. Having made himself master of the city on one of his raids, he carried off all the silver vessels in the church; and, as he could not burn the solid structure, he broke in the roof—probably a flat one, in Byzantine style—and left it a wreck. The terror caused by this ruffian is shown in a letter extant in the archives of the Cathedral, addressed by the

Emperor Ludwig the Pious, the son and successor of
Charlemagne, when on his way to Chur to cross by the
Splügen to Rome, in which he requests the bishop to
send soldiers to meet him, so that he may not fall into
the hands of this redoubtable Roderick. For 500 years
the bishop and people of Chur contented themselves
with a temporary wooden roof, until in the thirteenth
century, when gothic art had almost reached its purest
phase, the present roof was erected. The high altar
is a marvel of beauty and artistic skill. It is adorned
with scenes from Bible story, carved in wood, about
1490, by Jacob Russ of Lucerne. The material
he worked in was beechwood well soaked in oil, and
though nearly four centuries have passed away since
the figures were executed, they are still in wonderful
preservation. The forms are noble and natural, and
the colouring and gilding marvellously fresh. The
whole of the altar-screen rests upon a Romanesque
Mensa of the fifth century, so arranged that the
priest stood behind it and faced the congregation.
The Mensa, in its turn, rests upon the columns of the
old Mars' temple. It is strangely interesting to find
in one building the record and epitome of so many
generations.

The manuscripts treasured up in the sacristy, contain
amongst them one of Charlemagne's, written in beautiful characters, signed by his Chancellor Alcuin, and
sealed with the hilt of the Emperor's sword. It bears
the date of 784. Very interesting, too, is a letter to
the then bishop of Chur, from the celebrated Pater
Fidelis, one of the Catholic apostles, who, with the
help of Austrian soldiers, did his utmost to establish the counter-reformation in the Prättigau, early in
the seventeenth century. It was written from Seewis
the day before he was killed, when the inhabitants

rose against the hated papal and Austrian yoke.
With a grim play upon the words, as if conscious of
his approaching fate, he signs himself—*Ad vermes
Fidelis.*

Time would fail, and also I fear the patience of my
readers, were I even to enumerate the sacred vessels in
gold and silver and enamel, dating from different centuries, here kept.   One, however, I must speak of,
originating, as it did, in the childhood of Christian art—
a box to contain the sacred elements, dating from the
seventh century.   The sacristan, a man of between fifty
and sixty, has the boundless enthusiasm of a young poet
for everything relating to the church of which he takes
charge, and possesses a vast amount of antiquarian lore.
Upon its being remarked to him that he seemed to love
all these treasures in his keeping as if they were his
children, " Yes, indeed, I do," said he, " I don't know
how I could bear to leave them, or to adopt any other
manner of life."   " How was it," he was asked, " that
all this gold and silver did not find its way into the
melting-pot, when the French revolutionary armies
were at Chur at the end of the last century ? "   " Before the French came," he replied " the bishop carefully buried or otherwise hid away everything of value,
belonging to the cathedral.   He had been an officer
of Uhlans in his youth, and, when he had done his
utmost to put everything in safety, he mounted his
horse, and turning its head up one of the passes leading into Austrian territory, cried to the bystanders,
' The French will want to find me, and you need not
scruple to tell them which road I have taken, for whoever catches me must first ride boldly and well.' "
They did not catch him.   This prince of the church
was not equally careful of his own property.   Massena
established his headquarters in the episcopal palace,

and carried away from it everything that could be moved.

A day of intense heat was followed by pouring rain as we journeyed back again down the Rhine Valley, and very grand the mountains of Graubünden appeared, with the white mists rising upon their forest-clad sides, and climbing to their summits.

CHAPTER XXVI.

SUMMER AND AUTUMN AT SEEWIS.

Seewis in Summer—A natural bath—Variety of walks—Seewis to Grüsch—Seewis
to the Clushöhe—Inhabitants of Seewis—Cattle sent to the "Alps" in
summer—Return of Cattle from the "Alps"—Seewis in Autumn—Early
winter—Fruit harvest.

On the 13th of August, we returned to Seewis. The
flowers of early summer were gone, but the foliage
of the woods was fuller and richer than on our previous visit. The sun's heat on the dusty plain between
Landquart and the bridge at Felsenbach, at the narrowest part of the gorge, was tremendous ; but as our
carriage wound its way up the zigzag road to Seewis,
the air grew cooler and more refreshing. We had had
the carriage partially closed when we started, as a
protection from the blazing rays of the sun, and all the
way along the valley we had the unwelcome company
of a number of great *Bremsen* (gad-flies), of which, as fast
as we slew them, fresh relays came to take their place.
At Seewis we were joined by our two little girls, aged
respectively five and three, from whom we had been
separated for twenty months. Before we came, no
English guest had ever been at the " Kurhaus," and the
landlord had never seen either a Bank of England or a
Circular Note. Once settled in our secluded retreat at
Seewis, we were visited by many friends, one of whom
tendered our host a note of the world-famous institution
in Threadneedle Street in payment of his bill. With

SEEWIS

equal *naïveté* and trustfulness, he said the paper was unknown to him ; but if I would say it was good, he would gladly take it. Of many strange experiences in my life, this of guaranteeing the stability of the Bank of England was, I think, the strangest. Financially, it was the proudest moment of my existence.

One great charm of Seewis is that, within very easy distance, there are, in every direction, beautiful walks, commanding glorious mountain views. For the convenience of his guests, the proprietor of the " Kurhaus" has erected benches at all the principal points of view. The landlord of the " Scesa Plana " has followed suit, and the wholesome rivalry of the two innkeepers in this matter is highly conducive to the enjoyment of visitors.

The latter part of August and the whole of September, 1879, were fine and hot ; and upon our arrival I inquired anxiously of our landlord whether, in any of the mountain streams near by, a bath was to be had. He took me eastward through the village, and up a rugged ascent, as if to climb the Vilan, then along a path through meadows above the deep gorge of the Ganei Tobel, until we reached the summit of a knoll overgrown with great beech trees, one side of which descends steeply 700 ft. to the boisterous torrent of the Ganei Tobel or Bach. Just here a little stream comes foaming and dancing down to join the torrent in the gorge far below. To reach the brook from the beech-crowned knoll, we had only to descend about 40 ft. down a grassy slope, at this time dotted with the grass of Parnassus and, like all the meadows around, gorgeous with the autumn crocus. The stream is thickly fringed with beech, scrub, alders, and other trees, and through these Herr Hitz (the landlord) had a narrow path cut and a plank-bridge thrown across the stream, with steps leading down into a natural bath. In the course of ages the brook has here scooped for itself, out of the solid rock, an elliptical basin about 20 ft. long by 9 ft. wide and 3 ft. to 4 ft. deep, always full of sparkling crystal water. Into this the stream comes tumbling from above—a superb douche. As you watched the ferns waving from the rock above, or the harebells and other flowers being freshened by the spray, while the sunlight glinted through the leaves of the overhanging trees, it seemed the very ideal of a bath.

In seeking a walk, you can hardly go wrong at Seewis. In three minutes you reach a knoll well covered with trees, which received the name of Morgen-ruh because, on the hottest summer day, for four hours after sunrise, it affords shade and refreshing coolness. A similar retreat, a little further away, but affording a denser shade, was christened by my children the "Squirrel's Nest." One day we saw a beautiful little brown fellow with bushy tail, and watched him for some time running from tree to tree along the topmost boughs. The children thought if "we were very quiet he would come down to us, and let us stroke him." He probably was not quite assured of our pacific intentions, and did not come ; but the children consoled themselves by leaving a store of nuts at the foot of a tree for him to eat *when* he came down. Another favourite walk, but requiring much greater exertion, and unsuited for children, is to the bottom of the gorge which separates the base of the Vilan from that of the Fanasaberg. It is a very sharp descent of 700 ft. The gorge is so narrow that, looking across from Seewis to the village of Fanas on the mountain slope to the east, which is very con-spicuous by reason of its white church among the trees, you are hardly aware of any gorge at all. The way leads through orchards and meadows, until it stops altogether, and you reach a primeval forest through which it is difficult to penetrate safely to the stream which, for a great part of its course, runs between lofty precipices. The forest consists principally of pines and beech-trees, gnarled and twisted in a fashion most strange and weird—partly, perhaps, by the weight of the incumbent snow when the trees were young, and partly by wintry blasts sweeping down the gorge. This summer (1880) the woodmen have been very busy cutting down trees on all sides. As they cannot possibly bring the timber up to the road, they cut it into convenient lengths, and then tumble it over the rocks into the torrent by which it is carried down the gorge to Grüsch, where a barrier is thrown across the stream, and the floated timber (the *jetsam*) is arrested and stacked. The walk from Seewis to Grüsch is itself very interesting. Until quite recent years, when the zigzag carriage drive was constructed from Pardisla, this precipitous mountain path to Grüsch must have been the main, if not the only, road from Seewis to the valley. For some distance it skirts the tremendous gorge, the rocks on either side of which, being well grown with trees wherever they can find a foothold, present in autumn a splendid and varied show of colour. Before we reach Grüsch we come upon the ruins of what was once the strong castle of Solavers, whence, there is no doubt, in the "good old times," some noble family levied black-mail upon the travellers along the road below. The architect built his castle, with astonishing boldness, on a steep hill, the massive walls rising from precipitous slopes, where it would seem impossible for them to obtain the necessary foundation. The view from the ruins is very striking and varied, and

while the eye ranges over green Alp and forest up to the
snow-clad peaks, immediately below (so close, indeed, that
you could drop a stone on to it) is the high road of the
Prättigau, along which a constant traffic is passing
between Landquart and Davos. Grüsch itself is an
interesting and quaint little village with a curious
church, the body of which is separated from the tower
by the entire length of the grave-yard; and it has some
very fine old houses, many hundred years old, and once
the property of the Salis family, which, seen from above
the village, completely surrounded by orchards, look
very pretty. There is one other walk which I will
mention in this connection—that, namely, to the
Clushöhe. It is distant a short two miles from the
"Kurhaus." Passing through the western or old
picturesque and dirty part of the village, and leaving
to the right the forest which clothes the shoulder of the
Vilan, the visitor traverses the undulating and accidented
meadows until he reaches a purling brook that flows at
the foot of a rocky crag, forming one side of a wooded
eminence called the "Grupp spitze." This stream he
crosses, and then follows a narrow track through a solemn
forest of great straight pines, between the stems of which,
on a glorious day of Indian summer in 1879, murmured
a delicious autumn zephyr. Presently, attached to a
mighty pine to which the path leads us, is seen a
little board with "Clushöhe" painted upon it, and just
below stands a bench, placed there by our enterprising
host. Once seated, we can enjoy the view at our
leisure. One thousand feet below us is the narrow
gorge of the river Landquart, and so narrow does it look
that it is difficult to realise that a river flows through
the wooded cleft, and much more that there is also a
coach-road beside it. On the other side is the Haupt,
in its lower half a perpendicular face of rock rising

1000 ft. sheer from the abyss, while the remaining 1000 ft. is a regular cone, clothed with pines and other trees up to its summit. Looking down the gorge, you see the Rhine valley and the snow mountains beyond. From the other side of the Rhine comes the west wind, laden with the aromatic odour of the pines. It is the perfection of weather—all the brightness and glory of summer without its heat or glow. The hill-sides, clad with oak, ash, and beech, are fairly aglow with splendid autumn tints, which range from a bright yellow to fiery or blood-red crimson.

I know, however, how tedious descriptions of walks are liable to be when the breath of the Alps and the bright sunshine and the glorious autumnal tints are all necessarily wanting to the reader. I will, therefore, reserve to a subsequent chapter the description of some excursions of exceptional interest, and proceed to give some idea of the daily life of the little Alpine village of Seewis, as summer deepens into autumn, and autumn declines into winter.

Seewis contains about 900 inhabitants, including a small hamlet which adjoins Grüsch, and which curiously enough belongs to the Seewis Commune. After the terrible conflagration of 1863, Seewis was quickly rebuilt, and the picturesque old *châlets*, that were scattered about among the fruit trees in most admired confusion, just where successive generations of peasants had built them, connected by narrow, crooked, and dirty lanes, gave place to the comfortable modern houses already mentioned. Most of the old wooden houses that still remain have, carved upon them, the name of the builder, with the date, and some holy text or prayer. From these inscriptions we learn that many of them have stood for more than two hundred years.

It is the almost universal observation of summer visitors to Alpine stations that they see no cows or sheep, and they wonder where they all are. When we arrived in August this was the case at Seewis. Every morning at five o'clock the goatherd's horn sounded, and great numbers of goats ·came frisking from their stalls joyfully to answer his summons and to accompany him to the high grounds of the Vilan or into the neighbouring forests, whence they return home at sunset. But hardly a sheep or a cow was to be seen. Now as the principal wealth of Seewis is in its cattle and sheep, where were they? The answer is, three or four thousand feet above us, or from seven to eight thousand feet above sea-level, in the recesses of the mountains, wherever an oasis of verdure is to be found among the stunted pines and the barren rocks. Wherever a feeding ground of this kind is found at a great altitude it is called an " Alp," the word which has given the name to the immense congeries of mountains in Central Europe. To these " Alps," in the early summer, the flocks and herds are driven, each commune having its own, and sending a number of young men to look after them. These men live in rude huts and have a busy time. They rise about three, and find the physical labour of milking the kine and making the cheese sufficiently exhausting. Besides this, an accurate account of the quantity of milk and cheese has to be kept. The men remain three or four months, only coming down occasionally, when their stores require to be replenished. In this district no women are ever sent to the " Alp."*

* For a marvellous picture of strong human passions, working in the limited sphere of a Tyrolese Alpine village and a savage "Alp," let me recommend to the reader "Geierwally," by Madame von Hillern.

At the end of September, 1879, we had two or three days of bad weather, the rain being heavy and incessant, while the thermometer fell twenty degrees. What was rain to us was snow in the higher regions, and when the weather cleared, all was white very nearly down to our level. A solemn meeting of the Commune was held at the Schloss, and the decision was come to that the cattle should be brought down from the "Alps." Quickly the mandate was borne to the mountain-pastures, and very soon there was a constant sound in the village like that which greeted the ears of the prophet Samuel when he visited Saul after the discomfiture of Agag—a sound of the bleating of sheep and the lowing of oxen, mingled with the musical intonations of the cow-bells—the *Küh-reigen* or *Ranz des Vaches*. The fields around, which have already given two, and in some cases three, crops of hay, are now dotted all over with cows, mostly small, graceful creatures, reminding one of the Jersey breed. While the landscape is animated with their presence, the air is musical with the all-pervading tinkle of the cow-bells.

A strange breed of pigs has also come down from the "Alp," looking as though they were rather designed for coursing purposes than to yield fat bacon. These pigs are of a bright chestnut colour, with such glossy hides that they shine in the sun like polished bronze. The sheep, since their return from the "Alp," have been led out to pasture every day by a shepherd appointed by the Commune, and upon their return each afternoon, the court attached to the Schloss presents an animated appearance, as the little boys and girls of the village come to fetch away the sheep, and probably one or two lambs, belonging to their respective households. How they are able to distinguish one sheep from another is a puzzle to a stranger, but they evidently find no difficulty, as each quickly picks out his own sheep, or comes away with a lamb in his arms, its mother willingly following.

Every " Bürger " (citizen) of Seewis has more or less land, and throughout October all the men, women, and children who can possibly be spared, are out in the fields getting in the crops—hemp, maize, cabbages, and, most important of all, potatoes. In 1879 we had a magnificent summer and autumn here, while the whole season in 1880 was wet, the exact converse, I understand, of the weather in England. It is possible, however, that we may still have our Indian summer later—I am writing on the 15th October—and this is much to be desired for the sake of the poor people. They usually lock up their houses, often leaving the key outside for any one who chooses to enter, and the whole family betake themselves to the fields, where they remain from sunrise until sunset. In fine weather nothing can be pleasanter ; in spite of the hard work it is a regular family picnic. In one instance, I noticed a father and mother with their two children, probably two and three years old respectively, playing around a basket which contained the youngest born, a baby of a few months, who was evidently revelling in the sunshine. A similar group that I saw a few days since, returning early in the afternoon under a downpour of cold rain, did not present so comfortable or pleasing a picture. The people are all fairly well dressed, and the women, some of whom possess as much of the dark Italian beauty as rough field-work in all weather is likely to leave them, wear on their heads bright-coloured silk handkerchiefs, which look gay in the sunshine.

On the morning of the 16th October, 1879, after

wonderfully bright weather, the children woke me with
cries of delight that "Morgenruh was quite white." It
was true, and by the 18th we had four inches of snow
in the verandah, with the thermometer below freezing
point. As much of the fruit and crops were still out this
looked serious, but the inhabitants knew their climate
far too well to be alarmed. They said the snow would
do nothing any harm, and that it would quickly disappear, which it did. On the 20th October, the thermometer was at 52° in the shade, and from that date
until the 7th November, we had a perfectly blue sky,
in the day time flooded with sunshine, while at night
the stars blazed out from the empyrean with a
brilliancy that I have seldom or never seen equalled.
It is true there was pretty sharp frost at night, but the
climate by day was perfect. On the night of the
6th-7th of November, eighteen inches of snow fell, and
this time it did not go away.

No one can imagine, who has not seen it, the splendour of the sky at sunrise and sunset during this period
of Indian summer. When the king of day disappeared
in the west, the intense blue of the sky changed first to
a deep rose colour, and then to a dark blue purple,
against which the rocky mountain summits stood out a
pale cream colour. One curious effect of the frost, we
noticed. When we looked up to the forest above us
on the Vilan, after some sharp frosts in the night,
besides the yellow and brown and fiery red of the
beech, maple, and oak, there were a number of trees
whose leaves showed almost white as with the sheen
of silver. Upon examination these proved to be syca-
mores, the leaves of which had shrivelled and dried up
with the frost as though a scorching blast had passed
over them. The leaves of the hazel-bushes, a little
higher than Seewis, were all also similarly withered.

C C

Every villager is busy at this season drying apples, pears, and other fruit, in the sun for winter use, or washing and drying the fleeces of the sheep, which during the winter will be spun and woven by the women into cloth of astonishing durability.

CHAPTER XXVII.

THE REFORMATION AT SEEWIS.—THE POET SALIS.

The Reformation at Seewis—The Reformation in the Prättigau—Rising of the Peasants—Desperate fighting—Birth of the Poet Salis—His military career—His services to his country—Sweetest poet of Switzerland—Longfellow's translation of his poem " The Silent Land "—Estimate of his character—His tomb and epitaph.

To any one unacquainted with the history of the Prättigau, the derivation of the name Seewis would seem clear, if not self-evident. Formerly, immediately to the west of the village, there was a large mountain-tarn, which has since been drained. Now "See" in German means a lake, and "Wiese" a meadow ; what, then, could be more appropriate than to call the village close to this tarn, Seewis or the meadow by the lake ? Unfortunately for this derivation, we know that it is only within comparatively recent times that the Romansch tongue has given place to German, and it is difficult to believe that Romansch-speaking people gave a German name to their village. So late as 1540, Campell, an historian of the Republic of Graubünden, travelled in the Prättigau, and found that Seewis and Conteres were the only two villages where Romansch was still spoken. About 1590, Saluz, an energetic and able man, was pastor in Seewis. He paid great attention to the village school, if he was not its founder, weaned the people from their Roman Catholic views and popish practices, and was instrumental in causing the German language to be generally adopted.

But though from that time forth the Romansch language has been entirely supplanted by German in the conversation of the inhabitants, the melodious names of the mountains still tell of the original tongue of their ancestors—Scesa Plana, Gavadura, Fadära, Fanasa, Valzeina, and the like.   Now the village of 'Seewis was originally an upland appanage of the castle of Solavers, the name of which it probably took, and gradually it was softened by the villagers into Solwis and Seewis.

Like its parent castle, its faces the morning sun, so that the sunny village is an appropriate name.

Early in the sixteenth century the Prättigau adopted the doctrines of Zwingli.   Later came the counter-reformation under St. Charles of Borromeo, and in 1621 we find the Prättigau strongly held by an Austrian army, under General Baldiron, who behaved much as the soldiers of Tilly behaved in Protestant Germany. A noble of Graubünden, Pompeius Planta, who had renounced his Protestantism from the Valtellino, came breathing out threatening and slaughter against the Protestants of the Prättigau, and set a price upon the heads of their leaders.   They, however, were before-hand with him, having secured a trusty guide who led them by mountain-paths in the middle of the night through the fore-posts of Baldiron's army, and, in the grey of the morning, they reached the castle of Pompeius Planta, on the Rietberg.   His groom was just getting ready his horse to take him to Hanz, there to carry out his hostile intentions against the inhabitants.   The conspirators, it appears, were able to enter the castle unperceived.   They found Pompeius half-dressed, and pursued him from room to room until he finally took refuge in a chimney, where they slew him.   Strange to say, they were then all able to make good their escape. These desperate men were George Jinatsch, Blasius Alexander, Gallus im Ried, and Nicholas Charles von Hohenbalken, and they quickly became the leaders of the Protestant party in the Prättigau. Baldiron, however, brought up strong reinforcements, and there was nothing left for 1,500 Protestants of Graubünden but to take refuge in Zürich, whence most of them took service in the Protestant armies then fighting the Thirty Years' War in Germany. Preaching monks then occupied the pulpits of the churches in Graubünden, and the soldiers compelled the inhabitants to attend and listen to their sermons.

Meanwhile the exiled Protestant pastors continued, at the risk of their lives, to minister to their flocks in the forests and in the fastnesses of the mountains. The peasants, stung to madness by the oppression and outrages to which they were daily subjected, collected secretly in the woods, where they cut themselves clubs, which, studded with large nails and knives, were converted into most formidable weapons. They then sent out word among the villagers that on Palm Sunday a desperate effort would be made to strike down the oppressor. The garrison of Küblis, fearing an attack, withdrew to Putz, where they were surrounded by the insurgent peasants. A sortie which they made was repulsed, and eventually they capitulated and gave up their arms, when they were allowed by the peasants to retire. As soon as the men of Schiers heard that the Küblis garrison had retired to Putz, they, with the help of the men of Jenatz and other neighbouring villages, attacked the garrison of Schiers, who withdrew to the church-yard, whence they kept up a determined fire upon the villagers, using the church as their powder-magazine.

Whether by accident or design, this exploded and caused great confusion among the soldiers. This the peasants took advantage of, and men and women rushing in upon the soldiers with their clubs, slew them to a man. Salome Leonhard, a woman of Schiers, alone slew seven in the church-yard. That very morning Pater Fidelis had held early mass, and had preached in Grüsch, when the Baron of Völs commanded every one present to sign a recantation of the errors of Protestantism, and then, at the head of the mission and protected by the military police, Fidelis made his way up the steep and rocky road by the side of the gorge to Seewis. There he reached the church and was about to commence the service, when the cry of alarm raised by a sentry told of the explosion at Schiers. Shots were exchanged in the church-yard, and Völs prayed for quarter from Hieronymus von Salis and Ammann Martin Casper, who offered to protect him from the violence of their party. The soldiers rushed wildly down the rocky path to Grüsch. Pater Fidelis was charged to remain quietly in the church, in which case his safety was guaranteed. He, however, escaped out of it with the object of reaching Grüsch, when a youth named Rudolph Hildebrand struck him down, and Ulrich Bärtsch gave him the *coup de grace* with a pitchfork. Bärtsch is still the name of a family in Seewis. The spring close to which he was killed, still bears the name of the Fidelis Well. As was natural, the Catholics regarded Fidelis as a martyr, and his head, which was taken to the Capuchin Monastery at Feldkirch, was said to work many miracles. Arrived at Grüsch, the soldiers drew up on the bridge in order of battle under Ensign Crivelli, but their valour was in vain. The men of Grüsch made a determined onslaught, and forced living and dead into the rushing waters of the Landquart. The garrisons of Frakstein and Malans, lower down, first learned of the calamity that had befallen their comrades from the number of corpses that came floating down the stream. In all 350 soldiers fell in this insurrection. It is interesting to observe how in all these struggles for freedom the family of Salis, which first appears in history as early as the tenth century, always played a leading part on the popular side, and this brings me to the man whose name and fame are the chief glory of Seewis.

On the 26th December, 1762, was born at Malans, a village situated about four miles from Seewis, at the foot of the rocky heights of Fadära, Johann Gaudenz von Salis-Seewis. In common with so many members of noble Swiss families, he served in the Swiss bodyguard attached to the French monarch. Like most generous young men, he hailed the advent of the French Revolution with delight, as the dawning of a brighter day for humanity, and left the guard before the massacre of his comrades, on the 10th of August, 1792, commemorated by Thorwaldsen's Lion at Lucerne. In the winter of the eventful year 1789, he travelled in Germany, and enjoyed much personal intercourse with the great German poets, who were creating a new epoch in German literature —Gœthe, Schiller, Wieland, Bürger, and Herder— so that very soon he found himself in intimate relations, either of personal friendship or mental affinity, with all the leading literary men of the Fatherland. His little poem, " Das Grab," written when he was only twenty-one, made a profound impression upon Jean Paul Richter. Hoping against hope, that in spite of momentary excesses the French Revolution would yet serve the cause of freedom and humanity, he joined the army of the Republic, and served as captain on the general staff of the army that conquered Savoy. When, however, the head of the unfortunate Louis XVI. fell under the knife of the guillotine, and the independence of Switzerland was threatened by the younger and much more powerful republic, the young captain refused an offer to make him Chief of Battalion, and hurried home to place his brain and sword at the disposal of his threatened Fatherland. For the moment, however, the storm passed by, and a happy idyll of which he had long dreamed became a reality. He had for years been betrothed to Ursine von Pestalozzi, a lady belonging to one of those distinguished Italian families, exiled from their homes by persecuting bigotry at the time of the Reformation, who have conferred great distinction upon their adopted country. To her, under the name of " Berenice," Salis had addressed a number of touching odes. On the 26th December, 1793, his thirty-first birthday, they were married, and some years of most happy domestic life followed, the home of the young couple being at Chur. To this period of calm in his life belong some of his most charming lyrics. But young General Bonaparte was gaining his first laurels in Italy, and threatened to violate the neutrality of Rhaetia by traversing it to attack Austria. It was clear that the little Republic could not stand alone amid the war of giants that was raging around. Up to this time, Graubünden, though in alliance with the Swiss Confederation, had maintained its separate independence. A large party, at the head of which stood Salis, felt that the only hope of safety for the Fatherland lay in its incorporation with the Swiss republic. The Conservative and Catholic party would not hear of this, and, to prevent it, invited Austrian troops over the border into Graubünden.   As had happened in 1621, the heads of the Liberal party, including Salis, had no choice but to go into exile.   Salis took his family to Zürich and Berne, where he was appointed General Inspector of the troops of the Helvetic Republic, and served as Adjutant-General on the staff of Massena throughout the stirring campaigns in Switzerland with which the century opened.   In 1803 the influence of Napoleon caused the free state of Rhaetia to be incorporated in the Swiss Republic as the Canton of Graubünden.   Salis could now return home, and he lived by turns in Chur, Malans, and Seewis, serving his country with zeal and self-sacrifice, as member of the cantonal government, landammann, judge, and mayor, as well as in its military organisation, and in promoting education.   The period of poetic creation he felt was over, but when a young Rhaetian poet, J. R. Wyss, in the "Alpenrosen" called upon him, as the Rhaetian nightingale, to sing yet again, "Singe noch Salis ein Lied," he took up his harp and sang—

> "Mein bester Ruhm ist dass mich Edle lieben."
> "My highest fame is that noble souls love me."

Once again, at Christmas, 1821, when nearly sixty summers had passed over his head, he wrote a few touching lines "On the Thirtieth Anniversary of my Mother's Death," beginning :—

> "Du meine Mutter einst und Mutter auch noch drüben,
>   Dort wo kein Tod mehr ist, wo keine Thräne rinnt,
>   Dein denkt dein Sohn der hier so lang zurück geblieben
>   An Jahren alternd—doch im innern treues Kind."

> "Thou once my mother, and my mother ever,
>   Above where no death is, and no tear flows ;
>   Of thee thy son thinks, so long left here behind thee,
>   Ageing in years, but in spirit ever a true child."

One more extract and I have done : it is the closing stanza in the " Elegy to my Fatherland," written at Paris, in his twenty-third year :—

"Bleib durch Genügsamkeit reich und gross durch Strenge der
      Sitten ;
  Rauh sei wie Gletscher dein Muth ; kalt wenn Gefahr dich
      umblitzt ;
  Fest, wie Felsengebirge und stark wie der donnernde Rheinsturz ;
  Würdig deiner Natur, würdig der Väter, und frei."

" Remain rich through contentment and through moral purity great;
  Stern as a glacier thy courage; cool when the lightnings of danger
      play round thee ;
  Firm as a rock and strong as the thundering Rhinefall ;
  Worthy of thy nature, worthy of thy fathers, and free."

His long life was spent in a manner worthy of this youthful invocation to his country.. We have seen how ardent was his patriotism, how untiring his efforts for the common weal. It is, however, neither as general nor as patriot that his name will live, but as that of the sweetest singer that Switzerland has produced.

He sang principally of the simple Alpine life, to which he always turned with longing during his service in the French Guard in Paris, of the green upland pastures melodious with cow-bells, of the vast glaciers, and sky-cleaving peaks and everlasting snows of his native Graubünden. He sang also of the simple virtues of his countrymen, and his muse is always touched with the emotion of a fervent piety.

Readers of " Hyperion " will remember the noble rendering by Longfellow of " Das Stille Land." As, however, " Hyperion " is no longer read as it was thirty years ago, I think my readers will thank me for giving both the original and the translation :—

"DAS STILLE LAND.

"Ins stille Land
  Wer leitet uns hinüber?
  Schon wölkt sich uns der Abendhimmel trüber
  Und immer trümmervoller wird der Strand.
  Wer leitet uns mit sanfter Hand
  Hinüber, ach! hinüber
  Ins stille Land?

"Ins stille Land!
  Zu euch ihr freien Räume
  Für die Veredlung! Zarte Morgenträume
  Der schönen Seelen! künft'gen Daseins Pfand—
  Wer treu des Lebens Kampf bestand
  Trägt seiner Hoffnung Keime
  Ins stille Land.

"Ach Land! Ach Land!
  Für alle Sturm bedrohten;
  Der mildeste von unsers Schicksals Boten
  Winkt uns, die Fackel umgewandt,
  Und leitet uns mit sanfter Hand
  Ins Land der grossen Todten,
  Ins stille Land."

And Longfellow thus renders it:—

"Into the Silent Land,
  Ah! who shall lead us thither?
  Clouds in the evening sky more darkly gather,
  And shattered wrecks lie thicker on the strand.
  Who leads us with a gentle hand
  Thither, O, thither,
  Into the Silent Land?

"Into the Silent Land,
  To you ye boundless regions
  Of all perfection! Tender morning visions
  Of beauteous souls! The Future's pledge and band!
  Who in Life's battle firm doth stand,
  Shall bear Hope's tender blossoms
  Into the Silent Land.

> "O Land! O Land
> For all the broken-hearted,
> The mildest herald, by our fate allotted,
> Beckons, and with inverted torch doth stand
> To lead us with a gentle hand
> Into the land of the great departed—
> Into the Silent Land!"

But although the great American poet has rendered Salis-Seewis's lines into his own melodious verse, he can have known little about the active beneficent life of Salis, or he would never have written of him as follows in "Hyperion." Paul Flemming, in speaking of the poet Uhland, says :—" He is always fresh and invigorating, like a breezy morning. In this he differs entirely from such writers as Salis and Matthieson. 'And who are they?' asks Mary Ashburton. 'Two melancholy gentlemen, to whom life was only a dismal swamp, upon whose margin they walked with cambric hand-kerchiefs in their hands, sobbing and sighing, and making signals to Death to come and ferry them over the lake. And now their spirits stand in the green fields of German song, like two weeping willows bending over a grave. To read their poems is like wandering through a village churchyard on a summer evening, reading the inscriptions upon the grave-stones, and recalling sweet images of the departed.'"

This seems a very curious description of the young guardsman, enthusiastic for the cause of human free-dom, of the energetic Adjutant-General of the Revo-lutionary Army, or of the retired veteran, who for a great part of his life was the first magistrate in the district in which he resided. The estimate of his poetry, too, seems to me singularly misleading. I cannot remember exactly when "Hyperion" was written; but I am pretty certain that, at the moment when Longfellow describes the spirit of Salis as "standing in the green fields of German song like a weeping willow bending over a grave," the grand old soldier was still living and fulfilling all the duties of a country gentleman and magistrate. He died at Malans at the age of 72, in the house in which he was born, and his remains were brought for burial to Seewis, where he had passed a great part of his life, and the castle of which had been the seat of his ancestors for many generations.

A handsome marble slab, upon the outside of the southern wall of the old church at Seewis, marks the spot where the soldier and singer rests among the people and the Alps he loved so well. The inscription upon his tomb will suitably finish this chapter :—

"Selig sind die Todten die in dem Herrn sterben."

Ins stille Land hinüber gieng fest vertrauend an Christum,
JOHANN GAUDENZ VON SALIS-SEEWIS,
Gewesener Bundsland-Ammann Eidgenoessischer und
Kantons-Oberst
Geboren 26te December, 1762.
Gestorben 29te Januar, 1834.
Hier wo seine Leyer verhallte, Toene ein Accord durch
kommende Zeit.

Translation.
"Blessed are the dead who die in the Lord."

Into the Silent Land went, firmly trusting in Christ,
JOHANN GAUDENZ VON SALIS-SEEWIS,
Former Bundsland-Ammann and
Colonel of the Cantonal and Confederate Swiss Army.
Born 26th December, 1762.
Died 29th January, 1834.
Here, where his lyre ceased to sound, may an accord go
forth through coming time.

CHAPTER XXVIII.

SEEWIS IN WINTER.

ALL the seasons in the High Alps are beautiful. Spring comes, and, as soon as the snow has disappeared, the mountain-pastures are carpeted with delicate young grass, against the green of which show myriads of many-coloured flowers. With the summer the forests fully array themselves in their new foliage, and as the autumn deepens, the hill-sides blaze out with every shade of green, yellow, and fiery crimson. But how about winter? Surely, winter is cold, bleak, gloomy, and intolerable in the High Alps? Cold it no doubt is; and when the snow falls thick, and the winds sweep resistlessly down the Alpine gorges, it is pleasant to feel that you have a good substantial roof overhead, and a large hot stove, with plenty of wood wherewith to feed it. Gloomy, however, the winter is not.

The eighteen inches of snow that fell on the night of the 6th of November, 1879, were quickly followed by about 3 ft. more, so that the round iron tables on the verandah presented the appearance of gigantic bride-cakes, and the verandah itself was piled with snow up to the height of the railing that surrounded it. But when once the snow had ceased, the sun asserted its prerogative, and shone out with extraordinary brilliancy and power, from a cloudless deep-blue sky, upon the white Alpine world. The frost was often very severe, the thermometer ranging at night from the zero of Fahrenheit to 10° or 12° above ; but as soon as the sun, like a huge ball of fire, leaped up from behind the glaciers of the Piz Bija, he filled the air with light and warmth. Such a day was the 21st of November, when we drew the children upon little sledges for some miles over the snow. Everything was white and dazzling in the landscape save where the pine-trees stood out actually black by contrast, or where a larch had not yet shed its golden yellow spines. So hot was it that we were all glad to sit down upon the sledges, basking in the sun's light and warmth.

In the village the occupations of summer have given place to those of winter. The men have to look after the cattle and sheep, and keep them supplied with fodder. The women are busy weaving the wool into redoubtable home-spun garments. This home-spun is wonderful stuff. It seems as if it could not wear out. We were shown a gown that had been in wear for twelve years, and that appeared to have at least as long a lease of life before it. When the snow lies deep upon the ground it is a busy time in the great pine-forests of the Alps. All through the summer and autumn the woodman has been busy with his axe, and before him the sylvan patriarchs have come crashing down. But how remove them along rough and winding Alpine paths ? Except in winter it would be almost, if not entirely, impossible. But when four or five feet of snow lie upon the ground, a little traffic makes the paths and roads hard and slippery, so that the great trunks easily slide along when hooked to horses or oxen.

There is always one winter sport which visitors can pursue amongst the snow—that of sledging, now called "*toboggining*," a name imported from Canada. The *toboggin* is a flat oblong seat, about three feet long, raised about six inches from the ground upon wooden runners. The rider sits well back, with his legs stretched out one on each side. As gravity and the impetus you gain are the sole motive power, it is of course only possible to *toboggin* down hill; and it is well to choose a not too precipitous slope, with a good level piece to receive you at the bottom. Once started on a frozen slope, you bound—you fly. There is no stopping until long after you reach the level ground, unless, indeed, you are gliding along a narrow track with deep snow on either side, when you have only to let your sledge swerve by a hair's breadth to either side, and you soon stop. You shoot into and are buried in the snow; and when with great exertion you have picked yourself up and out of it, you find the snow has penetrated everywhere—snow in your mouth, snow in your ears, snow in your hair, snow gently thawing down the back of your neck, snow in your boots, snow in your pockets, snow penetrating into the most remote recesses of your garments. The sledge may be guided by a sort of wooden rudder worked by the hands behind; but this is high art to which I have never attained. The ordinary *tobogginist*, like many a soldier who has lived to a ripe old age, trusts entirely to his heels, touching the snow to the right or left according as he wishes the sledge to incline in that direction; and the greatest skill is displayed in touching the ground as little as possible, when you shoot through the air at an exhilarating speed. In addition to a certain skill or

knack, to ride a *toboggin* well it is necessary to be cool
and fearless; and these qualities mostly only come
with practice. It was pleasant to me to resume this
sport of my youth; for, some quarter of a century
back, at school among the Moravian Brethren in the
heart of the forest of Thuringia, sledging was our
favourite winter amusement. As we there had to ride
our sledges down narrow forest paths, accidents—and
sometimes very serious ones—were not uncommon.
Here at Seewis it is easy to choose ground for sledging
where the worst that can happen is a harmless, if igno-
minious, upset.

A time of snow and bad weather was favourable for
making inquiry of the Landammann (the principal
magistrate of the district) as to the social condition of
the people of Seewis. With the exception of the
Canton of Wallis (*le Valais*), Graubünden is probably
the most backward of the Swiss Cantons. You do not
find in it the beautiful homesteads and neatly-kept
gardens of Thurgau and Appenzell. Yet even in
Graubünden a substantial comfort and well-being
are universal which may well make an Englishman
sigh. Perhaps a few facts as to the village of Seewis
will convey more information than a disquisition upon
the state of the whole canton.

It is, however, fair to premise that Seewis is a somewhat exceptionally wealthy Commune. It contains, as
has been stated, somewhere near 900 inhabitants. The
timber in the forests, which belong to the Commune,
has been recently valued by a professional forester at
3,000,000 francs, or £120,000. This wealth it is
however impossible to realise, as, if the forests were
all cut down, not only would Seewis itself be exposed
to destructive avalanches, but the very soil of the
pastures would probably be washed away by winter

storms.   As a matter of fact, beyond supplying the
"Bürger" (citizens) of Seewis with timber for building
and with firewood, no very large profit has been
derived by the Commune from its timber.

The villagers among them possess about 1,000 cows
and oxen, 1,500 sheep, and 400 goats.   Almost all the
villagers, be they never so poor, possess the houses in
which they live and a certain freehold besides.   Thus,
early in September, 1880, a man of the name of Fausch,
who was engaged by the Commune to take care of the
cattle at one of the "Alps," for which he received his
keep and a payment of 100 francs (£4) for the entire
summer, was killed by the kick of a horse.   The visitors
at the Kurhaus made a small collection among themselves for his widow, as she was reported one of
the poorest people in the village.   We found that she
owned the wooden chalet in which she and her children
lived, together with a good-sized field planted with
potatoes, and a well-stocked but small orchard through
which flowed a mountain stream.   It is true that the
whole property was mortgaged to the bank at Chur,
for 4,000 francs (£160), but there is no doubt its value
much exceeds the amount of the mortgage.   Our contribution we found would be best applied towards
helping to pay the accruing half-year's interest.

In addition to its forests the "Alps" are of great value
to the Commune of Seewis.   Thither every citizen
may send as many cows, sheep, or pigs, for the summer
as he happens to possess.   I asked the Landammann "if he had 100 cows and some other citizen of
Seewis only one, was it fair that he (the Landammann)
should have one hundred times greater benefit from
the common pastures than the other?"   He replied
that this was rapidly becoming a burning question in
Communal politics, which would probably only be

settled by a fixed sum being paid into the Communal
Treasury for every cow pastured upon the "Alps." The
villagers divide themselves into four "Companionships"
(Genossenschaft), and each Companionship when the
snow begins to melt upon the mountains, sends the cows
belonging to its members to the special "Alp" allotted to
it—in the charge of four or five young men, appointed
to tend and milk the cows and to manufacture the
cheese. With them goes a "Schreiber," or book-
keeper, whose duty it is at every milking to weigh the
milk produced by the cows of each separate proprietor,
and to keep an exact record of the weights. At the
end of the season, when the cows come down from the
"Alps," the accounts are carefully made up, and the
cheese and expenses are divided in proportion to the
quantity of milk shown to have been yielded.

In addition to the "Alps" the Commune possesses
pastures at a lower level, where the cattle can graze
when the "Alps" have become inaccessible. I have
mentioned that what was once the old castle of the Salis
family has comparatively recently been purchased by the
Commune; with it were purchased considerable plots
of arable land. Every male citizen of Seewis upon his
marriage, or, if he remain single, at the age of fifty,
receives about 400 Klafter of this land—the Klafter is
36 square feet, consequently, 400 Klafter = 14,400
square feet. This allotment returns to the Commune
upon his death or upon that of his widow. The lands
thus held are called "Allmends." The Commune of
Seewis has set aside 35,000 francs, or £1,400, the
interest of which is applicable to the relief of the poor.
In the autumn of 1879, there were, however, only two
persons upon the books of the Commune, for poor
relief: a married couple, who received three francs a
week. In September of the same year died an old

man who at the time was receiving four francs a week.   These were at that time the only recent cases. The industry and frugality universally produced by the magic of possessing property are everywhere conspicuous.   There is very little waste of time and money in the public house, for everyone is anxious to save every franc he can make or spare, either to increase his freehold or to pay off the mortgage that may be upon it.

All the leaves of the ash trees are carefully collected, (the trees are sadly mauled and maltreated in the process), dried, and used as winter fodder for the cattle. When the leaves fall from the beech-trees, they are gathered and used as bedding for the cattle, and as stuffing for mattresses.   Late in the autumn we found women busy spreading manure on some upland pastures, 200 feet higher than Seewis.

With this general well-being, there is great simplicity and frugality.   The Landammann, the principal magisterial authority in the whole district, lives in a good house, it is true, but so do most of the peasants. His *ménage* is hardly to be distinguished from theirs. He is a man of considerable legal acumen, and was educated at the Universities of Munich and Heidelberg.   His name is Walser, and his ancestor, who lived at Schiers, had his land there so ravaged by the turbulent Landquart, that he determined to get beyond its reach, and so came up the hill to Seewis in 1740. There are now, of his descendants, fourteen families of the name of Walser in Seewis, and there are no less than twelve Andreas Walsers, which must be rather inconvenient.

What I have mentioned concerning Seewis will enable us to compare the condition of its inhabitants with that of the dwellers in an English agricultural

village of a like population, where the whole of the
land is owned by some great lord or squire, who
probably resides for one-half the year in a mansion on
his estate.   Near him, in a fine old parsonage, will
live the family of the rector or vicar, very possibly
diffusing much sweetness and light through the parish.
There may be half-a-dozen farmers, now, I fear, in no
very prosperous state.   The remainder of the inhabitants are labourers, or belong to the families of
labourers, with little or no property of any kind, and
with such small inducement to frugality that probably
each one, in the course of his life, spends in beer as
much money as would have purchased the freehold of a
cottage and an acre or two of land, if our land laws
made such a purchase possible.   What incentive, indeed,
has the English peasant to frugality and self-denial?
The advantages of saving, as represented by a small
hoard in an old stocking, or in a Post Office Savings'
Bank, are too remote and problematical to compete
successfully with immediate and tangible enjoyments.
Why should he deny himself to increase the convenience of, or to beautify, a tenement from which
he may at any moment be ejected?   The frugal and
the spendthrift, the sober and the intemperate, alike,
when old and worn out, have, it is true, a fine large
house to which to retire; but it is a workhouse,
and in entering it they proclaim themselves paupers.
It is, perhaps, a beautiful system, but must, one would
think, strike a foreigner as rather odd, especially
amongst a people who pride themselves upon being
the most practical and business-like in the world.

   To return to Graubünden and to Seewis, the
Landammann informs me that the sale and transfer
of land here are extremely simple and inexpensive.
On a purchase of 10,000 francs' worth of land in the

Commune of Seewis, there is a registration charge of 34 francs, and of 68 centimes (7*d.*) for drawing up a protocol; the entire expense on the purchase of £400 worth of land amounting thus to one pound eight shillings.

In former, though still quite recent times, the local authorities in the villages of the different cantons were able, in very arbitrary fashion, to forbid marriages which they deemed improvident, lest the offspring should come upon the commune for support. Now, however, the central government of the Confederation of Switzerland overrides any cantonal laws of that nature, and does not permit any restriction upon the marriage of adults beyond that of too close consanguinity.

There is no code of civil law applicable to the whole of Switzerland; and it is doubtful whether, in a congeries of peoples of different race, origin, and habits of thought, it would be wise to endeavour to establish one. The civil law in the German Cantons is based partly upon immemorial Allemanni custom and partly upon Roman law. In the French Cantons it has an entirely different origin, and there the Code Napoleon obtains.

In nothing is there so great a difference observable between the laws and habits of thought in England and, say, in the Canton of Graubünden, than in the laws that regulate the succession of property. In England —leaving on one side for the moment the laws of entail, settlement, and primogeniture—I know of no limitation to the right of bequest. It is taken for granted that it is inherently just for a man, even on his death-bed, to be able to do what he likes with his own. If no allegation of mental incapacity can be established against him, I presume a testator may, so far as his personal estate is concerned, disinherit

his natural heirs in favour of the Society of Jesus,
an asylum for homeless dogs, or that latest and
strangest development of the associative principle—
"The Tichborne Scientific Test Association;" and
however great the social obloquy attaching to his
memory, the law would declare the will valid.   Not
so among most other nations.   Among them the right
of bequest is brought within very narrow limits, and
the right of inheritance takes its place.   In Graubünden, if a testator have children of his own, he
must leave them nine-tenths of what he has inherited,
and two-thirds of what he may have added to the
inherited estate, he thus having the right of bequest
only in respect to one-tenth of his inherited property,
and one-third of what he has added to it.   If the
testator leave no children, but there should be relations descended from his own father and mother—*i.e.*,
brothers, nephews, nieces, &c., he has the right of bequest to the extent of one-fifth of what he inherited and
one-half what he has added to it ; the remainder must
go to his relations.   If the testator have no children,
nor relations descended from his father and mother,
but have relations descended from his grandfathers or
great-grandfathers, he has the right of bequest over
one-third of what he has inherited, and over the whole
of what he may have added to it ; but even to these
distant relations he must leave two-thirds of his
patrimony.   All children and all relations of the same
degree of consanguinity, inherit equally without regard
to sex, nor does the eldest son have any advantage
beyond the other children.   To an Englishman, this
abrogation of the right of bequest in favour of the
right of inheritance seems, on the first blush of it, a
monstrous injustice ; but should he try to argue the
question, he will find that there is more to be said in

favour of the Graubünden view of the case than he
would have deemed possible. I put a case to the
Landammann. "Suppose you had a worthless son,
could you not give away your property so that he
should not inherit it?" He replied, "No; the same
law applies to gifts as to bequests; and, moreover,"
he added, "if a testator were to say, 'I cannot
bequeath nor yet give away my property—at any rate,
I can spend it,' his relations, upon making proper
representations to the authorities, could, so to speak,
put his property in trust, only leaving him power over
a certain allowance." Many of my readers may, I fear,
find all this very dull; but nations make their laws,
and are in turn very much what their laws make them;
and it is interesting to note the radical difference
between the laws and habits of thought of England
and those of many other countries in this important
matter.

During the summer, when the assistance of the
children is much needed in the fields, the school is
closed, but in winter it is regularly open, and attendance
is obligatory, between the ages of seven and fifteen.
No payment whatever is made by the parents, unless
a curious survival of an old custom be regarded as
such. When once the cold weather has set in, each
child may be observed carrying to school, in addition
to his books, a good-sized billet of wood, to assist in
keeping the schoolrooms warm. · On visiting the
school, I was struck by the intelligent character of the
teaching, and the evidently great interest of the
children in what they were learning, Those of the
most advanced class were busy drawing upon their
slates from memory, maps of Graubünden, showing
its rivers and mountains. This they did with considerable exactness.

The " Pfarrer " or clergyman is a man of great importance in the village, but his social status is, of course, very different from that of a clergyman in England. As far as I can learn, the entire income of the Pfarrer, including certain perquisites, such as residence in the Schloss free of rent, an allowance of wood from the Commune, &c., does not exceed £100 to £120 a-year. This income will not admit of any very luxurious style of living, if, as is usually the case, a large family has to be maintained out of it. The present Pfarrer's wife is a very sweet-looking woman, with pleasing manners, and the deportment of a lady, but she cannot afford any servants whatever, and does all the housework herself, in addition to taking charge of her young family. The Pfarrer himself is a man of education and some cultivation ; in one respect, I should think, he must be almost unique—for it must be seldom, indeed, that a man can be met with who can preach in Italian, Romansch, and German. He and his wife spent a Sunday evening with us at the Kurhaus, and we were not a little pleased with their simple and unaffected manners, and their intelligent conversation. The former Pfarrer was a man who had studied philosophy deeply. The church is always well attended. The men sit on one side, the women on the other. All are decently dressed, the women very neatly in black ; the elder women wear caps, but the younger wear only their own very neatly plaited hair as head-dress. The thrifty habits of the Swiss show themselves in the choice of black, as well for weddings as for funerals. The one dress will do for either occasion or both. When the service is over, the women file out with the order and regularity of a regiment of soldiers, the clergyman then follows, and after him come the men.

Very solemn and impressive are the celebrations of the Lord's Supper which take place on the festivals of Christmas, Easter, Whitsuntide, and Harvest. The attendance at church is always good, but on these occasions no one who can possibly be present absents himself. The Sacrament is very simply, and, as it appeared to me, very worthily administered. At the close of the ordinary service the Pfarrer descends from the pulpit, and takes his stand by the stone font, which serves as Communion Table, on which are placed two white metal flagons of wine and a plate of bread. By the side of the Pfarrer stands the Elder, also in a gown, and then the whole congregation file past in regular procession, and partake of the elements.

In the Prättigau the women always come first, a privilege said to have been accorded to them as a recognition of their valour in the attack on the Austrian soldiery two hundred and fifty years since. The Pfarrer hands the bread and the Elder the wine, the latter in an ancient silver-gilt chalice, from which each in turn drinks. The whole scene is very solemn and impressive. The men, who often come to church in stout garments of home-spun, on these great occasions always appear in good black cloth. The women, of course, don their best, but as black is universally worn by the married women, and to a large extent also by the unmarried girls, there is little room for a display of finery. Married and single alike, without exception, wear a black alpaca apron. Both men and women are well and stoutly shod, and their whole appearance shews to how high a degree of comfort and prosperity a rural population can be brought by industry, frugality, and the magic of property. Except in the depth of winter, the young women almost always carry a little bouquet with them to church, and some of the elder men and women never appear there without a flower held jauntily between the lips. This is a curious custom, and must be very old and widely diffused.

After the service every Sunday, there is usually held a kind of open-air parliament, at the corner of the road leading down to the church, where such questions of communal politics as whether the cows shall be sent up to the "Alps" or brought down, are discussed with much eagerness and earnestness, the vote being taken by show of hands.

Of the moral condition of the village, I have done my utmost to obtain a correct idea by means of conversations with the Pfarrer, the Laudammann, and other leading villagers. So far as I can learn, there has been no illegitimate birth in the village itself during, at any rate, the past ten years, I say of the village itself, because I am not able to speak positively in respect to the small outlying hamlet of Schmitten, close to Grüsch, which appertains to the Commune of Seewis.* I wish I could speak as favourably of the cleanliness, as I can of the morality, of the inhabitants of Seewis. They come exceedingly neatly dressed and clean-looking to church, but I fear many of them have yet to learn the comfort to be derived from a plentiful personal use of soap and water. The lanes, also, in the older parts of the village, are in bad weather in a quite unnecessarily filthy state, as a few hours' labour on the part of two or three men, would effect a great and permanent improvement.

---

* Since the above was in print, the Landammann has been so obliging as to go through the register since 1870. From this it appears that there have been two illegitimate births in the village within that period. In the one case, the mother was a girl having nothing to do with Seewis, who simply came up from Chur for her confinement; the other was that of a Seewis girl, who had been away at service at Glarus. These exceptions seem to me to prove the rule.

During the height of the season the Kurhaus was so crowded that the proprietor was obliged to borrow one or two sofas and other furniture from the village. This furniture, we had painful reason to know, served as a means of immigration into the Kurhaus of considerable numbers of that wonderfully energetic and industrious, but ferocious and poisonous insect, the common flea. In this matter of cleanliness it must, however, be remembered that Graubünden is one of the most backward cantons in the whole of Switzerland.

As to the sobriety of the people, I can only say that it is very seldom that I have seen any of the villagers the worse for liquor. Everybody drinks a little " Most " or wine if he can get it, but it is but little ; and the clergyman told me there were only two or three old men in the village who were addicted to " Schnapps " (dram-drinking).

Apropos of cleanliness, I may perhaps mention that, having an application for the position of nurse to our children from a girl of seventeen from Grüsch, I visited her mother's house—a very small wooden châlet. The mother is a widow, and earns her living by very hard work as a hand-weaver ; but the house, which my sister and I visited without any notice, was exquisitely clean and neat. The personal habits of the girl leave nothing to be desired ; and, as showing what the compulsory education of the common schools does for the children, I may mention that her exercise-books show that she had acquired the rudiments of book-keeping, of free-hand drawing, and a little French, besides "the three Rs." As illustrative of the fact that even the very poorest possess their own homesteads, the girl told me that, although they had often been in great straits, " they had never, thank God, been obliged to part with their house."

A noteworthy feature of the social economy of the village is the night-watchman. On still and warm summer nights, the visitor whose windows are wide open, is more startled than pleased to be roused out of his sleep by the shrill sing-song of the watch-man. It must, however, be recollected that there is some good ground for this practice. In view of the great liability to fire in the case of all villages built for the most part of wood, it is satisfactory to know that it is the duty of some one to be constantly on the alert, and to give notice of the first approach of the dreaded enemy. To a Paterfamilias, at any rate, the vision of a great hotel in flames, and of wife and children rushing down the blazing staircase from an upper story, is not a pleasing prospect. In the possible presence of such a danger, it would be un-grateful to grumble at the too-audible evidence that some one is watching over our safety.

The rude rhyme, in barbaric German, sung by the night-watchman, I append for the benefit of the curious.

At 10 p.m. he sings :—

> " Jetzt tritt i üf die Abendwacht,
> Gott geb' uns Allen e' gueti Nacht ;
> Und löschend ab das Füür und Licht,
> Das uns der liebe Gott behüat."
> *Translation.*
> " Now I enter upon the evening watch,
> God give us a good night ;
> And putting out fire and light,
> May our dear God take care of us."

At 2 a.m. he sings :—

> " Stönd üf im Nama Jesu Christ,
> Der helle Tag vorhanden ist ;
> Der helle Tag, ünd das ist wahr,
> Gott geb' uns Allen en gueten Tag."

Translation.

" Stand up in the name of Jesus Christ,
  The bright day is at hand,
  The bright day and true it is,
  God give us all good day."

There are also special rhymes for eleven and for midnight, but the above will probably suffice as specimens.

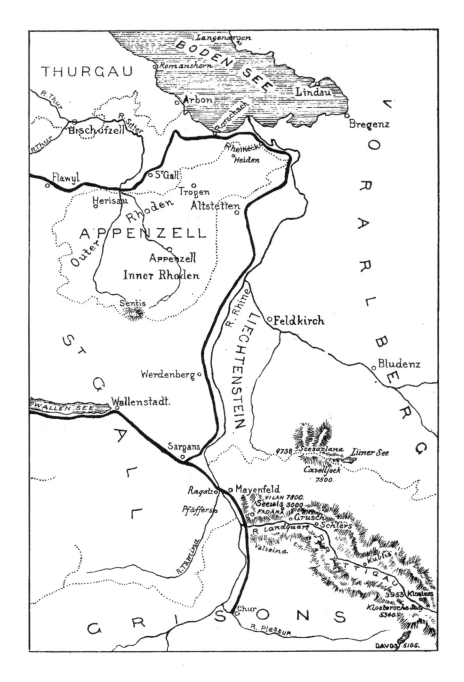

SKETCH MAP OF PRÄTTIGAU, WITH RHEINTHAL.

CHAPTER XXIX.

EXCURSIONS FROM SEEWIS.

Fadära Stein—Ascent of the Vilan—An early start—Venerable pines—Sunrise on the mountains—Monument near the summit—Magnificent view—The Scesa Plana—Excursion to the Lüner See—The baths of Ganei—National and patriotic songs—The Kuh-reigen, or Ranz des Vaches—An awkward piece—Benighted on the mountain—The "Douglas" Hut—Night-quarters—An uncanny goat—Dawn among the mountains—Summit of the Cavelljock—The return home.

I HAVE incidentally spoken of the abundance of beautiful walks around Seewis. It will here be convenient to mention two or three rather longer excursions than those already described,—and first that to the Fadära Stein. My readers will remember that the road from Landquart to Seewis runs through a narrow gorge, on either side of which tower rocky heights, and that when the gorge widens out into the valley of the Prättigau the road zigzags up to Seewis, which lies on the side of the Vilan, in a little hollow about 3000 ft. above sea-level, surrounded by gentle eminences, or knolls, clothed with wood or laid out in pastures. The Fadära Stein is the highest point of the great rocky ledge which overhangs the Rhine valley at a spot near to the gorge of the Landquart. The way from Seewis to Fadära lies through undulating meadow-land, with the valley of the Landquart below, and mountains upon all sides. A walk of one and a-half miles brings the visitor to what, within historical memory, was a mountain tarn, and which still retains the name "Zum See" ("At the lake"). At this point the view is very fine. On the right rise gentle undulations, with turf like that of an English park, all studded over with copses of oak, ash, beech, birch, maple, and hornbeam, until they are merged in the smooth green pyramid of the Vilan, nearly 4000 ft. above us, as we are nearly 4000 ft. above sea-level. On the occasion of my first visit, not being a good walker, I had hired of the landlord a powerful steed which would have made a good charger, and which cleared the ground with great strides, making nothing of the steepest hillsides. Surely the best position from which to enjoy scenery is from the back of a horse. Along devious paths through the woods we approached the "Stein." At last the path altogether ceased, and we rode at will across meadows, through copses, and up the green hillside. The hazel-bushes were laden with nuts, and the wild cherry, which here grows in abundance as a little bush, brightened the undergrowth with its brilliantly- . coloured, but intensely sour, fruit. As we reached the crest of the ridge the departing sun was just lighting up the landscape with golden light and throwing a crimson glory on the glaciers of the Ringel-Horn and the snow-fields of the majestic group of the Graue Hörner, far away on the other side of the Rhine valley.

Two thousand feet below is the village of Malans, whose church, and château, and houses look like toy structures, and whose people, as we see them through a field-glass, look like pigmies walking about in the miniature streets. Around Malans are vineyards, which now in autumn show a deep green, and from our point of view look like velvet upon a ground as of green silk formed by the meadows. Exactly below the rock on which we stand is a great beech wood, the foxes out of which commit serious depredations at the time of vintage among the vineyards of Malans. Carrying the eye a little further, past the village of Mayenfeld and to the other side of the Rhine, high above the gorge of the Tamīna, rise the conventual buildings of Pfeffers, now converted into a lunatic asylum. In a semicircle below, lies fashionable Ragatz. Looking southward up the course of the Rhine we see Chur, and rising behind it the huge wall of mountains separating us from Italy; while immediately below, the Rhine valley lies stretched out like a map, with ruins, rocks, old châteaux, and villages, here and there among its luxuriant crops. When we turned homewards the sun, though set to us, was still shining upon the great red rocky head of the Rhaetia-Horn, while the imposing and densely-wooded height of the Haupt, amidst the Valzeina mountain-land on the other side of the ravine of the Landquart, and the woody undulations around us, were all in solemn shadow.

It is impossible to visit Fadära without each time finding new beauties. Visitors never tire of it.

A rather longer excursion is that to the summit of the Vilan. Most visitors under-estimate its distance and think the ascent can be made in an hour, or an hour and a-half at most. As a matter of fact, the quickest walkers cannot reach the summit in less than two hours, while those who have seen their best walking days, or who, like myself, are obliged to avail themselves of horses, will find double or treble that time has passed before they reach the highest point. In summer, or during hot weather, the start should not be made later than 2 or 3 a.m., if you wish to avoid having to do the severest part of the ascent under a broiling sun.   At the latter end of May, 1880, we had a spell of splendid weather, very hot and bright.   Our landlord strongly advised us to take advantage of it to climb the Vilan, and accordingly, at 3 a.m. on the morning of May 27th, we started. We were a party of five—a gentleman from Sheffield, the old guide Jost, our landlord, and a boy to carry provender for the horse which I rode, and to lead it down when it could be no longer of service.   It was a lovely night, the waning moon shedding a silvery sheen upon mountain and valley, upon the châlets of the village, and the church with its tall, tapering spire. The air was soft and balmy, and, though the thermometer stood at 65°, it felt cool after the great heat of the previous day.   My good steed, which I firmly believe would refuse nothing in the shape of a hill, bore up the exceedingly steep rocky lane which leads out of the village, in grand style.   A few birds had already commenced their morning hymn, noticeably a blackcap that was pouring forth melody from a crab-tree near the path.   The murmur of the torrent at the bottom of the ravine which separates the Vilan from the Fanasaberg was a continual solemn bass to all other music.   As we ascended, our range of vision extended : peak upon peak, and range upon range, coming into view, which are invisible from the level of Seewis.   At four the moon began to pale her ineffectual fires before the approach of the king of day, and the snow-peaks on the horizon were touched with rosy light.   Leaving the lightly-wooded green pastures, up. the slope of which we had been climbing, we entered a pine forest, many of the trees of which are from 100 to 300 years old, and their great branches hoary with dependent moss.   Bearded and venerable are these pines; and, exposed as they are on this steep and lofty Alpine slope, the winter snows and wind-storms have caused many of them to assume weirdly-fantastic shapes.   The ground is strewed with giant stems uprooted by these storms, or cut down any time within the last fifty years, and left to rot when their removal proved too difficult.   The huge stumps are never grubbed up.   A better system of forest culture is said now to obtain, but the heart of a lover of trees almost bleeds to see how these sylvan monarchs have been causelessly and wastefully destroyed.   Just before five the golden disc of the sun rose above the mountains; and, as my gallant steed had already carried me to an altitude of 2000 ft. above Seewis, or 5000 ft. above sea-level, we halted, and he was allowed to have a long deep draught from a mountain-spring, and a loaf of black bread, which had been sliced for him as if he were a Christian.

The pines became more and more stunted, and at last ceased; and as we passed out of the forest and on to the bare mountain side, we reached a spot so immediately above Seewis, that it appeared as though you might drop a stone into that peaceful little nest upon which the sun had not yet risen.   Here we reached the first bank of snow.   The pasture exactly below it, and through which a stream from the snow ran, rivalled the snow itself in whiteness, for it was entirely carpeted with myriads of the fragrant white narcissus.

In this lovely spot stands a Senn-hütte—shepherd's hut—to which a cowherd and his family had just come up for the spring.   They were busy milking the kine when our party arrived, and a flat-bottomed vessel made of fresh pine-wood, and holding about three quarts of rich new milk, was handed to us—a

morning draught that was greatly appreciated. After
this welcome refreshment, we proceeded, and our
way became so steep that I was obliged to dismount ;
but the guide attached me by a rope to the saddle
of the horse, so that though he could not carry
me, he dragged me up. At one particularly steep
place the poor beast grazed one of his hind fetlocks
against a sharp stone, and giving a great start,
appeared for a moment much as though he were
going to roll down to Seewis. We were upon a very
steep ledge, on one side of which was a sheer descent,
and on the other a great bank of snow. Not wishing
to accompany my horse in any too hasty return home,
I sprang out of his way on one side, and found myself
up to my waist in the snow. The good horse, however, soon recovered himself, and the path becoming
less precipitous, he continued to do me yeoman's
service. Near the summit is a rude monument shaped
like a grave, with the inscription " Edward Hauser
von Zürich, 13th August, 1869," and a roughly shaped
anchor, carved upon a head-stone. He was a young
man from Zürich, who was staying at Seewis for the
benefit of his lungs. In attempting to climb the
Vilan, he died at this spot either from an apoplectic
seizure or from fatigue. Old Jost, an excellent
guide, and very deliberate, attributed the catastrophe
entirely to the fact of the doctor, who accompanied
the poor young man, being possessed of a mania for
taking people quickly up the mountain. We were
now within a quarter of an hour of the summit, and
as it was no longer possible for the horse to be of
service, he was sent home with the boy. A short
scramble along a narrow ridge of rock, with a bank of
snow upon one side and a precipice on the other, and
we had gained the summit. Beyond the cairn marking

the highest point is a tremendous chasm, reaching down into the Rhine valley. It is pleasant to throw yourself upon your face upon the turf, and to feel the mountain-top solid underneath you, forbidding the fear that it and you alike will incontinently slide over into the abyss. The only living creatures around us were great numbers of lustrous flies, about the size of bluebottles, with an occasional green beetle. Our landlord had brought up with him a supply of "proviant" that would have satisfied the eager appetite of that veteran campaigner, Sir Dugald Dalgetty; and the pure though not cold mountain air, combined with the fatigue of our climb, caused us to do ample justice to the viands. For two hours we lay basking in the sunshine and enjoying the view. And what a view lay at our feet and stretched around us! The sky was blue and the air perfectly clear, except in the west where, above the Lake of Zürich, there was a slight haze. The lake itself was plainly visible, and through a glass, the villages upon its shores. The summit of the Vilan commands a vast amphitheatre of snow-peaks. In the east, conspicuous among a thousand lesser heights, is the mighty Oertler Spitze, the highest mountain in Tyrol; just in front of it lay a huge glacier which sparkled in the sun. We could follow with the eye the course of the Landquart until near its source at Klosters, and see exactly where the road turns aside to Davos. In the same way we had the whole Rhine valley at our feet, and we could even follow it towards its source as it trends westward above Chur. The huge snow mountains through which wind the Splügen and Bernardino passes, shut out our view to the south, while westward are the peaks among which the Rhine begins his course, near the St. Gotthard. Comparatively near to the Vilan, but separated by a tremendous gulf, is the Rhaetikon chain, of which the Falkniss, the Tschingel, and the Scesa Plana are the highest points.   Though nearly 8,000 feet above sea-level, the sun was very hot ; but, as close to where we lay there was a great snow-bank, it was easy to keep cool with a handful of snow put inside one's hat. At eleven a.m., we slowly and somewhat reluctantly commenced our descent, collecting a few roots of Alpine plants as we went down.   Among these were the lovely *Primula Farinosa*, in both the pink and white varieties, here dwarfed to the tiniest dimensions, and bearing only one petal upon a stalk barely an inch long ;   the *Gentiana Nivalis*, a very lovely little yellow Auricula, a bright purple Pansy, and the delicately-fringed *Soldanella* which only grows just where the snow has melted,   When we sat down to rest we were cheered by the song of the mountain larks ; we watched a hawk, too, far below us, that probably also felt an interest in the larks.   Our guide and Mr. Hitz, the landlord, were very kind in helping me down ; but my good steed was gone, though even had he remained with us, nothing would have induced me to try and ride *down* such a mountain.   Deep draughts of sparkling cold water from a mountain spring put fresh life into us all, and after crossing a ravine, we were again shaded from the fiery rays of the sun by hoary pine trees.   Oh, the delight of lying prone under those grand old pines, that have braved the storms of centuries, and of gazing up through the white moss and green spines to the blue sky beyond, while with every respiration your lungs swell with the wholesome resinous breath of the forest, and a far-off murmur comes from the torrent 2,000 feet below, and a gentle breeze stirs the branches !

THE LÜNER SEE.

Largely availing ourselves of the rest and delicious shade which the forest offered, we did not reach the Kurhaus until four p.m. It was a rare day ; the ground was thirsting for rain after a long drought, during which the hot sun had baked it. The haze we saw over the Lake of Zürich was the sign of coming change, and proved the augury of a very wet summer. On the first day of June the thermometer fell from 68° in the shade to 40°, and the hills, including the Vilan, were covered afresh with snow.

Every visitor to Seewis frequently turns his eyes to the amazing wall of rock which rises up sheer to the north-east, and seems to deny a passage even to the most adventurous mountaineer. This rocky wall is the Scesa Plana, whose highest peak rises to a height of 10,000 feet above the sea-level, and separates the Austrian Vorarlberg from Switzerland. Among the bare and riven peaks of this wild and desolate region, there lies at a height of 6,500 feet, as it were in the very lap of the Alps, a little lake or tarn, about five miles in circumference, one-and-a-quarter miles in its greatest length, and three-quarters of a mile in its greatest breadth. Soundings have in some places proved a depth of nearly 400 feet. When the sun shines brightly upon its mirror-like surface, the deep indigo-blue of its waters makes the Lüner See appear like a dark glittering eye to the wild Alpine region in which it lies. To visit this secret recess of the Alps had long been my ambition, but there were difficulties in the way ; to walk there was beyond my strength, and I was told no visitor had ever attempted the excursion on horseback—if, indeed, it were possible for a horse with a rider on his back to climb the pass.

Early in September, a younger brother was spending a week with me at Seewis, before leaving for the

West Indies, and with him were three brother
Cantabs—all four, by a curious coincidence, being
Scholars of Trinity College. During the whole of
August the weather had been very unsettled, the
temperature ruled low, the sky was constantly draped
by dark clouds, and hardly a day elapsed without very
heavy rain. With the opening of September all this
changed, the barometer steadily rose, and the morning
of the 3rd—Cromwell's day—dawned bright and clear,
with a hot sun. In addition to those I have named,
a Scotch gentleman, who had been spending the
summer at Seewis for the sake of his health, and who,
like myself, was obliged to take a horse, and two lads
of seventeen, fresh from school, joined our party.
Old Jost, the guide, implored us to start early in the
morning, but one of the Cantabs, distinguished as a
Wrangler, who had beaten Jost as to time in the
ascent of the "Vilan," and who had just read in
Baedeker that the Lüner See could be reached from
Seewis in five hours, did not wish us to leave until
after our mid-day dinner or lunch. It was ultimately arranged that we should start promptly at
eleven a.m.; but the delays, almost inseparable from so
large a party, caused noon to have arrived before the
column really began to move. Old Jost went first,
with a heavy load of provisions, shaking his head, and
assuring us that we should be benighted. Mr. Hitz
himself came with us, together with one of the two
shoemakers of the village to help with the horses, and
besides these we had a second excellent guide named
" Fausch." Our party thus numbered twelve, and
two horses. The " old fogey " of the party ventured
to mention to the "Wrangler" how uneasy the
experienced old Jost was at our late start, to which
the Wrangler replied that old Jost was a humbug.

Passing through the new or eastern half of the village, we followed a narrow lane shaded by fruit trees, passed a saw-mill and waterfall, and then took a bridle-path, that winds up a bare slope where, generations since, must have been a great landslip, and where another landslip always seems to threaten. Soon we passed out of the hot sunshine into the solemn shadow of a pine forest. Steadily my brave old steed picked his way through mud, fetlock deep, among great stones, and along a pathway made, to a great extent, by plaiting branches of trees together along the side of a deep ravine. Then we crossed a mountain torrent upon a bridge made entirely of round logs laid transversely on great horizontal beams. My military saddle was as comfortable as an easy chair, and my black charger, with his cavalry-housings, looked quite handsome. His looks, however, our long and intimate acquaintance has taught me, are his least valuable point. My friend's horse was called "Fox," from his tawny coat, and though a decent beast, was not to compare with mine. After crossing the bridge, the road is cut sloping up the face of a great rocky scaur, and then through more pine-forest to Ganei. At each turn, fresh mountain peaks came into view, and we seemed more than ever oppressed by the enormous mass of the Scesa Plana in front. Ganei is five miles from Seewis, and up to fifty years ago was maintained as a rude bath by the Commune of Seewis. Its hot and mineral springs were supposed to have great virtues, and every "Bürger" of Seewis had the right to make use of the bath-house for a very small payment. Since then, successive avalanches of snow, and of earth and stones, have destroyed almost every trace of the bath-buildings. Here we crossed a bridge over the stream of Ganeibach, whose crystal waters came foaming and dashing over and between great stones. The proposition that we should bathe was received with acclamation, and we quickly swarmed down the steep banks, and were laving our limbs in the bright, sharply-cold water. From this point a number of highly picturesque peaks were visible—the Tschingel, the Geierspitze, the Yes (*sic*) Spitze, and others. From Ganei the road rapidly ascends, on the opposite side of the ravine from that by which we had come, and seems to zigzag back again through the forest—always, however, mounting higher. In this wood we found delicious wild strawberries and bilberries—a welcome refreshment. After a steep climb for half-an-hour, during which the horses had to flounder up a path deep in mud, with a log here and there to make it passable, we were all glad to come upon a stretch of level sward, where the forest became a park, the glades of which are studded with pines of extraordinary size and beauty. Close before us rose the bare rocks of the Scesa Plana, against an intensely blue sky. As we moved higher, we left the great trees behind us, and approached a murmuring, bubbling stream, flowing through a dense scrub of silver-birch and alder, with great patches of wild sage, ragwort and monkshood (*Aconite*), and occasionally a bright blue gentian. It was already five in the afternoon, and a halt was called. The provision bags yielded welcome treasures, the stream delicious cold water, of which we took deep draughts. The guides say that when a stream flows through moss, you may always be sure that the water is good. Of our party of eight, exclusive of guides, it was interesting to observe that there was only one who mixed the red juice of the vine of the Valtellino with the sparkling water. The guides were not so abstemious: the pure water did not make them oblivious of the virtues of " Schnapps."   Our *al fresco* entertainment was as picturesque as it was satisfactory : the horses with their girths loosened, and their heads freed from the bridles, ate slices of black bread and drank of the stream to their heart's content.   The travellers were scattered up and down among the brushwood, some sitting, some reclining, while some, not satisfied with their previous bath, had taken off shoes and stockings, and were cooling their feet in the stream.   A central figure in the group I will call the Entomologist, who, after doing his duty to the baskets and the stream, stood resting upon his Alpen-stock, with his butterfly-net fluttering over his shoulder.

Before we again started, our guides joined in some patriotic and national songs, the burden of one of which is the charms of the Seewis Alp.   Then followed the well-known " Volkslied" about the Swiss recruit in the French service, who, from the battlements at Strasburg, hears the sound of an Alpine horn—a call he cannot resist.   Caught while endeavouring to swim across the Rhine, he knows that in a few hours he will be shot for his attempted desertion.   The song begins,—

  "Zu Strasburg auf der Schanze da ging mein Trauern an,"

and proceeds to say that the " Alpen-horn" was " Schuld daran" to blame for all his trouble.   Feelingly sung in the deepening gloaming, with the Alps all around us, the song was very effective.   We were quickly again in motion, and, crossing the broad, stony bed of a dry torrent, were soon upon the sweet turf of an " Alp," or mountain pasture.   It is truly delightful, with a strong, brave horse under you, to ride over these soft, green slopes, following no path and needing none, but choosing a way at your pleasure.

Soon we were again among pines, many of which were perfectly dead either from disease or old age, cold or lightning. White, gaunt, and bare, they spread out their withered arms in the twilight. The peaks around were lit up with the peculiar glory of an Alpine sunset. Not a cloud was to be seen in the whole heaven, save just upon the western horizon, at the spot where the sun had gone down, where a few tiny, fleecy clouds, aglow with dazzling light, floated like golden Seraphim. At six o'clock we reached one of the principal "Alps" belonging to Seewis, and the men, who knew us, came to shake hands. The cows, in great numbers, were waiting to be milked, grouped near the buildings which served as lodgings for the men and as cheese factories. The sweet evening air was full of the music of the ·cow-bells (the Kuh-reigen), the sound or memory of which makes every Switzer's heart beat quickly. The twilight was now rapidly deepening into night, and the track (if "track" it could be called) became worse and worse— full of great stones and deep holes ; and, as the horses were no longer able to see, and were becoming distressed and terrified, we dismounted. One of the men returned with the horses to the "Alp ;" and as Mr. Hitz was obliged to be back at Seewis early in the morning, he went too.

This left us a party of ten, including the two guides. The stars were now shining out brilliantly, and helped us dimly to realise the difficulties of the journey we had still to make. It was past seven, and the hazy outline of the mountain-ridge we had yet to climb looked very formidable. At 8.30 we no longer had any track, and the two guides held frequent and earnest consultations, keeping their way along the side of a steep slope. The rest of us followed them as best we could, every now and again slipping and sliding most uncomfortably.

The darkness, the intensity of which the bright stars only faintly relieved, prevented us from seeing the gulf that yawned beneath. The "old fogey" of the party now became very crusty and savage, and indulged in many sarcastic speeches at the expense of the Mathematician, alleging that it was absurd to suppose, be one never so high a Wrangler, that, by means of the higher mathematics, one could tell the number of hours required for a mountain excursion, taken for the first time, better than guides—be they never so simple—familiar with that part of the Alps all their lives. The Wrangler took this all in good part, and he and an Irish Cantab, whose forte was the Classics, literally dragged the "old fogey" up the 1,500 ft. that had yet to be climbed before the summit of the Cavelljoch was gained, at nearly 7,500 ft. above the sea-level. Without their aid, he must have passed the night upon the mountain-side.

Great was the relief—not to say delight—of the whole party when we found ourselves upon the highest point of the pass, though even then the situation was not agreeable. Here we were, benighted in a region of gigantic rocks, precipices, and pathless Alpine wastes. To the galaxy of stars overhead had just been added Jupiter, which rose with extraordinary brilliancy; still there was only just light enough to make the darkness visible.

Beside us, like the sheeted ghost of a mountain, rose the inaccessible virgin peak of the Kircheli Spitz, so named from its supposed resemblance to a church-tower. Below, grey-white in the darkness, glimmered

the surface of the Lüner See ; and above its waters,
most cheering to our flagging spirits, was a light other
than the light of stars—the hospitable light of the
Douglas Hut, erected by the Austrian Alpine Club.
We hailed the light and our entrance upon Austrian
territory with ringing shouts ; and soon afterwards,
observing another light nearer to us upon the surface
of the lake, we hoped it might be a boat sent to meet
us by the people of the hut, who had heard our cries.
Soon, however, we sadly perceived that it was only
the reflection in the water of the light from the
windows of the hut. We had still nearly one thousand feet to descend without track of any kind, and
with the constant danger of falling over a precipice or
hurting ourselves in holes and against stones.   In the
darkness these seemed multiplied ; for the great white
thistles, of which I shall speak presently, could not be
distinguished from stones until you touched them or
leaned upon them for support, when you soon discovered your mistake.   Now the friendly light and
its reflection disappeared, hidden by a shoulder of
the mountain we had still to cross, and the way
seemed interminable.   Again we stumbled, slipped,
and slid, unable to find a path.   Happily the ground
was soft, and before long we found ourselves upon
the rocky margin of the lake.   At the last "Alp"
which we passed, a young goat had joined himself
to our party, and all over the Cavelljoch he kept with
us, flitting along at our side in graceful bounds, like
a white spectre, while we were stumbling forward,
awkwardly and with pain.   From the other side of
the lake, the light of the hut shone out brightly
through the perfectly clear air and against the deep
dark blue of the empyrean. And now on the lake
there appeared another light ; and this time it was

not a reflection, for the dip of oars reached our ears. Two of the party, tired out, had remained behind with one of the guides; the others, with old Jost, were already engaged in a toilsome circumnavigation of the lake along its rocky verge. Meanwhile the boat reached our shore. "Wie geht's Christine?" cried our guide Fausch, for the boat was manned by two girls. They did not come so much to fetch us, though they had heard our shouts, as to fetch a supply of milk from an outlying hut, where one or two cows were kept. The young women rowed us across the dark water in a few minutes. After landing, we climbed along a zigzag path up the face of a precipitous rock, and reached the hut long before our friends, who were wearily plodding round the rocky margin of the tarn. This welcome refuge is named after John Sholto Douglas, a Scotchman, formerly an extensive manufacturer in the Vorarlberg, who had much to do with the building of the hut. In September, 1874, he was killed by a fall while chamois hunting.

The hut is very strongly built, to resist the force of avalanches, one-half of it—that toward the mountain-side—is a solid mass of stone, against which the habitable part of the structure leans. This last consists of the "guest-room"—some 16 ft. long by 10 ft. wide, provided with a deal table, benches, and stools—behind which there is a very primitive kitchen, another room in which the caretakers of the hut live, besides two or three bedrooms (of which more anon), and the "Stroh-Dach." This last we thought, from the description, must be a shakedown of straw on the roof, which, the night being clear and brilliant, we thought would suit us very well. We found, however, that the "straw-roof" was a garret without windows, and with a sloping roof from one to three feet above the floor, which was thickly strewn with straw. Having inspected it, we were quite satisfied to leave its delights to our guides. Many of us were too tired to eat, but we were glad to partake of some Tyrolese wine and some *café au lait*. The " Guest-room " had some half-dozen books in it and a set of chess-men. Our faithful companion the goat, having been inhospitably refused admittance at the door, thrust his head and his two fore-feet in through the open window, and contrived to scatter the chess-men in all directions. This misdemeanor, however, we overlooked, and were not so insensible to the claims of comradeship as to forget to give him a supper of bread. When we made inquiry as to beds, we found that there was one room with four beds at our service ; and, in addition, there were two bedrooms, one occupied by five German gentlemen, with one spare bed, and the other by three German gentlemen, with three beds to spare. None of our party was in the least disposed to disturb the German gentlemen by thrusting his company upon them, so we mounted a sort of ladder to the four-bedded room, and proceeded to make ourselves as comfortable as the circumstances would admit of. It was no very spacious apartment for eight men, perhaps about the size of the guest-room below, with nothing but a sloping roof of wooden shingles above us, through which the wind whistled so merrily as to assure us of adequate ventilation. The men of Cambridge honours, like the fine young fellows they are, gave up two of the beds to the Scotchman and the " old fogey." The remaining two beds had each two occupants, and the two brothers of the party made a shakedown of pillows and "duvets" (the feather-beds used as bed-coverings on the Continent) on the floor.

Of undressing there was no thought; but what night-gear we had came in very usefully as turban-like wraps for our heads — a much-needed protection against the hurricane of wind that swept through the room. No sooner were we thus settled down than the goat commenced a *pas seul* upon the roof above us, and, from the unintermittent rattle of small stones on the shingles, appeared to be playing at marbles there. This was too much for our gravity, and we indulged in such shouts of laughter that the German gentlemen sent up Christine to beg us to moderate our mirth, which interfered with their repose. At length, in spite of the goat, the whistling and roaring of the wind effectually soothed most of us into profound slumber, when, at 2 a.m., the Scotch gentleman aroused us by inquiring affectionately, but with an earnestness that would accept no denial, how we were each individually sleeping. After informing us that *he* could not sleep, he lighted our only candle and took it away with him. The goat now became very vigorous overhead; and some of our party alleged that he was really not a goat, but a diabolical presentment; and that it was not marbles he was playing at up there, but chess against himself. Our Scotch friend not returning within half-an-hour, it was suggested that it was the manifest duty of some one of us to go in search of him, though some held that there was small chance of finding him, as there was too much reason to fear that he and the goat had gone off in a blue flame, after the fashion of Mephistopheles and Faust. At length the Irishman volunteered for this duty, and presently the shingles rattled over our heads; for he and the goat were having a *pas de deux* on the roof, and there seemed a great probability of both dancers coming through upon us. After a while the noise overhead ceased; but in its place we heard a great disturbance on the ladder leading to the bedroom, following upon which the classical Milesian reappeared, bringing the goat with him. It may have been inhospitable, but not all the Irishman's eloquence could induce us to let the goat stay. Our minds were much relieved by hearing that, so far from our Scotch friend having been spirited away, he was sitting in the "Guest-room" drinking "Tyroler." About five o'clock light began to stream in through the chinks of the roof, and, much refreshed by a not altogether undisturbed night, the "old fogey" arose. Upon his descending the ladder-stairs, water of crystal clearness, and of intense coldness, was brought him in a shallow pie-dish, together with a towel. The place of ablution was outside the front of the hut, and, in spite of the incompleteness of the implements, it was an enjoyment and a luxury. The wind that had seemed to rage all night was dying down at the approach of the sun. The tops of the bare and riven rocks around were just smitten with the dawn, the sky was intensely blue, but not so blue as the still lake below. All the mountains here are of the so-called Dolomite limestone, and present the strangely romantic and weird shapes peculiar to that formation. The hut itself, as seen by daylight, is just like a fisherman's cabin high upon the rocks, above the sea, say, on the West of Scotland or in Jersey. Nearly opposite to it, upon the other side of the lake, rise fantastic rocks, one of which presents an admirable likeness of a bishop in full canonicals in the act of giving the benediction. Here and there, great masses of snow rested upon the rocks, and noticeably so near the summit of the Scesa Plana. Towards sunrise there was a great calm, and all the peaks around glowed fervently, until at last the great round fiery disc of the sun showed itself above a wall of rock in the east. The air was delicious, crisp, and clear. About 7.30 all the party, except the Scotchman and the "old fogey," started to climb the Scesa Plana, taking the younger guide with them. Old Jost remained with us. After coffee, we went out to a flagstaff erected on the highest point of the headland on which the hut stands; and there for half-an-hour we basked in the sun, and drank in the stern and solitary grandeur of the scene. The rocks around are perfectly white, save where great black stains are visible, as though from the upsetting of a gigantic inkstand. Similar black streaks and stains are very striking on the precipices of the Black Monk opposite to Mürren. They are, there is no doubt, some very low form of lichen, nature always striving to clothe the bare places of the earth with life. Running through the limestone there are also red strata that look like jasper or porphyry. At nine we started to climb the Cavelljoch, the descent from which, in the darkness of the previous night, we had found so difficult. As before, we took the boat across the lake, so as to escape the long *détour* by the shore. Christine and her sister accompanied us to the boat, where they shook hands with us cordially, and hoped we should come again. A gentleman, who was crossing with a view to some mountain excursion, took the oars, and we were quickly ferried across the deep-indigo water. Then came what proved to be a very toilsome ascent, which lasted for an hour and a-half; and we wondered how we had got down in the dark with whole skins and sound necks. The slope we were climbing was too high for much vegetation; but innumerable thistles, with large white heads, presented the appearance of splendid flowers of the Cactus order.

Drawing honey from these were hundreds of the beautiful black and red butterfly, called by the Germans "Distelfalter," which is, I believe, the only butterfly common to Australia and the rest of the world. Myriads of large flies, having almost exactly the appearance of honey-bees, were also hovering around these blossoms. This somewhat desolate region was also beautified by the sturdy yellow flower of the Arnica Montana, and by several varieties of the Gentian.

At length we reached the highest point of the pass of the Cavelljoch (7,500 ft.), and threw ourselves upon the turf, to take repose and to revel in the view. Before us stretched a vast panorama of wild mountain-ranges, of snow-peaks, and glaciers. Behind us lay the lovely little lake, gleaming in the sunshine. Beyond, behind the jagged peaks of Saul (Saulenspitzen), was the Vorarlberg; and below the only trace of cloud to be seen upon the horizon, lay, though invisible to us, the eastern end of the Boden See. Close beside us, rising from the grassy ridge where we rested, stood the unconquered virgin-peak of the Kircheli Spitze, its precipitous rocks blasted and riven by a thousand storms. Further to the east was the more massive, but equally savage Drusenfluh; between which and the Kircheli Spitze there is a slight depression in the rocky wall, known as the "Schweizerthor," probably because, at some distant period, the Swiss penetrated into Austrian territory by means of this difficult pass. We had, before, with the help of a field-glass, seen our friends, like a string of black flies, crossing the great snow-field just below the summit of the Scesa Plana; and now, on the very apex of the mountain, our unassisted eyesight could see a party gathered. It proved, however, not to be our friends, but the five

German gentlemen whom our somewhat unseasonable hilarity of the previous night had disturbed. Where we had stretched ourselves on the Cavelljoch, there was a fine breeze blowing, which tempered the heat of the sun's rays; and it was with regret that we proceeded on our way, especially as at this point we had at once to bid farewell to Austrian territory and to the lovely Lüner See. Like poor Christian, when at last daylight dawned upon the horrors of the Valley of the Shadow of Death, we now first became fully aware of the dangers through which we had stumbled and slid on the previous night.

We now saw how easily we might have rolled down fully a thousand feet, and, indeed, such a fate might well have befallen us but for the skill and fidelity of our guides. In view of the accidents, at once so lamentable and so frequent, in Alpine districts, common prudence dictates that strangers should be guided implicitly by the advice of experienced mountaineers. At about eleven, upon our reaching the crest of a bluff, we came upon the man left in charge of the horses, and a boy from the " Alp," who had come to meet us. We had neglected Dalgetty's advice as to " proviant," so were right glad to find that the man had a little bread left; and when we arrived at the " Alp " at least one of the party revelled *ad libitum* in delicious fresh milk, which, followed by a collation of curds, made a capital dinner. Our walk and climb had tired us, so that it was a luxury to find ourselves again in the saddle, and right bravely did our good steeds bear us over rock and moss and fen. Before we entered the great pine-forests, the green sward of the " Alp " was here and there diversified with dwarf pine scrub. The mountain-sides, too, over hundreds, if not thousands, of acres, were covered with a dense thicket of dwarf alder, the foliage of which, in the bright sunshine, showed a brilliant blue-green. Huge blocks of rock, too, lie scattered over the " Alp," some as large as huts or houses. On and around these rocks, bushes of mountain ash, juniper, and Alpine rhododendron were growing in profusion. Perhaps, however, the most beautiful floral adornments of these mountain solitudes are the very frequent and extensive patches of monkshood (*Aconite*) with its dark green foliage and deep-blue flowers. As we rode along, we examined with great interest the precipitous face of the Scesa Plana, down which our friends were to come, and while we were giving our horses their loaves of bread, and were resting above the stream at Ganei, we heard a welcome halloo, and presently saw them scrambling down the mountain-side, accompanied by the ever-faithful goat, which had twice been to the summit of the Scesa Plana that morning—first with the five Germans, and then, on meeting them, with our friends.

As we came within two or three miles of Seewis, the ladies came out to meet us, and old Jost quite exulted in our long and triumphant procession of horse and foot, as we re-entered the village at about six in the evening.

CHAPTER XXX.

DAVOS AM PLATZ,

A sledge-drive to Davos—Küblis—Klosters—Unter-Laret and the Schwarz See
—Ober-Laret—Davos Dörfli—Davos am Platz—A village of invalids—The
air of Davos—Davos as a health-resort—Extremes of temperature—The Landwasser route—Davos Frauen-kirch—The Züger-strasse and Bärentritt—Wiesen
—Lenz—Chur—A mountain-ride in winter—Farewell and "Auf Wiedersehen.'

It is quite possible that my readers have already
had enough of these excursions : I will only inflict one
more upon them—a winter-trip from Seewis to Davos.

It was the early morning of the 10th November,
1879, and so much snow had fallen that Mr. Hitz
determined to drive me all the way from Seewis to
Davos, some thirty miles, in a sledge. The morning
was superb; the moon hung her luminous sickle high
in the dark empyrean, and was almost rivalled in brilliancy by Venus, her near neighbour. Orion was sinking
in the west, and Sirius blazing out just above the
Schloss. Mr. Hitz's sledge is a funny little box upon
runners, and (in expectation of a cold drive) I had put
on almost the whole of my available wardrobe. With
three shirts, two waistcoats, and—covering all—an
immense ulster that made the campaign in France
with me in 1871, I felt I might safely defy even
Arctic cold. We started on the stroke of six, and as
we glided down the zigzag road to Pardisla, the stars
grew pale ; and, in the west, the snowy peaks of the
Graue Hörner glowed, pink with the rosy light of the
coming sunrise. When we reached the valley, we
found that the road had been spoiled for sledge-

driving by the heavy traffic between Landquart and
Davos, and as far as Küblis our journey was heavy
work, especially for the horse.   Often, when the
weather was perfectly clear at Seewis, we had looked
down upon a sea of mist in the valley, and of this we
now found evidence in the thick rime that here
covered the ground.   Beyond Küblis the valley
narrows, and where the sun's rays could not penetrate,
the cold was intense.   The water that comes stream-
ing down the precipitous sides of the valley had been
frozen into icicles, and at one point they presented the
appearance of a vast organ.   About 2 p.m. we
reached Klosters, a well-built village, with about 1,500
inhabitants, which, although nearly 4,000 feet above
the sea-level, is in the very bottom of a valley.
There we dined, and gave our horse some much-
needed food and rest.   The Silvretta peaks and
glacier seemed close to us, but in the clear frosty air,
and with the pure white mantle over everything, the
distances were even more deceptive than is usual
among the Alps.   The sun was now shining with
great power, and water was running from all the roofs,
but the sun's heat seemed to have little or no effect
upon the deep snow in the streets.   From Klosters
the road to Davos winds up through a dark pine-
forest, the refreshing green of which was most
welcome after the intense glare of the sun upon the
snow.   Far below us on the left, flows an affluent of
the Landquart, on the other side of which rise precipitous mountains, whose sides are scarred by recent
avalanches.   The forest was full of weird and fantastic
shapes, for while the snow hung in great masses on
the branches of the larger pines, the smaller trees
and the stumps of felled trees were completely buried.
The top of a young pine, rising out of the centre of a

pure white hillock, like a gigantic broad-based sugar-loaf, showed how these curious hills of snow were formed. Often, however, no trace was to be seen of the little tree that served as skeleton, and no great play of fancy was required to see lions couchant, huge cats just seizing upon their prey, and bears sitting upon their haunches, all moulded in a material whose whiteness shames the marble of the quarries of Carrara. In the wood we met a jolly-looking carter, lying full-length face downwards, upon his sledge, with another horse and sledge following close behind, without a driver. He told us he had a third horse and sledge in his charge, lagging behind : " Would we whip the horse up ? " This we accordingly did, when we came up with the recalcitrant animal, and we saw him making up for lost time by following his master at a gallop through the deep snow down-hill. The wooded wall of mountain which we were crossing is called the Klosterser Stütz, and is the water-parting which separates the Prättigau from the valley of Davos. Near the summit of the pass we came upon a clearing in the forest, where stands the hamlet of Unter-Laret. Its little chapel is close beside a dark tarn called the Schwarz See, and above rises the gloomy and forbidding height of the Schwarz-horn. Unter-Laret is about 4,900 feet above the sea-level, and a more lonely or desolate-looking village it is impossible to imagine, with its few fields surrounded on all sides by pine forests. It was difficult to realise here that we were already quite close to what is fast becoming a resort for the consumptive patients of the whole world—Davos am Platz. Perhaps some ingenious doctor may shortly discover peculiar virtues in the air of Laret, in the waters of its tarn, and the resinous breath of its pine woods, when, *presto*, huge hotels and *pensions* would arise, and death-smitten men and women would hurry from all the ends of Europe, to take advantage of its healing properties.

Soon after leaving Unter-Laret, we passed through Ober-Laret, where we noticed a new house, just completed by the roadside, entirely built of round pine logs, the interstices between which are packed with moss. Mr. Hitz says these houses are very warm and comfortable. They have need to be, in such a climate. At 3.30 we reached the summit of the pass, Davos Kulm, nearly 5,300 ft. above the sea-level. Here there is a solitary little inn, but they do not receive *pensionnaires* in the winter. Our horse was now glad to exchange a toilsome ascent for a rapid descent through the forest, and we were soon swiftly gliding past the Davos Lake. The scene here was intensely arctic, but was not devoid of a stern beauty of its own. Beyond the dark water—soon, for at least four months, to be frozen up—rose a mountain-side clothed with dark-green pines ; all else was white and glistening in the still-powerful rays of the descending sun. Above was a perfectly blue sky. The lake passed, we were soon in Davos Dörfli, or the little village of Davos, thus called to distinguish it from the more important Davos am Platz lower down in the valley. Dörfli is finely situated, being to some extent protected from biting winds by the Schia Horn, and has a fine view up the Fluela Pass ; but I confess the place seemed to me to have a straggling, unfinished, and uncomfortable appearance.

Before leaving Seewis, I had undertaken to try and find quarters somewhere at Davos for two lady friends, ordered to winter there, who had spent the autumn with us at Seewis. All the hotels, in the least degree eligible, had their full complement of guests. At the

Kurhaus Dörfli I called to see a pastor's wife, who, up to within the last month, had been with us at Seewis. I was shocked to see how much worse she looked. She said the air was lighter than at Seewis, but more "angreifend" (biting). Poor woman! she was separated from her husband and three little children, and she had the look upon her face that those who have had to do with consumptive patients, know too well. Yet, although she seemed worse, and her cough had become exceedingly troublesome, she derived, I am told, great benefit from her winter's sojourn at Davos Dörfli. On the way from Dörfli to Platz we met many visitors walking or driving in sledges. Almost all had puggarees on their hats, and had, besides, umbrellas and coloured spectacles as a protection from the glare of the sun! Some looked like shadows, others seemed as robust as ordinary mortals. The situation and general appearance of Davos am Platz reminded me somewhat of Braemar as approached from Glenshee. The church is a picturesque structure; and the town itself, with its magnificent hotels, is laid out ·in broad thoroughfares, worthy of Cheltenham. In these hotels there were, at the time of my visit, about 800 visitors, of whom, probably, 700 were suffering from tubercular disease in some form or other. A place like Davos is pretty sure to remind you how small the world is. It is one of the pleasant features of such health-resorts that you are nearly sure to stumble unexpectedly upon acquaintances or friends. This was my agreeable experience. When our sledge was about half-a-mile from the town, a lady called me by name; and as soon as I had become accustomed to the disguise of dark-blue spectacles, I recognised a friend to whom I had said "good bye" twelve months before on the shores of Lake Leman, and whom I had supposed to be in Holland.

Davos is always so full of guests in winter, that to secure a night's quarters is often difficult. We put up at the Hotel Strela, where at first I was told there was no room ; but, upon learning that I was only going to stay two nights, the manager told me I could have the room of a visitor they were expecting—this, with the air of a man who was distinctly conferring a favour. It is curious to observe how the different nationalities affect different hotels. The hotels Buol and Belvidere have become exclusively English houses ; the Strela (where I stayed), entirely German and Dutch. It was painful to be told that, of the eighty ladies and gentlemen—some of them very fine-looking young men and young women—who sat down that evening to a plain but substantial *table-d'hôte* supper, there was hardly one who was not a consumptive patient. The manager of the hotel was evidently in a far-advanced stage. The book-keeper, who sat next me at table, looked emaciated, but otherwise healthy. He told me that he came from Thuringia, that he had been three years at Davos, and that if he even left this upland haven for a month or two on a visit to his friends, the disease made progress. The waitress who brought me my breakfast, a rosy-cheeked and pleasant-looking girl, told me that, being threatened with consumption, her doctor had sent her up here from her home at Lucerne, and that in this air she could do her work without strain or injury. The proprietors of some of the other hotels came to Davos, in the first instance, for their health. The shops are kept by *ci-devant* lawyers, professors, &c., who have fled up to this Alpine valley to escape death by consumption. The music-master, Herr von Radetzki, is a relative of the grim old Austrian Field-Marshal of that name. Herr Richter, the proprietor of the circulating library

was a lawyer in good practice in Germany. Davos is
a little over 5000 ft. above sea-level, and 2000 ft. higher
than Seewis ; and the air to me at first had the effect
of a good draught of champagne or an inspiration of
laughing-gas—it seemed fairly to pierce into me, and
about my temples there was a singular sensation, as if
something there were going to crack or burst. At the
time of my visit, early in November, the winter-cold
had not fairly set in ; and at 7 a.m. the thermometer,
just outside my window, stood at 23° Fahrenheit. I
cannot say that I felt the cold extreme, except in my
room, which I had somewhat imprudently declined to
have heated.

Having friends both at the Buol and Belvidere
Hotels, which are further away from the little town
than the Strela, I walked over to pay my calls. Both
hotels were quite full, and there seemed little prospect
of obtaining quarters at Davos for my friends. At
the Belvidere the sport of toboggining was being
pursued in spirited fashion, the straight carriage-
drive from the hotel into the high-road being admirably suited for the sport. The Germans at the
Strela, who affect sledging very little, were very
indignant at the reckless manner in which the English
came shooting into or across the high-road, at lightning
speed, on their sledges ; and doubtless it would be
better if toboggining could be confined to some
special slope, as several pedestrians were that winter
very unceremoniously bowled over, and bad accidents
might easily happen. In the evening I dined at the
Buol with an English clergyman, who had come here
with his family in the hopes that the air would benefit
his brain and nerves, which had been greatly injured
by a railway collision. I am sorry to say that his
residence at Davos was distinctly injurious to him.

The stimulating cold was trying, and, in addition, he was so unfortunate as to get a slight sun-stroke. And here let me enter a mild *caveat* against sending patients to Davos because it has become the fashion to do so. I speak as a layman : perhaps on that very account I can speak the more impartially. There is no doubt that, in certain stages of pulmonary disease, as well as in other disorders, the bracing, stimulating air of Davos is of immense service : in fact, I do not think I exaggerate when I say, I think in such cases it means life. Relatives of my own have found it such. On the other hand, many healthy persons cannot endure the stimulating air, or a temperature which ranges from 20° below Zero, Fahrenheit, on a cold night, to 120° in the sun on the following day ; and to many invalids to be sent to Davos is little short of a sentence of death. As a rule, those consumptive patients whose vital power is low, and whose strength is slight, would do well to consider whether Algiers, or Mentone, or Madeira, would not suit their case better than the snows of Davos.

Those who represent a residence in either of these places as a cure for consumption, are simply deluding the poor victims of that dreadful malady. All that either Davos or the balmy south can do, is to put the patients under climatic conditions which shall give nature a better chance of overcoming the disease than she has in the damp, the smoke, and the deadly fogs of England.

At 7.25 a.m., the next morning, the 12th of November, I found myself the sole occupant, of the Diligence for Chur, by the Landwasser route. For my ten or twelve francs I had all to myself, a well-appointed close carriage upon runners, with driver, conductor, and four good horses. The conductor did not require much persuasion to induce him to give me his seat upon the box in exchange for the inside, and I thus secured a fine position from which to see the country. The Föhn, or south wind, had been blowing for the past twelve hours, bringing rain into the valleys, and snow into these Alpine regions, so that, in place of the usual fiery-hot sun of Davos, I had a cloudy sky, overhead. We dashed along down-hill at a spanking pace, now passing a group of school-boys, with satchel on back, who greeted us with a cheery " Guten Tag," while anon some lasses, bareheaded, as always, started running when they saw the coach, to gain a cleared spot of ground, so that they might not have to turn into the deep snow to get out of our way.

At the little hotel at Davos Frauen-kirch, about an hour's walk from Platz, the coach stopped two minutes for the post-bags. Hitherto, I had been quite un-.successful in securing winter-quarters for my friends. As a last resource, without leaving my seat, I asked the landlord if he had any rooms still unlet. At first he said " No," and then, correcting himself, " Yes, one north room, with two beds " (the north rooms are exceedingly disliked at Davos, as having little or no sun). His price was exceedingly moderate, four francs each per diem, for the two persons who occupied the room, including board and lodging. I will just add that my friends took this room for three months, and were very comfortable. They were glad to be out of the vortex of Davos life, while at the same time the town was within a moderate walk. I mention this, because economy may be of importance to some one ordered to Davos, and, though the prices are likely enough to rise, they will probably always be less at Frauen-kirch than in the great hotels at Platz.

The road now follows the course of the Landwasser,

which rises in the lake of Davos, and ultimately finds its way into the Rhine. Sombre and dark were the pines, enwrapping the mountains on both sides of the pass, but among them were many larches fast shedding their golden-yellow spines, and making the snow underneath them a rich saffron colour. In the bed of the stream, or close upon its banks, were a few stunted alders. It was market-day at Davos, and we met many peasants, clad in stout homespun, bringing in their merchandise upon ox-sleighs. Every one was well clad and well shod, for in this favoured land there are no ·rags, and though there may be poverty there is practically no pauperism. About six miles from Davos the pass becomes much narrower, and the mountains on either side much higher. There is but just room for the Landwasser and the road, and from the lofty, almost perpendicular, Züge—the pass is called the Züger-strasse—frequent avalanches fall. Long tunnels have been blasted through the rock for the road, in order to escape these dangers, and at some of the most exposed situations, galleries of solid masonry have been built, while along the hill-sides a stout network of fascines has been placed, so that the soil may not be borne down in the rush of the snow. The cascades that, in summer, come dashing down, are now all turned to clusters of icicles. Arrived at a point on the Pass called the Bärentritt, there loomed immediately above us, through the mist—snowy, shadowy, and vast—the glittering crest of the Sand-hubel. The post-road along this pass was only completed between 1870 and 1873. It cost £25,000, and presented extraordinary engineering difficulties. It is of no great length, but no pass in Switzerland presents grander scenery.

At 9.30, after a considerable ascent, we reached the

little village of Wiesen, which stands about 4,700 feet above the sea-level, and contains 166 inhabitants. While the coach was changing horses, I found there were just two guests in the hotel, a Scotch missionary from India, recruiting shattered nerves, and his wife— they were just on the point of leaving this lonely station, and, curiously enough, in order to spend the winter at Davos Frauen-kirch. Wiesen is almost as high as Davos, and its situation is much finer. Below, in a deep gorge, flows the Landwasser, while imme diately opposite, rise, to the height of between ten and eleven thousand feet, the magnificently-shaped peaks of the Tinzenhorn, the Piz d'Aela, and the Piz St. Michel. Here the conductor took my place on the box, and requested me to get inside, as all the wits of both conductor and driver are needed in order to bring the coach safely down the rapid descent.

At eleven we stopped for twenty minutes in the Roman Catholic town of Lenz, where the snow was fast melting, and the street was full of little sledges ridden by school-boys. Again the road ascends, and we traversed the extensive forest called the Lenzer-Heide, the greater part of which lies as high as Davos. This forest is, during winter, a favourite resort of the Chamois, who find among the trees a shelter which the great icy peaks do not afford. Here a pitiless snow-storm overtook us, and I do not think the conductor was very sorry that I had previously again exchanged places with him. From the highest point of the Lenzer-Heide to Chur there is a descent of 3,200 feet, Chur being only 1,800 feet above sea-level. The distance is traversed by the coach in two hours, and at two in the afternoon our sledge was being dragged painfully over the stones and through the slush of Chur, while a deluge of warm rain was falling. It was certainly a striking change from Davos.

In closing these winter-pictures, and with them this book, I think I can hardly do better than devote a few lines to a description of how we left Seewis on the 5th December, 1879. Our landlord did not consider it would be safe to drive a close carriage upon runners, necessarily somewhat top-heavy, down the steep descent, so the luggage was all sent to Landquart on the previous day, and my wife and I, with our two little girls, were to follow in two small open sledges, than which, on a fine winter's day, it would not be possible to devise a more delightful mode of travelling. But the day of our departure was not fine, and before we started there were threatenings of a storm, which developed to a hurricane as we descended. Each of the little sledges would just hold two; so my wife took the elder child in the first, and I our little three-year-old in the second. The drivers sat in front. The final adieux having been said, the start was made. "Crack went the whip," though, unlike the chaise of John Gilpin, there were no wheels to go round, but, instead, the runners glided rapidly along the frozen road until we were out of sight of Seewis, and were rapidly descending the zigzag. The greater part of the way there was no fence of any kind to the road; and in the deep snow it was not always easy to make out the track, yet, if we missed it by an inch, our descent into the valley would have been swift indeed. The snow whirled around us in blinding gusts, and the oak leaves brought down by the storm went dancing over the trackless snow into the white abyss on the verge of which we were gliding. My little companion's spirits seemed to rise with the rising storm.

Everything was very "nipe." "What a 'nipe' horse!" "What a 'nipe' road!" an optimistic view of the situation which culminated in her describing the bitter driving blast, which I feared would take the skin off her face, as "What a 'nipe' wind!" Happily, in the expectation of a fine day and a hot sun, I had with me, in addition to a fur cap, a straw hat to serve as a protection from the sun (save the mark!), and, by holding this hat flat over her face, I was able to shelter her a little from the storm. More and more fiercely did it blow as we passed through the wild gorge of the Landquart, at the narrowest part of which the road was cut through an avalanche of snow that had fallen from the Clushöhe during the recent thaw. Though nothing can exceed the magnificence of the gorge in its winter dress of ice and snow, and especially when a hurricane is sweeping up it and lashing the waters of the Landquart into fury, it was with no ordinary feelings of relief and thankfulness that at last we drove across the bridge and into the inn-yard at Felsenbach, where a covered carriage awaited us.

By a curious coincidence, I am writing the closing words of this book upon the anniversary of the winter journey above described—on the 5th December, 1880. This year—from the middle of October until now—instead of frost and snow, we have had an almost unbroken Indian summer of perfect beauty. The sky has been of an unclouded blue, and our short winter-days have been flooded with sunlight. Old and young have spent as much time as possible in the open air, where the sunny warmth has rendered unnecessary any addition to our ordinary indoor clothing. At night there have occasionally been very slight frosts, but the climate has been more like that of an unclouded · English June, than of December. Yesterday, however, the thermometer fell considerably, and to-day dark and threatening clouds have gathered, so that probably within a few hours, the Alpine forests and pastures will be wrapped in a pure white shroud of snow, not to disappear until towards April.

And now, if any friendly reader has had the patience and perseverance to accompany me through all the pages of this rambling volume, he must allow me to wish him a cordial farewell, and, in German fashion, to add,—

"AUF WIEDERSEHEN."

THE END.

THOS. DE LA RUE AND CO., PRINTERS, BUNHILL ROW, LONDON.

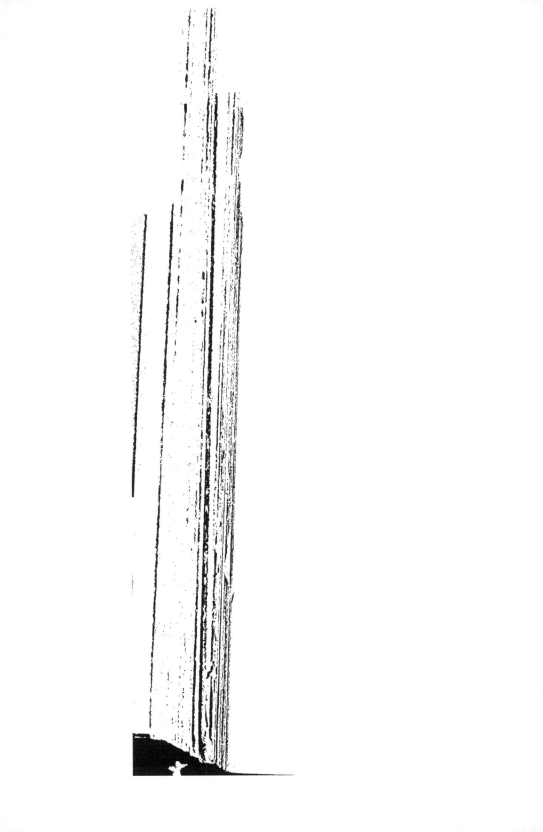

ADVERTISEMENTS.

THOS. DE LA RUE & CO'S ANNOUNCEMENTS.

In Two Handsome Volumes, Demy 8vo.

WITH A PORTRAIT BY PAUL RAJON, AND OTHER ILLUSTRATIONS,

THE LIFE OF SIR ROWLAND HILL,

K.C.B., D.C.L., F.R.S., F.R.A.S., ETC.

AND THE

HISTORY OF PENNY POSTAGE,

By SIR ROWLAND HILL,

AND HIS NEPHEW

GEORGE BIRKBECK HILL, D.C.L.,

AUTHOR OF "DR JOHNSON: HIS FRIENDS AND HIS CRITICS," ETC.

Demy 8vo.

COLONEL GORDON IN CENTRAL AFRICA,

1874-1879,

With a Portrait; and Maps of the Country, prepared under Colonel Gordon's supervision.

FROM ORIGINAL LETTERS AND DOCUMENTS.

EDITED BY GEORGE BIRKBECK HILL, D.C.L.,

AUTHOR OF THE "LIFE OF SIR ROWLAND HILL, K.C.B." "DR. JOHNSON: HIS FRIENDS AND HIS CRITICS," ETC.

Demy 8vo.

THE SHORES AND CITIES OF THE BODEN SEE.

RAMBLES IN 1879 AND 1880.

By SAMUEL JAMES CAPPER,

AUTHOR OF "WANDERINGS IN WAR TIME."

WITH A MAP; AND NUMEROUS ORIGINAL ETCHINGS ON STONE.

New Work by Dr. Guy, F R S.   Crown 8vo.

THE FACTORS OF THE UNSOUND MIND,

WITH SPECIAL REFERENCE TO THE

PLEA OF INSANITY IN CRIMINAL CASES,

AND THE

AMENDMENT OF THE LAW.

By WILLIAM A. GUY, M.B., F.R.C.P., F.R.S.

Consulting Physician to King's College Hospital; Honorary Vice-President of the Statistical Society; and formerly Professor of Forensic Medicine and Hygiène in King's College, London.

CLAY ON WHIST.

A new and improved Edition. Cap. 8vo. Price 3s. 6d.

LAWS OF SHORT WHIST,

AND A

TREATISE ON THE GAME.

By JAMES CLAY.

Crown 8vo. Cloth. Price 7s. 6d.

VOYAGES OF THE ELIZABETHAN SEAMEN.

A Selection from the Original Narratives in Hakluyt's Collection.

Edited, with Historical Introduction, by E. J. PAYNE, M.A.

FELLOW OF UNIVERSITY COLLEGE, OXFORD.

Crown 8vo. Price 5s.

HISTORY OF GERMANY.

POLITICAL, SOCIAL, AND LITERARY,

BROUGHT DOWN TO THE PRESENT DAY.

By THE REV. DR. E. COBHAM BREWER,

TRINITY HALL, CAMBRIDGE.

AUTHOR OF "HISTORY OF FRANCE," "GUIDE TO SCIENCE," ETC., ETC.

32mo. Price 2s. 6d.

THE SMALLER HISTORY OF GERMANY,

POLITICAL, SOCIAL, AND LITERARY,

BROUGHT DOWN TO THE PRESENT DAY.

BY THE

REV. DR. E. COBHAM BREWER,

TRINITY HALL, CAMBRIDGE.

AUTHOR OF "HISTORY OF FRANCE," "GUIDE TO SCIENCE," ETC., ETC.

In Royal 4to. Cloth. Extra Gilt. Price 6s.

NEW ILLUSTRATED CHILDREN'S BOOK.

THE STORY OF

PRINCE HILDEBRAND AND THE PRINCESS IDA.

BY

MAJOR T. S. SECCOMBE,

WITH UPWARDS OF 110 ILLUSTRATIONS BY THE AUTHOR.

THOS. DE LA RUE & CO'S PUBLICATIONS.

Crown 8vo, 2 vols. Cloth. Price 15s.

STRANGE STORIES FROM A CHINESE STUDIO,

TRANSLATED AND ANNOTATED

By HERBERT A. GILES, of H.M's Consular Service.

"This collection of Chinese stories is exceedingly curious as well as entertaining, and Mr Giles appears to be excellently qualified for the task he has undertaken."—*Times.*
"We must refer our readers to Mr. Giles's volumes, where, if they themselves bring to their perusal a spirit still capable of enjoying the marvellous, they will find a great deal that is full both of interest and instruction."—*Pall Mall Gazette.*

"Any one who reads this book with care will not only be delighted with the stories that are told in it, as works of art, but will get a much better knowledge of the true character of Chinese life than could well be got in any other manner."—*Scotsman.*
"Under this title Mr Herbert A Giles has translated and annotated a series of Chinese Stories, which are to the Chinese what the 'Arabian Nights' are to the Arabians."—*Trubner's Literary Record.*

Now ready Crown 8vo. Cloth. Price 10s.

A SIMPLE STORY, AND NATURE AND ART.

By Mrs. INCHBALD,

With a Portrait and Introductory Memoir by WILLIAM BELL SCOTT.

"Three generations have passed away since the 'Simple Story' was welcomed by the English public, with the unequivocal approval implied in a call for three editions in a few days Its charm is as fresh as ever; and many readers, sated with the slipshod sensational manner of some later novelists, will thank the publishers for introducing them to a work of fiction so original, so artistically contrived, and executed with so much literary skill No small praise is due, besides, to

the exquisite typography of the volume. The introductory memoir of the Authoress is one proof more that Mr. Scott can handle the pen as deftly as the painter's brush Nothing could be done in better taste than his account of Mrs Inchbald's career as a provincial actress, and literary lady. Her portrait, in the grotesque style of her period, is etched by Mr. Scott's needle."—*Bookseller.*

Crown 8vo. Cloth. With Portrait of the Author. Price 7s. 6d.

CARD ESSAYS, CLAY'S DECISIONS,

AND

CARD-TABLE TALK.

By "CAVENDISH,"

Author of "THE LAWS AND PRINCIPLES OF WHIST," &c., &c.

"Still retaining the familiar pseudonym of 'Cavendish,' but effectually dropping the transparent disguise by placing his portrait and autograph signature in the front of his book, its author now collects and gives to the world a remarkably pleasant and useful series of essays upon whist and its ways and surroundings."—*Saturday Review.*
"A volume of more than usual interest to whist-players. * * * * The author has made a reputa-

tion by his books on card-playing, and he may be described as the greatest living authority on card questions."—*Scotsman.*
"The 'Card Essays,' by 'Cavendish,' which Messrs. De La Rue publish, form a welcome volume."—*Athenæum.*
"An amusing book, full of curious pedantry and funny pedantic anecdote."—*Vanity Fair.*

Crown 8vo. Cloth. Price 7s.

BOSWELL'S CORRESPONDENCE WITH THE HON. ANDREW ERSKINE,

AND HIS

JOURNAL OF A TOUR TO CORSICA.

(Reprinted from the original editions.)

EDITED, WITH A PREFACE, INTRODUCTION, AND NOTES, BY

GEORGE BIRKBECK HILL, D.C.L.

Author of "DR. JOHNSON: HIS FRIENDS AND HIS CRITICS."

"The thanks of every one interested in the literature of the eighteenth century are due to Mr. Hill for this volume."—*Pall Mall Gazette.*

LIST OF PUBLICATIONS.—*Continued.*

Demy 8vo. Cloth. Price 25s. With Map, and Illustrations on Wood.

JUNGLE LIFE IN INDIA,

OR THE

JOURNEYS AND JOURNALS OF AN INDIAN GEOLOGIST.

By V. BALL, M.A., F.G.S.,

Fellow of the Calcutta University, and Assistant, Geological Survey of India.

"We can only allude to the many telling pictures of Nature in her more unfamiliar aspects; curious facts and discussions on vexed points in natural history; notes on the economical products of the country; traits of native character and manners, with other interesting matter, which, though scattered broadcast through the volume, is traceable by means of the index."—*Athenæum.*

"Mr Ball appears to have laboured both in and out of season, and as the result we have a work which forms an important contribution to the history of the fairest possession of the British Crown.—*Times.*

"This is a record of work of a peculiar and scientific kind, carried out in the teeth of great obstacles, manifold privations, and trials of climate. It introduces us to tracts little known except to political officers deputed to put down wicked customs, or to soldiers who have had to penetrate the fastnesses of some rebellious and wayward chief. And the story is told in a simple, straightforward, and unaffected style."—*Saturday Review.*

"This work is the day-to-day record of the experiences of a scientific man in parts of India which are little known even in these times of general travel and research. * * *."—*Pall Mall Gazette.*

A NEW EDITION, REVISED AND CORRECTED BY THE AUTHORESS, WITH SEVERAL NEW CHAPTERS.

Crown 8vo, 2 vols. Cloth. Price 10s. 6d.

AN ART-STUDENT IN MUNICH.

BY

ANNA MARY HOWITT-WATTS.

"A new and revised edition is announced by Messrs. De La Rue, of Bunhill Row, of 'An Art Student in Munich,' a work which will be remembered as having in the year 1853 first drawn attention in England and America to the Passion play at Ober-Ammergau."—*Athenæum.*

"'An Art-Student in Munich' is a new edition, but with so much of valuable addition as to be almost a new book."—*Art Journal.*

"Mrs Howitt-Watts's two-volume work, the 'Art-Student in Munich' has been long out of print. We are therefore glad to see that a second edition is now presented to the public, who will doubtless welcome it as it deserves. It is a brightly-written and agreeable guide to the great art city, of which Mrs. Watts is now, as she was twenty years ago, a devoted worshipper. The volumes form a charming record of pleasant experiences—perhaps the most pleasant experiences a woman of taste and culture can ever have, namely, those gained when, in the full glow of youth and enthusiasm, she enters upon the practical study of art."—*Daily Telegraph.*

"We give the most hearty welcome to a reprint of this book, which we have always looked upon, ever since its first appearance twenty-seven years ago, as the most charming of its class."—*Academy.*

"This is a new and enlarged edition of a very interesting book very favourably noticed in these columns some twenty-five years ago, and now long out of print. * * * * Though we cannot always agree with the writer, we can always enjoy her descriptions, and are grateful to her for the new chapters, which tell of the death of Kaulbach and of various other matters, adding new interest to a very charming book."—*Spectator.*

Crown 8vo, 2 vols. Cloth. Price 10s. 6d.

ERNESTINE.

A NOVEL. BY THE AUTHORESS OF THE "VULTURE-MAIDEN."

Translated from the German

By THE REV. S. BARING-GOULD.

"'Ernestine' has a great and real, if not extraordinary, pathos and power; and these it owes in a great degree to its intense earnestness of purpose, which infects the reader. It is the story of a nobly and strongly-natured woman plunged into every sort of moral and intellectual torment by the disbeliefs and other aggressive crazes of her time, and finally saved and made whole by finding that love and truth are higher than reason."—*Globe.*

"Though this story is certainly a good deal too long, yet we have read it with not a little interest. Had the translator been bold enough to cut it down by about one-fourth, he would have introduced to the English reader a very attractive work. Even as it is, we have to thank him for the way in which he has performed his part of the task."—*Saturday Review.*

WORKS BY "CAVENDISH."

THE LAWS AND PRINCIPLES OF WHIST.

THE STANDARD WORK ON WHIST. 8vo., Cloth, Gilt Extra. Greatly enlarged, and revised throughout. 13th Edition. Price 5s.

"We are happy to present him as a contemporary." —*Times.*
"'Cavendish' appears to possess a rare combination of attributes.'—*Bell's Life.*
"We know of no book on whist undertaken on so satisfactory a plan "—*Field.*
"I urge all those who desire to become whist players of the highest order to give a very careful study to 'Cavendish.'"—*J. C.'s Treatise on Short Whist.*

"An exquisite new edition of this master authority upon the King of Games has just been issued • •
• • It has been produced in a manner worthy of a book which is a very *bijou* among handbooks—'Cavendish' being indisputably *the* authority among Whist players "—*Sun.*
"Those who can learn Whist from books may learn it from this book with pleasure, the maxims being explained with great clearness."—*Pall Mall Gazette.*

THE LAWS OF PIQUET,

AS ADOPTED BY THE PORTLAND CLUB. Edited by "CAVENDISH;" with a TREATISE ON THE GAME, by "CAVENDISH." 2nd Edition. 8vo., Cloth, Gilt Extra. Price 3s. 6d.

THE LAWS OF PIQUET,

AS ADOPTED BY THE PORTLAND CLUB, printed in sheet, enamelled and varnished, suitable for framing and hanging up in Card Rooms. Price 2s. 6d.

THE SAME,

In neat Frame. Price 10s. 6d.

THE LAWS OF ÉCARTÉ,

ADOPTED BY THE TURF CLUB, with a TREATISE ON THE GAME, by "CAVENDISH." 8vo., Cloth, Gilt. Price 2s. 6d.

ROUND GAMES AT CARDS.

By "CAVENDISH." 8vo., Cloth, Gilt. Price 1s. 6d.

THE GAME OF BÉZIQUE.

8vo., Cloth, Gilt. Price 1s.

THE GAMES OF LAWN TENNIS
(WITH·THE AUTHORIZED LAWS)
AND BADMINTON.

Third Edition. 8vo., Cloth. Price 1s.

CARD ESSAYS, CLAY'S DECISIONS,
AND
CARD-TABLE TALK.

By "CAVENDISH." Crown 8vo., Cloth. With Portrait of the Author. Price 7s.6d.

LIST OF PUBLICATIONS.—*Continued.*

THE POCKET SERIES.—By "CAVENDISH."

PRICE SIXPENCE EACH.

POCKET GUIDE TO POLISH BÉZIQUE.
A pleasing variety of ordinary Bézique.

POCKET GUIDE TO BÉZIQUE.   POCKET GUIDE TO WHIST.

POCKET RULES FOR LEADING AT WHIST.

POCKET LAWS OF WHIST.   POCKET GUIDE TO ÉCARTÉ.

POCKET GUIDE TO EUCHRE.
The national game of the United States.

POCKET GUIDE TO SPOIL-FIVE.

POCKET GUIDE TO CALABRASELLA.

POCKET GUIDE TO CRIBBAGE.

POCKET GUIDE TO SIXTY-SIX.   POCKET GUIDE TO CHESS.

POCKET GUIDE TO DRAUGHTS AND POLISH DRAUGHTS.

POCKET GUIDE TO GO-BANG.

POCKET GUIDE TO BACKGAMMON AND RUSSIAN BACKGAMMON.

POCKET GUIDE TO FIFTEEN AND THIRTY-FOUR PUZZLES.

BILLIARDS.

By JOSEPH BENNETT, Ex-Champion.   Edited by "CAVENDISH."   With upwards of 200 Illustrations.   Second Edition, Demy 8vo. Cloth, Extra Gilt, Elegant.   Price 21*s.*   Whole Bound, in Russia or Morocco, Extra Gilt.   Price 35*s.*

THE SPOT-STROKE.
By the same Authors.   Price 1*s.*

THE LAWS OF CROQUET.
ADOPTED AT THE GENERAL CONFERENCE OF CROQUET CLUBS.   8vo. Paper Covers.   Price 6*d.*

DE LA RUE'S INDELIBLE DIARIES

AND

RED LETTER CALENDARS.

POCKET DIARIES.

DE LA RUE'S IMPROVED INDELIBLE DIARIES AND MEMORANDUM BOOKS, in three sizes, fitted in Velvet, Russia, Calf, Turkey Morocco, Persian, or French Morocco cases; plain or richly gilt, with gilt clasps or elastic bands, in a great variety of styles. All these Diaries are fitted with electro-gilt indelible pencils. Also supplied in enamelled paper covers.

A size.........3⅛ × 1⅞ inches.
B ,, ...3¾ × 2½ ,, also same size, F F (oblong).
C ,, ...4½ × 2¾ ,,   ,,   ,,   G G ,,

CONDENSED DIARIES AND ENGAGEMENT BOOKS.

In three sizes (**A, B, & C**, as above), and in a great variety of Plain and Ornamental leather cases; they are also published in enamelled paper covers, suitable for the Card Case or Purse.

COMPANION MEMORANDUM BOOKS.

For use with the Condensed Diaries; **A, B, & C** sizes, as above.

N B—All Condensed Diary and Calendar Cases (except the Tuck) are fitted with an extra elastic band for the reception of these books.

PORTABLE DIARIES.

Thin, light, and flexible, in a variety of leather cases, adapted for the Pocket. **A, B, & C** sizes.

DESK DIARY.

DE LA RUE'S IMPROVED DIARY AND MEMORANDUM BOOK; for Library or Counting-house use. **E** size, 7⅝ × 4¾ inches.

POCKET CALENDARS.

DE LA RUE'S RED LETTER CALENDARS AND ALMANACS, in three sizes (**A, B, & C**, as above), in enamelled paper covers, suitable for the Card Case or Pocket Book. Also interleaved; and in Russia, Persian, and French Morocco cases.

"FINGER-SHAPED" DIARIES AND CALENDARS.

In elegant sliding cases, extra gilt. Adapted for the Pocket or Reticule.

ORNAMENTAL WALL CALENDARS.

In great variety. Printed in gold and colours, from original designs. Royal 8vo.

MONTHLY TABLET OR EASEL CALENDARS.

Printed in Colours, in a variety of shapes and sizes. In Gilt and Nickeled Metal, Leather, and Leatherette Cases.

Lightning Source UK Ltd.
Milton Keynes UK
UKHW031943020219
336576UK00009BA/405/P